NELSON'S

ILLUSTRATED

WONDERS & DISCOVERIES

OF THE BIBLE

For my children,
Clare, Stephen and Jonathan,
with love

NELSON'S

ILLUSTRATED

WONDERS & DISCOVERIES

OF THE BIBLE

ALAN MILLARD

Publishers Since 1798

THOMAS NELSON PUBLISHERS
Nashville • Atlanta • London • Vancouver

This edition first published in 1997 by Thomas Nelson, Inc., Nashville, Tennessee.
All rights for this edition reserved.

Text copyright © 1985, 1990 by Alan Millard.

Illustrated edition copyright © 1985, 1990, 1997 Lion Publishing

Acknowledgements
Bible quotations are from the *Good News Bible,* copyright © 1966, 1971, and 1976
American Bible Society, published by the Bible Societies/Collins, and *The Holy Bible:
The New International Version,* copyright © 1978 by New York International Bible
Society published by Hodder & Stoughton.

A catalogue record for this book is available from the Library of Congress
Cataloging-in-Publication Data.

Printed and bound in Malaysia.

1 2 3 4 5 6 7 8 9 10 — 02 01 00 99 98 97

CONTENTS

PREFACE

For more than a hundred years people have been writing books to show what archaeological discoveries made in the Near East can tell us about the Bible. Some use archaeology to try to prove that the Bible is true; some think it is less important than other ways of studying ancient records. For more than a hundred years, too, thousands of people have flocked to the Holy Land to see the sacred sites—to 'walk where Jesus walked'. On Galilee's lake and hills the Gospel stories are easy to imagine; other places are greatly changed. What was it like to live in ancient Israel or in first century Palestine? How much can we learn about the days of Abraham or of Solomon? Discoveries made in the past forty years have given a much richer picture than earlier generations enjoyed, especially concerning the time of Jesus.

This book is a combination of two, *Treasures from Bible Times* and *Discoveries from the Time of Jesus*, which look at particular discoveries, at the sorts of things found, the ways some of them have been interpreted in the past and the ways they can be understood now. There are many more discoveries than can be presented here, but to try to include them all would have made the book too long, and perhaps too tedious, and archaeology's contributions to understanding the career of Paul and the early church lie outside my scope. For technical reasons, joining the two volumes has allowed only a few minor revisions of the earlier texts, but, although there are some interesting new discoveries which cannot be included, I find no reason to change the opinions given earlier.

Several friends and institutions have generously supplied photographs and I am grateful to them. The experience of living in Jerusalem as a Fellow of the Institute for Advanced Studies at the Hebrew University in 1984 and the kindness of friends in Jerusalem, especially the late Professor Nahman Avigad, stimulated the second part of this book. Dr Walter Cockle of University College, London, and Dr John Kane of Manchester University read and commented on several chapters and my friend Professor Kenneth Kitchen gave advice on Egyptological matters. My wife's unfailing encouragement and support has enabled me to complete this work, and I thank her most of all.

Alan Millard

THE LANDS OF THE BIBLE

Black Sea

ARMENIA

Lake Van

Lake Urmia

Caspian Sea

Harran

Gozan

Khorsabad

Nineveh

Aleppo

MESOPOTAMIA

ASSYRIA

Calah (Nimrud)

Ebla (Tell Mardikh)

Ashur

Nuzi

Ecbatana

Tadmor
(Palmyra)

Mari

Behistun

River Euphrates

Babylon

Kish

River Tigris

Susa

BABYLONIA

Nippur

SUMER

Tello

ELAM

Ur

ARABIA

Persepolis

Teima

Persian Gulf

THE LAND OF ISRAEL

Part 1

TREASURES FROM BIBLE TIMES

BIBLICAL ARCHAEOLOGY —
THE BEGINNINGS

Someone forgot to shut the door, and changed the history of Europe.
The Turks were attacking Constantinople in May, 1453. Its walls were strong, its defenders brave. Some had crept out through a little door for a hit-and-run raid, and failed to bar it when they came back. A group of Turks broke through, then a stream. Elsewhere they beat down the defenders, and soon the city was theirs.

Many citizens had already left, fearing a Turkish victory. Others, who could, fled afterwards. They were Greeks and they were Christians.
The only places where they could hope to find shelter were in Italy and France. Some of those who settled there were scholars who brought with them their inheritance from classical Greece. Under the influence of ancient Greek philosophy, coupled with other changes, the Renaissance flowered.

As interest in ancient Greece and Rome grew, rich men began to collect statues and coins found in the ruined cities. Scholars began to study and write about them. In a few cases connections could be made with the Bible, especially with the New Testament. People began to see that knowing about the ancient world and the way people lived could help them to understand ancient writings better.

Throughout the seventeenth and eighteenth centuries wealthy, adventurous young men travelled to Italy, Greece and Turkey exploring, describing and collecting from the remains of Greek and Roman cities.

A few went further, to Syria and Palestine. There they found the spectacular ruins of Baalbek, Palmyra and Petra, Roman cities with architecture derived from the Greeks.

Of course, pilgrims had been visiting the holy places for hundreds of years, but few had taken any interest in them as historical sites, or studied the ruins visible.

Ancient Egypt had drawn a few adventurers who brought back accounts of the enormous temples, painted tombs, and the pyramids. Beside straightforward travellers' reports, these journeys also brought ancient Egypt into the scope of fantasy-writers. They thought they could tell the future or learn some other secrets from the design of the pyramids — a false idea that is still current.

But if anything was known about ancient Egypt, it was the subject of mummies, the bodies of Egyptians carefully bandaged and preserved with natural chemicals. Powdered mummy was reckoned a powerful medicine!

With the opening of the nineteenth century, a new era dawned in the study of the ancient world. Exploration began in earnest in the lands where civilizations grew up before the time of classical Greece — in Assyria and Babylonia, and in Egypt. At first those cultures themselves were the objects of study. But when inscriptions were read which named kings known from the Old Testament a new interest was stirred, and the studies attracted a much wider audience.

Soon books were written to apply

Names from the Bible leapt to life with the discovery by archaeologists of palace walls carved with the triumphs of Assyrian kings. This stele shows the Assyrian king, Tiglath-pileser III.

The mystery of the great pyramids of Egypt has long haunted the imagination of travellers and writers of fantasy. Sir Flinders Petrie's accurate surveys put an end to much speculation.

In the seventeenth and eighteenth centuries adventurers first discovered the spectacular ruins of cities such as Palmyra, whose Roman builders derived their styles of architecture from the Greeks.

the new discoveries to the Bible. Suddenly names that had been almost meaningless became real. The Assyrian tyrants actually appeared, carved on palace walls, with their armies and their miserable captives. The great kings of Persia spoke through their own writings, and the pharaohs of Egypt could be identified.

All this gave a rich background for biblical history, the setting for the story of ancient Israel.

At the same time, views about the Old Testament were gaining ground which seemed to deny what the Hebrew books themselves said. Stories of Abraham and his family came, it was argued, from the times of the kings of Israel or later. Many of the laws attached to Moses' name grew up over a long period of time, some of them being the ideals of priests in the time of the exile. These, and related views, became very popular. They still are.

Some writers believed archaeological discoveries weighed against them, and began to use archaeology to 'prove' the Bible. But to do that, as some continue to do, is to ask archaeology to do more than it can.

Archaeology can neither prove the Bible nor disprove its major claims, for they are about God. There is no way archaeology could bring evidence to show that God spoke through Moses, for example, or that God sent Nebuchadnezzar to destroy Jerusalem. It is unlikely that anyone will ever find anything to do with, or written by, Moses.

Where archaeology can be helpful is over questions of human history and customs. If the Bible, or any other old book, says that people followed certain patterns of behaviour at a certain time, archaeological discovery may reveal whether or not they did.

If the results of archaeological discovery agree with the reports of ancient writers about an ancient practice, they still cannot prove that a particular instance mentioned in a text did take place. That would require independent written evidence about that occasion. But the fact that what the Bible states often agrees with ancient practices is a good basis for a positive approach to the biblical records (see, for example, *A Golden Temple, From Persian Postbags*).

Placing those records in their ancient setting is a major service of archaeology. It allows modern readers to appreciate them better on historical and cultural levels. Rarer discoveries, relating directly to passages in the Old or New Testaments, can give support to the witness of those passages, and add to them (see, for example, *No Hidden Treasure, 'The Assyrian Came Down...'*).

As all these discoveries increase our knowledge of the world in which the Bible was written, so they enable its distinctive religious message to stand out more boldly.

ENTREPRENEURS IN EGYPT

Napoleon Buonaparte invaded Egypt in 1798 and the team of scientists he took with him virtually founded modern Egyptology (see *The Mystery of Egyptian Hieroglyphs*).

Ancient Egypt became fashionable. The leaders of society bought furniture decorated in Egyptian style, and some imported ancient carvings from Egypt itself. Museum keepers, too, wanted fine objects. So people went to Egypt to bring back whatever they could.

One of the most unusual men involved was an Italian who had worked in a circus in London as a strong man, 'the Italian giant'. This man, Belzoni, had brains as well as brawn and invented a water-wheel much better, according to him, than any used in Egypt. In 1815 he displayed it in Cairo, but no one wanted it. He turned, instead, to transporting stone monuments from Egypt to England.

Belzoni's actions, breaking open tombs and ransacking temples, were deplorable when judged by later standards, yet he made many important discoveries and helped ancient Egypt to gain the hold on public imagination which it has never lost.

A number of other collectors and dealers in antiquities followed Belzoni's example. But there were scholars who worked more methodically. A German

The sun rises over the River Nile at Nag Hammadi, in Egypt.

team directed by Richard Lepsius worked from 1843 to 1845 investigating and making exact records of the tombs and monuments, at the same time collecting exhibits for the museum in Berlin. Lepsius edited twelve volumes of drawings and descriptions, *Denkmäler aus Ägypten*, which remain a basic source of knowledge.

Three Englishmen did a valuable job making copies of paintings and inscriptions which have since been destroyed or damaged. Some of their discoveries produced material for a famous book which one of them, Sir John Wilkinson, wrote: *The Manners and Customs of the Ancient Egyptians* (first published in 1837).

Bringing some order to archaeology in Egypt was the job a young Frenchman took on himself after a few years in the country. He was Auguste Mariette, who initiated the Cairo Museum in 1858, set up a local antiquities service and introduced laws to control the export of antiquities from Egypt. Mariette made a number of careful and important excavations.

Later in the nineteenth century,

excavation in Egypt was put on to a regular scientific basis by the energetic British archaeologist, Sir Flinders Petrie. Petrie was born in 1853 and educated by his parents and his own passion for collecting and arranging things. His father was a civil engineer who taught him the elements of surveying, which he then applied to ancient monuments in Britain.

In 1880 he went to Egypt in order to survey the pyramids, a task which took him the best part of two years. Tradition has it that he worked with only a walking-stick and a visiting-card, yet obtained very accurate results. Certainly he was a spartan, living on the barest necessities.

In 1883 the Egypt Exploration Fund, founded the year before, employed him to excavate in Egypt. Working there for most winters until 1926, he dug at about thirty different sites, making it a habit to publish a report of his work within a year of its completion.

Where earlier diggers had been seeking big buildings and objects for museums, Petrie gave his attention to the precise noting and comparison of small details. He was able to put earlier discoveries into their historical context, to rescue important evidence ignored by others, and make an orderly study of the amazingly varied things found in ancient Egypt.

When Petrie left Egypt, in 1926, there was no longer any room for archaeologists who ignored the humble potsherds or discarded animal bones. Archaeology had become a proper, scientific study.

It was Sir William Flinders Petrie who put excavation in Egypt onto a regular scientific basis, late in the nineteenth century.

CURIOSITIES FROM ASSYRIA

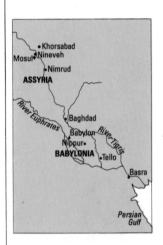

The name of Babylon never left people's minds, even after the place had turned into a wilderness. Babylon stood for luxury and evil living, for the Bible book of *Revelation* used its name for the centre of human wickedness.

What it was really like no one knew. A few Europeans who went to Baghdad saw the dusty mounds of Babil and picked up bricks with strange writing on them to bring home as curiosities.

The first to survey and describe the ruins was a remarkable young man, Claudius James Rich. At twenty he arrived in Bombay to work for the British East India Company, having travelled in Turkey, Egypt and the Near East. As well as speaking French and Italian, he could also speak Turkish, Arabic and Persian, and read Hebrew, Syriac and a little Chinese!

A year later the company appointed Rich to be their Resident in Baghdad, so he went there in 1807 with his eighteen-year-old bride. In 1811 they made an excursion to Babylon. Rich toured the mounds, making sketches and rough plans, and setting men to dig for inscribed bricks, seals and other objects.

His *Memoir on the Ruins of Babylon* was first printed in 1813 in Vienna and reprinted in London in 1815, 1816 and 1818, so much interest did it arouse. He made another visit in 1817 to check his earlier results, and published a *Second Memoir on Babylon* in London in 1818. Two years after that, the Riches made a long tour including Mosul, chief city of northern Iraq.

On the east bank of the Tigris, opposite Mosul, were the ruins of Assyria's former capital, Nineveh. Rich explored and surveyed these, and collected inscribed bricks and clay tablets. He kept notes of his travels but did not live to publish them. In 1821, while in Shiraz on his way to visit the ruins at Persepolis, he fell prey to a cholera epidemic and died, aged thirty-four.

His widow, who had gone ahead of him to Bombay, edited his diaries and they appeared in print in 1836 *(Narrative of a Residence in Koordistan)*. The British Museum bought the seals, inscriptions and manuscripts he had been collecting for £1,000 in 1825.

Rich's books were read widely. In France the government was persuaded to provide money for excavation in the promising mounds of Nineveh. Paul Emile Botta was sent to Mosul and opened his first trenches in the ruins of Nineveh in December 1842. He found very little during six weeks' work, so he was glad when local people told him of a place called Khorsabad, 22 km/14 miles to the north, where carved stones could be seen. Botta started digging there in 1843, continuing until 1845.

Only a little below the ground surface were the walls of a great palace. Lining the brick walls were slabs of stone carved with pictures and with cuneiform writing. At the main doorways stood enormous winged bulls, up to 4.8 metres/16 feet high.

Botta was delighted. He gathered more workmen to load the carvings on to carts, take them to the River Tigris to put them on rafts, and float them down to the port of Basra. Before packing them, Botta arranged for an artist to make drawings, thus recording them before any further damage could happen.

When the stones reached Paris they caused a sensation. Public interest rose higher when it was proved that the palace belonged to Sargon, the king of Assyria named in Isaiah 20:1, whose existence had been doubted because he was otherwise unknown.

In 1839 a twenty-two-year-old Englishman set out with a friend to walk from London to Ceylon, where a relative could find him a job. In 1840 they reached Mosul, then floated by raft down the Tigris to Baghdad. Soon afterwards they parted company.

One went on to finish his journey. The other, Austen Henry Layard, was spell-bound by the region and stayed behind. He spent some months in Persia, living among the tribesmen of the mountains, then returned to Baghdad. From there he was sent to the British ambassador in Istanbul with political messages. On the way he met Botta in Mosul.

The ambassador at that time was interested in antiquities so, after employing Layard on diplomatic errands, he gave him funds to begin an excavation in Assyria, with the approval of the Turkish sultan.

Late in 1845, Layard dug into the mound called Nimrud, which he had seen to the south of Nineveh. At once his workmen's shovels hit stone slabs lining the walls of rooms. Carvings in relief, cuneiform inscriptions, metal objects, and fragile pieces of carved ivory appeared.

Layard was convinced he had found Nineveh, and went home to London after eighteen months' work to write a best-selling book, *Nineveh and Its Remains* (1849).

Layard returned to Mosul in 1849 and began to dig in earnest in the mounds of Nineveh where he suspected more sculptures could be found, despite Botta's failure. He was right. During the years 1849-1851 he and his local assistant, Hormuzd Rassam, uncovered rooms lined with almost 3 km/2 miles of stone carvings. These belonged to the palace of Sennacherib (king of Assyria, 705-681 BC) and included his famous pictures of the siege of Lachish (see *'The Assyrian Came Down . . .'*).

In one room lay thousands of small

The Illustrated London News *publicized many dramatic finds by early archaeologists such as Austen Henry Layard.*

Decorating the palace of King Sargon of Assyria at Khorsabad was a great winged bull (left). Paul Emile Botta was the first to excavate the mound. When the carvings he found were taken to Paris, they caused a sensation.

Some of the most famous Assyrian carvings are those which show King Ashurbanipal and his courtiers hunting and killing lions.

clay tablets covered with cuneiform writing, part of the library of the palace. Important and exciting as the sculptures are, these documents supply the really vital information about Assyrian history, religion and society. All these treasures were shipped to England, to the British Museum. Layard finished his digging in 1851, becoming a politician, diplomat and art collector.

Assyria and Babylonia now became a hunting-ground for show-pieces to fill museum cases. In the south, only clay tablets, metal-work and other small objects were found, rather to the disappointment of explorers. Assyria continued to yield sculptured friezes to the spades of French excavators at Khorsabad and, supremely, to Rassam at Nineveh. There he found the palace of Ashurbanipal, the last great king of Assyria (669-627 BC). Another large collection of clay tablets came from it, and the magnificent scenes of the king hunting lions and other wild animals which are now so famous.

The pace of discovery slowed down with the Crimean War (1853-56) and other problems. Scholars worked to interpret and publish the discoveries. In 1872 George Smith, an assistant in the British Museum who was studying the clay tablets, identified on one a

Marsh Arabs with a cargo of reeds work their way across the River Euphrates. Their way of life in the southern part of the great kingdom of Babylon has changed little over the millennia.

story of a great flood very similar to the story of Noah's flood in Genesis (see *The Babylonian Story of the Flood*). This created a new wave of popular interest, and a leading newspaper, *The Daily Telegraph*, paid for new excavations at Nineveh.

Now more French scholars set to work in Babylonia, uncovering remains of the Sumerian culture from before 2000 BC. At Tello they found fine statues of a prince Gudea who ruled about 2100 BC.

A team from the University of Pennsylvania excavated in the Sumerian religious centre of Nippur from 1887, recovering thousands of cuneiform tablets, including many with myths and hymns about the gods and goddesses worshipped there.

At the very end of the century, a German expedition opened trenches in Babylon. Led by an architect, Robert Koldewey, it set new standards of precision in digging and recording.

Archaeology in Assyria and Babylonia had moved from a treasure hunt to become a scientific exploration of the past.

At Nimrud, close to Nineveh, Layard discovered rooms lined with stone slabs and doorways guarded by stone bulls. Arabs stare amazed at the first one to be unearthed.

IN THE LAND OF THE BIBLE

An American, Edward Robinson, stands at the beginning of archaeology in Palestine, although he never dug into an ancient site, and even thought that the mounds of earth *(tells)* which mask them were natural hills.

In two journeys to Palestine, in 1848 and 1852, Robinson and his friend Eli Smith explored the country and, by careful study of the landscape, identified a hundred places named in the Bible which had not been properly located before. This basic work, together with a description of the country, was published as *Biblical Researches in Palestine* (1841) and *Later Biblical Researches* (1856).

Mapping the land accurately was a major task. Another American, W.F. Lynch, made an essential contribution when he and his men sailed from the Sea of Galilee down the River Jordan in two prefabricated metal boats. The journey took them a week, 10-18 April 1848. He made the first detailed map of the river's twisting course, and found out that the Dead Sea's surface lies 1,300 feet below sea level.

The major work, the geographical survey of western Palestine, was done by the Palestine Exploration Fund, founded in London in 1865. British army officers were sent by the Fund to map Jerusalem and the countryside.

Between 1872 and 1878 C.R. Conder and H.H. Kitchener (later Lord Kitchener of Khartoum) surveyed over 6,000 square miles of country, marking more than 10,000 sites. Their maps, although replaced in recent years, underlie all others.

The Palestine Exploration Fund also made some excavations, especially around the edge of Herod's Temple in Jerusalem (see *Herod's Great Temple*). Not much productive digging was done, however, until 1890, when Flinders Petrie made a short visit from Egypt.

For six weeks he worked at a mound called Tell el-Hesy. There he saw the importance of relating the pottery, commonly lying on ancient sites, to the different levels of earth in which it was found. From the relative positions of the pieces he was able to work out which types were the oldest and so classify the pottery by age.

Thus he set the pattern for all later work in Palestine. Where there are no inscriptions or coins the pottery offers some clues about the date of the building in which it lies.

In Palestine there are none of the enormous stone temples or brick palaces of Egypt and Assyria. The Palestinian mounds demand much more attention from the archaeologist for fewer spectacular rewards. Observing and recording are vital. After Petrie's new approach, others gradually realized this.

An American expedition began to explore the site of Samaria in 1909 and 1910. King Herod's builders had destroyed much of the Israelite palace when they built a new temple (see *Herod, the Great Builder*), so it was very hard to trace the plan of the palace and its history. Happily G.A. Reisner, the director, was a meticulous and sharp-eyed excavator with

The hill-country of Judea and its small towns form the backcloth to much of the biblical record.

Dame Kathleen Kenyon was one of the most influential archaeologists to work in Palestine. She is most famous for her excavations at Jericho.

Petrie had the pottery found in his excavations at Tell el Hesy drawn on site before the objects were removed to the safety of a museum.

The aerial view (above right) shows the great 'tell' or city-mound of Lachish. The Bible records how the city fell to the invading Assyrians.

experience in Egypt. He noted the layers of soil with care, so that he could unravel the story. Reisner did not dig any more in Palestine and his methods were ignored by other excavators.

W.F. Albright, the leading American archaeologist, began to excavate in 1922 and refined the dating of pottery by comparing pieces from one site with pieces from all the sites, through his own unrivalled knowledge of them.

One of the most influential archaeologists to work in Palestine in the past fifty years was Dame Kathleen Kenyon (1906-1978). When she joined an expedition at Samaria in 1931 she used a technique of excavation she had learnt working in Britain with Sir Mortimer Wheeler. In her own excavations at Jericho (1952-1958) she applied this stratigraphic method of digging and recording with brilliant results, even though they proved disappointing for biblical studies (see *And the Walls Came Tumbling Down*).

The Kenyon excavations at Jericho, and her later series at Jerusalem (1961-1967), trained or influenced many of the archaeologists who have worked in Palestine since, although some Israeli scholars follow slightly different procedures. All are concerned to learn as much as possible from an excavation, aiming first to learn about the whole history of a place, and then looking at its value for interpreting the Bible.

DECIPHERING ANCIENT WRITINGS

The languages of the Bible, Hebrew, Aramaic, and Greek, have always been understood by some people, but the other languages of people who lived in biblical times were mostly forgotten. They are completely lost, of course, if their speakers did not write them down, and write them on stone or other materials that will survive over a long period of time.

These two factors mean that the scales are weighted against the recovery of ancient writings, yet they do survive in large numbers from certain places. From some places and some peoples we have no written documents at all. This is the case for the Philistines, for example. Their language is unknown, apart from one or two words and names preserved in the writings of other peoples (such as the Philistine name 'Goliath', recorded in the Bible).

The ancient written documents we read today survive by accident. Often they are not ones which modern scholars would have chosen if they had had any say. Accounts from Samaria tell us about administration and taxes in ancient Israel. There are no texts about the running of the king's court or dealing with crime, no hymns to Baal or letters from foreign kings.

Even when a wide variety of documents is available, as in Egypt or Babylonia, they are still a selection, and they give incomplete and unbalanced pictures. Often the letters sent to one man exist but his replies are lost, so their contents are a matter of guesswork.

Again, texts recovered in groups or archives tend to belong to the last generation or two of people who lived in, or used, the building. They threw away older documents unless they had a special value — as, for example, legal deeds and other family records.

Reading ancient writings is often difficult because they are damaged or broken. There may be more than one way to fill the gap, each resulting in a quite different sense. If part of the record is missing, its purpose or its date may be unknown, or the end of a story be lost.

To read the forgotten languages of the biblical world demands time and hard study, but all the major ones are now understood. Less than 200 years ago they were mysteries. Deciphering Egyptian hieroglyphs and Babylonian cuneiform was a great achievement of nineteenth-century scholarship, and the stories deserve to be told. There is now no doubt about the interpretation of most ancient texts. New discoveries serve as checks on older views, in language as much as in archaeology.

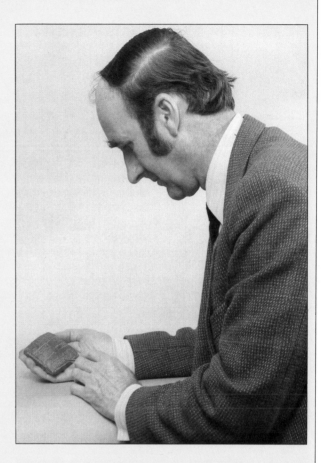

The author holds in his hand a clay tablet from Nuzi dating from about 1400 BC and written in Babylonian cuneiform script.

THE MYSTERY OF EGYPTIAN HIEROGLYPHS

Until the discovery of the Rosetta Stone no one was able to read the ancient hieroglyphic writing which could be seen everywhere on the walls of the tombs and temples of ancient Egypt.

A warship sailed away from the coast of Egypt. On board was Napoleon Buonaparte, with a small party of officers. It was August 1799.

Little more than a year earlier, Napoleon had invaded Egypt with a fleet and a large army. Now he was leaving his army, and the British Admiral Nelson had destroyed his fleet. Napoleon had hoped to make Egypt a French possession, so that he could move on to attack the British in India. His adventure was a failure in every way but one.

With his army had travelled 175 French scientists. They were to map and describe the land. They did their work thoroughly, returning to Paris with notes and drawings that were eventually published in twenty-four volumes as *Déscription de l'Egypte* (1809-1828). Their work was the foundation of modern Egyptology.

Among the large collection of ancient Egyptian carvings which Napoleon's men collected was a stone slab found near Rosetta on the River Nile. The stone itself, with the rest of the collection, was brought to London as a prize of war when the army Napoleon had left behind surrendered to the British. Drawings and plaster casts had already reached Paris. There the Rosetta Stone caused a lot of excitement, for it seemed to be the key to the mysteries of ancient Egyptian writing, the hieroglyphs.

At the top of the stone are fourteen lines of hieroglyphs, then thirty-two lines of a sort of Egyptian handwriting, demotic, and finally fifty-four lines of Greek.

Reading the Greek was not difficult. It was part of a decree issued by King Ptolemy V in 196 BC. But, try as they would, no one could make progress in reading the Egyptian, beyond two or three names.

Napoleon failed to conquer Egypt, but it was a Frenchman who was victorious in the struggle to decipher the writing of ancient Egypt. This man was Jean-François Champollion. Born in 1790, he showed himself a gifted child, studying Latin, Greek and Hebrew at the age of eleven.

Shortly after that, Champollion saw Egyptian inscriptions for the first time.

When he was told that no one could read them, he announced that one day *he* would. That became his passion.

He turned all his energy to learning ancient and obscure languages and to collecting everything he could about Egyptian history. At seventeen he went to Paris to study further, enduring poverty and the political troubles of turbulent France. When he was twenty-three he published a thorough history of Egypt (*L'Egypte sous les Pharaons*, 1814). Although he was chased from his university post, he never halted his study, and made himself a master of Coptic, the language of the church in Egypt.

Suddenly, in the autumn of 1822, Champollion saw the true explanation of the writing. Until then he had thought the hieroglyphs had some sort of symbolic meaning, used as letters only to write foreign names. Now, looking at recently copied texts, he recognized that the signs were used for sounds as well as for words. Within a few days he successfully made sense of many kings' names, and announced his discovery in Paris on 17 September 1822.

Copies of newly-found inscriptions reached him a few weeks later and he was able to apply his system to them, with success. In 1824 he set out a full account of his discovery in a book which gave birth to modern knowledge of ancient Egyptian (*Précis du système hiéroglyphique des anciens égyptiens*). It was quite clear he had deciphered the hieroglyphs correctly.

Champollion was appointed curator of the king's new Egyptian Museum in Paris in 1826 and led an expedition to Egypt in 1828-29. He made many discoveries and brought more objects home to France. He was highly honoured by his fellow-countrymen, but died of exhaustion in 1832 at the age of forty-one.

The Rosetta Stone was the key which unlocked the mysteries of ancient Egyptian writing. It records a decree of King Ptolemy V in three languages: Greek (bottom), Egyptian demotic script (middle), and hieroglyphs (top).

Ra' - mes - (s) sw

One of the groups of hieroglyphs that gave Champollion the key to deciphering ancient Egyptian was the name of Ramesses. The third sign is strictly unnecessary, simply helping to 'spell' the value of the second.

SECRETS FROM THE ROCK OF BEHISTUN

Travellers on the road going west from Tehran, through Kermanshah in Persia, towards Iraq, pass a great cliff known as the Rock of Behistun (or Bisitun).

Three hundred feet above the ground, men can be seen carved in the stone. A tall figure raises his hand towards ten standing men, and two others stand behind him. No one knew who they were. Guesses ranged from Christ and the twelve apostles to a school-master and his class!

Beside the picture the rock was polished smooth. Some who climbed near it reported that it was covered with arrow-head marks cut into the stone.

The same marks had caught the attention of visitors to parts of Persia from the seventeenth century on. The few Europeans who saw them made drawings of them which intrigued and puzzled the readers of their books. During the eighteenth century more men went to see them, and some began to decipher them.

There was agreement that they were a form of writing, not decoration, as some people had said. Cuneiform, 'wedge-shaped', was a name invented for them for French and English, derived from Latin (in German the name is *Keilschrift*).

First to make headway was the hardy explorer Carsten Niebuhr. Reading books about Persia had excited him. He learnt Arabic and led an expedition from Denmark in 1761.

He travelled through Arabia to India, arriving in Bombay with a doctor, the only other survivor of the party. Undiscouraged, he set off for Persia, where he spent three weeks copying the inscriptions at the ancient ruined capital, Persepolis (see *Persian Splendours*). After studying what he had seen, he published an account of his journeys and of the inscriptions in 1774-1778 *(Reisebeschreibung von Arabien und anderen umliegenden Ländern)*.

Niebuhr added to his copies an attempt to translate the writing. He saw that there were three different kinds, the simplest one being an alphabet. Out of the forty-two letters he recognized, thirty-two turned out to be right when the inscriptions were finally understood.

Neibuhr's work spurred a number of men to try to improve the understanding of this cuneiform alphabet. One correctly argued that it was written by the kings of the Persian Empire, Cyrus, Darius and their successors — but could not read it.

The one who succeeded was Georg Grotefend, a school-master at Göttingen in Germany. His hobby was to solve puzzles, especially puzzles with words. One day, about 1800, a friend who had been drinking with Grotefend made a bet that he could not read the Persian writing. In 1802 Grotefend announced that he had deciphered the writing and identified the names of Darius and Xerxes with words for 'son' and 'king'.

Unhappily, Göttingen University was not interested in Grotefend's work, so its full publication was delayed until 1805. He did not carry his work much further forward, that was done by other scholars.

Behistun and its inscriptions were the means of completing the decipherment of what we now call 'Old Persian' cuneiform. At the same time, they opened the door to deciphering the much more complicated Babylonian cuneiform writing.

An energetic Englishman squeezed the secrets from the Rock of Behistun.

Henry Rawlinson went to work for the East India Company in 1827, at the age of seventeen. He learnt Indian languages and Persian, served with the army in the 1st Bombay Grenadiers, and went to Persia in 1835 as military adviser to the Shah's brother, governor of Kermanshah.

Near the city were two inscriptions on rocks. Examining them, Rawlinson worked out the names of Darius and

Gigantic sculptured figures on the Rock of Behistun stand above the cuneiform inscription cut into the cliff face. Henry Rawlinson, copying the inscription into his notebook, did so at considerable risk. The prize was the deciphering of cuneiform signs for the first time.

Major General Sir Henry Rawlinson (1810-1895) was one of the great pioneers in deciphering Babylonian cuneiform.

Xerxes, apparently unaware of what Grotefend and others had done. Then he went to the Rock of Behistun.

In 1835 he began to copy. At the end of the year he was ill and spent some time in Baghdad where he evidently discussed ancient inscriptions with the British Resident. After military exercises, he returned to Kermanshah to find papers sent by the Resident explaining Grotefend's work.

Later in 1836, in 1837, and again in 1844 and 1847, Rawlinson copied the texts at Behistun. It was not easy to reach parts of them.

He described the work on the cliff face: '. . . ladders are indispensable . . . and even with ladders there is considerable risk, for the footledge is so narrow, about 18 inches, or at most 2 feet in breadth, that with a ladder long enough to reach the sculptures sufficient slope cannot be given to enable a person to ascend, and if the ladder be shortened in order to increase the slope, the upper inscriptions can only be copied by standing on the topmost step of the ladder, with no other support than steadying the body against the rock with the left arm, while the left hand holds the note-book and the right hand is employed with the pencil. In this position I copied all the upper inscriptions and the interest of the occupation entirely did away

Rawlinson's notebooks, preserved in the British Museum, show how he worked to achieve his decipherment. This is a detail from one page.

with any sense of danger.'

In another passage he told how a ladder he was using to bridge a chasm came apart and left him hanging over a precipice to be rescued by his friends. Such was the price of decipherment!

Rawlinson sent a first essay to London, translating and commenting on 200 lines of the inscription in 1837. His major study, *Memoir on the Persian Version of the Behistun Inscriptions*, appeared in 1846 and was completed in 1849. With that, the study of Old Persian was firmly founded.

Rawlinson guessed that the two other sorts of cuneiform writing on the cliff gave translations of the Persian inscriptions. In one of the scripts there were over 100 signs, too many for it to be an alphabet.

Grotefend identified a few signs, and a Danish scholar, Niels Westergaard, several more, using examples of the same writing found elsewhere in Persia.

It was Rawlinson, again, who made the major contribution. He sent his copy of the text to London, with a translation and notes, and it was printed in 1855 after careful editing and improving by Edwin Norris of the Royal Asiatic Society.

The language of this second sort of cuneiform writing was named Susian or Elamite, because it was found mostly at Susa, capital of ancient Elam (see *Persian Splendours*).

With two of the three writings deciphered, Rawlinson turned to the third. This is the most complicated and was the most awkward to reach of the inscriptions at Behistun. In 1847 Rawlinson paid a local Kurdish boy to clamber across the sheer rock face, hanging by a rope, banging wooden wedges into cracks to gain a foothold.

The boy reached the right part of the rock where, dangling in a rope cradle, he took an impression of the engraved signs with large sheets of damp paper. Little more than a year later, Rawlinson felt he could understand the sense of the inscription.

He spoke about his work in London in January 1850.

Other discoveries of cuneiform inscriptions had been made, and other men were trying to read them. In a quiet Irish rectory an Anglican clergyman, Edward Hincks, devoted himself to the mystery. Already, in 1847, he had published lists of signs with their values, and the meanings of some words. Hincks deserves great credit beside Rawlinson as a pioneer in deciphering Babylonian cuneiform. It was he who told Layard the meaning of the inscriptions he unearthed in Assyria (see *The Price of Protection*).

The papers by Hincks and Rawlinson were sent to other scholars who interested themselves in cuneiform, so that all could share in the work. There were many mistaken attempts before everyone accepted that Hincks was right in claiming that the signs stand for syllables (*ba, ad, gu, im,* etc.), although some of them could also be words (*an* is also 'god', *ilu*).

Hincks also observed that the signs were originally invented to write a different language from the Semitic Assyrian and Babylonian. Later, the language was revealed to be the quite unrelated Sumerian.

Were Rawlinson, Hincks and others right, or was their decipherment mistaken?

1 ya - ú - a son of

1 khu - um - ri - i.

One of the first Assyrian inscriptions to be deciphered was on the Black Obelisk which bears a picture of tribute sent by a king named as 'Jehu, son of Omri', one of the kings of Israel (see The Price of Protection).

In 1857 one man interested in the subject, Henry Fox Talbot, a pioneer in photography, proposed a test. A text should be sent to the decipherers for each to translate independently, the results being submitted to an independent judge.

Rawlinson, Hincks, Talbot and a French scholar, Jules Oppert, took part. The translations were so similar as to make it certain the script had been deciphered.

Now the publication and translation of the inscriptions could go ahead. The records of Assyria and Babylonia could speak again, 2500 years after they had fallen silent.

DIGGING UP THE PAST

Villagers have dug into the mound on which their present village is built, disclosing layers of earth and an ancient brick wall.

Stories of buried treasure are common all over the world. For as long as people have built houses and lived in towns and villages, they have been finding things their forebears lost or buried.

Usually these things are found by accident, and most of them are so uninteresting, they have simply been thrown away. The only things people have kept are objects of gold and silver, or things which they can admire.

This is still true today. Farmers ploughing fields will keep anything they think is valuable that their ploughs turn up, and throw away the rest. People combing the beach or countryside with metal-detectors hope to find money or valuables. They leave behind the nails and other odds and ends their machines locate.

Archaeologists are scientific

treasure-hunters. When they find gold and silver, or beautiful works of art, they are pleased. But everything people have used is valuable to them.

In certain circumstances a single piece of broken pottery may tell the archaeologist more than a gold ring. If, for example, the pottery was marked as an import from a country overseas, it could be a sign of foreign relations through trade or warfare.

Equally important are the ruined buildings, houses, temples, palaces, fortresses that people have built in the past, and the tombs they dug for their dead.

Digging ancient remains out of the ground can be exciting and rewarding. But simply pulling a jar or a jewel out of the earth, or clearing the rubbish down to the floor of a building, destroys valuable evidence.

Observing exactly where the things

lie, the different colours and textures of the soil, and how they are arranged in the ground, can reveal a great deal.

Was this pot underneath the earth floor or on it, or in the rubbish lying on it? If the first, it is older than the floor. If the second or third, it is likely it belonged to the people who used the building. If it was on top of rubble fallen into the house, it could belong to a much later date. Even if it was below the level of the floor, careful inspection might discover that it lay in a pit dug from a higher level long after the building was forgotten.

In the same way, following the layers or strata of earth may show that one wall was built earlier than another, if the layer of soil running up to the first wall was cut through by the foundations of the second.

It is as vital for the archaeologist to observe and record all of these matters

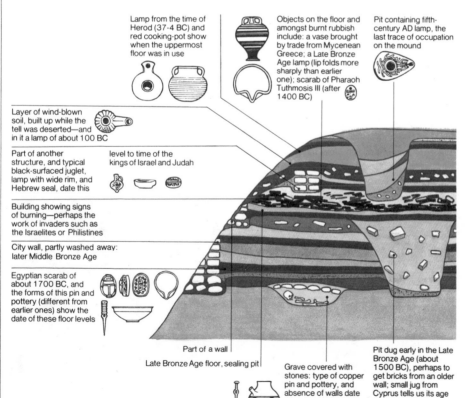

Lamp from the time of Herod (37-4 BC) and red cooking-pot show when the uppermost floor was in use

Objects on the floor and amongst burnt rubbish include: a vase brought by trade from Mycenean Greece; a Late Bronze Age lamp (lip folds more sharply than earlier one); scarab of Pharaoh Tuthmosis III (after 1400 BC)

Pit containing fifth-century AD lamp, the last trace of occupation on the mound

Layer of wind-blown soil, built up while the tell was deserted—and in it a lamp of about 100 BC

Part of another structure, and typical black-surfaced juglet, lamp with wide rim, and Hebrew seal, date this

level to time of the kings of Israel and Judah

Building showing signs of burning—perhaps the work of invaders such as the Israelites or Philistines

City wall, partly washed away: later Middle Bronze Age

Egyptian scarab of about 1700 BC, and the forms of this pin and pottery (different from earlier ones) show the date of these floor levels

Part of a wall

Late Bronze Age floor, sealing pit

Grave covered with stones: type of copper pin and pottery, and absence of walls date this to early Middle Bronze Age, about 1900 BC

Pit dug early in the Late Bronze Age (about 1500 BC), perhaps to get bricks from an older wall; small jug from Cyprus tells us its age

approximate dates

50 BC

100 BC

900-600 BC
1400 BC
1500 BC
1550-1200 BC
1800-1700 BC

about 1950 BC

The excavation of a town mound ('tell') shows the layers of earth and remains of previous buildings, with buried objects which may provide clues to the date.

in notes, photographs and drawings, as it is for him to describe the objects and the building he finds. All excavation is destructive; disturb the soil and it is impossible to replace it as it was before. What the archaeologist's eye misses is lost.

These essential facts have gradually become obvious over the last century and a half. In recent years all sorts of refinements have developed, and a wide range of techniques have entered archaeology from physics and chemistry, all aimed at extracting as much information as possible from what is found. In the end, the observant eye of the archaeologist is still the most vital tool.

In the lands of the Near East, where most of the Bible was written, people have been building their houses of stone and brick for more than 7,000 years. The stones may have fallen from their places, but they often survive. Bricks, however, were made of mud dried in the sun, not baked in a kiln, and so they usually disintegrate quite quickly, unless they are buried in the ground.

The life of a simple mud-brick building, therefore, might span only thirty years or so before the walls started to give way. Where this was the normal building material, repairs and total rebuildings were frequent.

That is the process which built up the great mounds of ruined towns and villages visible all over the Near East, one house rising upon the remains of the earlier one. (The same process can be seen in many other lands; in cities of Europe, for example, streets of the Roman period lie 3–7 metres/10–20 feet below the modern roads. The stumps of walls and the debris of medieval and later times make up the difference.)

The need to observe all the time digging is in progress, and the need to record all that is found, makes excavation a slow and demanding task. Consequently, the excavation of an entire town is very rare. Expeditions may concentrate on the buildings of one period or, more commonly, dig in selected areas.

The archaeologist may choose to dig where a farmer has uncovered a carved stone, or explorers have noted the lines of walls or large quantities of pottery. He may hit a part that has always been important, perhaps as the highest quarter of the town, or the best situated for sun and wind. On the other hand, he may miss the chief buildings, learning much about the houses of the poorer people.

So the restricted areas cleared, as well as the amount of destruction worked on the ruins over the course of

Carved stones from earlier buildings, like the bull (below right) were often reused by later builders on the same or nearby sites.

At Nimrud in Iraq, workmen dig and basket boys carry away unwanted earth.

Excavation is in progress at a Sumerian burial site in northern Iraq.

centuries by mankind and the elements, mean that the complete history of a site is beyond recovery. What is found can never be more than a part, a sample of what once existed.

This is an important condition to keep in mind when reading any study based on archaeological discoveries. Unless the evidence is very soundly established and is evaluated in the light of other knowledge of the time and region, it may be misleading. And what applies to archaeological discoveries also applies to written documents. They, too, are only a sample of all that was written in ancient times. Although thousands of them lie in modern museums, many thousands more have been lost.

Few buildings, few texts, and few objects were made in order that they should last for distant generations to

read. The majority survive by accident and are found by accident. Indeed, some things found may not even be typical of their kind. This means that a new discovery can force scholars to change their accepted positions completely, or to revise them.

To take just one example, the recent finding of a palace at Ebla in north Syria with thousands of clay tablets written about 2300 BC is opening new areas of study in history and language (see *Headline News: The Lost City of Ebla*).

As farming and towns spread across parts of the Near East where no one has lived for centuries, ancient sites risk destruction. Excavating these places has priority, but others can be studied at leisure. There is much work yet to be done, and many more discoveries to be made.

A DAY ON A DIG

It is dark when we get out of bed. After a quick wash in a basin of cold water, we walk across the courtyard of the mud-brick house to a long room. This serves as the expedition's meeting-place and dining-room. Cups of tea, pieces of bread, and a tin of apricot jam are on the table, a snack before the day's digging starts. Chattering and clattering in the court-yard tell us that the workmen have come to collect their shovels and pick-axes, and baskets for carrying earth.

Sleepily, we pick up our notebooks, pencils, tape-measures, labels, paper-bags and boxes, and walk out after them across the mound to the trenches. The sun is about to rise. Over the hill to the east shines a rosy glow, then, quickly following, the sun's disk blazes light over the countryside.

After the workmen had left yesterday, we had assessed progress to decide where to dig deeper, and where to stop. Now we show the two pick-men the area for today's work. Part of a brick wall is showing, and we want to follow it down to the floor, then trace its course across the area of our trench. At first the work is heavy, vigorous digging, to clear away mud-bricks that have fallen from the wall and weathered into a mass of hard mud with nothing else in it. The picks swing, the mud-bricks give way and soon there is a pile of loose earth.

The two men stop, and step aside to rest. In their place come the four shovel-men and the basket boys. They scoop up the earth, two or three shovelfuls to a basket. The boys swing the baskets to their shoulders and pad away to tip the earth over the edge of the mound. (Excavating is often done after harvest, when the men have little work to do in the fields and the boys are on holiday from school.)

We watch, checking that the earth is nothing but decayed brick, until the picks strike into different-coloured soil. Under the fallen bricks is a layer of rubbish. Perhaps we are near the floor. The pick-men wait while we test the ground with trowels. The dark, ashy soil is several inches thick and stretches for some distance. All the fallen brick-work has to be cleared away before deeper digging is done.

As the picks hack into it we describe the change in the notebook, give a number to the new layer and prepare a bag, marked with the number of the trench, the layer and the date, ready for any finds. At last the sterile brick-mass is gone. The wall stands clear at one side, patches of fine mud-plaster still sticking to it.

Now the pick-men dig very gently into the ashy level. They are trained to detect any hardness or object in the ground by the feel and sound of the steel point as it touches the earth. Often, the soil will fall away from a stone or a pot as soon as it is loosened. The paper bag begins to fill as pieces of pottery come out of the ground. Less earth is being shifted, the basket boys need not run so fast!

As we are examining the pottery, one of the pick-men calls. He has hit a black square a few inches long; it is a piece of wood, charred in a fire. Is it only a piece of wood? Is it shaped or carved? It is too delicate to handle. With trowel and knife we cut it from its place in a block of mud and lay it on a cotton-wool bed in a cardboard box to be taken to our make-shift laboratory.

Expert treatment can solidify it before it is studied. Even if it is simply a lump of wood, botanists can identify the tree and atomic physicists can measure its age by the Carbon 14 test. (All living organisms contain a radio-active carbon isotope, C14, in a regular proportion. After death this substance begins to decay at a known rate, so that half of it will have disappeared after 5,730 years. Measuring the proportion of Carbon 14 in the material enables its age to be calculated.) There is a great deal of broken pottery — ancient people were very careless and very untidy. Two bags are full, we need to commandeer a basket to hold all the pieces.

A lot more wood is uncovered, bigger pieces from the beams of a roof or floor, so more samples have to be taken and the position of each one measured and noted on a sketch-plan. Putting their picks aside, the workmen scrape and dig gently with trowels and knives.

As well as pottery and wood, there are green spots in the ground at one place. Very slowly the earth is cut away. Lying there, complete, though badly corroded, is a copper ring with an Egyptian scarab as its stone. Before we lift it, its position is noted, for

A Danish archaeology student sieves earth, looking for coins, at the site of a fifth century AD Jewish village on the Golan Heights.

that may help to tell us why it was lying just where we found it. Everyone is pleased. We have made a good 'find'.

Hardly is the ring packed in a clearly labelled box, when one of the basket-boys comes running back. As he tipped his load away, his sharp eyes saw a flash of bright colour. In the palm of his hand he holds a tiny bead of polished red stone. It goes into an envelope, is duly labelled, and a note is entered in the book. The boy's name is written on the envelope, too — a good mark for him!

We've been busy and three hours have passed. It's time for breakfast. Back at the dig house we eat eggs, boiled or scrambled, bread and more apricot jam, with tea or coffee to drink. There's half an hour to rest, discuss finds and progress, warn the registrar that more finds may be coming. His job is to draw and describe them for the records of the expedition and of the national Department of Antiquities.

In the second half of the morning the pace of work slows as noon approaches. Soon it will be time to end the digging for the day. In the strange way things happen, a few minutes before work finishes the pick-man stands up, nursing something in his hands, and comes to us. He has picked up something he has never seen before.

Everyone gathers round to stare at a small lump of brown mud. One flat side has little marks impressed all over it. It is a Babylonian cuneiform tablet, an outstanding discovery, a written document perhaps bringing names and personalities to the mute walls and potsherds. But as we gingerly take it from him we see that two edges are newly broken. Are the other parts still in the ground, or did we all miss them?

The man's face falls; he goes back to look, the shovel-men and the basket-boys sift the loose soil. Soon they are all happy. One piece was in a basket ready to be carried away to the tip, two more were still in the ground. The positions of the pieces are recorded, then all are solemnly borne to the house, where the news has already spread.

Hurrying from the other side of the mound comes the epigraphist, the expert in writing and languages, who has spent a miserable three weeks without a single inscription to study. With paintbrush and pin he cleans the dirt away from the first two lines, a grain at a time. Everyone is waiting. What does it say? It is a letter addressed to a king, the king of the city everyone has believed the place to be. Now there is no room for doubt.

Dinner is ready, an interruption, but a welcome

An artist makes a careful copy of a relief portrait of Pharaoh Tutankhamun, on site.

one. Discussion goes on around the table. Records from other cities speak of this king and his contemporaries, so we can give him an approximate date. How long after that did the tablet stay on a shelf in the building? Is it the palace we are digging into? Will there be more tablets, more rings?

After dinner most of the expedition takes a siesta for an hour or two, to wash and shave, write letters. Refreshed, we continue to clean and draw the finds, sort and mend the pottery, draw plans, take photographs and pore over the tablet. The sun sets, paraffin lamps are lit. The cook has a special supper ready — frogs' legs from the nearby river — a change from tinned meat bought in the town twenty miles away. Contented, we retire to bed, stumbling across the rough courtyard in the moonlight, to dream of more tablets, more pots, palaces, rings and archives. The mound has many more treasures waiting to be found!

The 'day on a dig' describes the traditional way of excavating in the Near East. A director with a small team of experts from Europe, or America, or from the near eastern country itself, works with local labour. In recent years, some directors have welcomed students and other volunteers to work on their sites, almost completely dispensing with local workmen.

'OF COURSE, IT'S THE FLOOD!'

Leonard Woolley, the archaeologist in charge at Ur, instructed his workman to dig a small pit, to find the ground surface on which the first settlers had built their reed huts. That would mark the birthplace of the great city Ur of the Chaldees.

The workman dug down to a clean bed of clay, with no broken fragments of pottery. 'That's the bottom sir,' he shouted. But Woolley was not so sure.

The workman was still standing more than 2 metres/6 feet above sea-level and Woolley reckoned that was also the original level. Unwillingly, the man agreed to dig deeper. He dug and dug, through 2.5 metres/8 feet of clean soil, and then more pottery began to appear. At last he hit true virgin soil, 1 metre/3 feet below modern sea level, and about 19 metres/62 feet from the surface of the ruin mound.

What was this thick layer of sterile soil?

Woolley thought he knew, and when two assistants could give no answer, he turned to his wife.

'Well, of course, it's the flood,' she remarked.

When the soil was analysed, it was shown to be silt deposited by water. On the basis of that, and related discoveries, Leonard Woolley claimed he had found physical evidence of the great flood which Sumerian, Babylonian and Hebrew stories recall.

All sorts of writers took up Woolley's discovery. Some seized on it as proof of the biblical story of Noah. Others saw it simply as the remains of one of the many floods that overwhelmed the cities of Babylonia.

News of the flood-level at Ur had hardly broken before another excavator claimed he had found a layer of silt left by the flood. He was working at Kish, 220 km/137 miles north of Ur.

Now the debate began.

The Ur layer, deposited about 4000 BC, was much older than the one at Kish. Did either represent the flood?

Excavations at other places in

Babylonia produced clean levels like those at Kish, and belonging to roughly the same date, about 2800 BC.

None of the levels at other sites belonged to the same time as the level at Ur. Many scholars now argue that some of those later deposits mark the time of the flood.

They argue this because the date fits information preserved in Babylonian traditions. Some of the lists of early kings begin with the gods setting up kingship. After a few reigns the sequence is broken — 'Then came the flood' — and a fresh start follows. Other lists begin with the first king after the flood. Not so very long after that king, and within his line of succession, we meet a ruler whose own inscriptions survive. Since they have an archaeological date of about 2600 BC, the floods can be set a century or two earlier.

There is no doubt the flood was a catastrophic event that stayed in human memory as long as Babylonian civilization lasted. A variety of writings refer to it as a point in time. It was evidently more than a small local flood, the sort of thing most of the low-lying riverside towns of Babylonia could expect. Yet we are still not sure that these deposits of silt and clay are traces of it.

At Ur, Woolley admitted, the silt did not cover the whole site. The great depth of clean soil he dug through appeared to be the result of water running against part of the ruin mound, perhaps over a long period of time. Some of the other deposits, too, seem not to have destroyed or drowned the buildings where they are found. Perhaps Mrs Woolley was wrong, after all, and it was only a flood, not *the* flood.

The snow-capped peak of Mt Ararat, in eastern Turkey, reaches to the sky. The Bible says it was on the mountains of Ararat that Noah's 'ark' came to rest, after the flood.

Another exciting discovery about the flood was made long before the excavations at Ur. In the 1850s Sir Henry Layard dug out of the ruins of Nineveh thousands of pieces of clay tablets. They were once the library of the Assyrian king Ashurbanipal, and were left lying broken and forgotten when his palace was destroyed in 612 BC. Layard brought the tablets to the British Museum in London. Over the years scholars catalogued and identified the pieces, making their work known in books and learned journals.

In 1872 George Smith was busy at this task when he realized the fragments on his desk belonged to a story of the flood. This was no ordinary flood, nor just a story of a flood. It had striking resemblances to the story of Noah in the biblical book of Genesis.

Smith described his discovery to a meeting of the Society for Biblical Archaeology, and it created a sensation.

The Babylonian story and the biblical one clearly shared so much that there could be no doubt there was a strong connection between them. But what was it? Did the Hebrew story derive from the Babylonian, the Babylonian from the Hebrew, or did both have a common source?

Ever since the discovery was announced, the first possibility has won greatest support. The second is held to be unlikely because the Babylonian account dates back to at least 1600 BC, well before the Hebrew one was written.

A small number of scholars have always taken the third position, that the stories have a common origin. Abraham's migration from Ur to Canaan could have carried the story westward; many scholars think the Israelites learnt it from the Canaanites.

What is the Babylonian Flood Story? Chapters 6–9 of Genesis tell of the flood as part of the continuing story of God's relations with mankind. The story George Smith found is also part of a longer tale. It is in the eleventh, and last, tablet of the Epic of Gilgamesh.

This epic tells how the ancient king Gilgamesh tried to win immortality. After many adventures he reached a distant land where lived the only man who had become immortal, a man named Ut-napishtim, the Babylonian Noah. He told Gilgamesh about the flood to explain why the gods gave him his eternal life. After the story was told, he showed Gilgamesh that he could not hope to become immortal, and sent him home.

Several details and oddities suggested that the Babylonian Flood Story did not begin as part of the Gilgamesh Epic. Thanks to the discovery of another poem, known as the Atrakhasis Epic, the story can now be seen in its proper setting.

Like Genesis, the Atrakhasis Epic tells of the creation of man and his history to the time of the flood and the new society which was set up after it. Here the reason for the flood is clear, which it is not in the Gilgamesh Epic. Mankind made so much noise that the chief god on earth could not sleep. The gods, having failed to solve the problem in other ways, therefore sent the flood to destroy these troublesome humans and silence them for ever.

The similarities between the

Records of the excavations at Ur, published in 1956, include this cross-section of the pit which cut through a thick layer of silt. Leonard Woolley claimed this was evidence of the flood.

Buildings of reeds, on the banks of the Euphrates, serve as reminders of a low-lying riverside area prone to flooding.

Babylonian and the Hebrew stories are easy to see. But there are notable differences which should not be overlooked. The basic one lies in the monotheism of the Hebrew account contrasted with the many gods acting in the Babylonian story. Equally different is the moral attitude. Details differ, too, about the form and size of the ark (the Babylonian one, a cube, would be unlikely to float on the water), the duration of the flood, and the sending out of the birds.

The similarities in the stories and the recognizably Mesopotamian background imply that they had a common origin. The archaeological evidence for floods in Babylonia, and the strong tradition of one major, disastrous flood, taken with the stories about it, point to a catastrophic event early in history. When it comes to the interpretation of the event the biblical record clearly stands apart from the others, supporting its own claim to be not just a human tale but the revelation of God.

THE BABYLONIAN STORY OF THE FLOOD

The Babylonian Flood Story, as it is told in the Epic of Gilgamesh, occupies almost 200 lines of poetry. The following extracts show how the story runs and give the flavour.

The gods in council decided to send the flood, and Ea, the god responsible for creating man, took an oath with them not to tell mankind about it. Ea, however, wanted to warn his worshipper Ut-napishtim, and so spoke to his house:

'Reed-hut, reed-hut, wall, wall!
Reed-hut listen, wall pay attention!'

He was really addressing Ut-napishtim:

'Pull down the house, build a ship!
Leave riches, seek life!
Spurn possessions in order to stay alive!
Take the seed of all creatures aboard the ship.
The ship you are to build
Its measurements shall equal each other
Its width and its length shall be the same.'

There follows a discussion about how Ut-napishtim should explain his work to his fellow citizens, and how he is to know when the flood will come. The solution was to hide the facts from them, and lead them to think the gods would bless them. Then the building of the boat is described. When it was made, Ut-napishtim continued:

'Whatever I had I put aboard it,
Whatever silver I had I put aboard it,
Whatever gold I had I put aboard it,
Whatever living creatures I had I put aboard it.
I made all my family and relatives board the ship.
The domesticated animals and the wild,
All the craftsmen, I made go aboard . . .
The fixed time arrived . . .
I looked at the pattern of the weather,
The weather was terrifying to see.
I boarded the ship and closed the door . . .

This seventh-century BC inscribed clay tablet, the eleventh tablet of the Assyrian version of the Epic of Gilgamesh, contains a Babylonian account of the flood.

With the first glow of dawn,
A black cloud rose up from the horizon.
Inside it the storm-god thunders . . .
The god of the underworld tears out the posts of the dam.
The warrior-god leads the waters on.
The gods raise the torches,
Setting the land on fire with their blaze.
The fearful silence of the storm-god reached the heavens,
And turned everything bright to darkness.
[   ] of the land shattered like a pot.
For one day the tempest [raged]
It blew hard . . .
Like a battle the divine might overtook the people.
No one could see his neighbour.
The people could not be recognized from heaven.
The gods were frightened by the flood.
They went off up to the heaven of the chief god.
The gods cowered like dogs, crouching outside the door.
The goddess Ishtar cried out like a woman in labour . . .
The gods weep with her . . .
For six days and seven nights
The wind, the flood, the storm overwhelmed the land.
When the seventh day arrived, the storm and flood ceased the war
In which they had struggled like a woman in labour.
I looked at the weather: it was still,
And all mankind had turned to clay.
The countryside was flat as a flat roof.
I opened the window, light fell upon my cheek,

Crouching down, I sat and wept . . .
On Mount Nisir the ship grounded . . .
When the seventh day came,
I sent out a dove, releasing it.
The dove went, then came back,
No resting-place appeared for it, so it returned.
Then I sent out a swallow, releasing it.
The swallow went, then came back,
No resting-place appeared for it, so it returned.
Then I sent out a raven, releasing it.
The raven went and saw the waters receding,
It ate, it flew about, to and fro, it did not return.
I brought out sacrifices and offered them to the four winds,
I made a libation on the peak of the mountain,
The gods smelled the savour,
The gods smelled the sweet savour,
The gods clustered like flies around the sacrificer.'
When at last the great goddess (Ishtar) arrived,
She lifted up the big fly (beads) which the chief god had made to amuse her.
"All you gods here, as I shall never forget my lapis lazuli necklace,
I shall remember these days, and never forget them . . .".'

Following a dispute over the survivor and advice to punish individuals for their sins, the gods ordained immortality for Ut-napishtim and his wife.

The biblical story begins in Genesis 6. Its tone and flavour is quite different from the Babylonian.

'God looked at the world and saw that it was evil, for the people were all living evil lives.

God said to Noah, "I have decided to put an end to all mankind. I will destroy them completely, because the world is full of their violent deeds. Build a boat for yourself out of good timber; make rooms in it and cover it with tar inside and out. Make it 133 metres long, 22 metres wide, and 13 metres high. Make a roof for the boat and leave a space of 44 centimetres between the roof and the sides. Build it with three decks and put a door in the side. I am going to send a flood on the earth to destroy every living being. Everything on the earth will die, but I will make a covenant with you. Go into the boat with your wife, your sons, and their wives. Take into the boat with you a male and a female of every kind of animal and of every kind of bird, in order to keep them alive. Take along all kinds of food for you and for them." Noah did everything that God commanded . . .'

'The Lord destroyed all living beings on the earth — human beings, animals, and the birds. The only ones left were Noah and those who were with him in the boat. The water did not start going down for a hundred and fifty days.

God had not forgotten Noah and all the animals with him in the boat; he caused a wind to blow, and the water started going down. The outlets of the water beneath the earth and the floodgates of the sky were closed. The rain stopped, and the water

gradually went down for a hundred and fifty days. On the seventeenth day of the seventh month the boat came to rest on a mountain in the Ararat range. The water kept going down, and on the first day of the tenth month the tops of the mountains appeared.'

ROYAL TREASURES FROM UR

The golden head-dress of flowers and leaves once belonged to a queen of Ur.

Sir Leonard Woolley had been excavating at Ur for only a few days in 1923 when one of his workmen dug out a small hoard of gold and stone beads. The men were new to the work, untrained, and Woolley was afraid that the sight of the gold might lead to secret digging and smuggling. He knew there was more to be found, but he stopped the digging at that spot for four years, until 1926.

He was uncertain, too, about what the man had found. No one had seen jewellery like this before. One experienced archaeologist reckoned it belonged to the Middle Ages and was 5–600 years old. Woolley himself thought it might be 2,000 years older, from the Persian period or just before.

When Woolley put the men to work in that place again the result was astonishing. They found a cemetery with hundreds of graves dug over a period of several centuries into an older rubbish tip. The majority of the burials were quite simple. Each grave contained a skeleton with a few pots, perhaps a little jewellery, some tools or weapons.

Sixteen burials were very grand. Great pits were sunk some 9 metres/ 30 feet from the surface to make a space up to 11 × 5 metres/32 × 16 feet at the bottom.

To reach the bottom, the tomb-builders cut a sloping shaft leading in at an angle. On the floor they built a small stone- or brick-vaulted chamber for the dead man. But these great shafts were designed to hold more than one body. To the excavator's amazement, dozens of bodies were lying on the floor of each shaft. Near the foot of the ramp were skeletons of oxen, once harnessed to a wagon. The reins had decayed, but some had been threaded through beads which were still on the lines where the reins ran.

Human skeletons beside the oxen Woolley identified as their grooms. Other bodies belonged to guards with spears and helmets stationed at the foot of the ramp. Still more were the court attendants. Musicians had their harps and lyres, the ladies wore bright headdresses of flowers and leaves cut from gold and silver sheets.

All the bodies were so neatly placed, Woolley concluded the people had walked down the ramp to their positions, lain down, and drunk poison from a small cup. (Some of the cups were beside the bodies.) Undertakers then tidied the scene, killing the oxen, some of which lay on top of their human attendants, and left. With great ceremonies and offerings, the shaft was refilled with earth.

Ancient robbers had tunnelled into the tombs and disturbed the central burials. They took all they could, still leaving plenty for Woolley's men. What was left made it clear these had been the tombs of kings. Royalty had to pass into the grave with all the trappings of state they had enjoyed in life. Their servants had to go with them, too, and it was probably an honour to be chosen.

Processes of decay had destroyed the clothing, basketry, leather and woodwork, yet, with brilliant makeshift techniques, Woolley was often able to preserve traces of rotten wood, or at least record them. If his workmen found a hole in the ground, he poured plaster of Paris down it. When the plaster had set, they would chip away

the soil to see what had been there. In this way the shapes of harps and lyres, spear shafts and many other wooden objects were recovered.

Through Woolley's skill and observation more was learnt about the culture of Ur about 2500 BC than any other Babylonian city of that time.

The Royal Tombs of Ur reflect the wealth of the city. Kings and queens drank from gold and silver beakers. For

Music as well as art was part of the cultural life at Ur. Only the gold bull's head and mosaic decoration of this lyre (below, left) could be recovered, but Woolley's careful records of the decayed woodwork made this reconstruction possible.

One of the finest treasures of Ur is the figure of a goat (below), decorated with gold, silver, lapis and shell.

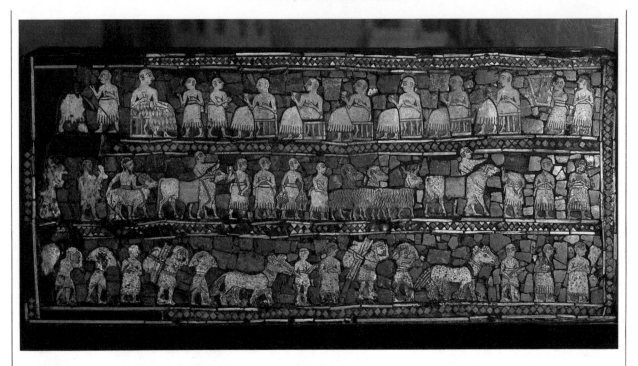

The 'standard' from the Royal Tombs at Ur is a mosaic of shell, red limestone and blue lapis lazuli. One side shows scenes of war, the other (pictured here) shows the victory feast and parade of booty. Several hundred years before the time of Abraham, the craftsmen of Ur were able to produce work of consummate skill.

The gold tools are also from the Royal Tombs at Ur.

show, the kings wore daggers with golden blades, the queens exquisite jewellery of gold and coloured stones. As they feasted they listened to singers accompanied on strings and pipes.

Metals and stone are not found in Babylonia. These had come by trade or conquest from foreign lands, the blue lapis lazuli from distant Afghanistan. In some of the tombs were the owners' seal-stones with their names and titles engraved on them. These allowed the dead people to be put in their historical setting.

The treasures of Ur have no direct connection with the Bible. Like many less spectacular discoveries they reveal the craftsmen's consummate skill and hint at the beliefs of the time — in this case a form of self-sacrifice abhorrent to both Judaism and Christianity. They date from several centuries before Abraham's time, reminding us that the beginning of Israel's history is set, not in an age of primitives, but in a world of men already highly civilized.

HEADLINE NEWS
The Lost City of Ebla

Week after week the workmen toiled under the hot Syrian sun. Italian archaeologists hired them for two months each year and they dug into the mounds they and their fathers called Tell Mardikh. 1964 saw the first season; 1965, 1966, 1967 came and went.

Obviously, an important city lay hidden here. A high bank all round the site marked the city wall, and a strongly-built gateway led through it at the south-west. A local man turned up a carved stone by the hill in the centre of the enclosure, and the archaeologists found more, large stone basins ornamenting a big temple.

All these buildings belonged to the Middle Bronze Age, 2000 to 1600 BC. Yet no one knew the city's name. In 1968 an answer came. Builders in the Persian era, about 500–400 BC, had found part of an old statue and taken it as a useful stone. Written on it was the name of the king who had had it made over 1,000 years before. He presented the statue to Ishtar, goddess of love and war, the Babylonian Venus. Beside the king's name was his title, 'King of Ebla'.

Ebla was the name of a city the powerful Babylonian kings Sargon and Naram-Sin claimed they conquered about 2300 and 2250 BC. Scholars had been looking for it for years. Usually they looked near the River Euphrates, 160 km/100 miles from Tell Mardikh. Of course, a king could travel a long way from home to set up a statue in another city, so this single stone did not prove that Tell Mardikh was Ebla.

In 1975 the answer was made certain. In a building below the big temple thousands upon thousands of cuneiform tablets were uncovered and they made the identity of the place clear beyond doubt. Ebla was found!

The tablets lay in a pile on the floor of a small room at one side of a courtyard. They were the archives of a palace that had flourished for a few generations, then burnt down. In the heat of the flames the brickwork was baked, and the tablets too, so that both were stronger to stand the wear of time.

Enemy soldiers did not leave visiting-cards but, because we have no reason to doubt the boasts of conquest by Sargon and Naram-Sin, we can assume the army of one of them sacked Ebla's palace. They looted it hastily, leaving behind plenty of things precious to the archaeologist. Pieces of stone statues modelled in Babylonian styles, morsels of gold plating and intricately carved woodwork, charred by the fire, had fallen to the floors to be covered by the crumbling building.

Ebla hit the headlines when a leading Italian expert began to study the tablets. Valuable as the other discoveries are, the written words bring life to the picture. Dates, names and personalities add vividness to the dusty objects and broken walls. The very first news from the tablets was intriguing. In the oldest written documents ever found in north-west Syria the language was closer to Hebrew than to Babylonian.

Then the names of some Eblaites were announced. Among many strange ones were some which had a more

familiar sound: Ishmael, Adam, Daud (David). Some names ended in *el*, the word for 'god', and some in *ya*. Was this a pattern, like the biblical name 'Michael', meaning 'Who is like God?' and 'Micaiah', 'Who is like the Lord' (Jehovah, or Yahweh, shortened to Yah)? Was this *ya* really the name of the God of Israel (see *The Engraver of Seals*)?

The expert asserted it was so, and some scholars agreed with him. He went further. Places Ebla ruled, or had some power in, covered a large area, even to Hazor, Megiddo and Lachish in Canaan, and the cities of the Dead Sea plain, Sodom and Gomorrah.

One king of Ebla had the name Ebrium. Might his name be the same as Abraham's ancestor, Eber, mentioned in Genesis 10:21, or as the word 'Hebrew'?

Journalists seized on this news. Ebla featured in magazines of all sorts and was hailed as 'proof' of the Bible. The tablets themselves had not been made accessible to other scholars. Only reports from the one in charge were circulated. Irresponsible writers then imagined that the modern political prejudices of the Near East were hindering the flow of information, a charge which was untrue.

The Ebla tablets are one of the outstanding archaeological discoveries of the 1970s. Regrettably, its size and its novelty led the Italian scholar to move too fast, to neglect normal precautions in dealing with a strange language. Now, an international team of experts, principally Italian, with representatives from Belgium, Britain, France, Germany, Iraq, Syria and the USA, has the responsibility to edit the entire collection. They have discarded most of the sensational claims.

Canaanite places do not occur in the tablets. Ebla had no contacts so far south, certainly not with the cities of the Dead Sea plain.

Names ending in *ya* may be short forms like Jimmy, Tommy, or the names may be read another way. There was no god Ya at Ebla, and no connection with Israel's God.

Ebrium was a high official, but not king. His name might be the same as Eber, but there is

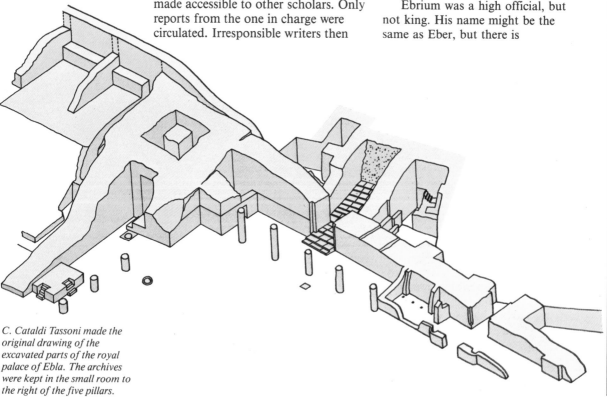

C. Cataldi Tassoni made the original drawing of the excavated parts of the royal palace of Ebla. The archives were kept in the small room to the right of the five pillars.

no reason to connect the two men. An association with the term Hebrew is unlikely.

Even the language of the tablets may prove closer to a Babylonian dialect than to Hebrew, although some citizens of Ebla did speak a language belonging to the same West-Semitic group as Hebrew.

Ten thousand documents written in a place from which none were previously known may well be full of difficulties. Long years of research will be needed for solving them. Meanwhile, the tablets are valued for their evidence that Babylonian writing spread to north Syria before 2300 BC, for their evidence of a readiness to write down every sort of administrative and legal activity, to write letters and literature, even to make dictionaries of different languages, and for their witness to the presence of West Semitic people there at that early date.

The later remains at Ebla illustrate the biblical texts more directly.

In its plan the big temple foreshadows Solomon's, with a porch, inner hall, and holy room. The proportions, however, are different.

Local royalty were buried in tombs hollowed out underneath a palace of the same period, 1800–1650 BC. Robbers had plundered the burials, but some treasures escaped them. Finely-worked gold beads were threaded for necklaces. There were gold bracelets, and a sceptre with a pharaoh's name spelt out in gold hieroglyphs.

A beautiful ring of gold, covered

with minute golden balls, had hung in a lady's nose. One may imagine the ring Eliezer gave to Rebekah at Harran was like it.

Ebla was a flourishing city in the days of the patriarchs.

Great discoveries often create rumours which excite false hopes and mislead people. In due course it is possible to make a balanced judgement and see what is really important. This is the case with Ebla.

When the dust raised by the first reports has died away, Ebla will be seen as a key site in early Syrian history, giving a brilliant insight into the level of culture there before the days of the patriarchs and during their period. The tablets will make knowledge of the early Semitic languages clearer, and so broaden our understanding of Hebrew.

It was the discovery of thousands of clay tablets, the palace archives, which made the identity of the 'lost city' of Ebla certain.

UR: CITY OF THE MOON-GOD

The train trundled through the night, privileged passengers asleep in bunks, others dozing on hard seats. With a jolt it stopped; bleary eyes looked out of the windows. The station's name, 'Ur Junction', had an air of unreality. We climbed down to the ground and spent the last part of the night in a convenient rest-house. Next morning, a mile or two across the flat plain, we reached the ruined city, Ur of the Chaldees.

The place is marked by a massive block of brickwork which can be seen from miles away. This was the temple of Sin, god of the moon, the chief god worshipped by the people of Ur.

Although the temple is even older, the bulk of the building standing today was erected by a king of Ur over 4,000 years ago. He made it as a series of platforms, one on top of another, each smaller than the one below. On the third platform stood the chapel where the people believed the god would live.

The Babylonians called the tower a ziggurat, meaning a mountain peak. A temple like this was a typical feature of a Babylonian city (see *The Glory that was Babylon*), rising above the flat countryside, a landmark to honour the gods and display the wealth of the king. In the city around the temple are ruins of other temples, palaces and

The temple of the moon-god dominates the ruins of Ur. It is more than 4,000 years old and was built as a series of stepped platforms with the house of the god on top. The biblical 'tower of Babel' was probably a temple tower of this kind.

tombs, and the houses of rich families.

When Sir Leonard Woolley, the archaeologist in charge of the excavation at Ur, cleared the dirt and fallen bricks from the houses, he found two areas quite well-preserved. A king of Babylon had destroyed Ur about 1740 BC, setting fire to some of the buildings. The inhabitants ran away, and only some came back to live in the houses again. Woolley was able to draw the plans of many streets, houses, shops and small chapels set among them. From his discoveries he was able to reconstruct their appearance and imagine life in the city.

In a typical town house the street door opened into a small lobby, perhaps provided with a jar of water for those arriving to wash their feet. A doorway at one side gave onto a courtyard. There were other rooms around the sides of the courtyard, among them store-rooms, a lavatory

and a kitchen. In the kitchen there might be a well, a brick-built table, an oven, and grinding stones for making flour, as well as the pots and pans the last owners left behind. A long room at the centre of one side could have been the reception room.

Arab houses built in recent times in the towns of Iraq follow almost the same plan. All the rooms may be on the ground floor. Houses in Babylonia 1,000 years later than those at Ur were also single-storey dwellings. In the houses at Ur there is usually a well-constructed staircase at one side of the courtyard. None of the walls stands high enough to prove there was an upper storey, but it seems very likely there were upstairs rooms.

The furnishings did not survive. Carvings, pictures on seal-stones and models made in clay, probably as toys, represent the folding tables and chairs,

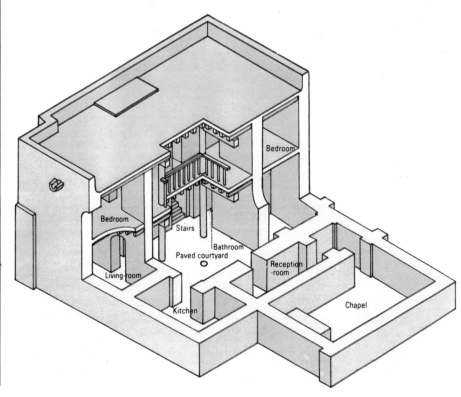

At the time of Abraham some well-to-do citizens of Ur may have lived in two-storey houses built in this style. In the centre was a paved courtyard, with bathroom, kitchen, chapel and other rooms around it.

wickerwork and basketry containers, wooden bedsteads and rugs that made the houses comfortable.

In larger houses one room could be set apart as a shrine. An altar of mud-bricks, carefully plastered, stood in one corner. An installation like a hearth nearby had a flue reaching to the ceiling, possibly for burning incense, and a mud-brick bench served as a table for cups of drink and dishes of food. Nothing reveals the sort of worship carried on in the houses. But probably the owners made offerings, praying to their family gods and commemorating their ancestors. Family feeling is demonstrated in twenty of the sixty-nine houses excavated. Vaulted chambers under the floors were tomb chambers. They might hold the remains of ten or a dozen people, earlier burials being pushed aside to make room for later ones. A proper burial, the Babylonians believed, prevented the dead from haunting the living.

Clay tablets left in the houses, some in small archive rooms, tell what the occupants of those houses were doing. Among them were merchants who traded to the south down the Persian Gulf, east into Persia, and north-west up the River Euphrates to Syria. There were local businessmen, priests and others in the service of the temples.

A beautiful gold dish was among the treasures discovered in the Royal Tombs at Ur.

A great flight of steps led up to the first level of the temple.

Their records deal with the sale and purchase of houses and land, slaves and goods, with adoption, marriage and inheritance, and all the affairs of a busy city.

In a few houses there were scores of tablets of a different sort. On round balls of clay, flattened to a bun shape, pupils had copied the teacher's handwriting in exercises to learn how to form the cuneiform signs. The next stage was to copy out the inscriptions of earlier kings, or hymns and prayers to gods and goddesses, or myths and legends about distant days.

We owe our knowledge of Sumerian and Babylonian literature to the activity of these teachers and their pupils. To help them learn the old Sumerian language they had tables of verbs, and for arithmetic they had tables of square and cube roots and reciprocal numbers. Tablets from other cities of the eighteenth century BC in Babylonia display a correct understanding of 'Pythagoras Theorem' — 1,200 years before Pythagoras formulated it!

Citizens of Ur between about 2100 and 1740 BC were able to enjoy quite a high standard of living in their prosperous city. So it is no surprise to find that they felt superior to the nomads who lived in the semi-desert beyond the areas watered by the River Euphrates. People who had 'no fixed abode', who ate raw meat and did not give their dead a decent burial were hardly human!

The nomadic people were called Amorites and seemed to come from Syria. They came in such large numbers that kings of Ur built a wall across Babylonia to try to keep them back.

More and more Amorites came, overran the wall and brought to an end the rule of Ur over Babylonia in about 2000 BC. Gradually, the newcomers took up city life and lived in places like Ur alongside the original inhabitants. These Amorites spoke a language more like Hebrew than Babylonian, but the scribes still wrote Babylonian, since it was a more respectable language. Hammurabi, the famous king of Babylon (see *King Hammurabi's Law-code*) belonged to an Amorite family.

The names of Abraham and his family are very much like these Amorites' names. The biblical records point to a date about 2000 BC, or a little before or after, for Abraham's career. The book of Genesis, chapter 11, tells us that Ur of the Chaldees was his birthplace. So it is against this background that we should set his early life.

How stark is the contrast with the life he turned to. At the call of God, Abraham left the sophisticated city, with all its security and comfort, to become one of the despised nomads!

The New Testament letter to the Hebrews (chapter 11) puts its finger on the key to this remarkable response:

'It was faith that made Abraham obey when God called him to go out to a country which God had promised to give him. He left his own country without knowing where he was going. By faith he lived as a foreigner in the country that God had promised him. He lived in tents, as did Isaac and Jacob, who received the same promise from God. For Abraham was waiting for the city which God has designed and built, the city with permanent foundations.'

THE PALACE OF THE KINGS OF MARI

Nomads leave very little evidence of their existence for archaeologists. Once they have pulled up their tent-pegs and moved away, a few stones in a circle blackened by fire may be all they leave. So it is only from contacts with settled farmers and town-dwellers that something can be learnt about the nomads, and their opinions may be rather biased. However, there is one discovery which is giving direct information about the nomads in Mesopotamia about 1800 BC.

In 1933 a party of Arabs dug into a hill by the River Euphrates in order to make a grave. They dug out a stone statue. They reported their find and before the end of the year a team of French archaeologists began work. They soon dug out more statues, and read the name of the city of Mari inscribed on one of them in Babylonian. Other records showed that Mari was an important place, but it had not been found until this moment. Excavations have continued in the ruins, with some interruptions, to the present time.

Temples, a palace, statues, inscriptions and a jar of buried treasure, all dating from about 2500 BC, are signs of Mari's importance at the time when the kings of Ur were buried with such magnificence. Long after that flowering, Mari had another short spell of power. About 1850 BC an Amorite chieftain took over the city and made it the centre of a kingdom controlling trade along the River Euphrates between Babylonia and Syria. With the income from taxes on this trade, and from other business and farming, the kings of Mari were able to

build themselves a huge palace. This ranks as one of the major discoveries in the Near East.

The palace of Mari covered more than 2·5 hectares/6 acres of ground and had over 260 rooms, courtyards and passages. Enemies had ransacked the place and set it on fire. Then the desert sands filled the rooms until they were entirely covered. Thus the walls were still standing 5 metres/15 feet or more high when the archaeologists dug into them, and now a roof has been erected over parts of the palace to protect the walls, so that visitors can walk into a most impressive ancient building.

After shifting the tons of sand from each room, the excavators hoped for great rewards. Some rooms were empty, some rooms were stores: rows of great jars stood ready for oil, wine or grain. There were living-quarters — spacious for the king, his wives, and his family, more cramped for officials and servants. We can imagine craftsmen were busy in workshops, secretaries in their offices, pastry-cooks in the kitchens. There were even singing-girls practising to entertain the king's foreign guests.

As always, the most informative discoveries are the written documents. Clay tablets were scattered on the floors of various rooms. One in particular was the archive room where they were stored. Altogether over 20,000 cuneiform texts awaited the archaeologists in the palace of Mari.

The scribes kept their eye on every detail of palace life. Tablets record the amounts of food coming into the palace, grain and vegetables of all sorts, and several hundred list the provisions provided for the king's table each day.

Hundreds of letters carry news to the king from all over his realm. One official reports progress in making musical instruments the king had ordered, another that there is not enough gold to decorate a temple as the king wanted. A small group of letters brings accounts of messages given by the gods to prophets or to ordinary people. Some advise the king to act in a certain way, others assure him of divine protection.

The nomadic tribes and their movements were a serious matter for military officers. They constantly reported about them to the king. Tribesmen moving in hundreds were a threat to small farming towns and even to Mari itself. They stopped traffic on the trade-routes and pinned down the king's forces. In attempts to keep the

The statue of a bearded man found at Mari and dating from the eighteenth century BC is inscribed with the name Ishtup-ilum, king of Mari.

peace, treaties were agreed with some groups who were allowed to settle in parts of the territory of Mari. This is one picture of a situation that has repeated itself throughout the history of Mesopotamia.

The letters name several of the tribes. All fall under the blanket-term 'Amorites'. When scholars first studied these texts they were excited to read one name as 'Benjaminites'. Was this the Israelite tribe, or an ancestor of it? Later research decided the name was actually 'Yaminites', meaning 'southerners' (like the Yemen in the south of Arabia). Another name means 'northerners', and they both seem to have to do with the origins of the tribes. There is no reason to see a biblical connection here.

In the same way, the initial enthusiasm of discovery led to a claim that the name David was current at Mari

The great palace at Mari was enlarged and rebuilt by King Zimrilim in the eighteenth century BC. The complex includes state reception rooms, apartments for the royal family, rooms for scribes, and an inner sanctuary.

Store-rooms

Store-rooms

Inner sanctuary and hall

Main court

Court with wall-paintings

Main entrance

Oven
Audience-hall with wall paintings
Throne-room
Steward's offices

Scribal school

Royal residence

Privy-chamber

0   20 metres
0   20 yards

as a title 'chieftain'. On that, theories were built about David's name originally being a different one, 'David' only adopted when he became king.

A long-standing problem could be solved by this means. According to 1 Samuel 17, David killed Goliath, whereas Elhanan killed the giant according to 2 Samuel 21:19. If 'David' was a title, David and Elhanan could be the same person. It is now certain the word at Mari is not a title and not related to David (it is a word meaning 'defeat'), so this solution disappears. (Although there are difficulties, the simplest answer may be to suppose the Philistines had more than one champion named Goliath.)

Apart from David, hundreds of Amorite names occur in the Mari tablets. Similarities with Hebrew names abound, notably in names of the patriarchal age. Sometimes the names are identical, as in the case of Ishmael, but this does not mean a reference to the same man (see *Headline News: The Lost City of Ebla*), simply that the name was common, perhaps fashionable at the time.

Mari's great palace displays the organization and the bureaucracy of a small though powerful state. Its archives give a wealth of unexpected knowledge about the life of nomads in the eighteenth century BC. Despite diplomatic alliances with other kings and with the tribes, Mari fell to the forces of Hammurabi of Babylon soon after 1760 BC. Other towns flourished in the area from time to time, the nearest today is Abu Kemal. But none was as great as Mari.

Among discoveries at Mari was a life-sized statue of a goddess. She holds a vase through which water flowed, and her robe is decorated with representations of streams in which fish are swimming. The statue dates from the eighteenth century BC.

THE PATRIARCHS: AN ARGUMENT FROM SILENCE

Abraham and his father Terah lived at Ur in southern Mesopotamia and at Harran in the north. Nowhere, in those two cities or in any other Babylonian city, have their names appeared in ancient texts. Harran is unexcavated; the early levels lie beneath the medieval castle and mosque. Ur, as we have seen, has produced hundreds of written documents.

Once out of Mesopotamia, the patriarchs' story is set in Canaan. There, Genesis 21 records, Abraham had a quarrel with the king of Gerar over water-rights. The quarrel ended with a peace treaty. Abraham's son, Isaac, had the same trouble, and reached the same solution. Today we can read a variety of ancient treaties, is it not surprising that nothing is known about these outside the Bible? Canaanite cities have not given any sign at all of Abraham's presence.

At one stage Abraham went to Egypt. The pharaoh took his wife Sarah from him, then, faced with God's disapproval, gave her back, sending Abraham away with rich gifts (the story is told in Genesis 12). Later, Isaac's grandson, Joseph, rose from slavery in Egypt to become the pharaoh's right-hand man. He brought his father, Jacob, and his family to live with him in Egypt. What do the Egyptian hieroglyphs have to say about these events? Again, the answer is: 'Nothing!'

Silence about the patriarchs from all sources except the Bible leads some writers to conclude that the patriarchs never existed: they are inventions by

Jewish patriots exiled from their land, seeking to create a national history; or they are legendary men, figures of folk-lore without any reality at all. Arguments for views like these may follow several lines. Those who use archaeology as a platform for such a conclusion are, however, failing to look at the evidence properly.

To find Abraham's treaty with the king of Gerar, for example, would require archaeologists to locate the palace in Gerar and discover records which include that king's reign.

To find the treaty would require, first, that it was put into writing, then that it was written on a lasting material, stone, or a clay tablet. Yet Gerar was in the south of Canaan, near Egypt. So scribes who worked there are more likely to have written in the Egyptian way — on papyrus, which decays quickly — than in the Babylonian way on clay.

On top of this, the likelihood of archaeologists finding the right records is small. When a palace is dug out, as at Mari, the things found in it usually belong to the reigns of the last two or three kings who lived in it before it was abandoned. So the reign of Abraham's

ally would need to have fallen near the end of a period in the history of Gerar.

Even if all these demands could be met, there is no guarantee that every document buried in an archive survives intact and legible; exposure, damp, falling brickwork, careless excavation, can all destroy the writing on clay tablets.

The possibility of finding that treaty is remote. At present it would be an accidental and unexpected discovery, because no one can even be quite sure where Gerar is!

In Egypt the perishability of papyrus always presents a serious problem to historians (see *Any Sign of Moses?*). For the 500 years from 2000 to 1500 BC the monuments of kings in temples and tombs and the memorials of their servants are almost the only sources of information. Very few papyrus documents have escaped the rotting effects of damp. Fragments of one report on conditions in the south of Egypt, others deal with the affairs of a single town.

Once more, it is most unlikely any record will be found about Abraham or Joseph in Egypt. Unlike

other leading men, Joseph did not have a tomb in Egypt carved or painted with the significant moments of his career. Genesis 50 states that his embalmed body was to be carried back to Canaan.

Even though it provides no direct references to the patriarchs, archaeology may still offer help in studying the background to their lives. Are the stories in keeping with what we know about the period 2000 to 1500 BC in which the Bible seems to place them, or do they show signs of another era?

If they were written in the middle of the first millennium BC they might be aware of the Assyrian or Babylonian Empires, of the Arameans in Damascus, of the general use of iron and of horses. In fact these things are absent, except for Joseph's chariots in Egypt, presumably horse-drawn.

Other facts point to the earlier half of the second, millennium as the most appropriate period. Egypt was then receiving a constant inflow of Amorites and others from Canaan, and some of them rose high in the pharaoh's service. In the end, some of these foreigners ruled Egypt for a

while (the Hyksos kings). Joseph's career and his family's emigration suit this time well.

Although the nomadic way of life (which the Mari tablets have documented) was widespread and common in more than one period, it certainly makes a dating for the patriarchs at 2000 to 1500 BC feasible.

Ancient Egyptian scribes copied out a story of an Egyptian who fled from the court and had many adventures in Canaan, eventually returning to honour and proper burial at home. The copies date from 1800 to 1000 BC. The story is set 150 years before the earliest copy. Egyptologists assert that it is based on fact and is in accord with the period it describes. The hero of the story, Sinuhe, had no national position. His tale was popular, it seems, as an adventure story.

In Genesis the Hebrew writers presented the stories of their nation's origin. Archaeology can shed light on their background. It cannot bring proof that they are true. Neither can it prove that they are baseless legends. What it can show is that similar stories were told, and appear to be reliable reports.

An Egyptian nobleman was proud of the day, about 1900 BC, when he introduced a party of foreigners to the Egyptian court. He had the scene painted on the wall of his tomb at Beni Hasan. A dark-skinned Egyptian scribe (to the right of the picture shown here) holds a placard announcing the visitors as

Asiatics from the region of Shut, bringing galena for the black eye-paint Egyptians liked. The leader is named 'foreign chief Abushar'. This group from Sinai or southern Canaan gives a visual description of the way the patriarchs could have appeared.

A PEOPLE REDISCOVERED
Who were the Hittites?

'Look, the king of Israel has hired the Hittite and Egyptian kings to attack us!'

This suspicion was enough to cause panic in the army of Damascus. The troops fled, suddenly releasing Samaria from a siege which had brought the city's inhabitants to starvation-point (the story is told in 2 Kings 7).

The ancient Egyptians have left too deep an imprint on humanity ever to be forgotten. But who were the Hittites? Until a century ago no one could answer that question. The Hittites, if they had ever existed, had vanished along with the Hivites, Perizzites, Girgashites and other peoples named in the Old Testament.

Yet although the Hittites are often mentioned simply as one of the list of nations which occupied Canaan — nations the Israelites were to destroy as they conquered the Promised Land —

Until late in the nineteenth century nothing was known of the Hittites outside the Bible. Their rediscovery is one of the most remarkable achievements of archaeology. This statue, from the eighth century BC, is of a late Hittite king.

the incident mentioned above and another, telling that Solomon sold horses 'to all the kings of the Hittites and the kings of Syria', suggest they were more important.

Nevertheless, because they were unknown and often classed with other unknown groups, some commentators believed that there must have been a mistake: at least in 2 Kings 7 the biblical historian was meaning the Assyrians.

In 1876, however, the rediscovery of the Hittites began, through the work of A.H. Sayce. An English scholar, Sayce spent much of his life travelling in Egypt and the Near East from his house-boat home on the Nile, returning to Oxford each spring to give the lectures his position demanded. Sayce realized that picture-writing on stone blocks reused in medieval buildings at Hama and Aleppo in Syria was the

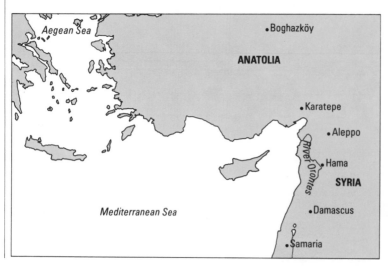

same as writing carved on rocks in Turkey. In 1876 he related these writings to the Hittites of the Old Testament and the 'Kheta' named in Egyptian texts.

From the Egyptian references there was no doubt the Kheta were a 'great power'; one of their kings made a treaty with Pharaoh Ramesses II as an equal. Explorers roaming Anatolia now began to pay more attention to these carvings and to the ruins of old cities scattered across the Turkish plateau.

Largest of all the ruins was a place called Boghazköy, about 160 km/100 miles due east of Ankara. Local people had sold pieces of clay tablets they found there to foreign visitors. The writing on the tablets was Babylonian, but the language was not. Two other tablets in the same language had come to light in Egypt in 1887, with Babylonian letters, including one from a Hittite king (see *Relatives of the Hebrews?*). But for a few years the language defied the scholars.

Boghazköy was the obvious place to learn more about the Hittites. In 1906 an expedition from Germany, led by H. Winckler, began to excavate the ruins. Success came immediately. In the burnt ruins of a range of store-rooms there were more than 10,000 pieces of cuneiform tablets, baked hard in the

Stone lions, about 3,500 years old, guard the gateway of the ancient Hittite capital, Hattusha, near Boghazköy in Turkey.

fire. Most remarkably, one of the documents proved to be a Babylonian version of the treaty between Ramesses II and the Hittite king. This, with other Babylonian texts, proved that Boghazköy was the capital city of a powerful kingdom. Its ancient name was Hattusha.

An outline of its history and the names of its kings for the period 1400 to 1200 BC emerged quickly from the Babylonian tablets. Hittite scribes had used that language for state records and international correspondence. They were able men, some of them specialist translators. In addition to Babylonian, six other languages are represented in the cuneiform texts. The most important is the one now called Hittite, written beside Akkadian in state documents, and used extensively for religious and administrative records.

Less than ten years after Winckler's discovery, study of the tablets led a Czech scholar, Bedrich Hrozný, to publish his conclusion that the Hittite language is a relative of Greek and Latin, French, German and English, a member of the Indo-European family of languages. Another scholar had suggested the same thing some years earlier, about the two tablets from Egypt. No one had believed him, and people were reluctant to believe Hrozný, but further research proved him right. Hittite now has a central place in the study of Indo-European languages and the history of the people who have spoken them.

The other languages used on the tablets at Boghazköy were one spoken by the pre-Hittite inhabitants, two related to Hittite (one of them, Luwian, used quite widely) and Hurrian which was current in eastern Turkey and northern Mesopotamia. Hurrian-speakers played a big part in the Hittite kingdom. A few phrases are all that remain of a seventh language, one connected to Sanskrit.

In variety of content and language the tablets from Boghazköy are unrivalled. Other discoveries in the city disclose the culture and skill of the Hittites in numerous ways. (The excavations by Winckler lasted from 1906 to 1912; they were resumed under K. Bittel in 1931, interrupted in 1939, and have been continuing since 1952.)

The city of Hattusha covered more than 120 hectares/300 acres. A stoutly constructed wall of stone and brick defended the city, and instructions for the sentries are among the texts in the archives. At the east side is a high rock which was the fortified citadel.

In the city area five temples have been uncovered. The largest (64 × 42 metres/70 × 46 yards) was surrounded by rows of store-houses, doubtless to hold offerings brought to the god. A considerable organization was needed to staff the temples, and the texts give details of the rites and ceremonies the priests performed, some involving the king. Elaborate and lengthy services were carried out to consecrate a new temple or to purify people from sin.

It has been standard practice amongst Old Testament scholars to claim that the Hebrew laws of Exodus, Leviticus, Numbers and Deuteronomy are too 'advanced' or too complicated for so early a date as Moses' time, no later than 1250 BC. But the Boghazköy texts, and others from Egypt and from recent French excavations at Emar on the Euphrates, clearly dispute this: the ceremonies which Israel's Law prescribes are not out of place in the world of the late second millennium.

Beside the gateways of the city stood lions carved in stone, magical figures to keep enemies out. In a narrow gorge nearby a shrine was made for the gods and goddesses whose pictures are carved on the rock faces. Other rock-carvings and stone sculptures proclaim Hittite control in several parts of Anatolia.

The Hittites built their power from about 1750 BC. From about 1380 to 1200 BC the Hittite ruler was 'the Great King', overlord of numerous princes as far west as the Aegean and as far south as Damascus. Through this extensive empire the name of the Hittites was famous in antiquity. To control their subjects, the Hittite monarchs made treaties with the subject kings. Two dozen of these treaties, in whole or in part, have been pieced together among the tablets from Boghazköy. An analysis of them made in 1931 revealed their basic form, and this has provided a fruitful basis for investigating treaties in the Old Testament (see *Treaties and Covenants*).

On the Hittite sculptures, and on the seals impressed on the clay tablets, we can see the type of picture-writing known as Hittite hieroglyphs. These hieroglyphs look something like the Egyptian ones, and the Hittites may have taken the idea from Egypt, but the writing is not the same. In a few examples, mostly on the seals of the kings, the hieroglyphs stand in parallel with Babylonian cuneiform to spell the royal name and titles.

Using the Babylonian script as key, some of the values of the hieroglyphic signs became clear. The discovery in 1947 of much longer parallel texts, in Hittite and Phoenician, at a place called Karatepe, put understanding of the hieroglyphs on a firm footing.

Hattusha and the Hittite Empire came to an end soon after 1200 BC in the disturbances that afflicted many areas of the eastern Mediterranean (see *The Philistines*). Hittite traditions lasted longer. In small states in Anatolia and north Syria, local kings

On this relief carving of the eighth century BC from the Hittite centre at Carchemish is shown a baby prince in his nurse's arms, with a goat beside, perhaps to supply milk. The Hittite hieroglyphic writing gives the prince's name and title.

continued to have their inscriptions written in Hittite hieroglyphs and in the Luwian language as late as 700 BC (the date of the Karatepe inscriptions). Some of these kings may have traced their ancestry back to the Hittite Empire, some were not Hittite at all. But to other ancient nations, to the Assyrians and to the Hebrews, they were still Hittites.

At the time when the army of Damascus fled from Samaria, there was a strong 'Hittite' king a little further north, at Hama on the River Orontes. He could have been a threat to Damascus, especially if he was allied with other kings. This is the reality behind the biblical historian's report.

Rediscovering the Hittites is one of the notable results of Near Eastern archaeology.

TREATIES AND COVENANTS

Ancient kings were always suspicious of their neighbours. Would they attack to take over the kingdom? Or were they open to attack by more distant enemies? One way to get security was to make sure the neighbours were on good terms and did not threaten the frontiers or other interests. Strong kings might make treaties with each other as equals, by 'parity treaties', or they might persuade or force weaker kings to accept them as their overlords, by 'suzerainty treaties'.

Among the tablets discovered in the ruined Hittite capital city at Boghazköy are the texts of at least two dozen treaties, some very badly preserved. One of them is the famous agreement made between Ramesses II of Egypt and Hattusil III of the Hittites in 1259 BC. This is a parity treaty. The kings are brothers: they will respect each other's interests not fight each other, help each other against mutual enemies and send back fugitives.

In Egypt, the counterpart of this treaty was carved in hieroglyphs on the wall of a temple at Karnak. The Egyptian version even includes a detailed description of the silver tablet, engraved with the terms of the treaty and bearing the royal seal, which was shown on it. Men can never rely fully on one another, so formal curses were declared on any future Egyptian or Hittite king who broke the terms of the pact. The gods of both countries were called to witness and safeguard it.

Suzerainty treaties were more common. In return for the protection the Great King could offer, the junior king promised to be loyal, not to have any dealings with the Great King's enemies, nor with any foreign rulers unknown to the Great King. If the Great King went to war, the junior king would supply men for his army, and each year he would send a tax to the Great King. He was expected to send back any refugees from the Great King's realm, but the Great King could keep refugees from his land.

A careful analysis of these treaties was made in 1931. All followed the same basic pattern. After an introduction, there is an account of events leading up to the making of the treaty, then the requirements of the treaty, arrangements for its safe-keeping and public reading, the names of the witnesses, blessings on all who kept it and fearful curses on those who broke it. This was not a cast-iron pattern; some elements could be left out or put in a different order. It is, however, clearly the normal arrangement.

It was not until 1954 that an Old Testament scholar, G.E. Mendenhall, realized that the pattern also occurs in the Old Testament. Treaties as such are not quoted there, but they are reported at length. The accounts of the treaty, or covenant, which God made with Israel and which established the people as a nation under his care, are especially extensive. Parts of this appear in Exodus 20–31; and Deuteronomy presents a complete renewal. Joshua 24 also shows the basic elements of the treaty pattern, and they appear in Genesis 31:43–54 and in other passages.

What is significant about the emergence of this pattern in the Hittite and in the Hebrew texts is the dating. Shortly after 1200 BC the Hittite Empire ended. When other treaties become accessible to us, in Assyrian and Aramaic texts of the eighth century BC and later, the pattern has changed. At that time the introduction was followed by the names of the witnesses, then the requirements, and curses, with variations in order. The account of events leading up to the making of the treaty is missing (there is one very poorly preserved tablet that may have had it), and blessings are all but absent.

Despite various attempts to undermine it, the strength of the comparison between the Hittite treaties and those in the first five books of the Bible remains. It does not prove they were all written at the same period, but it makes it very possible. To suppose, as many commentators do, that the biblical texts did not come into being in their present form until 600 years later, requires the survival in Israel of an old-fashioned pattern, a pattern different from that of the treaties which Israelite and Judean kings accepted with the Aramaean kings of Damascus and with the kings of Assyria and Babylon. Still more research is needed on this subject, both with regard to the dating and to comparison of the patterns and the language.

RELATIVES OF THE HEBREWS?

An Egyptian peasant woman was busy grubbing in the mounds of earth near her village in 1887. She was looking for the marly earth that was good for enriching her field. The marly earth was the decayed rubbish and brickwork from an old town.

Sometimes, as the villagers dug into the mounds, they would find things left behind in the ruins which they could sell for a few pence to antiquity-dealers who would take them to Cairo for European collectors to buy. What they liked were carvings in stone, decorative glassware, metal statues, and the little beetle-shaped charms, 'scarabs'.

As the woman dug she came upon a lot of lumps of hard clay. They were of no use to her, and she had not seen anything like them before. A neighbour bought them from her for a few pence.

The lumps of clay were, in fact, cuneiform tablets, and there were 400 or more of them. Some were taken to Cairo, but no one there was sure whether or not they were really old. No cuneiform tablets had ever been found in Egypt before, so uncertainty and suspicion were natural.

For a few weeks Egyptian dealers hawked the tablets about the country, trying to get a good price. At the very end of 1887, Wallis Budge arrived from the British Museum with instructions to buy whatever he thought should be added to the museum's collections. He heard rumours about new discoveries of papyri and the unusual tablets, so he took the train south from Cairo, then transferred to a steamer at Asyut for the rest of the journey up the Nile to Luxor.

There, a dealer brought a few of the clay tablets to him. Budge could see they were not the sort of tablets familiar to him from Assyria and Babylonia, yet he was convinced they were not forgeries. When a second lot reached him he was able to recognize them as letters sent to kings of Egypt in the fourteenth century BC.

He bought eighty-two of them, which are now in London after being smuggled through Egypt. One hundred and ninety-nine tablets passed to the State Museum in Berlin, fifty stayed in Cairo, and a score or so came to rest in other collections. The total number known at present is 378.

Between the peasant woman's discovery and the safe housing of those tablets in museums some

Pictorial as well as written records have been discovered at El-Amarna, in Egypt.

damage occurred, and an unknown number were lost. There is a story about one very large tablet. Its owner was taking it to Cairo. As he climbed on to the train, hiding the tablet under his robe, he slipped, and the tablet crashed to the ground. He picked up most of the pieces, and they are now in Berlin. It is a list of treasures accompanying a foreign princess who went to marry the pharaoh.

Excavations carried out at the site of the discovery, El-Amarna, recovered a few more, broken, tablets. They had all been left behind when the Egyptian government moved back to the old capital under Pharaoh Tutankhamun. Apparently, they were unwanted files from the foreign affairs office.

Kings and princes all over the Near East wrote to the pharaoh, and he sometimes replied in Babylonian. Kings of Assyria and Babylonia wrote, so did princes of Syria and Canaan, rulers of cities like Tyre and Beirut, Hazor, Gezer and Jerusalem. They speak of international affairs, of local problems, of the loyalty of the Canaanite kings. Those who proclaim their faithfulness to pharaoh most vigorously are the ones who accuse their neighbours of disloyalty!

A problem these rulers faced was the menace of foreigners who roamed the

Tablets from El-Amarna, written by Canaanite kings to the Egyptian pharaoh, mention the problem of attack from roving bands of foreigners — the 'Habiru'. Were these the Hebrews of the Old Testament?

From earliest times the River Nile has been the great highway of Egypt, forming a fertile corridor through the deserts which lie to the east and west.

countryside, attacking the towns. They were bandits, criminals, fugitives of all sorts. They were not normal tribes of nomadic shepherds. The letter-writers called them Habiru. When this word was read in the Amarna Tablets a debate began which has not yet ended. Were these Habiru, who fought the Canaanites, the Hebrews of the Old Testament?

If the Israelites moved into Canaan in the thirteenth century BC as most people think, the Habiru of the Amarna Tablets could not be them, because they belong in the century before. If, on the other hand, the date of the exodus is put about 1440 BC, as some prefer, the Habiru *could* be the same as the Hebrews.

No connection can be

established between the events and people mentioned in the letters and those in the Old Testament. Although the places are well known, the kings and princes in each source are different. There is a different background, too, for all the letters from Palestine are from rulers subject to Egypt, which is not the background we find in the books of Joshua and Judges.

Since the Amarna Tablets brought the Habiru to prominence, many more texts have come to light which refer to them. The Habiru appear in Egyptian, Hittite, Ugaritic (see *Conquered Cities of Canaan*) and Babylonian records. In large numbers they could be a threat; as individuals they were unimportant. Egyptian generals took

them prisoner in Canaan and they hauled stones or served wine as slaves in Egypt. In Babylonia they could sell themselves into slavery in return for food and shelter.

They are most common in documents written between 1500 and 1200 BC, but they appear 2–300 years earlier in Babylonia. All these texts combined indicate that Habiru became a name for homeless people, displaced persons.

Abraham and his descendants fall into that category; the name Hebrew is used mainly in the early part of Israel's history, down to the reign of Saul. The Habiru were not Hebrews, but they help to explain what the Hebrews were!

TUTANKHAMUN'S TREASURE

Lord Carnarvon was an extremely wealthy man, but he had paid for 200,000 tons of Egyptian sand and stone to be shifted and after six seasons of digging they had still found nothing. It was a waste of effort to carry on. He decided to end the work. He called Howard Carter to his country home to tell him. It was Carter who had proposed and directed the excavation beause he was convinced there was one royal burial place still to be found in the Valley of the Kings. Tombs existed there for all the rulers history suggested should be there, except for one — Tutankhamun.

Carter persuaded his patron to support one final attempt. Hardly an inch of the valley floor remained to be cleared of rubble. Just one area, which had been left so that tourists could visit another tomb easily, was still unexplored. Surely it would be worth

clearing that, too! So, in November 1922, Howard Carter returned to his task — and to his triumph.

The workmen cleared away the stones and the ruins of huts which builders of another tomb had made. Beneath them, cut in the rock, was a staircase leading downwards. After sixteen steps there was a sealed doorway, and some of the seals bore Tutankhamun's name. Although in ancient times thieves had broken through, the royal cemetery-keepers had filled up the hole they made. Had the thieves left anything of value behind?

Beyond the door was a passage about 9 metres/30 feet long, then another sealed doorway.

On 26 November Lord Carnarvon, his daughter and an assistant pressed round Carter as he made a hole in the blocking and held a candle inside. What could he see?

'Wonderful things', he replied.

Carter was looking into the largest of four underground chambers. Three proved to be packed with objects, the equipment the king would need in his next existence. The fourth chamber housed the body of the king.

The robbers' hole, and the disturbance they had made searching in the tomb for precious things they could carry away, show how Tutankhamun's treasure was almost destroyed centuries ago, just after it was buried. The vigilance of the ancient guards foiled their attempt. Soon after, the entrance disappeared under the rubble of the valley floor, and the later workmen's huts hid it completely. That is how the

In November 1922 Howard Carter broke through the sealed door which stood between him and the richest treasure trove of all. Tomb robbers of past centuries had failed to find the burial chamber of King Tutankhamun of Egypt. Holding a candle to the opening Carter could see 'wonderful things' within. It was the only shrine of a pharaoh ever to be found intact.

tomb of an unimportant pharaoh escaped the looting which all the tombs of Egypt's greatest kings suffered.

Tutankhamun's tomb gives a glimpse of the glory that Egypt's kings enjoyed when the nation's power was great. Gold flowed into the treasury as booty or tribute from foreign countries, and from gold mines in the south of Egypt. Tutankhamun's tomb shows how the gold was used to honour the king.

The bird with its clutch of eggs is another of the treasures from Tutankhamun's tomb.

King Tutankhamun, the young Egyptian pharaoh of the fourteenth century BC, is known today by the spectacular gold mask made for the royal mummy, one of the treasures from his tomb.

A dog, representing Anubis, the Egyptian god of mummification and rebirth guarded a doorway in the tomb of King Tutankhamun.

What Carter saw in his first glimpse included a gilded wooden bed, a gilded statue and may other pieces of furniture decorated with gold. As they gradually emptied the tomb, the archaeologists were constantly amazed at the variety of the objects they found, the high quality of workmanship and the high level of art.

There is, for example, a wooden throne, the legs ending in lions' claws, and topped at the front by lions' heads, the whole encased in gold. The arms are carved as winged serpents, protecting the king, and the gold plating of the back shows the queen attending the seated king. The sheen of the gold is relieved by details picked out in silver and glass, coloured blue, green and reddish-brown.

Four chariots had been dismantled and laid in the tomb. The wooden body of one was cased in gold, beaten and engraved with pictures of Egypt's enemies tied together. The dead king owned many pieces of fine jewellery, too, of gold and semi-precious stones. He had a dagger of solid gold, and a more effective one with a blade of iron, a rarity at that time. Twenty-nine bows lay in the tomb, some of them bound or plated with gold. The catalogue of precious possessions seems endless.

Most magnificent of all, and most well known, are the solid gold coffin and the golden mask that enclosed the pharaoh's body. Inside the four shrines (see *Tutankhamun, the Tabernacle and the Ark of the Covenant*) was a yellow stone coffin. Within this coffin was another, mummy-shaped, of wood covered with gold leaf. A second gold-plated wooden coffin fitted inside the first and, when it was opened, the astonishing gold coffin was revealed. The metal is 2.5 to 3 mm/$\frac{1}{8}$ to $\frac{1}{10}$ in. thick, beaten to the shape of the body and inlaid, like the second one, with coloured glass and stones. The body had been mummified and on it, between the layers of careful bandaging, were dozens of amulets and jewels in precious metal.

The inside of the back of King Tutankhamun's throne shows the king with his queen. The throne is of wood overlaid with gleaming gold, silver, blue faience, calcite and glass. It is one of the richest treasures of Egypt.

In effect, the royal tomb was furnished with all the king had needed or used in his life-time, so that his spirit could maintain the same life-style in the next world. To ensure the welfare of the spirit, various magic texts were engraved in the tomb, and carved figures of gods and goddesses were placed in it. Great care had been given to do everything that was right and would benefit the dead Tutankhamun.

He had died about 1350 BC, within 100 years of Moses' lifetime. In the treasures of his tomb, therefore, we can see the style of the Egyptian court where Moses was educated, and the luxury that surrounded him. Although the ordinary Egyptians would not have shared in these riches, various discoveries make it clear that a considerable number of royal officials, soldiers and administrators did.

From those people, in the main, we may assume, the Israelites 'borrowed' the gold and silver they took when they left Egypt after the tenth plague.

Exodus 12 records: 'The Israelites had done as Moses had said, and had asked the Egyptians for gold and silver jewellery and for clothing. The Lord made the Egyptians respect the people and give them what they asked for. In this way the Israelites carried away the wealth of the Egyptians.'

Later, in the wilderness, according to Exodus 38, the Israelites gave nearly thirty talents of gold for decorating the Tabernacle (see *Tutankhamun, the Tabernacle and the Ark of the Covenant*) and making its equipment. Taking the talent as about 30 kg/66 lbs, this amounts to about 900 kg/1,980 lbs.

Some people are sceptical of so large an amount, yet it gains plausibility in the light of Tutankhamun's treasure. His solid gold inner coffin weighs about 110 kg/243 lbs, rather more than three and a half talents, and there are numerous other objects in his tomb which are made of gold or overlaid with gold. It is impossible to weigh the gold plating, but if 180 kg/400 lbs is a reasonable guess for the total weight of

A wooden chest from King Tutankhamun's tomb at Thebes is painted with scenes from life. The king in his chariot rides out against his enemies. On the lid he is shown hunting.

gold in the tomb, then it was about one fifth of the amount the Israelites carried off.

Tutankhamun's treasure is the most spectacular of all archaeological discoveries. Although there is no direct link between this discovery and the Old Testament, it illustrates the wealth of Egypt and the background for the Exodus story. It also demonstrates the quantity of gold available and how it was used.

TUTANKHAMUN, THE TABERNACLE AND THE ARK OF THE COVENANT

Tutankhamun's treasures help us understand more clearly two things which are described in the Bible. Both belong to the time of the Exodus, that is, within a century of Tutankhamun's burial.

The first is the Tabernacle, the sacred tent-shrine where God was present. This was a prefabricated structure that could be dismantled, carried in pieces from place to place, and reassembled. Its walls were a series of wooden frames linked together by cross-rails running through rings on the vertical posts.

All the wooden parts were covered with gold, and the posts stood on silver sockets. A set of ten curtains, brilliantly embroidered, hung round the sides and over the top of the framework.

To make it weather-proof, a covering of skins was stretched over the whole thing.

Egypt's craftsmen had been making prefabricated portable pavilions and shrines for many centuries. One lay in the tomb of a queen from the time of its burial, about 2500 BC, until its excavation in 1925. A gold-plated wooden frame provided a curtained shelter for the queen on her journeys.

In Tutankhamun's tomb four gold-plated wooden shrines protected the king's body. The largest is 5 metres/18 feet long, 3.3 metres/12 feet 9 ins wide and 2.3 metres/7 feet 6 ins high. A second shrine fitted inside the first, a third inside the second, and a fourth inside again. Each side was made of a wooden frame fitted with carved panels, covered with thin sheets of gold.

The undertakers had brought the parts separately along the 1.6 metre/5 foot 3 inch-wide entrance passage of the tomb, then fitted them together in the burial chamber. In their haste they had not matched all the parts correctly!

Covering the second shrine was a linen veil decorated with gilt bronze daisies representing the starry sky. The roofs of two of the shrines reproduce a very ancient form. They are made in wood with gold covering but, long before, at the beginning of Egyptian history, the shrine of a leading goddess had a light wooden frame roofed with an animal skin, and it is this that these two shrines reproduce in more splendid materials.

None of these things is identical with the Israelite Tabernacle. All of them show that the idea itself and the methods of construction used in making it were familiar in Egypt at the time of the Exodus.

The second thing which Tutankhamun's tomb illustrates is the ark of the covenant. This was a box holding the basic deeds of Israel's constitution, the laws of God which his people promised to obey, and was kept in the inner room of the Tabernacle. A gold ring was fixed at each corner for poles to be inserted for carrying.

Also amongst Tutankhamun's possessions was a wooden chest, a beautiful piece of joinery, which had poles for carrying it. Probably it was made for heavy royal robes. There were four carrying poles, two at each end, and when the box was at rest they slid in rings underneath it, so that they did not project at all. Each had a collar at the inner end so that no one could pull it out from the base of the box. Although this was a little more sophisticated than the ark, it shows a similar pattern of construction.

A wooden box with rings and carrying poles, found in King Tutankhamun's tomb, illustrates the biblical 'ark of the covenant', the sacred box in which God's laws were carried.

In King Tutankhamun's tomb, four gold-plated shrines protected the embalmed body, each fitting inside the other, and all made to take apart — like the Israelite Tabernacle.

IN THE BRICKFIELDS OF EGYPT

Visitors to Egypt stand in amazement before the great pyramids near Cairo, then travel over 322 km/200 miles south along the Nile to gaze at the great temples of Karnak. These tremendous monuments are built of stone. Gangs of men were organized to quarry the stones in the hills at the edge of the Nile valley and bring them by sledge and by boat to the building site. There the masons would trim and shape them ready for use.

Although the stone structures still stand to impress the tourist (and there have been tourists visiting them for a very long time — the Sphinx and the pyramids were already an attraction in the time of Moses), bricks were the usual building material in ancient Egypt.

Each year the River Nile rises about 7.5 metres/25 feet to flood its valley. The flood begins in July and the waters gradually subside from the end of October. As the river rushes down from the mountains of Ethiopia, it brings tons of mud, suspended in the water. This rich black soil settles on the ground as the water moves more slowly across Egypt, leaving a new deposit to make the earth very fertile for farming. With mud all around them, it was natural for the Egyptians to use it for building.

Their earliest shelters may have been simply reeds woven and plastered with mud. Buildings of this sort were made for a long while, until the people discovered the advantages of bricks, some time before 3000 BC. The idea may have reached them from Syria or Palestine where bricks were common much earlier, as they were in Babylonia.

Making bricks was simple. Labourers dug out suitable mud and carried it to a yard where they mixed it with water, treading it in or turning it with a hoe to get the right consistency. Mud alone will make a brick, but adding chopped straw gives strength and makes the substance less crumbly. Nowadays, about 20 kg/44 lbs of straw are needed for every cubic metre of mud, and sand is often included as well.

After mixing and kneading, men carried the brick-earth to the brick-makers. They pressed it into rectangular wooden frames held flat on level ground. Then they lifted the frames off and left the bricks to dry. After two or three days in the hot sun, the bricks were hard and ready for the builder.

The work was messy, even when the bricks were dry. An ancient Egyptian scribe praised his own profession above all others. The builder, he said, had a miserable time: 'The small builder carries mud . . . He is dirtier than . . . pigs from treading down his mud. His clothes are stiff with clay . . .'

Bricks found in Egypt often show the pieces of straw still in their make-up. When they were soft, bricks destined for a special building might be marked with a stamp. Cut in the wooden stamp would be the name and titles of a pharaoh or a high official (see also *The Glory that was Babylon*). The bricks for houses measure about 23 × 11.5 × 7.5 cm/9 × 4½ × 3 ins. For bigger buildings they might be

Models found in ancient tombs show Egyptians making bricks nearly 2,000 years before Christ.

larger, up to 40 × 20 × 15 cm/16 × 8 × 6 ins.

Several records present accounts of brick-making for official purposes. They list gangs of twelve workmen, each under a foreman. In one case 602 men produced 39,118 bricks. That is only sixty-five each; the modern rate for a group of four men is 3,000 bricks each day. Other accounts give the numbers of bricks of various sizes — 23,603 of 5 palm-breadths, 92,908 of 6 palm-breadths — in all, 116,511 bricks. A detailed account from the thirteenth century BC lists forty men with the target '2,000 bricks' opposite each. Then the actual numbers delivered are entered, one being 'total 1,360; deficit 370'. We are not told the penalties for failure!

All this produces the same picture as the Bible gives in Exodus (chapters 1 and 5), describing Israelites making bricks for pharaoh before the Exodus.

'The Egyptians put slave-drivers over them to crush their spirits with hard labour. The Israelites built the cities of Pithom and Rameses to serve as supply centres for the king. But the more the Egyptians oppressed the Israelites, the more they increased in number and the further they spread through the land. The Egyptians came to fear the Israelites and made their lives miserable by forcing them into cruel slavery. They made them work on their building projects and in their fields, and they had no mercy on them.'

'Moses and Aaron went to the king of Egypt and said, "The Lord, the God of Israel, says, 'Let my people go, so that they can hold a festival in the desert to honour me.'" "Who is the Lord?" the king demanded. "Why should I listen to him and let Israel go? I do not know the Lord; and I will not let Israel go." Moses and Aaron replied, "The God of the Hebrews has revealed himself to us. Allow us to travel for three days into the desert to offer sacrifices to the Lord our God. If we don't do so, he will kill us with disease or by war." The king said to Moses and Aaron, "What do you mean by making the people neglect their work? Get those slaves back to work! You people have become more

Stamped into the top of the mud-brick (top) is the name of Pharaoh Ramesses II, on whose great building projects it is likely that the Israelites slaved.

Painted on the walls of tombs from ancient Egypt are scenes of brick-making. A mixture of mud and straw is placed in the wooden moulds. They are dried in the sun, then carried to the building-sites. Brick-making was dirty work — an obvious for slave labour.

A modern brick 'factory' outside Cairo still uses the age-old methods and materials: mud from the Nile, and the hot sun to bake the bricks.

numerous than the Egyptians. And now you want to stop working!"

That same day the king commanded the Egyptian slave-drivers and the Israelite foremen: "Stop giving the people straw for making bricks. Make them go and find it for themselves. But still require them to make the same number of bricks as before, not one brick less. They haven't enough work to do, and that is why they keep asking me to let them go and offer sacrifices to their God! Make these men work harder and keep them busy, so that they won't have time to listen to a pack of lies."

The slave-drivers and the Israelite foremen went out and said to the Israelites, "The king has said that he will not supply you with any more straw. He says that you must go and get it for yourselves wherever you can find it, but you must still make the same number of bricks."

So the people went all over Egypt looking for straw. The slave-drivers kept trying to force them to make the same number of bricks every day as they had made when they were given straw. The Egyptian slave-drivers beat the Israelite foremen, whom they had put in charge of the work. They demanded, "Why aren't you people making the same number of bricks as you made before?"

Then the foremen went to the king and complained, "Why do you do this to us, Your Majesty? We are given no straw, but we are still ordered to make bricks! And now we are being beaten and you are responsible." The king answered, "You are lazy and don't want to work, and that is why you ask me to let you go and offer sacrifices to the Lord. Now get back to work! You will not be given any straw, but you must still make the same number of bricks." The foremen realized that they were in trouble when they were told that they had to make the same number of bricks every day as they had made before.'

Here are the mud and straw, the moulds, the foremen and the taskmasters, and the daily quotas. The biblical narrative illustrates the human suffering and toil behind the figures of the Egyptian accounts. No wonder the people of Israel wanted to escape!

Their demand was for permission to leave to worship their God. That was in order; notes about workmen carving the tombs of the pharaohs in the Valley of the Kings report many men taking days off for religious festivals and worship.

Straw made better bricks: the Israelite labourers had to find their own, after their petition to pharaoh. An Egyptian official in a remote border-post complained, 'there are no men to make bricks, and no straw in the region.'

For thousands of years men have made bricks in Egypt; the Exodus record and the Egyptian sources give vivid pictures of the processes and hardships involved in the second millennium BC.

THE STORE-CITY OF PHARAOH RAMESSES II

When Egyptian kings wanted to honour their gods and preserve their own fame by some great building work, they always built in stone because mud-brick buildings did not last nearly as long. The stone had to be quarried in the hills and brought to the towns.

This was a very costly business for any buildings sited in the Nile Delta, in the north of Egypt. So, when one of the pharaohs ruling at a period when the country was weak, about 900 BC, wanted to build in two Delta towns, he could not afford fresh stones. Instead, his men took the stones they needed from the ruins of earlier palaces and temples.

The new buildings were put up at Tanis and at Bubastis. Excavations at Tanis, now called San el-Hagar, uncovered large quantities of carved stonework in the buildings of Osorkon II (about 874–850 BC). On many of the blocks are the names and titles of the great Pharaoh Ramesses II, who ruled 400 years earlier.

When they were first discovered, the excavator jumped to the conclusion that Ramesses himself had erected these important temples and palaces. He was known to have built a new city in the Delta, named after him, Pi-Ramesse, and believed to be the 'Ramesses' which the Israelites toiled to build (see Exodus 1:11; the identity of the other place, Pithom, is uncertain).

But Ramesses' stone-work at Tanis is clearly not in its original position. Some of the inscriptions are

Stone blocks inscribed with the name of Ramesses II were transported to Tanis and reused there, to the confusion of archaeologists trying to identify the site of pharaoh's store-cities.

77

built in the walls upside down, or facing the interior of the wall. Nowhere on the ground at Tanis were there any foundations of Ramesses II's buildings, or any blocks in their proper places.

Since the excavations at Tanis, other work has been done at a place 30 km/ 18 miles to the south, now named Qantir. Today there is almost nothing to be seen there above ground.

From time to time, brightly glazed bricks and tiles came out of digging done in the area. Some had decorated a summer palace that Ramesses' father, Seti I, had had constructed. Much belonged to a great reconstruction of the palace for Ramesses. His name and titles stood out in blue on white and white on blue, with scenes of his victories in other colours, and figures of defeated foreigners on the steps of the throne.

Obviously, this had been an elegant palace, making up in decorative brick-work for the lack of the carved stone featured in palaces further south.

Study has disclosed that the palace at Qantir was part of a city — the city called Pi-Ramesse. There were temples for the chief

gods, and one for the Canaanite goddess Astarte, houses and offices for the government staff, and military barracks. Small houses and workshops accommodated large numbers of servants, craftsmen and labourers.

A canal led water from a branch of the Nile at one side of the river to join it at the other, so setting the town on an island. Ships from the Mediterranean could easily sail to the port created on the canal. Storehouses were built to contain goods imported and exported, and to hold the taxes the pharaoh's customs' men exacted.

All this was Ramesses' work, some of it done hastily. An ancient town, Avaris, lay beside the new one, so Ramesses had pillars carried from older temples there to complete one of his new ones, just as a later king, in turn, took Ramesses' stone blocks and pillars for his buildings at Tanis.

Pi-Ramesse was plainly a commercial centre. It was also a well-located military centre. Under Ramesses II, Egypt kept control over Canaan and part of Lebanon. After twenty years of battles and cam-

paigns in Syria-Palestine, Ramesses made a peace-treaty with the Hittite king whose army had marched as far south as Damascus (1259 BC).

From Pi-Ramesse there was easy communication with Egyptian governors in Canaan by land and sea, and the Nile led on through Egypt, giving access to the old capitals at Memphis and at Thebes, far up-stream.

No Egyptian accounts for the construction of Pi-Ramesse are known. The extensive, labour-intensive works would need many gangs of men, clearing sites, making bricks, and raising the walls. A large alien community living in the neighbourhood would be an ideal pool for the essential man-power. And that is exactly what the book of Exodus describes.

Even without precise details of the labour-force from Egypt, we can see how the discovery of Pi-Ramesse illuminates the biblical record, and endorses it. From Pi-Ramesse the oppressed Israelites did not have to go far to cross the frontier and escape into the Sinai Desert.

The head of Ramesses II, the pharaoh whose image dominates so many of the great ruins of ancient Egypt.

A colossal statue of Ramesses II lies among the palms at Memphis.

ANY SIGN OF MOSES?

One of the most important events in the Bible story is the Exodus of Israel from Egypt. Without it there would have been no nation of Israel, and so no Bible. And without a great leader to guide and encourage them, the escaping slaves would not have united to survive the desert and force their way into another country.

Moses, the book of Exodus relates, was brought up in the royal household of Egypt as an Egyptian. He fled from the country after he had murdered an Egyptian who was beating one of Moses' people, the Hebrews.

After a long absence, he came back, took the leadership of his people and tried to persuade the pharaoh of Egypt to let the Hebrews leave the land.

When the pharaoh refused, Moses, as God's agent, brought a series of plagues, the tenth one killing the oldest son of every Egyptian family. The pharaoh relented and the Hebrews left, but they were not out of Egyptian territory before he changed his mind and sent his army to stop them.

As the chariots appeared on the horizon, the waters of the Red Sea parted. The Hebrew tribes crossed safely; but as their enemies chased across the sea-bed after them, the waters ran back and drowned the Egyptians.

We might expect sensational events like these to leave their marks in the archaeological evidence. For a century or more people have been looking for them. They have made various claims.

The body of one pharaoh was said to be covered with salt, the result of his drowning in the sea. But this was soon seen to be a chemical salt produced during the embalming of the pharaoh's body.

Great brick buildings have been enthusiastically identified as the 'store-cities' where the Hebrews laboured before the Exodus, but nothing has been found to prove the bricks were made by Israelites rather than any other workmen.

Various pharaohs have been put forward as the oppressor of the Israelites because they were not followed on the throne by a first-born son. But in days when many babies died, it would not be unusual for a first-born child to die before its father, so that cannot identify the pharaoh of the Exodus.

When we look for information in the thousands of Egyptian inscriptions that survive, again, there is nothing known that can be related to Moses and the Exodus.

Since so rich and well-known a land as Egypt has failed to give us anything that can be clearly associated with the biblical story, some people suppose the story has no historical basis. They find it inconceivable that such disasters could have struck so well-organized a people as the Egyptians without their writing about them.

Great pharaohs carved their deeds on the walls of the temples, their servants had their biographies written in their tombs. Stewards and treasurers kept accounts of income and expenditure for the palaces and temples, and secretaries made lists of workmen, noting their days of work, holiday, and illness. So it certainly does seem odd, at first, that there is nothing in all the surviving records of Egypt about the events of Exodus.

But it is wrong to jump to the conclusion that the lack of evidence from Egypt implies the Bible story is baseless. What it really shows is how little we know about that country's history, and how small an amount of ancient writings actually survives.

Kings had their titles cut in stone, lists of conquered enemies, accounts of the battles they won. Some of these still stand, but many have been knocked down by later kings.

This was the fate of a great palace which Pharaoh Ramesses II built at Qantir, in the west of the Nile Delta (see *The Store-city of Pharaoh Ramesses II*).

Very many royal inscriptions have disappeared in this way. Yet even if we recovered every one, we would not expect to read in any of them how the army of Egypt was overwhelmed in the sea. The pharaohs, not surprisingly, did not present descriptions of their defeats to their subjects or to their successors!

If the royal monuments cannot help, the disruption Egypt suffered through the plagues and the loss of a work-force could result in administrative changes. Like any centralized state, Egypt's government consumed vast quantities of paper, papyrus, and much of its documentation was stored for reference. But this does not help either, for, as we have seen, the documents have virtually all perished and the likelihood of recovering any that mention Moses or the affairs of the Israelites in Egypt is negligible.

Once we understand the reasons, therefore, the complete absence of Moses and his people from the Egyptian texts is not surprising. Certainly it does not give any ground for arguing that he did not exist.

Indeed, famous leaders in the early history of many peoples are known, like Moses, only through documents handed down in native tradition, but more and more historians are treating them as notable men. The very sceptical attitudes formerly held are giving way to a more positive approach to what those traditions say, whether there is archaeological support for them, or not.

KING HAMMURABI'S LAW-CODE AND THE LAW OF MOSES

French archaeologists digging in the ancient city of Susa in western Persia in 1901–1902 made a surprising discovery. Amid ruins of buildings abandoned at the end of the second millennium BC they found finely carved stone monuments made hundreds of years before. They were not local Elamite sculptures, they were memorials that famous kings of Babylon had set up in their own cities.

In a short-lived moment of triumph, a king of Susa had raided Babylonia, carried away these pieces as trophies, telling about his victory in his own inscriptions, and writing his name on some of the prizes. The stones were shipped to Paris where they now adorn the Musée du Louvre.

Chief among these monuments is a black stone pillar. It stands 2.25 metres/7 feet 5 ins high and has a carving 60 cm/2 feet high at the top. Hundreds of lines of cuneiform writing are carefully engraved over the rest of the stone. Details of this discovery, with a translation of the text, were issued within a year, and so the world came to know about the Laws of Hammurabi.

There was great excitement, for here was a series of laws very much like the 'Laws of Moses' in many respects. Here are translations of paragraphs which find their closest similarities in Exodus 21–23.

'If a son has struck his father, they shall cut off his hand.' (no. 195)
'Whoever hits his father or his mother is to be put to death.' (Exodus 21:15)

The stela of Hammurabi of Babylon is inscribed with the king's laws. Although he lived several hundred years before Moses, the two law-codes invite comparison. The differences are as remarkable as the similarities.

'If a citizen steals a citizen's child, he shall be put to death.' (no. 14)
'Whoever kidnaps a man, either to sell him or to keep him as a slave is to be put to death.' (Exodus 21:16)

'If a citizen has hit a citizen in a quarrel and has wounded him, that citizen shall swear "I did not strike him intentionally," and he shall pay the doctor.' (no. 206)
'If there is a fight and one man hits another with a stone or with his fist, but does not kill him, he is not to be punished. If the man who was hit has to stay in bed, but later is able to get up and walk outside with the help of a stick, the man who hit him is to pay for his lost time and take care of him until he gets well.' (Exodus 21:18,19)

'If a citizen has hit a citizen's daughter and she has a miscarriage, he shall pay ten shekels of silver for her miscarriage. If that woman dies as a result, they shall put his daughter to death.' (nos. 209, 210)
'If some men are fighting and hurt a pregnant woman so that she loses her child, but she is not injured in any other way, the one who hurt her is to be fined whatever amount the woman's husband demands, subject to the approval of the judges. But if the woman herself is injured, the punishment shall be life for life, eye for eye, tooth for tooth, hand for hand, foot for foot, burn for burn, wound for wound, bruise for bruise.' (Exodus 21:22–25)

'If a citizen has put out a citizen's eye, they shall put out his eye. If a citizen has broken a citizen's bone, they shall break his bone. If a citizen has knocked out his equal's tooth, they shall knock out his tooth.' (nos. 196, 197, 200)
'Eye for eye, tooth for tooth, hand for hand, foot for foot.' (Exodus 21:24)

'If an ox has gored a citizen while going along the road and has caused his death, there shall be no penalty in this case. If the ox belonged to a citizen who had been informed by the authorities it was likely to gore, and he has not removed its horns or kept it under control, and that ox gored a citizen to death, he shall pay half a mina of silver (30 shekels).' (nos. 250, 251)
'If a bull gores someone to death, it is to be stoned, and its flesh shall not be eaten; but its owner is not to be punished. But if the bull had been in the habit of attacking people and its owner had been warned, but did not keep it penned up – then if it gores someone to death, it is to be stoned, and its owner is to be put to death also. However, if the owner is allowed to pay a fine to save his life, he must pay the full amount required. If the bull kills a boy or a girl, the same rule applies. If the bull kills a male or female slave, its owner shall pay the owner of the slave thirty pieces of silver, and the bull shall be stoned to death.' (Exodus 21:28–32)

'If a citizen has stolen an ox, or a sheep, or an ass, or a pig, or a boat, if it is the property of the temple or of the crown, he shall give back thirty-fold, but if it is the property of a dependant he shall give back ten-fold. If the thief has no means to make repayment, he shall be put to death. If a citizen has committed a robbery and is caught he shall be put to death.' (nos. 8, 22)
'If a man steals a cow or a sheep and kills it or sells it, he must pay five cows for one cow and four sheep for one sheep. He must pay for what he stole. If he owns nothing, he shall be sold as a slave to pay for what he has stolen. If the stolen animal, whether a cow, a donkey, or a sheep, is found alive in his possession, he shall pay two for one. If a thief is caught breaking into a house at night and is killed, the one who killed him is not guilty of murder. But if is happens during the day, he is guilty of murder.' (Exodus 22:1–4)

Hammurabi was king of Babylon about

1750 BC, several hundred years before the time of Moses. His laws deal with many of the same offences because Babylonians were mostly farmers living in small towns, as the Israelites were to be. Some of the similarities are so striking that there is little doubt the Hebrew laws draw on a widely known tradition.

This is most apparent in the laws about the dangerous ox. Another collection of Babylonian laws, slightly older than Hammurabi's, has a ruling he does not include, yet which is close to a biblical command: 'If an ox has gored another ox to death, the owners of the oxen shall divide between them the value of the living ox and the body of the dead ox.' ('Laws of Eshnunna', no. 53)

'If one man's bull kills another man's bull, the two men shall sell the live bull and divide the money; they shall also divide up the meat from the dead animal.' (Exodus 21:35)

The differences between these Babylonian laws and the biblical ones are just as striking as the similarities.

In the Babylonian laws property and possessions are as important as people. Crimes to do with either have the same range of punishments.

In the biblical laws only crimes against the person carry physical penalties, offences over possessions are penalized in money or goods.

The fate of the thief who cannot make repayment under Hammurabi's law (no. 8) is death, whereas Exodus 22:1–4 requires him to be sold as a slave. The Hebrew laws set a higher value on man than the Babylonian.

Hammurabi's laws, as far as can be discovered, were never exactly enforced. Although Babylonian scribes were still copying them in Nebuchadnezzar's time, well over a thousand years after Hammurabi, no Babylonian reports of legal cases refer to them. Their influence may have lain in their principles rather than their practice.

In this, too, they are interestingly like the Old Testament laws. Although they are recorded as given by Moses, scholars commonly claim there is little trace of them in the history books of Samuel and Kings. They could have existed for centuries, as Hammurabi's did.

This famous monument shows that Hebrew laws shared many concerns with the older Babylonian ones. The Hebrew laws may have inherited certain solutions for particular problems from the Babylonians. The comparisons also point to deep-seated distinctions in concepts of human life and values, drawing attention to an aspect of Hebrew thought which still influences modern civilized society.

UNDER THE PLOUGH
The Buried City of Ugarit

A farmer ploughing his field hit a large stone. When he heaved it out of the way, he saw a passage leading to an underground room. It was an ancient tomb, with the belongings of the dead man still in it. The farmer took them out and sold them to an antiquities dealer.

News of the discovery leaked out, reaching the government's officer in charge of ancient monuments, who sent one of his staff to inspect the tomb. His report, older studies of the area, and local stories that a great city stood there once upon a time, led to the decision to excavate.

This is the classic way for a great discovery to be made — and it was.

The country is Syria; the site is on the Mediterranean coast, north of the port of Latakia; the year of discovery was 1928. The French controlled Syria at that time, so it was a French team, led by Claude Schaeffer, that began excavations in 1929. With an interruption from 1939 until 1948, there has been work in the neighbourhood almost every year, and it still continues.

Under the farmer's field spread the ruins of a harbour town. Here were the houses and work-places of merchants, with their tombs beneath the floors, the factories and warehouses of a busy port. Hundreds of pottery bowls, jars and vases lay in them, including some foreign pieces imported from Cyprus, Crete, or the Greek islands. Contacts with Egypt were evident in styles of bronze axes and ivory cosmetic boxes. The whole place had been deserted suddenly, the buildings crumbling over the centuries to be hidden by a few inches of earth. From the styles of pottery, Schaeffer could date the life of the port to some time between 1400 and 1200 BC.

In this site there was plenty to be found and studied but, after only five weeks' digging, Schaeffer took his men to a *tell* 1,200 metres/three-quarters of a mile inland, overlooking the harbour. At this place, local people told him, golden objects and tiny carved stones had been found. The *tell* is a big mound, up to 18 metres/60 feet high, spreading over an area of over 20 hectares/50 acres. Its modern name is Ras Shamra.

Starting at the highest point of the mound, the excavators soon cleared the walls of a large building. Carefully-cut stone blocks formed the walls, and inside were pieces of stone sculptures. On one was the name of an Egyptian pharaoh, on another was a dedication, written in Egyptian, to a god, 'Baal of Saphon'. Near the building had stood a stone slab bearing a picture of the storm-god Baal. These objects, together with the plan of the building, indicated that it had not been a house or a palace, but a temple, presumably for the worship of Baal.

At a short distance to the east were the walls and pillars of another building. This was a fine house, with a central court open to the sky, and paved rooms leading from it. A stone staircase suggested there had been an upper storey. Under a doorstep in this house was a hoard of seventy-four bronze tools and weapons, swords, arrowheads, axes, and a tripod decorated with pomegranates, each one swinging from a loop (like the ornaments of the Israelite high priest's dress, described in Exodus 28:33,34).

It was in a room of this house, in 1929, that Schaeffer made the most significant discovery. Tumbled on the floor were a quantity of clay tablets bearing cuneiform writing. Happily, the director of the ancient monuments service, Charles Virolleaud, was an expert in Babylonian. He was able to see at once that some of the tablets were the lists of words belonging to Babylonian schools. But not all the tablets were written in Babylonian.

The cuneiform writing on forty-eight of them was of an unknown kind. Virolleaud quickly made drawings of them which were published less than a year after the discovery, so other scholars were able to puzzle over them. The honour of deciphering the newly-found script belongs to Virolleaud, another French expert, E. Dhorme, and a German, Hans Bauer.

Between them, working independently but with Virolleaud receiving the results of the other two, they were able to work out the values of the thirty different signs used in the script. They thought the language was a Semitic one, so they then sorted out

The harbour town of Ugarit, on the Syrian coast, flourished in the years just before the Exodus. It was suddenly deserted and completely disappeared. Claude Schaeffer began the excavations which yielded many remarkable discoveries. Among the finds was a gold bowl (left) with a design showing a wild-bull hunt.

The seated goddess from Ugarit, modelled in bronze (below), dates from about the fourteenth century BC.

the most common letters used to start or end words in West Semitic languages such as Hebrew. Their scheme gave translations that were sensible (a vital test!), and worked with other tablets found later.

Virolleaud had charge of the tablets and quickly translated them as they were unearthed. The language they preserve is known as Ugaritic, for they showed that the name of the city was Ugarit. In almost every season of excavation more tablets have come to light, so that now over 1,500 are known in this Ugaritic writing and language, and there is a large number in Babylonian (see *Canaanite Myths and Legends*).

The remains of the palace entrance at Ugarit give some hint of its former glory. Kings here lived in style, using beautiful furniture inlaid with carved ivory, brought by foreign princesses as part of their dowry.

A clay tablet (below) shows the alphabet in the Ugaritic script. Fifteen hundred tablets using this form of writing have now been discovered.

With the appearance of the documents, the history and culture of the city began to come to life. Enthusiastically, Schaeffer opened trenches in other areas of the mound. Everywhere, the ruined buildings lay immediately below the surface of the soil.

In one place were houses and workshops of weavers, stone-workers, smiths and jewellers, with many of the tools and products left just where their owners had dropped them as enemies set fire to the city. In other parts there were grander houses for the wealthy men of Ugarit. Some had their own archives of cuneiform tablets.

The fabled treasures of local tradition became real, too. Gold and silver jewellery, copper statuettes of gods and goddesses, plated or decorated with gold, were hidden in several houses. One trench, dug in 1933, produced a dish and a bowl of gold with elaborate designs hammered in relief. Bowls of silver and gold also came out of excavations in the 1960 season.

By far the most impressive of the

buildings at Ugarit was the royal palace. Like the rest of the city, it had been burnt. Although the timbers disintegrated, the stone walls still stand 2 metres/6 feet or more above the ground.

A stepped entrance with two pillars supporting the lintel led to a small vestibule, then a large courtyard. Here, a well supplied water so that visitors could wash before entering the king's presence. A stone slab set in the floor was where they stood to have water poured over their hands and feet; a drain carried the water away.

King after king had added new courts and suites of rooms during the two centuries or so in which the palace existed. The archaeologists have detected twelve stages of building. Quite late in this process a garden was planted in one court, and in another was set a large, shallow pool where we may imagine fish were bred. Several rooms had been stores for palace records.

Cuneiform tablets in Babylonian and Ugaritic reveal the business of day-to-day government. Some report foreign affairs, treaties with neighbour kings, or imposed by the Hittites, even the case of a foreign princess who was married to the king of Ugarit being executed, probably for adultery.

Foreign princesses brought rich dowries with them, duly listed on certain tablets. In the palace were pieces of some of the furniture they describe. A bed had a head-board of ivory, carved with animals and hunting scenes and with pictures of the king and queen embracing, flanking a figure of the mother-goddess suckling two young gods. A round table had an elaborate inlay of ivory carvings of fantastic animals, sphinxes and lions with wings.

Other pieces of furniture had legs and feet of ivory in the shape of lions' legs and paws. Quite exceptional is a piece of elephant tusk cut as a support for a piece of furniture and carved as a human head, perhaps the likeness of a king or queen of Ugarit.

Ugarit's wealth came from trade. The city stood at the end of a road from Babylon, up the Euphrates and across to the Mediterranean. From Ugarit ships sailed to Cyprus and Crete, to the southern coast of Turkey, and down the coast of Canaan to Egypt. Not surprisingly, influences from all these regions appear in the art and culture of Ugarit.

They are most obvious in writing, for beside Babylonian and Ugaritic, Hittite and Hurrian were also written in cuneiform, Egyptian appears on metal and stone (and surely was more common on papyrus), while the Hittite hieroglyphs and a syllabic script from Cyprus are also found at Ugarit.

The peasant's plough opened an inexhaustible store of treasure in the ruins of Ugarit. Although the city lies outside the borders of Canaan, it gives a rich picture of the life that flourished in Canaan before the arrival of the Israelites. It was a society of wealthy land-owning kings and courts, and a host of peasant farmers.

CANAANITE MYTHS AND LEGENDS

The books people read and the songs they sing often reveal their hopes and beliefs. In biblical times only a few people's ideas were written down, and even fewer survive.

From the people who lived in Canaan before the Israelites there is almost no information of this sort at all, probably because they used papyrus as their writing material (see *The Alphabet*).

To the north, at Ugarit, clay tablets were more commonly used. Many have survived, and some contain stories about gods and heroes, rituals and prayers for the worship in the temples.

Although Ugarit is outside the boundary of Canaan, the people there revered the same gods and goddesses. Local variations may have existed in their beliefs, but it is safe to assume a general similarity.

El, the chief god (his name means simply 'god'), was thought of as an old man — helplessly drunk on one occasion — whose place as the vigorous, active god was taken by Baal.

Baal was god of rain and storm. He had two rivals.

One was Yam, the sea. Yam had a palace, but Baal did not. One of the myths gives an account of how Baal got a fine palace, perhaps after he defeated Yam.

Baal's sister, Anat, was his main supporter. At one stage she slaughtered the people of two towns:

'Lo, Anat fought in the valley,
She fought between the two towns,
She smote the crowds by the coast (?),
She silenced the men of the east.
Under her feet heads were like balls,
Palms of hands were like locusts about her,
The palms of warriors like heaps of corn (?).
She hung the heads at her waist,
She bound the palms to her belt.
She plunged up to her knees in the blood of heroes,
The hems of her skirts in the warriors' gore.
She drove out the old men with her staff,
With her bow string . . .
. . .
She fought hard, then looked around,
Anat struck, and laughed,
Her heart filled with joy . . .'

When she had finished her fighting, Anat bullied El into allowing Baal to have a palace built where he could sit in state.

Baal had another enemy

Baal was the Canaanite god of rain and storm. In contrast to the chief god, El, he was vigorously active, challenging rival gods with the aid of his sister, Anat.

A tablet in the Ugaritic script contains a series of spells to charm serpents.

to face, Mot, 'Death'. A broken tablet tells how Mot gained power over Baal, who entered the underworld. Anat mourned her brother, found Mot, his murderer, ground him like corn, burnt him, and scattered him over the earth. Meanwhile, the goddess Asherah, El's wife, suggested that another god should take Baal's place on the throne. He did, but he was too small to sit on it properly!

Baal, at the entry to the underworld, mated with a cow who immediately gave birth to a boy. When Mot was dead, Baal reappeared, killed Asherah's sons, and took his throne again.

Seven years later, Mot reappeared to open another fight. Neither won, for El stopped them, leaving Baal as king.

Gods like these do not commend themselves to people today. As far as the Israelites were concerned, they were a dangerous distraction from their one God. Canaanite gods had no moral scruples. They behaved and acted just as they pleased.

Followers of Baal performed all sorts of rituals to win his favour, usually through offering sacrifices. A prayer for a time of danger is preserved on one tablet:

'If a powerful enemy attacks your gate,
If a mighty one attacks your walls,
Lift your eyes to Baal:
''O Baal, drive away the powerful one from our gate,
The mighty one from our walls.
We consecrate a bull for you, O Baal,
We offer to you, O Baal,

what we have vowed,
We consecrate a bullock for you, O Baal,
We offer a sacrifice, O Baal,
We pour drink-offerings, O Baal,
We go up to your temple, O Baal,
We come along the paths to the house of Baal.''
Then Baal will hear your prayers;
He will drive away the powerful one from your gate,
The mighty one from your walls.'

Among the heroes of old in the legends of Ugarit was a King Keret. He lost his wife and family, and was mourning them when the god El, 'father of mankind', came to him in a dream to solve the problem.

Keret was to gather an army to march to the city of a king who had a beautiful daughter and demand her hand in marriage. After a long journey and a long conference, the wedding was arranged. In due course the princess bore many sons and daughters.

Yet all was not well. Keret fell ill, and his land suffered a drought. Eventually El intervened again, to cure him, or at least to give him a longer life.

Keret's son had hoped to be king, so he tried to persuade his father to retire because he was no longer capable of ruling: 'You do not judge the widow's case, nor do you give justice to the oppressed.' But Keret had enough spirit left to curse his son and keep his throne.

These stories, and several more, express the problems of life. Baal, Yam, and Mot personify the

forces of nature. Baal's death signifies the annual disappearance of rain and water in the summer's heat, to return in the autumn rains.

Directions on the tablets prove that they were read aloud, perhaps in annual festivals, to ensure that Baal would return.

Keret's story shows how the god cares for the king, and how the prosperity of the land depends on his health and success. Family rivalries and the problem of old age also play a part, although the end of the story, which may have told how they were solved, is missing.

This summary gives a small taste of Canaanite literature. Even to read all that survives can only bring partial knowledge, for many tablets were destroyed in ancient times, and a lot of the stories would have been kept alive by word of mouth alone, never being written down.

Still, there is sufficient for us to see the sort of beliefs the Israelites met in Canaan.

The records that survive have a value for Hebrew studies in another way. Their language is similar to Hebrew, and has helped us to understand more clearly some words and passages in the Old Testament.

The form of the poetry, with pairs of lines, the second almost repeating the first, is common in both literatures, showing how Hebrew poets took up the styles that were well known when they wrote psalms and hymns for their God.

The figure of Baal is made of bronze and dates from about 1400-1200 BC.

THE ALPHABET

The majority of languages written in the world today are written with an alphabet. Only those using Chinese and Japanese characters and their imitations are not. At first sight it is hard to believe that the Roman alphabet, the Hebrew alphabet, the Arabic alphabet and the Ethiopic alphabet are connected. Yet they are all descended from one parent. One of the contributions of archaeology in the regions of Palestine and Syria is the discovery of the early history of the alphabet.

In the hills on the south-western side of the Sinai Desert the ancient Egyptians had mines where they dug out a blue stone, turquoise, which they used in their jewellery. (It is still a favourite today, as a 'lucky' stone to ward off 'the evil eye'.) Egyptians were responsible for the production of the turquoise. The labourers in the mines were local nomads or men brought from Canaan. Both the supervisors and the workmen made offerings to the mother-goddess and other divinities. They commemorated special moments with inscriptions on stone.

Egyptian inscriptions follow the standard patterns. Beside them are others which, when Sir Flinders Petrie found them in 1905, no one could understand at all. In them were about thirty different signs, each a picture like the Egyptian hieroglyphs, but not the same as them.

After some years, the eminent British Egyptologist Sir Alan Gardiner perceived that these characters were a sort of alphabet. He was able to progress further by making the assumption that each sign stood for the initial sound of its name. Children learning the alphabet said, 'A is for apple, D is for dog'. Gardiner reasoned that the signs he studied were created on the reverse of this principle, that is to say, 'apple is for A, dog is for D'.

In 1915 Gardiner announced he had worked out the values of nine of the signs. Less cautious scholars rushed ahead, one claiming that there were links between the inscriptions and Moses. Even the most distinguished expert who attempted to read all of them found his results received with great scepticism. It is still not possible to read what the writings say, mainly because they are all very short. They are clearly dedications to the goddess and other religious records.

Finding these inscriptions, about thirty of them, in the Sinai Desert was an archaeological accident. When the mines were abandoned there was nothing but the weather and occasional visitors to damage them. The same sort of writing was used in Canaan itself, a meagre handful of examples assure us. One or two may be older than those from the Sinai, others slightly later. From such meagre sources

the early history of the alphabet can be deduced, at least in general terms.

Between the years 2000 and 1500 BC strong cities arose all over Syria and Canaan, usually on the ruins of those destroyed late in the third millennium. With the cities came a growth in trade all over the Near East, with contacts renewed between people speaking many different languages. Babylonian cuneiform and the Egyptian scripts were the normal forms of writing for inter-national communications. Both were complicated, with hundreds of signs, some with more than one meaning.

The coast of Syria-Palestine was a meeting-place for all these languages. It was there, perhaps at the busy port of Byblos, that a scribe hit on the idea of the alphabet. He was a genius, who saw a way to write which was very simple and very adaptable. His invention also displays an advanced attitude to his language. Babylonian scribes examined their language to make lists of syllables and the forms of verbs. The unknown originator of the alphabet separated each distinct sound in his language for which he could draw a picture on the 'dog is for D' pattern.

His language was a West Semitic one, probably a form of Canaanite which developed into Phoenician. In that language no word began with a vowel, so he

The inscription on the stone sphinx from the Sinai desert is an example of early alphabetic writing.

			Name	(Meaning)	Value
			'aleph	ox	'
			beth	house	b
			resh	head	r
			'ayin	eye	'
(1)	(2)	(3)			

Signs in forms found in the Sinai mines (1) and in Canaanite writing of the thirteenth and twelfth centuries BC (2 and 3).

			Semitic value	Greek name	Greek value
			'	alpha	a
			b	beta	b
			r	rho	r
			'	omicron	o
(1)	(2)	(3)			

Signs in forms found in Phoenician about 1000 BC (1), in Moab (2, Mesha's stone, see No Hidden Treasure), and in early Greek about 700 BC (3).

The Gezer calendar is the oldest continuous text written in the alphabet found in the land of Israel. It probably dates from the time of King Solomon.

did not make signs for the vowel sounds. They had to be supplied by the reader after each consonant, according to the sense. This is still the case in two descendants of that alphabet today. In Arabic and in Hebrew the vowels are either not written, or are marked by extra signs above and below the letters.

If this account is right, the clever scribe was most likely already an expert at writing Egyptian with a pen and ink on papyrus. That would explain why the new script ran from right to left: it was the Egyptian way (as it still is for Arabic and Hebrew). That also explains why so few specimens of the alphabet in its early stages survive. They were almost all on papyrus, so any left in ruined buildings in Canaan will have rotted away.

At Ugarit, the Babylonian system of writing on clay was common; papyrus had to be imported from Egypt, which made it more costly. When knowledge of the early alphabet spread, a scribe trained in the Babylonian tradition saw its advantages and created an imitation, using wedge-shaped strokes on clay tablets. The tablets that survive at Ugarit bear witness to the way scribes there were ready to use this cuneiform alphabet for every form of record. There is no reason to doubt that the original alphabet was used with equal freedom in Canaan to the south.

As Israel gained control of Canaan, the alphabet was taking on a settled form, so that it could be understood wherever it was used. The oldest texts, apart from the very short ones of 1600–1200 BC, are Phoenician ones. They were engraved in Byblos on stone slabs, statues, and a coffin about the time David

and Solomon were ruling Israel. From that time onwards a number of inscriptions on stone, metal, and pottery enable us to trace the rise of local forms of the alphabet: Aramaic, Hebrew, Moabite, Phoenician.

The advent of the alphabet did not bring literacy to everyone, but it did make reading and writing easier and so available to far more people than the specialist scribes who wrote cuneiform and Egyptian.

In the centuries after 1000 BC the Greeks adopted the Phoenician alphabet. Their language has many words beginning with vowels and so they needed to write the vowels as well as consonants. To do that, the Greeks took letters for Phoenician sounds they did not need and used them to denote the vowels they did need (for example, the Phoenician gulping sound

named 'ayin was taken for 'o'.)

From this Greek alphabet, through the Romans, come the modern roman letters used throughout the Western world today.

CONQUERED CITIES OF CANAAN

Mediterranean Sea
Hazor
Megiddo
Beth-shan
CANAAN
PHILISTINES
Jericho
Jerusalem
Lachish

Digging into the ruin mounds of Palestine, archaeologists have hit a level of buildings destroyed by fire. At site after site their reports are the same: 'a thick layer of ashes showing the level was brought to an end by a great fire . . . before the close of the thirteenth century BC' or '. . . the fortress . . . was completely razed by fire. The thickness of the destroyed layer was 1.5 metres/5 feet. The city was apparently destroyed in the second half of the thirteenth century BC.'

A number of cities destroyed about the same time points to a widespread enemy attack. The date fits the time when the Israelites are most likely to have entered Canaan. Many have drawn the obvious conclusion: the Israelite soldiers burnt these places.

Unfortunately for archaeologists, enemy armies left the smoking ruins and moved on. They seldom left a notice or a monument declaring, 'We, the Israelites, destroyed this city called Bethel', or anything like that. So it is impossible to be certain these ruins were made by Joshua's tribesmen. There is also another complication; beside the Israelites, there were Philistines trying to gain control of Canaan from the coast and Aramaeans from Syria in the north. Any of these people may have attacked the Canaanite towns and cities. Nor should the Egyptians be forgotten. Pharaoh Merenptah's forces were active at the end of the thirteenth century BC (see *Record of Victory*). Without written evidence we cannot place the blame on one group rather than another.

The pottery styles and a few objects inscribed with names of Egyptian kings give the clues to the dates of the destructions. These cannot be very precise, for a fashion may last longer in one place than in another, and some evidence may be missed.

The picture emerging at present is of several attacks on the Canaanites, some overwhelming several towns at once, some taking place occasionally at intervals of several years. This is in keeping with the age of disruption which the biblical book of Judges describes. Different armies, Israelite, Philistine, and others, would raid and burn a city here and a city there.

At the time of their first invasion, the Israelites did not burn the Canaanite towns wholesale. They needed them to live in! According to the Bible, only Jericho, Ai and Hazor were burnt by Joshua.

In the ashes and the ruins many possessions lie where their owners left them. Pottery is always the most common. The Canaanite potters made a variety of bowls and dishes, mugs and jars. Although by the thirteenth century BC their wares were not as good as they had been a few centuries earlier, the potters still enjoyed themselves painting animals and birds on some of the pieces they made.

One type of two-handled jar, about 57 cm/2 feet high was used to export Canaanite oil and wine. These jars were taken in trade or tribute to Egypt, and as far as Mycenae and Athens in Greece. Typical pottery from those countries came to Canaan in return.

Most striking are the pots painted with horizontal stripes of red or brown, produced by the potters of Greece. They were fashionable among well-to-do Canaanites, and so local potters made rather second-rate copies for poorer people. The fashions in this imported Mycenaen ware are a major key to the dates of the places where they are found, because the shift from one fashion to another can be linked to the reigns of certain pharaohs.

Canaanite craftsmen were skilled in casting and engraving metals — silver and gold for jewellery, copper and bronze for tools and weapons and other utensils. As at Ugarit, there were some who carved ivory with great skill, and a few who engraved stones as seals. In their art the Canaanites display their magpie instincts, mixing ideas from Egypt and Babylonia, from Turkey and Syria.

A similar mixture of local with foreign ideas is also seen in Canaanite religion. Small figures of gods may wear Egyptian crowns; the goddesses may have the curls of the Egyptian mother-goddess, Hathor. At the same time, Canaanite priests tried to tell the future in the Babylonian way, looking at the livers of animals they sacrificed. Clay models of livers, used to teach them how to do this, have been found.

The temples where sacrifices were made, and the gods worshipped, have been uncovered at several sites. At Lachish, a small shrine outside the city wall was rebuilt three times. Each new temple buried the old one and anything left in it. Scores of bowls in and around the temple had held offerings, probably of flour baked into bread in the ovens standing nearby. A bin to the left of the altar was full of animal bones, the sacrifices given to the god and his priests. Almost all were the bones of the right foreleg of a sheep or goat, the shoulder which was the priest's part of the Israelite peace-offering (described in Leviticus 7:32). This shrine and the city were burnt, perhaps a few years after 1200 BC.

Another Canaanite city burnt by enemies was Hazor. The destruction there may be dated a little earlier. Yigael Yadin's excavations from 1955 to 1958 cleared several temples used during the Late Bronze Age and violently destroyed. One was a single room with a recess opposite the doorway. Entering the shrine, the worshipper would see facing him a rough stone slab serving as a table for offerings. Behind it, in the recess, were a seated stone statue of a man, and ten stones stood upright in a row. On the middle one was carved a crescent moon and a disk, with a pair of hands reaching up to them. These seem to be symbols of the moon god and his wife.

The other stones may be memorials to dead people, or to great events. Pillars had this purpose in many periods and places, from Jacob's 'pillow' (in Genesis 28) to the present day. For the Canaanites they had become objects of worship, so Israel was told to destroy them: 'Do not bow down to their gods or worship them, and do not adopt their religious practices. Destroy their gods and break

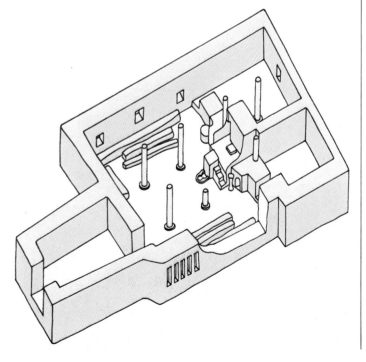

At Lachish a small temple building was discovered. It was burnt, with the rest of the city, probably a little after 1200 BC.

Yigael Yadin's excavations at Hazor revealed a Canaanite shrine. The carvings on the central standing stone are thought to be symbols of the moon-god and his wife. Temples in use during the Late Bronze Age had been violently destroyed.

God promised his people a land 'flowing with milk and honey' — the land of Canaan. From Mt Tabor the view extends over the fertile Valley of Jezreel.

down their sacred stone pillars.'

A much larger temple had three main rooms, a porch, a middle room and a sanctuary, an arrangement which parallels Solomon's temple, although the proportions are different. Strewn among the ashes on the floor of the sanctuary were stone tables with hollows for liquid offerings, an altar for incense, basins, a number of stone seals and bronze figures, a small stone statue of a seated man, and part of a larger statue of a god. Professor Yadin identified him as the god of the storm, Hadad or Baal to the Canaanites.

In these Canaanite cities, where new buildings were put up above the ashes of the destructions, they were usually very different from the old ones. Only in Egyptian garrison towns at Beth-shan and Megiddo did life continue much as before well into the twelfth century.

Whoever came to live on top of the ruins did not care for the old religion.

The temples were not rebuilt, and the Canaanite figures of gods and goddesses made of metal or pottery soon disappear entirely.

Canaanite pottery styles were carried on, with less skill, but the buildings were very much poorer, sometimes little more than squatter huts, with many pits 2 metres/6 feet deep or more, used for storing foodstuffs. Eventually these poor levels give way to better-made houses with finer pottery.

Setting all this archaeological evidence beside the biblical records, there seems little room for doubt that some of these changes, at least, mark the arrival of the Israelites. They were less accustomed to town life, and were supposed to have a very different religion from the Canaanites, with only one God and no local temples. There was no place for separate city-states when a single nation had control of the land.

This bronze plaque of a Canaanite was found at Hazor.

AND THE WALLS CAME TUMBLING DOWN

CANAAN

Jericho •

• Jerusalem

Dead Sea

Ancient walls serve as a reminder that Jericho is one of the oldest cities in the world going back to before 6,000 BC.

The Bible tells us that, at the time of the Israelite conquest of Canaan, Joshua's soldiers marched round Jericho, and when the walls fell flat they killed the inhabitants, took everything worth having, and set the city on fire. If any event in Israel's history can be traced by archaeology, surely this one can!

Jericho was one of the first places in Palestine to attract the early archaeologists. The first team sent from London by the Palestine Exploration Fund, a group of Royal Engineers led by Charles Warren, dug shafts deep into the ruin mound in 1868. Everyone was hoping for great stone carvings like those recently brought back from the Assyrian palaces. Finding nothing but earth and mud bricks, the diggers decided there was nothing worth searching for, and moved on.

Forty years passed before more excavations were made at Jericho. In the interval there was some progress towards a better understanding of the ancient cities in Palestine. German archaeologists, directed by E. Sellin, uncovered part of the city wall and houses within it during the years 1907–1909. They found nothing they could say was the result of Joshua's attack.

That was left to the third expedition, from 1930 to 1936. Led by John Garstang of the University of Liverpool, the excavators had the search for remains of Joshua's Jericho as a major aim. After digging for a few weeks, Garstang amazed the world. He pointed to masses of mud-bricks

and the stumps of walls. These, he claimed, were the very walls that fell before Joshua and his men. Garstang's discovery was accepted by other archaeologists and became a stock example of how archaeology 'proves' the Bible's record true.

There were two walls, parallel, with a space of 4.5 metres/15 feet between them. Buildings had rested across the tops of these walls. A violent destruction by fire had overtaken the city. According to Garstang this happened about 1400 BC, a date he reached on the evidence of Egyptian scarabs from tombs he opened around Jericho. None of the scarabs was later

96

than the reign of Pharaoh Amenophis III, then dated about 1411–1375 BC. This date is in agreement with the earlier of the dates proposed for the Exodus (see *Relatives of the Hebrews?*).

In addition to this city belonging to the Late Bronze Age, Garstang's work proved that Jericho had been an important place at much earlier periods, in the Middle Bronze Age, in the Early Bronze Age (about

3000–2300 BC), and in the Neolithic Age, before man used metal. It was about this very early time that the fourth series of excavations at Jericho had most to reveal, but they also related to the question of 'Joshua's Jericho'.

In 1952 Miss Kathleen Kenyon of the University of London opened new trenches at Jericho. She wanted to clear up some problems about Garstang's

The great mound, all that is left of ancient Jericho, shows clearly from the air.

conclusions. Other excavations in Palestine had produced results which did not agree entirely with Garstang's, quite apart from the question about the date of the destruction of the city. Very few scholars accept the date Garstang used, about 1400 BC, preferring the late date in the thirteenth century.

Kathleen Kenyon examined the walls and houses Garstang found, and was able to show he had dated them wrongly. By minute, painstaking study of the layers of earth running beneath them, up to them, and over them, and of the broken pottery in those layers, she demonstrated that the walls were about 1,000 years older than Garstang had thought. Earthquakes had made them tumble long before Joshua's day. The rubbish of later buildings piled up over the ruins and Garstang's excavations failed to separate them.

Kathleen Kenyon found the same evidence for destruction by fire as Garstang had done. With better knowledge of the pottery fashions, the fruit of an extra twenty years' research by many archaeologists, she demonstrated that the fire happened

some decades before 1500 BC. After that, Jericho lay desolate until about 1400 BC or soon after.

What buildings existed then, and how long they stood, is very hard to say. Certainly there was never a great city at Jericho again. Over many centuries, wind and rain have scoured the mound, washing away the ruined mud-brick walls. The city which was burnt before 1500 BC had a great rampart all round it with a brick wall on top. Erosion had taken away every part of that wall, except at one corner, and there only the foundations had escaped. At other points up to 6 metres/20 feet of the height of the sloping rampart had vanished, too. In the light of this evidence, Kathleen Kenyon could suggest that erosion had removed almost all traces of the lost Jericho.

However, she found a small part of a building which she dated before 1300 BC, and Garstang had found pottery belonging to the same time or a little later. There is enough to show there were some people about at Jericho somewhere near the time of

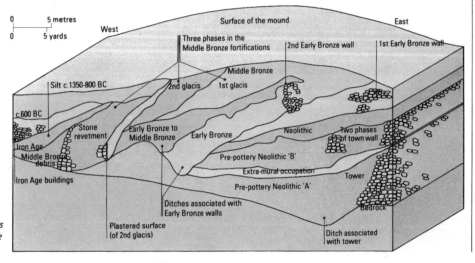

Kathleen Kenyon's main excavation at Jericho is shown in the cross-section. Erosion has removed almost all traces of the lost Jericho.

THE PROBLEM OF AI

After the fall of Jericho, the biblical book of Joshua recounts the Israelites' march against Ai, and their capture of the city after an initial failure.

In 1838 Edward Robinson, the American pioneer of exploration in Palestine, suggested Ai might be an imposing mound called Et-Tell, although he preferred another place.

Another great American scholar, W.F. Albright, argued in favour of Et-Tell in 1924, and his arguments have convinced most people.

A French team dug into the mound from 1933 to 1935, and an American team from 1964 to 1970. Both excavations found remains of a large town with a strong city wall still standing 7 metres/23 feet high at one point. Inside the town was a fine temple, houses and a reservoir. Its life began about 3000 BC and it was finally destroyed about 2400 BC. Neither expedition found any pottery or buildings that they could date between then and about 1200 BC.

Here archaeology presents a problem to the historian: how is he to explain the ancient record? Three answers are possible.
● Et-Tell may not be ancient Ai. There are no inscriptions to prove its identity. Yet attempts to find another site which fits the biblical description of Ai as well have not succeeded so far.
● The story may be a 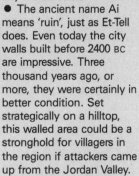legend, a popular explanation for the people living there after 1200 BC of how the great old walls they could see were broken down. This overcomes the archaeological difficulty, but denies the Hebrew narrative any factual basis.
● The ancient name Ai means 'ruin', just as Et-Tell does. Even today the city walls built before 2400 BC are impressive. Three thousand years ago, or more, they were certainly in better condition. Set strategically on a hilltop, this walled area could be a stronghold for villagers in the region if attackers came up from the Jordan Valley.

To the present writer this last is the most satisfactory explanation of the problem of Ai.

Joshua's attack. But what the place was like cannot be discovered.

Jericho is a good example of the limitations archaeologists may face. The excavations have revealed nothing that really agrees with the biblical history. The best one can say is that erosion has obliterated the ruins of Joshua's Jericho. But the absence of ruins is taken by some Old Testament scholars to support their view that the biblical account is a piece of legend or folk-lore, a story which need have no factual content at all.

In the case of Jericho, archaeology can contribute nothing for or against this view. For a historian, however, it is most unsatisfactory, for it opens the way to treating ancient records in any way the individual pleases. He may even remodel them to suit his own theories.

The book of Joshua preserves the story in its ancient form. Like any other ancient record it deserves serious historical consideration. The fact that archaeological discoveries have been reinterpreted warns us against treating them as crystal clear evidence.

RECORD OF VICTORY
The 'Israel Stele'

'Canaan has been plundered in every evil way,
Askelon has been brought away captive,
Gezer has been seized,
Yenoam has been destroyed.
Israel is devastated, having no seed,
Syria is widowed because of Egypt.
All lands, they are united in peace,
Everyone who roamed, he has subdued him,
By the king of Egypt . . . Merenptah.'

These words stand at the end of an Egyptian inscription on a stone slab. The monument was found in 1896 at Thebes where it had stood in the temple honouring the Pharaoh Merenptah. From the appearance of 'Israel' in it, the stone is called the 'Israel Stele'.

Merenptah was a son of the great Pharaoh Ramesses II, and followed him on the throne of Egypt about 1213 BC. He was not as great a soldier or builder as his father, and although Egypt had enjoyed several years of peace there were still enemies abroad.

The Libyans threatened Egypt from the west, and Merenptah defeated them. This inscription celebrates that decisive victory, won in the fifth year of his reign. At the end come the lines quoted, as a final note of praise to the king, naming an earlier victory.

The name of Israel is clearly recorded on a stone slab (right) found at Thebes which records the military triumph of Pharaoh Merenptah. It is the oldest evidence for the existence of Israel outside the Bible.

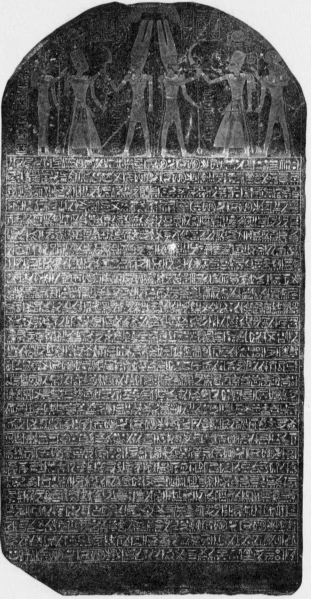

That the name 'Israel' is on this slab is beyond doubt, despite an attempt to disprove it. Also beyond doubt is the fact of military action between Merenptah's forces and peoples and places in Canaan, although some scholars have tried to argue there was none. In a separate inscription the same pharaoh is given the title 'he who binds Gezer'.

The 'Israel Stele' is valuable because it gives the oldest evidence for the existence of Israel outside the Bible. The next inscriptions to mention Israel are Assyrian and Moabite, written nearly 400 years later (see *No Hidden Treasure, The Price of Protection*). Without the Old Testament, the history of Israel in those four centuries would remain unknown.

Here is an example of the chance element in archaeological discovery; without the 'Israel Stele', and apart from the Old Testament, there would be no evidence that Israel existed as early as 1200 BC.

The words of the stele do not make it quite clear whether the name Israel applied to a people settled in a definite territory, or to a nomadic group. Israel is clearly in Canaan, and it is most satisfactory to set the conflict in the period when Israel was settling their Promised Land, after the death of Joshua. The phrases 'destroyed, is devastated, having no seed' are part of the usual way of claiming a complete victory. They should not be interpreted literally.

In fact, Merenptah's reign lasted only ten years, and then Egypt's power grew weaker, so the success did not have lasting effect as far as Israel was concerned. That may be one reason why the biblical writers did not report this incident. It may have been a single battle in which the Egyptians drove Israel out of part of Canaan for a short time.

There is one other point arising from the 'Israel Stele'. If Israel was in Canaan by 1213 BC or soon afterwards, the Exodus from Egypt clearly happened earlier.

Before the stele was discovered some historians had claimed the Exodus took place in Merenptah's reign. Unless the Bible's timing is wrong, or its picture of Israel moving in a single body from Egypt to Canaan is wrong, Merenptah could not be the pharaoh of the Exodus. There is a strong possibility that this pharaoh was in fact Merenptah's father, Ramesses II.

Pharaoh Merenptah or his father, Ramesses II, storms the fortress of Ashkelon in the south of Canaan. It is typical of the strong, fortified cities faced by Joshua and his army.

THE PHILISTINES

The head of a Philistine soldier was carved at Thebes in Egypt. It dates from the twelfth century BC.

Pharaoh Ramesses III was pleased. His army had won a great victory. For years there had been bands of strangers sailing across the Mediterranean to Egypt. Some had settled peacefully, some had joined Egypt's old enemies, the Libyans, to the west. The mighty Ramesses II conquered one attacking party at the very beginning of his reign and made some of them fight for him at the great battle of Qadesh, when he faced the Hittites in 1275 BC. After Ramesses, Merenptah also captured some of these foreigners.

Both kings tell us the names of tribes or parties of these people: there were Sherden and Sheklesh, Lukka and Aqaiwasha. They are all described as 'foreigners of the sea'. Unlike the Egyptians themselves, they were uncircumcised. Modern scholars refer to them as the Sea Peoples.

Ramesses III faced a bigger threat than earlier kings, so his success was greater. How many of the Sea People he killed or captured we do not know; Merenptah killed over 2,000, Ramesses III killed over 12,000 Libyans in a one-year war. It was in his fifth year, about 1175 BC, that he joined battle with the Sea People. They were arriving by ship in the Nile Delta and trekking overland along the coast of Syria and Canaan in ox-drawn wagons. More tribes came than before. Some were the ones already known, and there were Tjekker and Weshesh and Peleset. The Egyptians probably did not really know who all these people were. To them they were aliens and enemies, and we know little more today. The only name we

can identify for certain is the last one in the list, the 'Peleset', who were the Philistines of the Bible.

Even though these were strange and despised enemies, the Egyptians took note of their appearance and their equipment. Ramesses wanted a record of the triumph, so he had pictures of the battle carved on the walls of this temple. Visitors to Medinet Habu, on the opposite bank of the Nile to Luxor, can view them still.

One scene depicts the land battle. Many Sea People lie dead or dying beneath the feet of their fellows who are vainly fighting the ranks of the Egyptian infantry. Here and there in the battlefield are the Egyptian light chariots and horses and the heavy wagons and oxen of the Sea People.

Pharaoh's artists took care to make the differences between the Egyptian soldiers and their foes clear. Egyptian soldiers carry oblong, round-topped shields, heavy tipped clubs and short daggers; the chariots carry archers. In contrast, the Sea People have spears and long, tapering swords, round shields, and head-dresses of feathers or hair standing straight up on their heads. One group, fighting on the Egyptian side in these pictures, wears helmets with a pair of horns on top.

Another scene illustrates the war at sea. Egyptian archers, in ships with oars and a sail used for moving up and down the Nile, shoot at Sea People in sailing ships. One of those has overturned, and the water is full of drowning Sea People with both kinds of head-gear — but not one Egyptian.

The sculptures of Ramesses III and their captions state plainly that the folk with the horned helmets were the Sherden, whom some writers link with Sardinia. Wearers of the plumed hat included the Philistines.

After their defeat, the Sea People evidently broke up. Egyptian army units absorbed some, as they had done earlier, and they may have been posted to Canaan where, it appears, other Sea People clans had settled. The Old Testament refers to the presence of the Philistines in the south-west of Canaan, on the coast, and the very name 'Palestine' is proof that they were once present there in force. At about 1100 BC

an Egyptian traveller found members of another group, the Tjekker, a little further up the coast, at Dor.

There could hardly be better evidence for the arrival of the Philistines and their occupation of part of Canaan. For a long time archaeologists have related these events to a series of discoveries in sites all over the eastern Mediterranean area.

In Turkey, the empire of the Hittites collapsed, attacked by enemies from the west and east. At Ugarit, letters written just before the city was burnt speak of all the ships going west to help the Hittites, and of the damage a few enemy vessels had done. From

The Bible makes frequent mention of the Philistines as the enemies of Israel. They were one of the 'Sea Peoples' who invaded Egypt itself. Captured Philistines, wearing feathered head-dresses are shown on an Egyptian relief which records the pharaoh's victory.

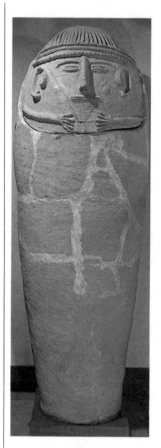

An anthropoid clay coffin (above) found at Bethshean, Israel, seems to wear a similar head-dress to the Philistines on Egyptian reliefs.

The characteristic style of pottery illustrated by the jug (right) is associated with the Philistines.

Ugarit southwards, at place after place, heavy deposits of ash and hastily evacuated buildings support the remark in Ramesses III's Egyptian text that the Sea People destroyed the Hittites, Carchemish, Cyprus and the Amorite land.

Ugarit and some other places did not recover. Where towns did rise from the ruins there is often confirmation of a change in population. The buildings have different plans and, most noticeably, there are new fashions in pottery. They are closely connected to styles of pottery current in Greece, Crete and Cyprus.

Towns flourishing before the destructions had imported older styles of this pottery. Now there was much more, and the local copies were almost as good as the originals. A particular pattern featuring a bird was popular, and has become the characteristic by which this pottery is recognized. The pottery is found mainly in the region in which the Bible places the Philistines, and so it is named Philistine pottery. This is one of the few cases where a particular type of pottery can be associated with a specific people.

That unusual fact almost exhausts archaeological knowledge of the Philistines. They left no recognizable writings, and too little has been found in their towns to build a picture of their culture. One other type of object found in the Philistine area and commonly called Philistine is a clay coffin with face and hands modelled in relief. Above the face are horizontal bands with vertical lines rising from them which echo the Sea People's head-dress. Examples from Transjordan and southern Egypt could be relics of Sea People squadrons in Egyptian garrisons. These clay coffins obviously imitate Egyptian mummies.

According to the Israelite historian, the Philistines controlled iron-working in the land, and it may be that they introduced this skill. The time of their arrival, and of the destruction of so many cities, coincides, in archaeological terms, with the end of the Bronze Age and the beginning of the Iron Age.

A GOLDEN TEMPLE

The Temple built by King Solomon as a house for God in his capital city, Jerusalem, was not very big, but it was certainly spectacular. For, inside, everything was gold. There were dishes and bowls, lamps, lampstands and tongs of gold. The door fittings were gold, and so was the table for the sacred bread.

Gold has always been one of the things people have given to their gods. Cathedrals in Europe and South America, temples and shrines in Asia, still display chalices and lamps and other equipment for worship made of solid gold.

But Solomon's Temple had more than a wealth of golden furnishings. The priests, mounting the steps to go inside, would see nothing but gold — and a rich curtain at the far end.

The biblical description in the first book of Kings, chapter 6, says: 'Solomon built the Temple . . . he lined its walls inside with cedar boards . . . he overlaid the whole interior with gold . . . he also covered the floors of both the inner and outer rooms of the temple with gold.'

A golden temple! The idea is breathtaking.

Building temples or renovating old

King Solomon's Temple, like this miniature shrine of King Tutankhamun, was a glory of gold.

An artist's reconstruction of King Solomon's Temple, based on the measurements and description given in the Bible. The building was quite small — just 27 × 9 × 13.5 metres/ 89 × 30 × 44 feet inside. It was intended as a house for God, rather than a great cathedral in which his people could meet.

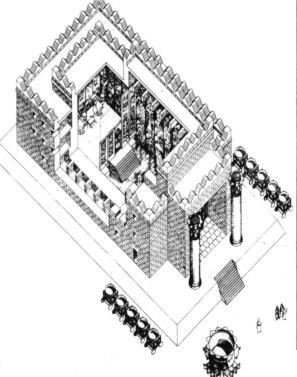

Are the nail-holes in these stones evidence of sheets of gold once pinned to temple and palace walls, so that they shone like the sun?

ones was a regular activity for ancient kings. They wanted to win the favour of their gods and popularity with their people, and to win fame for themselves. The stronger and richer they were, the more lavishly they decorated the buildings they put up.

Over the centuries local people have pillaged the ruins of these great temples for bricks and stones. And long before that all the moveable furnishings of any value had been carried off. Yet still today, when only the basic walls remain, visitors to the temple-towers in ancient Babylonian cities such as Ur, or to the Egyptian temples at Karnak, cannot help being impressed by their grandeur of size and design.

Sometimes the kings who had these temples built left inscriptions telling of their work. When we read them, we have to remember that they were written to impress their readers, in particular to tell future generations how great and how pious their ancestors had been. They may have exaggerated in some cases, or claimed more than their due, but there is no good reason to doubt them over all.

We need not doubt the word of kings of Assyria and Babylonia when they boast of covering the walls of temples with gold like plaster, or of plating them with gold so that they shone like the sun; nor of the pharaohs who told how they put sheets of gold on the walls of their temples in Egypt.

From Egypt there also appears to be some physical evidence of the gold sheets covering parts of temples. One temple built by Pharaoh Tuthmosis III, about 1450 BC, bears inscriptions that record its splendour: certain doorways, shrines and pillars were plated with gold.

When an eminent French Egyptologist closely examined the ruins of the building he noted unusual narrow slits in some of the stone columns, the bases on which they stood, and the capitals that crowned them. These slits are too narrow to be of any use in the construction, and they add nothing to the carved decoration. Their function, the Egyptologist deduced, was to take the edges of sheets of gold hammered over the stonework and folded round into the slits to hold them in position. Other stone blocks have rows of small holes which could have held nails fixing the golden sheets to the flat walls.

What the Egyptian inscriptions describe appears to be supported by the stones of the temples; the gold was there, adorning their walls, not as gilding to highlight parts of the design but as sheets covering whole surfaces.

So there is good contemporary evidence that the Bible's account of King Solomon's golden Temple is no mere invention, or even exaggeration. It falls into the known pattern of ancient practices.

SOLOMON'S BUILDINGS

The most remarkable of the buildings assigned to Solomon's time are the gateways leading through the walls of three cities. There are no foundation stones or documents to say who built them. But the pottery found there can be dated to Solomon's reign, showing that the buildings were certainly in use at that time.

One was discovered at Gezer in excavations from 1902 to 1909, another at Megiddo in 1936–37, and the third at Hazor in 1955–58.

Progress in the techniques of excavation and better knowledge of pottery types led Yigael Yadin to assign the gate he excavated at Hazor to Solomon's time. He then took a further look at the ruins at Gezer and especially at Megiddo, which the original excavators had not associated with Solomon at all.

Yadin was able to show that all three gates have a nearly identical plan and very similar dimensions. The pottery fragments belonging to the moment when the gates were constructed and in use belong to Solomon's time — the middle of the tenth century BC.

Yadin turned his attention to Gezer and Megiddo after the Hazor gateway had come to light because he recalled a passage from the Bible that relates Solomon's building activities at important towns in his kingdom. 1 Kings 9:15 records: 'King Solomon used forced labour to build the Temple and the palace, to fill in land on the east side of the city, and to build the city wall. He also used it to rebuild the cities of Hazor, Megiddo, and Gezer.'

In addition to the uniform plan of the gateways in each city Yadin found that the adjoining city walls were also of identical design. They were what is called 'casemates' — that is, a double line of wall with cross-walls making a series of long narrow rooms.

At each site the stone-work of the walls above floor level was of very high quality. The blocks in each face of the walls were carefully squared and laid, giving an imposing solidity to the structures.

The similarities between these three gateways, and the quality of their masonry, suggest they were built to a design circulated by a central authority with considerable resources at its disposal. The evidence of the pottery indicates a tenth century date for the building work.

When these points are placed beside the biblical report, the conclusion that these gateways are indeed Solomon's work becomes almost inescapable. Short of inscriptions on the stones themselves, it would be hard to make a stronger case.

At Megiddo there were traces of extensive buildings within the city belonging to the same date. Unfortunately, their stone-work was so good that later builders demolished the walls to re-use the blocks, with the result that the palaces, offices and houses of the time are little known.

At Gezer and at Hazor, too, very little could be learnt about the Solomonic cities because later occupants had disturbed and destroyed their ruins.

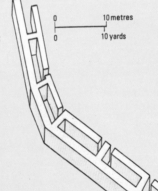

| 0 | 10 metres |
| 0 | 10 yards |

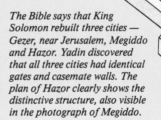

The Bible says that King Solomon rebuilt three cities — Gezer, near Jerusalem, Megiddo and Hazor. Yadin discovered that all three cities had identical gates and casemate walls. The plan of Hazor clearly shows the distinctive structure, also visible in the photograph of Megiddo.

A FORTUNE IN SILVER AND GOLD

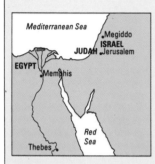

Pharaoh Shishak invaded Judah and plundered the Temple at Jerusalem. This bracelet belonging to the pharaoh's son may have been made from the Temple gold.

Soon after King Solomon died, the Bible book of Kings reports, 'Shishak king of Egypt attacked Jerusalem. He carried off the treasures of the temple of the Lord and the treasures of the royal palace. He took everything . . .'

This is the earliest incident in Israel's history which documents outside the Bible also reflect.

Shishak was the founder of a new dynasty of kings in Egypt, the twenty-second. In previous years the land had been divided among kings, local chieftains, and priests. The new pharaoh united Egypt under his rule, then set out to gain control over his neighbours Judah and Israel, which had once been

the Egyptian province of Canaan.

As long as Solomon was on the throne, Israel was probably too strong for Shishak to attack. Once Solomon's kingdom had split in two, with Judah ruled by Solomon's son Rehoboam, and Israel under the rebel Jeroboam, it was too weak to defend itself.

Shishak's men marched through the land, visiting, sometimes destroying, as many as 150 towns and villages. Returning home victorious, Shishak set about building temples at Memphis in the north and Thebes (Karnak) in the south. Only the Theban one survives.

There, a length of wall still stands around a great

courtyard. Near one gateway the stones are carved with a huge picture of the pharaoh in triumph. Beside him are the names of the towns and villages he conquered in Israel. He claimed he had brought them back under Egyptian control, as they had been 200 years before. To remind the conquered people of his victory, Shishak had a stone slab set up in Megiddo with his name and titles engraved on it. A small piece of this was found in the ruins of Megiddo, happily a piece bearing Shishak's name to guarantee its identity.

Shishak died a year or so after his victory. His son was not strong enough to follow his example as a conqueror. One damaged inscription details the gifts Shishak's son gave to the gods of Egypt. They amounted to much more in gold and silver than any other pharaoh records giving. By weight they totalled to about 200,000 kg/200 tons of gold and silver.

Study of other Egyptian documents shows no reason to suppose these amounts are exaggerated. Other pharaohs also gave magnificent presents to their gods, even if none were as large as this.

Nothing tells where this wealth came from, but it seems reasonable to suppose that much of it was the gold which Shishak carried away from Solomon's Temple and palace in Jerusalem.

IVORY PALACES

We knelt on the dry, dusty soil, working slowly with penknives and paintbrushes. Embedded in the mud on the floor of a palace store-room were scores of pieces of carved ivory. They had grown brittle, lying there for nearly 3,000 years, and the weight of fallen brickwork had cracked them. Each one had to be lifted separately in the block of earth around it. But as we carefully cut one free others would appear beneath or beside it. So the task took a long time.

In the expedition house we gently chipped away the mud with scalpels and needles, and sponged it off the smooth surfaces with moist cotton-wool. We watched with amazement as superb miniature works of art emerged from the dirt. The pieces were creamy-white, cut and polished smooth. Some were inlaid with stones or glass coloured red or blue. A few still had pieces of gold foil stuck to them.

What were these ivory carvings?

Another store-room made the answer clear. There, fifteen or more chairbacks stood in rows across the floor. Great panels of ivory had been fixed to the wooden frame or backing, so that the woodwork was invisible. The furniture appeared to be made of ivory.

Some parts were simply strips of

Ivories carved with sphinxes show the influence of Egypt.

Furniture inlaid with carved ivory was carried as booty to Assyria. It was high fashion among the wealthy in Israel, whose extravagance and exploitation of the poor called down the wrath of God's prophets.

The ivory of a woman at a window is typical of the Phoenician style.

ivory cut and polished to give a smooth surface at the edges of beds and chairs. Some pieces were solid blocks of ivory carved or turned on a lathe to make decorative supports and finials.

Most of the pieces were plaques that fitted into a frame to make a decoration. The majority of these were carved in relief. Their designs were chosen for their magical and symbolic values, as well as for their beauty. Figures grasping a plant or tree represent fruitfulness. The winged disk of the sun shows divine care. Men fighting dragons depict the triumph of order over chaos.

Very often the carvings show clear signs of Egyptian influence. There are sphinxes and palm-fronds and lotus flowers, and there are unmistakably Egyptian gods and goddesses. But the pieces we dug out did not lie in the ruins of an Egyptian palace, they were in an Assyrian city.

It was clear that most of the ivory furniture came to Assyria as booty, or as tribute from countries the Assyrian armies had conquered. The soldiers sent the furniture home for their kings to use. The royal apartments were adorned with many of these costly products. In fact there was so much that it also filled several palace store-rooms.

Assyrian kings have left records of this conquered city or that subject prince sending ivory beds and chairs to them. Hezekiah of Judah was one, according to Sennacherib (see *'Like a Bird in a Cage'*). Ivory furniture was obviously expensive, a luxury item for the houses of the very rich, a status symbol that an enemy would want to take away.

That is how it appears in the Old Testament. King Solomon fetched ivory to Jerusalem when his ocean-going 'ships of Tarshish' went on their voyages (recorded in 1 Kings 10). He used the ivory to make a throne. This would be a wooden frame sheathed entirely in ivory.

Two hundred years later, ivory furniture was fashionable among the nobles of Samaria. They would squeeze every penny out of their debtors, and more, in order to spend all their money on ostentatious extravagance.

'Woe to those who loll on beds of ivory,' shouted Amos, the shepherd-turned-prophet from Judah, 'they'll be left with only the corner of a couch or the leg of a bed,' useless relics of their squandered wealth.

Israel's rulers, one of them at least, encouraged the fashion. 1 Kings 22 reports that King Ahab made an 'ivory house'. This may mean a house panelled with ivory, or more probably a house provided with ivory furniture. The discoveries in Assyria illustrate the sort of decoration, intricately-carved ivory panels, some enriched with coloured stones and covered with gold foil.

To modern eyes the effect might be rather bright and gaudy, but that was

what the ancient people liked. In the Song of Solomon a girl describes her lover as having a body of ivory inlaid with blue stones.

At Samaria, ruins of the Israelite palace were unearthed. In them, smashed and scattered on the ground were over 500 fragments of ivory, more than 200 of which were carved. Some scholars think they belong to the reign of Ahab, about 860 BC. Others date them a century later. Whether or not they are from Ahab's time, they show the sort of furniture he would have had, and it is just like many examples found in Assyria.

Phoenician craftsmen set the chief style for ivory-carving. And Ahab's wife, Jezebel, came from the Phoenician city of Sidon. It was in Phoenicia that local Canaanite concepts were mixed with some from Egypt and other places to produce the designs on the ivories. Imported into Israel, these pagan patterns can hardly have helped God's people to remember the commandment not to make carved images.

When invaders ransacked the palaces of Samaria, and later of

Assyria, they smashed the ivory furniture. They could not carry away large numbers of couches and chairs, so they stripped off the gold overlay and left the wood and ivory parts behind. What the archaeologist now finds is, in Amos's words, just 'the corner of a couch or the leg of a bed'. Yet even these are enough to show how splendid this furniture was when it stood in all its beauty in Ahab's 'ivory house'.

An ivory bed-head from Nimrud vividly recalls the words of Amos, the shepherd-prophet who pronounced God's judgement on Israel. 'Woe to those who loll on beds of ivory.' When the kingdom fell to the Assyrians it was seen as God's punishment.

THE ENGRAVER OF SEALS

Israelite craftsmen were kept busy meeting the needs of the ordinary people. There were carpenters and blacksmiths, weavers and dyers, potters and masons. Their work was essential, but in almost every case it has disappeared because of destruction either by man or by nature. Only the potter's products are still plentiful.

Along with ordinary pieces of craftsmanship, the work of the experts also disappeared. Hardly any Israelite jewellery has come to light, perfumes and cosmetics vanished long ago. But one sort of object made by experts does survive in fairly large numbers: the seal-stone.

Before the Babylonians created their cylinder seals, people had carved designs on small stones as a mark of personal identification so that they could make an impression on a piece of clay to seal a box or jar. In Egypt and Canaan this shape of seal was normal, and the Israelites also adopted it.

Anyone with the money could buy a seal from the jeweller. It would be a small stone, perhaps a gem-stone — amethyst, agate, or cornelian — hard and with a pretty colouring. Cheaper seals were made of local limestone.

The engraver, or his apprentice, would polish the stone, cut it to give an oval or round shape at one end, and smooth that end until it was almost flat. Through the middle of the stone, or at the other end, he would drill a hole so the seal could hang from a necklace or be fixed into a ring.

Now the stone was ready for the engraver. He had to work on a polished surface normally less than 2.2 cm/1 in across. With fine drills and tiny wheels with sharpened edges he would cut into the stone the chosen design.

The customer wanted a design he and other people could recognize as his, distinct from anyone else's. So the engraver would offer a choice. Would his client like a picture of a griffin, or a sphinx, or a scarab beetle in Egyptian style, or a plant, or a person in an act of

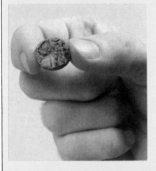

The author's hand gives an idea of the size of the tiny seals on which the ancient engravers worked with such skill.

Seals dating from the eighth to sixth centuries BC are inscribed in the ancient Hebrew script, many of them made from semi-precious stones. They carry the owner's name and were used to impress the lumps of clay which sealed containers and papyrus scrolls. Several of these sealings are shown on the right.

worship, or a god or goddess? All of these can be seen among the hundreds of seals in modern collections.

Some people wanted a seal that was theirs only, that no one else could use. For that they had to have their name inscribed on the stone, assuming they could read.

So far almost a thousand seals have been discovered which carry their owners' names in the old 'Phoenician' alphabet, seals made between the tenth and fourth centuries BC. The seals belonged to members of all the nations in the area, Arameans and Phoenicians in Syria and Lebanon, Ammonites, Edomites and Moabites in Transjordan, Israelites and Philistines in Palestine.

Often the seal-engraver would add a person's name in a space around the design, and so the majority of the seals have a picture or pattern and an inscription.

The majority of the seals which we can identify as Hebrew are different. They bear an inscription only. Although there are Aramaic seals without designs, and several from Transjordan, the proportion is far higher for the Hebrew seals. The

reason could be an attempt to follow the command recorded in Exodus 20, 'You shall not make an image.'

Usually the seal bore its owner's name and his father's name. Sometimes a title follows the owner's name, 'servant of the king', 'steward of X'. The few seals engraved for women have the same pattern, 'daughter of X' or 'wife of Y'.

How can we decide whether or not a seal is Hebrew? Study of the writing can give a clue, but the names themselves are the best guide. Israel and her neighbours worshipped God as El ('god'), using his name to make their own: for example, 'Ishmael', meaning 'God heard', 'Elnathan', 'God gave'. Names like these could be Hebrew or could belong to a neighbouring nation.

When the personal name includes the special name of the national deity, the origin of the seal's owner is clear. 'Chemosh-sedek' and 'Chemosh-nathan' were evidently Moabites, for Chemosh was the chief god of Moab. Seals of 'Jeremiah', 'Jehoahaz', 'Gedaliah', equally clearly belonged to Hebrews, whose God's name was shortened to

'-iah' or 'Jeho', or 'Yaw'.

In these seals, more than in any other excavated objects, we are brought into touch with the men and women of ancient Israel. The engraver's skill has kept their names alive.

Seals were hung from necklaces, or set into rings. The ring seal (top) belonged to a man named Shaphat.

One seal which has survived (above) belonged to 'Nehemiah, son of Micaiah', names familiar from the biblical records and obviously common at the time.

PRIVATE HOUSES

The luxurious 'ivory houses' of kings produce exciting discoveries, which catch the imagination and bring fame to those who dig them up. Less sensational, but just as valuable for our knowledge of ancient times, are the ruins of houses which once belonged to ordinary townspeople.

Excavators have uncovered the remains of houses built during the days of the kings at many places in Israel. These round out the information supplied by written records and, together with observation of recent country life in the Near East, give us a picture which is surprisingly complete.

In most towns Israelite houses were built to the same basic plan, but the arrangement of the rooms naturally depended on the shape of the building plot. It is those whose work brought them an adequate livelihood, making them moderately prosperous, who lived in the typical 'Israelite' house. (The poor lived in one- or two-roomed hovels which have left little trace.)

The entrance opened from the muddy, unpaved street on to a small courtyard, perhaps cobbled. On one side a row of roughly squared stone pillars supported a low roof, forming a byre where animals might be tethered at night. (They could not be left unguarded in the fields in case wolves, bears, or other wild animals savaged them.) Another row of pillars might stand opposite, with stones or bricks between them to make a wall, or there might simply be a wall, with a doorway into the long narrow room.

At the end of the courtyard the space across the width of the house was enough for two more rooms. These were the main living and sleeping quarters. All the rooms could be divided by inserting cross-walls.

In the courtyard, the householder could arrange a hearth and an oven as he wanted. Ovens were often built of mud bricks, plastered smooth inside. Flat cakes of moist dough, stuck on the inside walls of the oven, were cooked by the heat the walls absorbed from a fire lit in the bottom.

Baking was a daily task in every household. Most would have their own stores of grain, kept in small pits in the floor, lined with stones or basketry. A stone quern or mill was all that was needed to grind the barley or wheat into flour.

Other basic supplies were stored in the houses, too. Large jars set into the floor, or standing on special brick

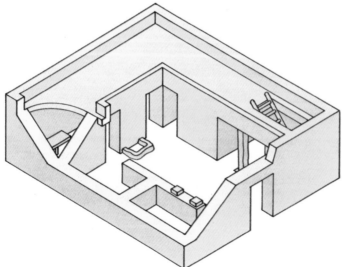

The typical Israelite house consisted of rooms built around a central courtyard. A flat roof with a parapet gave extra space.

pedestals, could hold oil or wine or water, or be used for dry goods. Oil was crushed from olives in special stone pressers.

A group of these in one town suggests that a particular household supplied several of its neighbours. Other people spun thread from wool or flax, and wove it into cloth. Clay weights for the spindles and for holding threads taut in the looms have been found lying on the floors.

The roofs of the houses were flat. Tall trees were uncommon, so the roof beams were quite short, making the rooms fairly narrow, rarely much more than 2 metres/6 feet 6 ins wide. Branches and twigs were laid over the beams, then several layers of mud plaster were packed on top and made solid by pressing with a stone roller.

Mud plaster was also used on the stone and brick walls. A fresh coating was applied each summer to help make the building water-proof. It also gave a surface that could be decorated, or at least whitewashed (this is referred to in Ezekiel 13). The mud bricks were not baked in a kiln, only dried in the sun, and without proper care they soon crumbled, and the wall collapsed. A well-tended house could stand for thirty years or more.

In the summer, the flat roofs were convenient for all sorts of domestic activities. Joshua (chapter 2) records that in Jericho Rahab laid the flax there. On warm nights the family often slept on the roof. A wise law (recorded in Deuteronomy 22) demanded that every house have a parapet around its roof to prevent anyone moving about at night from falling off.

Rooms could be built on the roof to provide extra accommodation, but some houses did have an upper storey, perhaps set above the rooms at the end of the courtyard. Stairs led up to these

Every home had its simple pottery lamp (above) filled with olive oil.

Houses line a narrow street in Iron Age Beersheba (left).

rooms from the courtyard, or, occasionally, from the outside of the house. It was a room of this sort that a well-to-do lady prepared for the prophet Elisha (the account is in 2 Kings 4). She furnished it with a bed, a table, a chair and a lamp, which was probably as much furniture as any room would have.

The lamps were shallow pottery dishes, pinched at one place on the edge to make a lip. A wick of rush or rag would lie in the lip, drawing fuel from the pool of oil in the dish. The pottery was simply earthenware or terracotta. Glazes were not in use, but the better quality wares were given a high polish before they were baked. This resulted in a very smooth surface which was easy to keep clean.

The potters made bowls and basins of all sizes; large deep ones for cooking, small, open ones for eating. They made a great variety of jugs for oil, wine, and water, and small ones for the perfumes needed frequently in the hot weather. Although the pottery was plain, it was expertly made, and the simple shapes have real elegance.

Although no one can claim, 'This was Elisha's house', or 'This was Jeremiah's', the ruins that have been found remind us that the Old Testament describes the deeds of real people who were once alive, and show us the sort of houses they lived in, and how their basic needs were met.

IN THE DAYS BEFORE COINAGE

To buy something in ancient Israel you had to have something else to give in exchange because there was no coined money (see *Jewish Coins*). Even if a shop-keeper set his prices in silver shekels, he might take a sheep or a shirt of the right value instead.

For paying in silver people needed scales and weights to check the amounts. The silver could be scraps of metal, or rings and other pieces of jewellery. So it was necessary to have a system of weights that everyone would know.

In Jerusalem, and other towns, numbers of ancient weights have been found. These weights are mostly of stone, cut and carefully smoothed to a rounded shape with a flat base and a domed top. Tiny fractions of a shekel may be only

1 cm/½ in in height and diameter, weighing 2 or 3 gms/0.06 or 0.09 ozs, while in contrast weights of 4,500 gms/10 lbs may represent 400 or 500 shekels.

Although the weights look well-made, even those which ought to weigh the same vary. As a result, the exact weight of the shekel is not certain. It was probably 11.4 gms/0.34 ozs.

In order to identify them easily, the smaller weights were often inscribed with their value. This might be a number with a sign for 'shekel', or it might be the name of a smaller weight. The writing was probably the work of the seal engraver.

Apart from the shekel, two other weights mentioned in the Old Testament are identifiable among those found. The

first is the *beqa'*, the half-shekel which each adult Israelite paid as a tax to God's shrine.

No one knew the second weight until examples came to light and were related to a biblical verse. On these weights is engraved the word *payim*, meaning 'two thirds' of a shekel. In 1 Samuel 13:21 this word stands in the Hebrew text, but no one had understood it. The Authorized Version and the Revised Version translate it as 'a file', with a note of doubt.

When the passage was read with knowledge of these weights it became clear, so translations now read, 'the charge was two thirds of a shekel' imposed by the Philistines on the Israelites for repairing their iron tools.

Before there was coined money, payment in silver was made by weight. This meant a system of weights that everyone knew. The bronze lion-weights from Assyria (top) are inscribed with the name of the king for whom they were made.

The value of the weights (above) is marked on them in Hebrew. The second from the right is a payim weight.

NO HIDDEN TREASURE
The 'Moabite Stone'

Sheep — hundreds and hundreds of sheep! The king's secretaries had been sent out to check that the right number had arrived. Now they reached the total: 100,000 sheep. Besides the sheep, there was wool from another 100,000 rams. The king of Israel was pleased. All this was tribute from his subject, the king of Moab.

Naturally the Moabites resented this tax. They resented Israel's control. Eventually the moment came when they could reject it.

The man who had put Moab in this position was Omri, the king of Israel who had built the new capital of Samaria. Ahab, his son, maintained control, but at the end of his reign he joined with other kings in an inconclusive battle against the Assyrians, and soon afterwards he was killed when fighting the king of Damascus. The son who followed him fell from a window and died.

Here was an ideal opportunity to assert Moab's independence. Mesha, king of Moab, rose in rebellion. Ahab's second son Joram, now king of Israel, led a campaign to put down the revolt. Although his army reached the Moabite capital, they withdrew without taking it. Moab was free.

The Bible and Assyrian records give us this information. More comes from the Moabite side.

Mesha, king of Moab, was able to throw off Israel's rule, win back some

Moabite territory and rebuild some of its towns. He was so proud of his deeds that he had the story engraved on a stone slab. He then erected this stela in the citadel at Dibon, his home town.

Like many other ancient royal inscriptions, it starts by introducing the king: 'I am Mesha, son of . . . ,

king of Moab, the Dibonite.' The recital goes on almost entirely in the first person. 'I fought, I killed, I took, I built.'
But the king did not believe he won entirely by his own power. He explains that he built the high place where the stela stood for Chemosh, the national god of Moab. The king was

Thinking it must contain treasure, local people used fire and water to break open the 'Moabite Stone'. But the 'treasure' was the Stone itself and the inscription.

In ancient times it was often the job of the scribes to count and record tribute. These two scribes come from Assyria.

honouring his god 'because he delivered me from all kings and because he let me have victory over all my enemies'.

He says that Israel ruled Moab as a consequence of Chemosh being angry with Moab in time past. Now Chemosh had told him to fight Israel and so re-establish Moab. In particular, he told Mesha to capture the town of Nebo from Israel. Mesha went at night, fought all morning, took the city and slew 7,000 people. He devoted it as an offering to his god. Objects in it belonging to Yahweh, Israel's God, Mesha carried off to present to Chemosh. He conquered other places and the prisoners he captured were set to work on the citadel at Dibon.

The inscription is written in old Phoenician letters, also used for writing Hebrew. Its language is very much like the Hebrew of the books of Judges, Samuel, and Kings. Ideas in it are similar to ideas the ancient Israelites held.

When their God was angry with them, enemies such as the Philistines

attacked and ruled them. Then he inspired leaders to free his people — the Judges, Saul and David.

Like Mesha, Israelite kings also set enemy prisoners to work on their buildings. As Mesha devoted the town of Nebo to Chemosh, so Joshua set Jericho apart. Everything in it belonged to God.

Mesha's inscription presents some problems for the modern interpreter. This is not uncommon when we read ancient texts and compare two accounts of events written from different points of view. Mesha did not name the king of Israel at the time of his victory. To the annoyance of historians, his words are vague: 'Omri took possession of the territory of Madeba and (Israel) lived there during his days and half the days of his son, forty years.' Omri reigned for twelve years (about 884–873 BC), his son Ahab for twenty-two (about 873–853 BC) — much less than forty years altogether. Should we understand 'forty years' as a ·round number, or as a 'generation'? Do the words 'son' and 'half' mean simply 'descendant' and 'part'?

In fact, forty years from some time in Omri's reign end in the reign of Joram (about 852–841 BC), Ahab's son who failed to reconquer Moab. Mesha could have had his monument made soon after that.

Mesha's monument, now known as the 'Moabite Stone', stands in the Louvre in Paris. Originally it was over 1.15 metres/3 feet 9 ins high, and 68 cm/27 ins wide at the foot. Now it is a battered group of fragments

of black basalt. Yet when it was found it was nearly complete. The story of its discovery illustrates the dangerous life of many ancient monuments.

In 1868 a German missionary saw the stone at the ruins of Dibon. It had probably been incorporated into a later building. The next year a French scholar in Jerusalem had an Arab copy some lines of the writing. These made him realize how important the stone was. Next he had a paper squeeze or impression made of the whole stone, and set about trying to buy it.

To the local people, it was only a stone. The writing meant nothing to them. There must be treasure inside it, they thought. So they heated the stone over a fire, then poured cold water over it. It shattered, as they intended, but there was no hidden treasure.

The Frenchman, Clermont-Ganneau, determinedly collected all the pieces he could, buying them from the villagers. Although he recovered only about three-fifths of it, he was able to restore the missing parts from his paper squeeze, and so read the story of Mesha's triumph.

The 'Moabite Stone' is the only monument of its kind known to survive from Israel, Judah, Edom, Moab, or Ammon. If there were others, which is likely, they are either still buried or destroyed, as Mesha's so nearly was.

THE PRICE OF PROTECTION
The 'Black Obelisk'

The excavation had gone on for days. Nothing of interest had come to light. It was November 1846. Henry Layard, who was directing the work, had to leave the ruin-mound on an errand.

Before he left he talked with the workmen. They had dug a trench more than 15 metres/50 feet long. The soil was hard and dry, they were dispirited. Layard told them to dig for one more day, until he returned. Then he rode away.

He was hardly clear of the mound when a panting workman overtook him. Something had been found in the trench. He should stop to see it.

Layard rode back, dismounted, and climbed down into the trench. There at the bottom lay a block of polished black stone, carved and inscribed. As Layard watched, eager hands hauled it out with ropes. It was a four-sided pillar or obelisk, 2 metres/6 feet 6ins high, with five panels of small pictures on each face, and line upon line of finely engraved cuneiform signs.

Layard himself made careful drawings of the pictures and the writing, and had it packed and sent off to England. Today it stands in the British Museum in London with other monuments Layard unearthed.

If he had listened to his men and stopped the digging before he left that day, the 'Black Obelisk' might still be buried in the ruins of the ancient Assyrian city of Calah (now called Nimrud).

When the obelisk came to light, Layard could not read the inscriptions, nor could anyone else. He had the drawings printed quickly, and sent them to scholars who were trying to decipher the cuneiform writing. At almost the same time two of them were able to read some of the words on the stone.

The first was a shy Church of England rector, Edward Hincks, who lived in Ireland. He studied quietly in his rectory, and occasionally at the British Museum. His parishioners were probably quite unaware that their rector, who spent so much time with large books in foreign languages, was unlocking one of the long-closed doors of ancient history. Hincks and Layard were friends, and it was Hincks who was able to tell Layard the meaning of many of the inscriptions he found.

The other great decipherer at this time was Henry Rawlinson (see *Secrets from the Rock of Behistun*).

Both men recognized that the 'Black Obelisk' records the triumphs of an Assyrian king, and that the writing above each row of pictures describes them.

As they worked through the text, the decipherers found that the first row of panels is labelled as the tribute of a king from north-west Persia. This king, or his ambassador, is shown kneeling in front of King Shalmaneser, whose officers stand behind.

On the other panels, attendants lead a horse and two camels, and porters carry other things as examples of the tribute this king is giving to Assyria.

The second line of pictures proved to be the most exciting. In the first panel another figure kneels to kiss the dust at the feet of the king of Assyria. Thirteen men follow the Assyrian courtiers bearing the tribute. Above the pictures the label reads, 'Tribute of Yaua son of

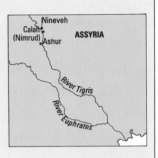

In 1845 men working for Henry Layard on the site of the ancient Assyrian city of Calah (Nimrud) uncovered a block of polished black stone, carved and inscribed. The 'Black Obelisk' records the triumphs of the Assyrian king, Shalmaneser.

The first panel in the second line of pictures (above, right) proved exciting. The text above the kneeling figure lists tribute brought to the king from 'Yaua son of Humri', that is, Jehu, who took the throne from a descendant of Omri, king of Israel. The Assyrian monument throws interesting light on the reign of a biblical king.

The 'Black Obelisk' is the only monument so far discovered which shows Israelites (pictured above) bringing tribute to an Assyrian king.

Humri: I received silver, gold, a golden bowl, a golden beaker, golden goblets, golden pitchers, lead, a royal staff, a javelin.'

It was not hard to identify the name of the king who sent these presents. Yaua is the Assyrian writing of Jehu, king of Israel, and Humri is Omri who set up the Israelite capital at Samaria.

Here is an important link between an Assyrian monument and the Bible — a fact that Hincks and Rawlinson realized immediately.

Before we look further at this matter, we should notice the other pictures. No more kneeling envoys appear, but there is a variety of tribute. Row three has two camels, three horned creatures, an elephant, two monkeys and two apes. These came from Egypt, the horned creatures perhaps including a rhinoceros, and were intended for the royal zoo. The Assyrian kings loved to collect unusual animals and plants.

Following a scene of a lion felling a stag, the fourth row of pictures illustrates the tribute of a king living by the middle section of the River Euphrates. It is much like the first two sets of tribute, with the addition of folded clothes.

In the final row the procession of porters bears the tribute of a state on the coast of Syria, very similar to Jehu's tribute.

Assyrian stone-carvers may not have seen some of the animals sent from Egypt before, and so may not have cut their pictures very accurately in the stone. They did take care, on the other hand, to give each group of tribute-bearers different clothing, and it is likely they were trying to depict the various native costumes.

In the 190 lines of inscription at the top and bottom of the pillar, Shalmaneser relates his triumphs from the first year of his reign (857 BC) to the thirty-first (826 BC). It was in the sixteenth year, 841 BC, other records of Shalmaneser explain, that Jehu paid his tribute. Now Jehu was not a royal prince of Israel. He was a soldier

who killed King Joram, a descendant of Omri. At the same time Jehu killed the king of Judah. The second book of Kings, chapter 9, tells the story.

Shalmaneser's other records and the biblical records, when taken together, indicate that Jehu's murder of the two kings, and his seizing the throne in Samaria, happened in the same year as he paid homage to Assyria. He may well have thought he could make his position more secure by having Assyrian protection. The Bible does not tell us about this aspect of Jehu's reign; it was not relevant to the Hebrew historian's purpose.

The 'Black Obelisk' remains the only monument with carvings of Israelites bringing tribute to an Assyrian king. From the time of the first studies by Hincks and Rawlinson it has held a major place among the Assyrian documents relating to the Old Testament, as well as being an important work of art in its own right.

'THE ASSYRIAN CAME DOWN...'

In a British Museum show-case in London stands a hollow brown clay prism. On each of its six faces is line after line of neat cuneiform writing. This dull-looking piece of pottery, almost 37.5 cm/15 ins high, is one of many inscriptions recording the successes of King Sennacherib who ruled Assyria from 705 to 681 BC. The British Resident in Baghdad, a Colonel Taylor, acquired this example at Nineveh in 1830 and it entered the museum in 1855, to be known as the 'Taylor Prism'.

Assyrian kings had such records written to bury in the foundations of the temples, palaces, and city-gates they built or repaired. They hoped their successors would find them in due course, read them and realize what great men they had been. In this way the memory of a king such as Sennacherib would be kept alive. That explains the tone of the inscriptions. They sound very boastful and conceited, telling of nothing but the king's prowess and the victories he won, the enemies he executed and the loot he took home.

A closer study suggests that these kings were not quite such blatant, bullying imperialists as they seem at first sight. They justified their wars quite often with the claim that their national god commanded them to fight. Often, too, they fought to put down rebellious subject kings. That is the reason for all the wars of Sennacherib which the 'Taylor Prism' describes.

Among those Sennacherib attacked was Merodach-baladan, king of Babylonia. After earlier battles, he had accepted the Assyrian presence in Babylonia, but when Sennacherib became king he had made an alliance with enemies of Assyria to the east. He also tried to win support from other subjects of Assyria, including King Hezekiah of Judah, far to the west.

The biblical book of Kings tells how Hezekiah received Merodach-baladan's messengers with honour, and it may be that their visit was one of the reasons for Hezekiah's rebellion against Assyria. For Hezekiah did rebel and, after dealing with the Babylonian

In the time of King Hezekiah of Judah, the Assyrians hammered at the gates of Jerusalem itself. The capital did not fall — but Lachish, to the south, was taken after a siege. King Sennacherib decorated his palace walls in Nineveh with scenes of the dramatic finale. Here the inhabitants leave as missiles fall.

The ambassador of King Merodach-baladan of Babylonia (the king pictured below) was made welcome at King Hezekiah's court. A century later Babylon, not Assyria, was the chief threat.

trouble, Sennacherib marched west.

The Assyrian king reports how he moved down the Mediterranean coast in 701 BC, meeting various local kings who bowed before him. Eventually he reached Philistine territory, south-west of Israel and Judah.

One king, the king of Ashkelon, refused to submit, so Sennacherib deposed him and packed him off to

The might of proud Assyria is expressed in this statue of King Ashurnasirpal II, from the ninth century BC.

Assyria with all his family. A man who had ruled Ashkelon previously, under Assyrian protection, was made king.

Another Philistine city, Ekron, was also in revolt. Some of the leading citizens had tied up their king who was loyal to Assyria, and handed him over to Hezekiah, king of Judah, in Jerusalem. The rebels called on Egypt to help them, but the Assyrian army won the battle at Eltekeh, and Ekron was overwhelmed. Sennacherib executed the leaders of the rebellion, and took their supporters prisoner, but allowed the rest to go free. Then he set back on the throne the king who had been imprisoned in Jerusalem.

Although Sennacherib's inscriptions describe these events one after another, the release of the king of Ekron may have taken place only after the final stage of the campaign.

One rebel remained defiant.

Hezekiah of Judah, evidently a leader of the revolt, was holding out in his capital, Jerusalem. Sennacherib overran the whole of Judah and encircled the capital. His record tells the tale (see *'Like a Bird in a Cage'*).

There are several notable points. Although his troops surrounded Jerusalem so that no one could enter or leave the city, there is no account of an attack made on it as there is for the 'forty-six strong walled towns', or for other rebel cities. Sennacherib claims Hezekiah gave in to him, paying a heavy tribute, yet he makes no mention of his soldiers entering Jerusalem, or of meeting Hezekiah himself.

The most striking fact comes at the end. Hezekiah sent his messenger, and all the tribute, to Sennacherib 'later, to Nineveh'. The Assyrian army did not carry them home in triumph in the usual way.

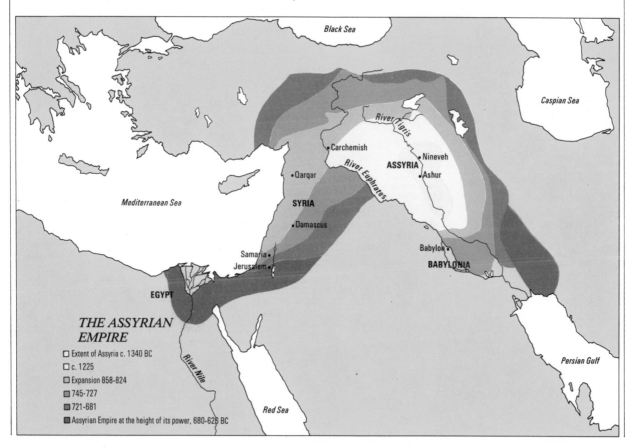

THE ASSYRIAN EMPIRE

☐ Extent of Assyria c. 1340 BC
☐ c. 1225
☐ Expansion 858-824
▨ 745-727
▨ 721-681
■ Assyrian Empire at the height of its power, 680-626 BC

'LIKE A BIRD IN A CAGE'
Sennacherib Attacks Jerusalem

King Sennacherib's attack on Jerusalem is recorded on the 'Taylor Prism'.

This is a translation of the report Sennacherib left for later kings to read about his attack on Judah:

'As for Hezekiah, the Judean who did not submit to my yoke, I surrounded and conquered forty-six of his strong walled towns and innumerable small settlements around them by means of earth ramps and siege-engines and attack by infantrymen, mining, breaking through and scaling. I brought out from them and counted as spoil 200,150 people of all ranks, men and women, horses, mules, donkeys, camels, cattle and sheep. He himself I shut up in Jerusalem, his royal city, like a bird in a cage. I surrounded him with watchposts and made it impossible for anyone to go in or out of his city. His cities which I had despoiled I cut off from his territory and gave to Mitinti king of Ashdod, Padi king of Ekron, and Sil-Bel king of Gaza, so reducing his realm. I added to their previous annual tribute a tribute gift befitting my lordship and imposed it on them. Fear of my lordly splendour overwhelmed that Hezekiah. The warriors and select troops he had brought in to strengthen his royal city Jerusalem, did not fight. He had brought after me to Nineveh, my royal city, 30 talents of gold, 800 talents of silver, best antimony, great blocks of red stone, ivory-decorated beds, ivory-decorated armchairs, elephant hide, tusks, ebony, box-wood, valuable treasure of every sort, and his daughters, women of his palace, men and women singers. He sent his messenger to pay tribute and do obeisance.'

This episode is known to us from the Old Testament, too. The story is told at length twice, in 2 Kings 18 and Isaiah 36 and 37 (and in summary in 2 Chronicles 32). Reading the biblical accounts beside Sennacherib's shows that there are many differences. Yet both clearly deal with the same events.

The differences are not surprising since the accounts come from opposing sides. In addition, none of them necessarily follows the actual order in which the events took place.

According to the Hebrew writers, Sennacherib threatened Jerusalem, tried to persuade the citizens to open the gates, and tried to bully Hezekiah into surrender, but failed. Jerusalem remained intact. Hezekiah had assurances from God, through the prophet Isaiah, which encouraged him to resist. And he did not fall!

A famous verse states the Hebrew historian's interpretation: 'the angel of the Lord went out, and smote in the camp of the Assyrians an hundred fourscore and five thousand: and when they arose early in the morning, behold, they were all dead corpses. So Sennacherib, king of Assyria departed, and went and returned, and dwelt at Nineveh' (2 Kings 19:35,36, in the Authorized Version).

What exactly happened we cannot

discover. There is no good reason to doubt this report of a catastrophe cutting short the Assyrian campaign. Understandably, Sennacherib would not record such a disaster for his successors to read, for it would discredit him.

A sudden sharp drop in the strength of his army, leading to a quick withdrawal, would explain why Sennacherib does not claim to have captured Jerusalem, and why he received Hezekiah's submission by messenger, in Nineveh.

One other fact suggests Sennacherib failed to capture Jerusalem. In his palace at Nineveh one room was decorated with carved stone slabs illustrating the campaign in Judah. They are concerned with the capture of one city, and that is not Jerusalem, but the stronghold of Lachish to the south. If the Assyrians had captured Jerusalem, that could be expected to feature on the palace walls. But it did not. Lachish was given the prominence.

Sennacherib's 'Taylor Prism', and its parallels, give the most extensive example of a piece of Hebrew history told from the enemy's point of view. It is very valuable as an aid to understanding the biblical texts, and in the way it corresponds to them.

In this scene from the time of Assyria's greatest influence, King Ashurbanipal leads the lion-hunt.

KING HEZEKIAH'S TUNNEL

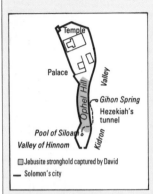

The tunnel wriggles its way through the rock from Spring to Pool.

In 1880 a boy noticed some writing scratched on the wall of the tunnel which led to the Pool. It records how two gangs of workmen, starting from opposite ends, broke through the rock to meet deep underground.

For years women of Jerusalem had washed their clothes in the pool at the south of the city. Water came into the pool from a tunnel and the children used to splash in the water. Some of the boys crept a little way into the dark passage.

One day in 1880 one of them, holding a light, went further than usual. By the flickering flame he noticed some writing scratched on the rocky wall. He came out to describe his discovery.

Nobody had seen this inscription before, so soon it was studied carefully. Water running down the tunnel wall had left deposits of lime over the writing, but when they were cleaned off, six lines of clear Hebrew writing appeared.

They describe how two gangs of men cut a tunnel through the rock. The gangs began work at opposite ends and eventually met deep underground. The text says one gang heard the sound of the other hacking at the rock, so they knew which way to go.

The tunnel runs to the pool from a spring on the east side of the city, in the Kidron Valley. People had known about it for a long time when Edward Robinson, a famous American explorer of Palestine, made the first accurate survey of it in 1838. He demonstrated that the water ran from the Virgin's Fountain to the pool, not the other way as some had thought.

With his friends, he managed to make his way through the whole length of the tunnel. At some places it was 4.5–6 metres/15–20 feet high, at others it was so low the explorers could only wriggle through, lying at full length and dragging themselves along on their elbows. Since that time the silt has been cleared from the bottom and it is not as difficult to walk through.

Robinson had expected the tunnel to be about 366 metres/1,200 feet long on an almost direct line. So he was surprised when his measurement reached 534 metres/1,750 feet. The reason is clear. The tunnel bends like an S. There is another double bend near the middle which is evidently where the two gangs of tunnellers met. Had they not heard each other's pick-axes, the plan suggests they might not have met at all!

Why the tunnel has so twisting a course is not certain. Despite their lack of compasses, the ancient engineers could have kept a straight line by sighting from the ends. Possibly they followed an underground stream and faults in the rock for parts of their work.

The tunnel was dug to take water from one part of the city to another. That is obvious. The inscription which the local boy found nearly fifty years after Robinson's survey points to the time when the tunnel was made and the reason for making it then.

The engraving is a fine example of the ancient Hebrew handwriting current before the Exile. From the time of its discovery, scholars have linked it with King Hezekiah of Judah, just before 700 BC. In recent years the recovery of other early Hebrew documents has shown that the shapes of the letters belong to this date. Among them is an impression on clay of a seal owned by one of Hezekiah's officers, 'Jehozerah son of Hilkiah, servant of Hezekiah'. (Hilkiah is mentioned in 2 Kings 18.)

The link with Hezekiah follows from records in the Old Testament about Hezekiah making a reservoir and a canal in Jerusalem. 2 Kings 20:20 records: 'Everything else that King Hezekiah did, his brave deeds, and an account of how he built a reservoir and dug a tunnel to bring water into the city, are all recorded in *The History of the Kings of Judah.*'

2 Chronicles 32:3–4 says:

'he and his officials decided to cut off the supply of water outside the city in order to prevent the Assyrians from having any water when they got near Jerusalem. The officials led a large number of people out and stopped up all the springs, so that no more water flowed out of them.'

Verse 30 adds: 'It was King Hezekiah who blocked the outlet for the Spring of Gihon and chanelled the water to flow through a tunnel to a point inside the

walls of Jerusalem. Hezekiah succeeded in everything he did.'

Today the pool is open to the sky, and lies outside the Turkish wall of Jerusalem. When Hezekiah's men dug it, the pool may have been open, reached by steps cut around the sides, or it may have been entirely underground. At that time it was within the walls of the city, for the oldest part of Jerusalem was built above the Virgin's Fountain, the Gihon Spring of the Old Testament, which provided the citizens with water.

A Greek who hoped to become rich by selling the inscription chopped it out of the rock in 1890 and broke it. The Turkish authorities, who then ruled Jerusalem, confiscated it, and it is now on exhibition in the antiquities museum in Istanbul.

The pool is called the Pool of Siloam, but it is not certain if this is the pool mentioned in the Gospel of John, chapter 9, as the one Jesus sent the blind man to wash in. That could be another pool, slightly to the south.

To safeguard Jerusalem against siege, King Hezekiah had a tunnel cut through solid rock to bring water from the Spring of Gihon (above, left) within the city walls. The Spring was then sealed off.

The tunnel now channels water to the Pool of Siloam (above).

'WE CAN'T SEE THE SIGNALS'

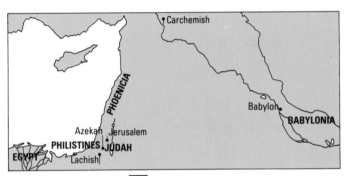

The tiny kingdom of Judah was in trouble. Her pious king Josiah had been killed in a battle he should never have fought. His conqueror, the king of Egypt, put Josiah's son on the throne as his subject king.

Only four years later the army of Babylon defeated the Egyptians at Carchemish, far to the north. The Babylonians then moved on south to take control of the cities of Phoenicia, the Philistines, and Judah. So Judah's king was now subject to the king of Babylon.

Although its armies were strong, Babylon was far away. Egypt, on the other hand, was next door to Judah. After the Babylonians had gone home, Jehoiakim, king of Judah, listened to the pharaoh's messengers as they urged him to break the treaty that bound him to Babylon and join the Egyptian side again. In Jerusalem, the prophet Jeremiah tried to persuade him not to agree, without success. The Egyptian alliance was renewed.

As the prophet had warned, King Nebuchadnezzar of Babylon took swift action. He sent local forces to bring the rebel to heel. When their attacks had no lasting effect, the Babylonian army marched to Jerusalem to set matters right.

Jehoiakim died in Jerusalem, and his son Jehoiachin became king. He had ruled for only three months when the Babylonians captured him and his capital. They took the young king and his leading men captive to Babylon, and set his uncle, Zedekiah, on the throne.

Incredibly, Zedekiah did just what Jehoiakim had done. He joined Egyptian intrigues and the Babylonians were roused again. Nebuchadnezzar could not allow the people of Judah to have a king of their own any longer. Their continual defiance must be ended.

His army laid siege to Jerusalem and took it. The soldiers broke down the city walls, ransacked Solomon's Temple, and set it on fire. They caught Zedekiah as he tried to escape, killed his sons as he watched, then blinded him. All the well-to-do and skilled people were taken in exile to Babylon, and a local governor was left in charge, under Babylonian supervision.

That is the history of the last twenty-five years of the kingdom of Judah as the Bible and Babylonian documents tell it.

Archaeology can add to their accounts. From 1932 to 1938 a team of Britons dug into an impressive mound between Hebron and Ashkelon. The ruins are believed to be those of the ancient city of Lachish (see also *'The Assyrian Came Down . . .'*). At one

place on the edge of the mound the spades quickly struck the stumps of stone walls. They were the remains of the city gate. The floor of the guard-chamber was covered with rubble and ash, evidence that they were destroyed by fire. The fire had also ravaged some poorly-built houses nearby.

From the style of the broken pots lying in these gateways it is almost certain the destruction was the result of one of the Babylonian assaults on Judah. Most archaeologists believe it was the last one, when Jerusalem was sacked. The burnt walls and broken vessels are a reminder of the disaster such an invasion brought to the ordinary people of Lachish. Their homes were never rebuilt.

A few potsherds found in the gatehouse bring the situation to life. A junior officer in the Judean army

On this 'tell', the ruins of ancient Lachish, burnt walls and broken vessels are a reminder of the disastrous attack its people suffered at the hands of the Assyrians.

On pieces of broken pottery found in the gatehouse are reports from a Judean soldier to his commanding officer at Lachish. News was sent by smoke signals.

had sent reports from his outpost to his commander in Lachish. They were short messages written in ink on pieces of broken pottery. Their language is good Hebrew, just like the language of the Old Testament. Their writing shows how Hebrew appeared at that time. This is what the written prophecies of Jeremiah and Ezekiel would have looked like. Apart from a list of names discovered on a potsherd in Jerusalem, these were the first examples of ordinary ancient Hebrew writing unearthed in Judah. Others have been recovered since at different places.

The letters are simple. In one, the officer seems to say he is not as stupid as his commander suggested, he really is able to read! Another notes the arrival of a general on his way to Egypt, an echo of the intrigues between Judah and the pharaoh. There is also

mention of a prophetic warning that had come by letter, which the writer is forwarding.

There are eighteen letters, some of which are very poorly preserved, the ink has faded or been washed away. One may come from the last moments of the garrison. The officer reports he had put down all he was instructed on a writing-tablet or a column of a scroll, a certain man has been taken to the city (perhaps Jerusalem) as a prisoner, and ends 'we are watching for the beacon from Lachish, following the signals you, sir, gave, but we do not see Azekah.'

These last words apparently refer to a system of sending news from place to place by smoke signals or bonfires. Azekah is identified as a place about 15 km/9½ miles north of Lachish. The officer was at a place where he could see both. Smoke signals would be especially important as a warning of invasion. (A chain of beacons was set up in Britain to serve exactly the same purpose if Napoleon invaded in 1803.)

The prophet Jeremiah warned King Zedekiah to change his policies at a moment 'when the army of the king of Babylon was fighting against Jerusalem and against all the cities of Judah that were left, Lachish and Azekah, for these were the only fortified cities of Judah that remained.'

It is tempting to think this insignificant-looking piece of pottery carries a message from those last days as the Babylonian forces closed in.

'NEBUCHADNEZZAR, KING OF THE JEWS'

Excavators digging into the ruined palaces of Sennacherib and other Assyrian kings all tell the same story. The magnificent halls and courtyards lined with sculptured slabs of stone were looted and burnt, and left desolate. What the plunderers could not carry away, they left to wild animals and the elements. The glory of Assyria vanished.

In place of Assyria, Babylon rose to rule. A few Babylonian tablets, the Bible, and some Greek reports describe these events. After 640 BC Assyria grew weak. From the east, from the hills of Persia, Medes and their allies attacked. From the south came the forces of Babylonia, commanded by successors of Merodach-baladan, the king whom Sennacherib had defeated.

Following several battles, these forces joined to bring Assyria's power to an end by capturing Nineveh in 612 BC. The victors shared the Assyrian Empire, the Medes taking the hill-country to the east and north, the Babylonians holding Mesopotamia, Syria, and Palestine.

A third power, Egypt, tried to win some of the spoils, but the Babylonians thoroughly defeated the Egyptians at Carchemish, in 605 BC. Commanding the Babylonian army in that battle was Nebuchadnezzar. He became king of Babylon in the same year and reigned for forty-three years, until 562 BC.

Nebuchadnezzar did not leave long descriptions of his victories on the walls of the temples and palaces he built, as the Assyrian kings had done. The inscriptions he did leave speak almost solely of what he did for the gods he worshipped. As a result, the history of his reign is not very well known. Some inscriptions name places in his empire, showing how large it was, and two groups of cuneiform tablets supply more detailed information.

The first group is the Babylonian Chronicles. Two tablets cover events in the reign of Nebuchadnezzar's father, and two in his own reign (other tablets deal with earlier and later kings). The two tablets for Nebuchadnezzar, unfortunately, only refer to the first eleven years of his rule. The remaining thirty-two are almost entirely without record. It is possible other tablets will

The 'Hanging Gardens' of Babylon were among the seven wonders of the ancient world.

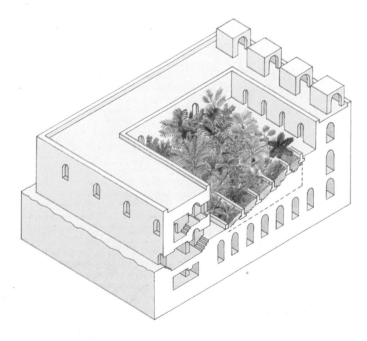

be found one day. Those known at present were bought by the British Museum late in the nineteenth century, but the two about Nebuchadnezzar lay there awaiting publication until 1956.

Why the tablets were written is not explained; they seem to be extracts from a fuller account of each year's events. These chronicles are not boastful descriptions of bloodshed and victory, like the Assyrian kings' monuments. They are plain, factual, and, scholars agree, reliable. They tell us about the rise of Babylon to power and the fall of Assyria, of the battle of Carchemish and Babylonian successes in Syria and Palestine.

One short entry states: 'The seventh year, the month of Kislev, the king of Babylonia mustered his forces and marched to Syria. He encamped against the city of Judah and on the second day of the month of Adar he took the city and captured the king. He appointed a king of his own choice there, took its heavy tribute and brought them to Babylon.'

Enough is known for these dates to be translated exactly. The month of Kislev in year seven was December 598 BC. The second of Adar was 15/16 March 597 BC. Here is the Babylonian report of the attack on Jerusalem which ended with Nebuchadnezzar making Zedekiah king in place of young Jehoiachin, whom he took prisoner to Babylon (see also 'We Can't See the Signals'). These kings were under Nebuchadnezzar's control. He was really 'Nebuchadnezzar, king of the Jews', as the nursery rhyme says!

The Babylonian soldiers transported Jehoiachin and his courtiers to Babylon. There they lived under guard in the royal palace. During excavations in that palace some cuneiform tablets

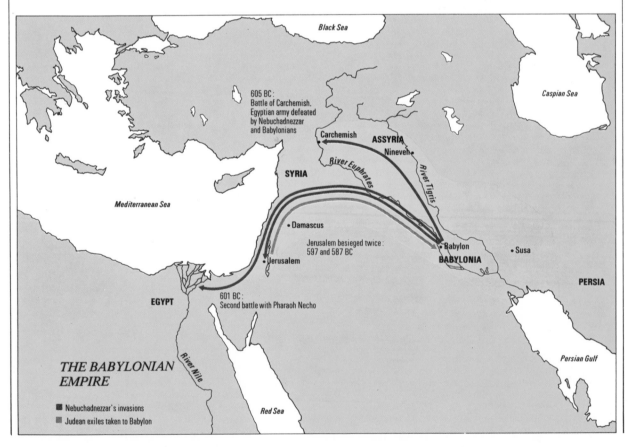

605 BC:
Battle of Carchemish.
Egyptian army defeated
by Nebuchadnezzar
and Babylonians

Caspian Sea

Carchemish ASSYRIA
Nineveh

River Euphrates

SYRIA

Mediterranean Sea

River Tigris

Cyprus

Damascus

Jerusalem besieged twice:
597 and 587 BC

Babylon
BABYLONIA

Susa

PERSIA

Jerusalem

EGYPT

601 BC:
Second battle with Pharaoh Necho

River Nile

THE BABYLONIAN
EMPIRE

Persian Gulf

■ Nebuchadnezzar's invasions
■ Judean exiles taken to Babylon

Red Sea

came to light which list rations issued to all sorts of people living there. The tablets are dated by years of Nebuchadnezzar's reign, between 594 and 569 BC.

Among those who received grain and oil were Medes and Persians, Egyptians and Lydians, all with their own distinctive names. There were men from Phoenician cities — Byblos, Arvad and Tyre — from Philistine Ashkelon, and some from Judah. Most of them were officials or craftsmen, sailors, boat-builders, carpenters, and one Egyptian was a keeper of monkeys (see also *The Price of Protection*).

From Ashkelon there were sons of the king, but from Judah there was the king himself. Four tablets list rations for 'Jehoiachin, king of Judah', for his five sons and, probably, for four other Judeans — one a gardener bearing the good Hebrew name 'Shelemiah'.

Nebuchadnezzar kept Jehoiachin in his palace throughout his reign. His son, 2 Kings 25 relates, released him and gave him a privileged place at his table.

Nebuchadnezzar made Babylon a splendid city (see *The Glory that was Babylon*). He had a very large palace, heavily defended, at the north end of the city. Its main entrance opened into a great courtyard almost 66 metres/220 feet long × 42 metres/140 feet wide. At either end were rooms for guards and other personnel. Opposite the main entrance the visitor would pass through a hall into the second court, a rather smaller one with many rooms at the ends. A suite at the southern end may have served the highest officials under the king for receiving petitioners.

A monumental gateway led west from that courtyard into the main one, nearly 60 metres/200 feet long × 55 metres/180 feet wide. Bricks covered with blue glaze bearing tree and flower designs in yellow, white, red, and blue, covered the south wall of the main

courtyard. Below the trees ran a frieze of lions.

A central doorway led through this wall to the king's throne-room, a hall 52 metres/170 feet long × 17 metres/56 feet wide. The king's throne probably stood opposite this main door, partly recessed into the wall. This was presumably the room in which Belshazzar may be imagined sitting when the hand wrote his doom on the plaster of the wall. Beyond this central courtyard and throne-room lay two more courtyards with many more rooms. In some the royal women may have lived.

At the north-eastern corner of the palace was a structure with thick brick walls and long, narrow vaulted chambers. (The ration tablets of Jehoiachin were found here.) These may have been store-rooms, but the thick walls suggest this was a high building. The excavator proposed to identify it with the 'Hanging Gardens'.

Greek historians explain how a Baylonian king created a mountain-like garden to please his Median wife. She came from a hilly land and was homesick in the flat plains of Babylon. The vaulted rooms could have supported terraces of brickwork for these gardens.

Nebuchadnezzar had a long reign in which to enjoy his glory. Less than twenty-five years after his death the Persians conquered Babylon and the city gradually lost its importance.

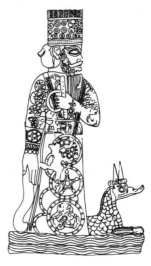

Nebuchadnezzar embarked on building work which made Babylon a splendid city. Even the bricks (above, left) were stamped with his name.

King Nebuchadnezzar paid due attention to matters of religion. He rebuilt several temples, including that of the god Marduk (above). This may be the god he honoured with a golden statue 27 metres/89 feet high, according to the book of Daniel.

THE GLORY THAT WAS BABYLON

For hundreds of years people living on the banks of the River Euphrates in Iraq had dug into the mounds of ancient Babylon for the hard baked bricks used in the old buildings. Most of the villages along that part of the river, and the town of Hillah, were largely built with Babylonian bricks. Yet, although the ruins were pillaged in this way, the city was so great that much remained.

Major excavations began at Babylon under German auspices in 1899. Robert Koldewey was in charge of the work, summer and winter, for eighteen years. His men uncovered city-walls, palaces, temples and houses. In them were pots and pans, metal objects, stone carvings and cuneiform inscriptions. Almost all belonged to the Chaldean period, 626–539 BC, when Nebuchadnezzar ruled.

The Ishtar Gate (left) stands as a memorial to the glory that was Babylon.

The plan (page 137) and artist's reconstruction of 'great Babylon' at the time of King Nebuchadnezzar give just a glimpse of its magnificence.

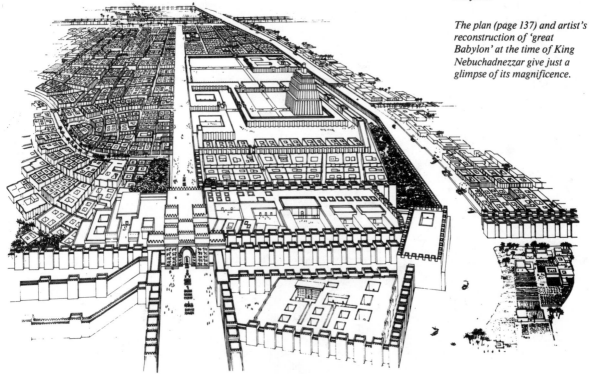

Ruins of earlier buildings lie below these, but the nearby river makes the water-table too high for them to be excavated properly. Consequently what visitors to the site see today is the work of Nebuchadnezzar and of later builders. It was his work that left its mark most strongly on Babylon.

When Nebuchadnezzar became king he pressed forward with the rebuilding his father had begun. Babylon stood on the east bank of the Euphrates, with a suburb across the river.

Two lines of walls protected it. The inner line was made up of two parallel walls 6.5 metres/21 feet and 3.72 metres/ 12 feet thick with a space between them 7.2 metres/24 feet wide serving as a roadway. These walls ran for about 6 km/3½ miles along the north, east, and south sides of the city, the river guarding the west side. Similar walls enclosed the suburb.

Outside the walls a moat some 80 metres/262 feet broad gave added protection. The outer walls were even bigger (7.12, 7.8 and 3.3 metres/23, 25 and 11 feet thick), with another great moat beyond. They enclosed an area of triangular shape occupied by suburbs and another royal palace. Their length was slightly over 8 km/5 miles.

Anyone entering the inner city

Over 200 animal-images decorate the great Ishtar gateway, faced with glazed tile, at the entrance to the processional way that led to the temples of the gods.

passed through impressive gateways in these walls. By far the most splendid was the Ishtar Gate, beside the palace at the north. This gate controlled a processional road leading to the main temple. Nebuchadnezzar rebuilt the Ishtar Gate three times. In each case the walls had a decoration of magical animals moulded in relief in the brickwork, but in the last stage the bricks were glazed, yellow and brown animals against a blue background.

Although brick-hunters had demolished all of the glazed walls, enough bricks remained loose on the ground for the reconstruction now standing in the State Museum in Berlin. The earlier, unglazed walls can still be seen at Babylon.

Flanking the street leading to the gateway, the walls were also covered with glazed bricks with lions moulded in relief. For the pavement of the road,

white limestone slabs were laid, each more than 1 metre/3 feet square, with red and white veined slabs along the sides. This road ran straight from the Ishtar Gate for almost 900 metres/half a mile to the temples of the god of Babylon. He was Marduk, commonly called Bel, 'Lord'.

Little could be discovered about the two central temples of Babylon. One was a tower built in diminishing stages. This great mass of mud-brick had been a rich quarry for the local brick-hunters. Nothing remains of the tower but a large hole in the ground and a few foundations. Its base was about 91 metres/100 yards square, with a long staircase at right angles on the south side for access to the upper stages.

Other information about the tower comes from Babylonian tablets which give measurements for each stage, and from Greek descriptions. The sides of

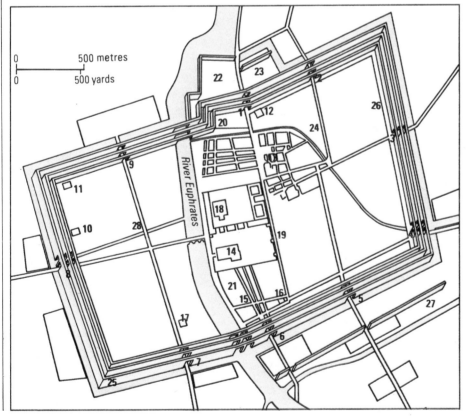

1 Ishtar gate
2 Sin gate
3 Marduk gate
4 Zababa gate
5 Enlil gate
6 Urash gate
7 Shamash gate
8 Adad gate
9 Lugalgirra gate
10 Temple of Adad
11 Temple of Belitnina
12 Temple of Ninmah
13 Temple of Ishtar
14 Temple of Marduk
15 Temple of Gula
16 Temple of Ninurta
17 Temple of Shamash
18 Temple tower
19 Processional way
20 Palace of Nebuchadnezzar
21 Esagila
22 Northern Citadel
23 Citadel
24 Southern Citadel
25 Outer wall
26 Inner wall
27 Nebuchadnezzar's outer wall
28 Canal

the stages were painted in different colours, the shrine at the top, perhaps 190 metres/300 feet above the ground, was covered with the blue glazed bricks. A great courtyard surrounded the tower, with dozens of rooms for priests and stores, and shrines for less important gods.

The second temple was named Esagila. Koldewey could not excavate it properly for it is buried under almost 21 metres/70 feet of debris, and a Muslim shrine stands on top of the mound. Nebuchadnezzar's own records and the report of the Greek writer Herodotus show it was a magnificent place.

The Babylonian king covered the walls of the holy place with gold and provided a great gold-plated bed and throne for the god. There were two golden statues of Marduk, Herodotus states, one sitting and one standing. Local priests told Herodotus that over twenty tons of gold had been used for the temple and its furniture.

Chiselled on the paving stones of the processional way and stamped on many of the bricks were inscriptions proclaiming, 'I am Nebuchadnezzar, king of Babylon, son of Nabopolassar, king of Babylon.' This is the claim echoed in the Bible book of Daniel, 4:30: 'Is not this great Babylon which I have built . . .?'

The ruins reveal the grounds for the king's boast. The period of madness which followed, does not appear in Babylonian records, but, as we have noted, hardly any exist to tell of Nebuchadnezzar's last thirty years' kingship.

THE WRITING ON THE WALL
Belshazzar — Man or Myth?

The book of Daniel is famous for its stories of heroes. They were men who stood firm for what they believed was right. They were protected by the power of God when the pagan kings persecuted them. Daniel himself was kept safe in the lion's den. His three friends stepped out alive from the burning fiery furnace . . .

A different story is just as famous — the story of the writing on the wall. It became so well known that the phrase 'the writing's on the wall' has gone into the English language.

Belshazzar, king of Babylon, held a feast for his courtiers. They ate and drank, using the gold and silver vessels brought from God's temple in Jerusalem.

As they revelled, a hand appeared.

The hand wrote on the wall in front of the king. The words it wrote did not make sense: MENE, MENE, TEKEL, PARSIN.

The king's scholars tried to find a meaning. They failed. Daniel was brought in. He saw at once what the words indicated, gave the king a warning, and told him his reign was about to end.

It seems the writing was the equivalent of 'Pounds, pence' - units of money or weight. Daniel's interpretation played on the meaning of each unit's name (as one might say 'pound' means 'beat, crush'). This was one of the methods Babylonians used for interpreting old books by which they tried to tell the future.

'Mene (number): God has numbered the days of your kingdom and brought it to an end.'

'Tekel (weight): you have been weighed on the scales and found to be too light.'

'Parsin (divisions): your kingdom is divided up and given to the Medes and Persians.'

The prophecy came true. The ancient historians record how Cyrus the Persian diverted the course of the River Euphrates and brought in his men along the river-bed to take the impregnable city of Babylon.

Belshazzar is remembered for his feast. Rembrandt and other great artists have painted pictures of it, and Sir William Walton used its theme for his famous modern oratorio 'Belshazzar's Feast'. Yet Belshazzar's name was not to be found outside the book of Daniel.

As a result, some scholars have promoted the idea that the whole story is fiction. It was made up, they argued, to give encouragement to Jews fighting for their independence in the second century BC. Indeed, they claimed, the whole book of Daniel was written then, and has no historical foundation. The supposed King Belshazzar was one of several historical mistakes the author made.

One eminent German wrote in his commentary on the book of Daniel that Belshazzar was simply a figment of the author's

imagination. That commentary was published in 1850.

In 1854 a British consul explored ancient ruins in southern Iraq on behalf of the British Museum. He dug into a great tower built of mud-brick at an ancient city ruin. The tower was part of the temple of the god of the moon, and dominated the city. Buried in the brickwork he found several small clay cylinders. Each one is about 10 cm/ 4 ins long inscribed with sixty or so lines of Babylonian writing.

When the consul took his finds to Baghdad, his senior colleague was able to read the inscriptions, for, fortunately, he was Sir Henry Rawlinson, one of those who had deciphered the Babylonian cuneiform script. Rawlinson immediately saw the importance of the clay cylinders.

The inscriptions had been written at the command of Nabonidus, king of Babylon, 555– 539 BC. The king had repaired the temple tower, and the clay cylinders commemorated the fact. The words they carried proved that the ruined tower was the temple of the city of Ur. The words were a prayer for the long life and good health of Nabonidus — and for his eldest son. The name of that son, clearly written, was Belshazzar.

Here was clear proof that there was an important Babylonian called Belshazzar, so at least he

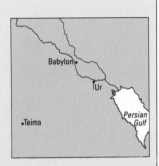

was not an entirely imaginary person. But this prayer spoke of him only as crown-prince. Since 1854 several more Babylonian documents have been unearthed that refer to Belshazzar. In every case he is the king's son or the crown prince; he is never given the title 'king'.

In fact, other records make it clear that Nabonidus was the last native king of Babylon. Belshazzar never came to the throne. So the majority of scholars concluded that the author of Daniel had still made a mistake in calling him king — although the mistake was not as bad as they originally thought.

Yet even that may not be right. Some writers have drawn attention to the reward Belshazzar offered to Daniel if he could interpret the writing on the wall:

'You will be clothed in purple, and have a gold chain placed around your neck, and you will be made *the third highest ruler* in the kingdom.'

If Belshazzar was king, why could not Daniel be given second place, like Joseph in Egypt? But if Belshazzar's father was king, Belshazzar himself would be second, and able to offer only the next place to Daniel.

The Babylonian texts support this idea. They reveal that Nabonidus was an eccentric ruler. Although he did not ignore the gods of Babylon, he did not treat them in the approved way, and gave a lot of attention to the god of the moon at two other cities, Ur and Harran.

For several years of his reign Nabonidus did not live in Babylon, but in the distant oasis of Teima in northern Arabia. During that time Belshazzar ruled in Babylon. According to one account of events, Nabonidus 'entrusted the kingship' to him.

That being the case, it is quite in order for him to be called 'king' in unofficial documents such as the book of Daniel. He acted as king, even if he was not legally king, and the distinction would have been irrelevant and confusing in the story.

The cylinders from Ur and other Babylonian texts do not tell us any more about 'Belshazzar's Feast'. But they do tell us about Belshazzar. They show that Daniel was not just telling

fables. And if he got these odd details right, perhaps we should listen to his message, too: God was in control. And even with kings, God knew the end from the beginning.

The records name as last king of Babylon Nabonidus, who is shown here. So was Belshazzar, who figures in the biblical book of Daniel, merely a myth?

PERSIAN SPLENDOURS

Three merchants from central Asia were travelling to India in May 1880. Coming into northern Afghanistan with bags of money to buy tea and other things in India, they were told the local chief was taking a heavy tax from all travellers. The chief wanted money to build up his army. (He got enough to do that, later becoming ruler of Afghanistan.)

But he failed with these merchants.

Someone told them there was treasure for sale, a treasure of gold and silver objects. The merchants bought those things and sewed them into packages to look like merchandise and so escape the chieftain's greedy eyes. All was well. They travelled across the country, through Kabul, and on. They were making for the Khyber Pass and Peshawar.

Then disaster fell on them.

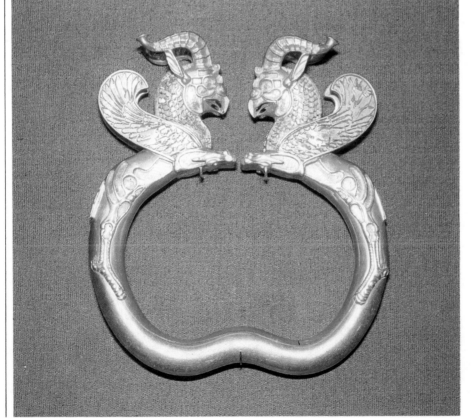

No one knows where the Persian 'Oxus Treasure' was found. The story of its discovery is one of high romance, involving chieftains and merchants and robber bands. Small wonder lives were lost in a struggle to possess such treasures as the beautiful gold bracelet (left).

Above the lines of human figures on the palace stairway at Persepolis are carved the symbols of religion. The bearded sphinx (below) was a frequent choice of sculptors.

Bearded bull-figures, in Assyrian tradition, guard the Porch of Xerxes (opposite) at the Persian capital, Persepolis.

Persepolis was sacked by Alexander the Great and left to decay. But it has yielded some treasures to the archaeologists, among them a silver goat (below, right).

The bowl of beaten gold (below) is another of the treasures from the Oxus. It dates from about the fifth century BC.

Somehow, rumours had spread about their load of gold. Robbers attacked, carrying off the merchants and their packages. But a servant escaped, made his way to a British political officer nearby, and reported the robbery.

Taking two men, the officer caught the bandits by surprise at midnight. They had been fighting over the share-out: four lay wounded on the ground. They handed over most of their loot to the Englishman. He heard of a plan to attack him, hid all night, went back to his camp, and threatened to lead his men to hunt down the robbers. Frightened, they brought more of the gold to him: only about a quarter was lost. He gave the treasure back to the three merchants, keeping one magnificent armlet which they could hardly refuse to sell to him in gratitude.

At length, the three men arrived in Peshawar, went on to Rawalpindi, and

there sold the treasure to local dealers. From them, a British general and another collector bought all they could, and the treasure eventually came to the British Museum.

No one knows exactly where the treasure was found. The merchants said it came from a place where a river running into the great River Oxus cuts through the ruins of an ancient town. In 1877 the river's waters washed out the objects and the local people were delighted to find them scattered over the sand. How many pieces they found is also unknown. Some were lost, a few were cut up to be shared. What remains is called the 'Oxus Treasure'.

It is not a set of table-ware or jewellery, it is a mixed collection. Three gold bowls and a gold jug stand beside a gold dagger sheath, sixteen gold and silver figures of men and animals, thirty or so gold bracelets and collars, a series of gold sheets with human figures on them, and a number of other objects. The most likely source for such a collection is a temple. People would have left them as gifts to the god or goddess. Whatever their purpose, these objects display the skill of the goldsmiths who worked during the Persian Empire. There is no doubt all the pieces belong to the fifth and fourth centuries BC.

Other examples of Persian

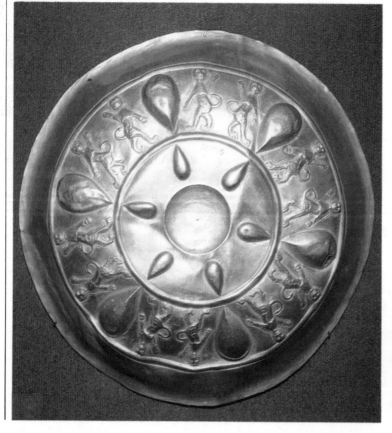

goldwork have come to light from time to time. They show clearly what the biblical book of Esther describes: 'drinks were served in golden goblets'. They illustrate the tremendous wealth of the Persian Empire. When Alexander the Great marched into Susa, one of the capital cities, Greek tradition says he took 40,000 talents of gold (that is about 1,200,000 kg or 1,180 tons). And there was more in other Persian cities.

Persian kings were great builders. Their empire stretched from India to Greece and south to Ethiopia, so they could draw on the skills and resources of every land. King Darius (522 – 486 BC) had an inscription written about the palace he built at Susa. Babylonians made the bricks, he said, men of Ionia and Sardis carved the stone, Assyrians brought cedarwood from Lebanon, gold came from Sardis and from the east, to be worked by Medes and Egyptians . . .

Little can be seen of the splendid palace of Susa. The description in Esther chapter 1 rings true in the light of what is known. The king is holding a banquet in the palace gardens: 'The courtyard there was decorated with blue and white cotton curtains, tied by cords of fine purple linen to silver rings on marble columns. Couches made of gold and silver had been placed in the courtyard, which was paved with white marble, red feldspar, shining mother-of-pearl, and blue turquoise.'

Much more survives of the new palace Darius began at Persepolis. He probably designed it as the centre

Privileged visitors seeking an audience with the Persian king at Persepolis climbed a great stairway lined with elaborate carvings. Persian guards lead the great procession to the throne.

Following the guards and nobles come representatives from all parts of the Persian Empire bringing tribute to the Great King.

Carved on the rock-face at Behistun is an awe-inspiring portrait of the Persian king, Darius I.

for the annual festival at the New Year. It was also a centre for administration and storing treasure. Once Alexander's soldiers had sacked it, it was left to decay until archaeologists began to study it. An important expedition from the University of Chicago worked there from 1931 until 1939, and further studies and restoration work have taken place since.

To achieve the greatest impact, Darius set his palace on a stone terrace partly cut in the rock, partly built artificially. Visitors would climb a wide stone staircase to a gateway, then pass into a great courtyard. Rising from this court was another stone platform 2.6 metres/8 feet 6 ins high which supported the audience hall. To reach it, privileged visitors climbed more stairs. These had elaborate carvings on the walls.

In low relief, long lines of men move towards the centre. They are the royal guards, horses and chariots, the nobles of the Persians and the Medes, and then representatives of all the provinces of the Persian Empire, each one carrying the special products of his land as tribute to the Great King. Arabs lead a dromedary, Ethiopians carry elephant tusks, an Indian bears jars probably filled with gold dust.

At the top of the stairs was a pillared porch leading to the audience hall. This was square, each side 60.5 metres/200 feet long, its roof held up by slender stone columns 20 metres/ 65 feet high, topped by elaborately carved bulls' heads.

Here the Great King sat in state, as a famous carving shows. The hall was bright with colour, paintings and woven hangings on the walls, carpets on the polished stone floors. The courtiers moved in ceremonial dramas, wearing heavily embroidered robes and massive gold jewellery. Seated on couches covered with gold, at banquets they ate and drank from dishes and flagons of gold and silver, like those of the Oxus Treasure.

Next to nothing remained of the treasure once housed at Persepolis. But the buildings themselves, and fine bronze work and stone vessels which the Americans found in their excavations, point to the high quality of everything made for the palace. They show why Persia represented the greatest degree of luxury for the ancient Greeks.

From the walls of King Darius' palace at Susa (Shushan) comes this Persian guard. The Persian Empire was vast — stretching from India to Greece, and south to Ethiopia.

THE KING'S ORDERS — IN EVERY LANGUAGE

Wherever the Persian king was, there was the government, for everything depended upon his decrees. What he said was law. So when he made an announcement it had to be carried to every part of his empire that was affected.

Routes used for centuries connected the ancient cities which Cyrus conquered from the Babylonians in 539 BC.

Couriers sped along the great roads of the Persian Empire taking the king's orders to every corner of his domain. The peoples he governed spoke many different languages. The stele from the temple at Xanthos (right) is inscribed in Greek and in the local Lycian language.

The tomb of Mausolos at Halicarnassus, decorated with fine sculptures, was one of the seven wonders of the ancient world. The figure pictured below may be Mausolus himself.

When he took control of western Turkey, the Persian surveyors mapped a new road from Sardis, the capital of Lydia, to Persepolis, covering some 2,600 km/1,600 miles. This was called the Royal Road.

Along these roads a well-organized messenger-service linked all the major cities. At regular stations 25–30 km/15–20 miles apart there were rest-houses with stables. Here, fresh horses awaited the couriers, so that they could speed on their way, or hand over their messages to a fresh messenger.

By this means, the Great King's orders could be made known throughout the empire. Equally, news of the state of affairs in each province would swiftly

reach the ears of the king. Agents throughout his empire kept him well-informed. They were known as 'the eyes and ears of the king'.

The Persian kings divided their great empire, which stretched from India to Greece, into provinces. A governor or satrap ruled each one. These men spent part of their time in their provinces and part with the king. When they were away with the king, more messengers had to travel between them and the provinces.

The king and the leading satraps were Persians, but they governed an empire containing a mixture of peoples speaking many different languages. There had always been

plenty of work for interpreters in the Near East. They are listed at Ebla as early as 2300 BC (see *Headline News: The Lost City of Ebla*).

In the Assyrian Empire the language problem was reduced with the spread of Aramaic. This language was current in Syria and spread widely as the Assyrians conquered small kingdoms such as Arpad, Hamath and Damascus.

2 Kings 19 records the Assyrian king's threatening words to King Hezekiah of Judah: 'My ancestors destroyed the cities of Gozan, Haran, and Rezeph, and killed the people of Betheden who lived in Telassar, and none of their gods could save them. Where are the kings of the cities of Hamath, Arpad, Sepharvaim, Hena, and Ivvah?'

Under the Persians, Aramaic became the ordinary language for the royal officials all over the empire. That is why letters to and from the Persian kings are recorded in Aramaic in Ezra 4–7.

A discovery made by French archaeologists in 1973 is a good illustration of the way Aramaic was used. The excavators were clearing a Greek temple at Xanthos in south-western Turkey. There, lying at the foot of a wall, they found a stone block carefully cut and finished. It is about 1.35 metres/4 feet 6 ins high, almost 60 cm/2 feet wide and nearly 30 cm/1 foot thick.

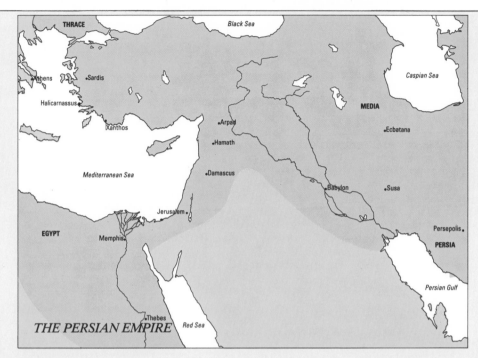

THE PERSIAN EMPIRE

Originally it had stood somewhere in the temple. On three sides of the stone there are finely engraved inscriptions.

On one of the wider faces the writing and language are Greek. The French scholars could understand it straightaway.

This stone was the foundation charter for the worship of two gods. The citizens of Xanthos agreed to build an altar for them, appoint one man and his descendants as priests for ever, and give property and an annual grant to maintain the shrine. They would sacrifice one sheep each month and one ox each year. The citizens swore to carry out their promises, and curse anyone who upset the arrangements.

On the opposite side of the stone the inscription is written in the local language, Lycian. Earlier discoveries gave examples of Lycian, mostly written on tombs, but very little of the language was understood.

Reading this monument, scholars soon saw that the Greek and the Lycian texts say almost the same thing. As a result, the Lycian language is becoming less mysterious; it proves to be a lingering survival of the language the Hittites spoke (see *A People Rediscovered*).

This Lycian inscription appears to be the original agreement about the new shrine, afterwards translated for the sake of the Greeks living in Lycia.

Any new cult like this had to have permission from the Persian power. A public meeting-place, supported by public funds, could easily turn into a centre for troublemakers and rebellion.

So the citizens of Xanthos took their agreement to the Persian governor for his approval. He was not a Persian. He was a brother of Mausolos whose famous tomb at Halicarnassus was one of the seven wonders of the ancient world.

Despite his local associations, the satrap was acting as the representative of the Persian king. He accepted the citizens' request, and so the new shrine was set up.

The satrap's approval is the third inscription on the stone from Xanthos. It is given in an Aramaic text set between the Greek and the Lycian on the narrower side of the stone.

It begins, 'In the month of Siwan year one of Artaxerxes, in the citadel of Xanthos, . . . the satrap said . . .

A summary of the citizens' request follows, then the satrap's assent, 'This law he has written'. Eight lines of curses by the gods of Xanthos and other places warn everyone against interfering with the agreement.

This, the official Persian deed, is proclaimed in the official language of the empire, with due attention to local circumstances.

When the Jews were rebuilding the temple in Jerusalem in the reign of Darius, the governor Tattenai wanted to stop them. He asked Darius if the Jews had official permission, and the king replied that they had, ordering Tattenai to help in every way.

At the end of his letter, recorded in Ezra chapter 6, Darius curses anyone who hinders or destroys the work, and he calls on the God of Jerusalem: 'May the God who chose Jerusalem as the place where he is to be worshipped overthrow any king or nation that defies this command and tries to destroy the Temple there. I, Darius, have given this order. It is to be fully obeyed.'

Scholars could not accept that the Persian king should acknowledge the Jewish deity, and concluded that Jewish scribes had changed the text. The Xanthos decree shows that they were wrong.

At Xanthos the gods of that place were asked to protect their own interests; the king does precisely the same in Ezra.

FROM PERSIAN POSTBAGS

The Persian governor of Egypt was living in Babylon, but there were all sorts of problems in his province. He would have to send his officer to put things right.

It was a long journey and it could be dangerous. Ezra thought of asking the king for a guard when he went from Babylonia to Jerusalem. He says (chapter 8), 'I would have been ashamed to ask the emperor for a troop of cavalry to guard us from any enemies during our journey, because I had told him that our God blesses everyone who trusts him.'

The governor had three other members of his staff who ought to go to Egypt, so they would all travel together, with the officer's ten servants.

The governor wrote a letter to the officials in the main towns on the way. He ordered them to draw on his accounts to supply the party with food. They were to have flour, wine or beer, and a sheep each day. But if they stopped longer than one day anywhere, they could not draw extra rations.

We know about this because the governor's order was kept in a leather bag with some other letters, and an Egyptian found it somewhere, about 1930. The order, and fifteen or more letters, were written on leather in Aramaic, in Babylonia. The bag may have been the postbag in which the officer had carried some of them to Egypt, and then he or someone else used it for holding other letters as well.

In his letters the governor asked about the income from his estates, about the staff on them, and about a sculptor who was to carve a figure of a horse and rider.

These letters open a small window into the affairs of a Persian administration. They also show what sort of letters were written in Babylonia in the fifth century BC and what the Aramaic language spoken there was like. No leather letters buried in Babylonia's damp soil could last so long. Through these letters it is possible to picture the letters reported in the biblical book of Ezra.

Another collection of Aramaic letters and legal deeds adds to the picture. These are written on papyrus and were discovered, odd as it may seem, on an island in the middle of the River Nile.

The island is Elephantine, which lies opposite modern Aswan, 700 km/430 miles south of Cairo, just north of the famous High Dam. It was a frontier post throughout Egyptian history, guarded by troops drawn from many places.

During the sixth century BC, some of the garrison were Jews and Syrians, and their families lived there until about 400 BC. The papyrus documents

When there was trouble with the local Egyptians, Jews at Elephantine applied to the Persian governor for permission to rebuild their temple. Excavation is carried out on the site, in Egypt.

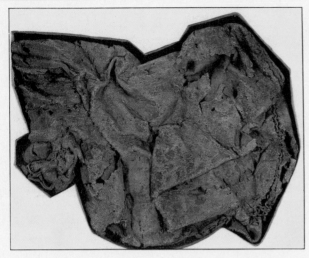

The leather postbag was once a diplomatic bag used for official communications in the Persian Empire.

Aramaic, the language in which the letter is written, was used by royal officials throughout the Persian Empire, a fact reflected in the way letters from the Persian king are recorded in the biblical book of Ezra.

belonged to them.

Deeds recording the sales of houses, marriages and marriage gifts, divorces, gifts and loans make up the majority of the collections found in the ruined houses. There are also letters and a few examples of literature.

Several of the Jewish people had names familiar from the Old Testament, especially with the name of God in them (see *The Engraver of Seals*).

Not all of the Jews at Elephantine were orthodox in their religious beliefs. They worshipped other gods, inherited from the Canaanites (the goddess Anath, for example), borrowed from other peoples, or invented by themselves.

Such situations aroused the prophet Jeremiah's indignation (chapter 44): 'They offered sacrifices to other gods and served gods that neither they nor your ancestors ever worshipped. I kept sending you my servants the prophets, who told you not to do this terrible thing that I hate.' Even so, the chief god was still the God of Israel.

What surprises the reader of the texts is to learn that these Jews in the south of Egypt had a temple where they worshipped Israel's God. They offered sacrifices, burnt offerings, flour offerings, and incense. It was a fine building with a cedar-wood roof, cut stone doorways, and gold and silver dishes, and they were proud of it.

The Jewish worship annoyed local Egyptians, and, in 400 BC, the priests of the chief Egyptian god of Elephantine, Khnum, destroyed the Jewish shrine and stole its treasures.

The attack was made when the Persian governor was away with the king. Clearly it was against official policy, but it took some years for the Jewish leaders in Elephantine to win permission to rebuild their temple.

They wrote to the Persian governor of Jerusalem about it and to the sons of Sanballat, governor of Samaria, as well as to the High Priest in Jerusalem.

After three or four years,

Sanballat's sons replied with advice on approaching the governor of Egypt. It would no longer be a temple that they had, but an 'altar-house' where they would offer flour and incense, no longer, it appears, burnt offerings.

The papyrus letters and draft letters which supply this history make an instructive parallel case to the history in Ezra.

Jews trying to rebuild Jerusalem's temple faced local hostility, and Sanballat of Samaria was a leading enemy. They had to petition the Great King, and he took the same attitude present in the Elephantine situation: local people should be allowed to worship peacefully as they wished, especially if they followed a good, well-established precedent. (Ezra 5:6–6:7 records the correspondence with the king.)

Another papyrus illustrates the same position. A problem arose in Elephantine about observing the Passover, perhaps a problem about the exact date. The letter reports the king's decision

about the question, giving the exact dates for observing both the Feast of the Passover and of the Unleavened Bread.

The words of the letter echo the words of Exodus 12-13 which records the institution of these festivals, and were evidently presented to the king for his approval, very much like the agreement at Xanthos (see *The King's Orders — In Every Language*).

From this it appears that for King Darius to write a letter about the Temple in Jerusalem, with the details which Ezra 6 contains, was not out of keeping with Persian practice.

Before the papyri were read, scholars had stated authoritatively that the documents quoted in Ezra were Jewish forgeries, or adaptations of Persian documents.

Now there is no reason to doubt that they are copies of the official letters.

THE WORK OF THE SCRIBE

Copies made by scribes were checked by counting the number of words or lines. Mistakes could then be spotted and corrected. In this Aramaic treaty engraved on stone, words that have been missed out are written in between the lines.

Being able to read and write was a rare qualification in the world of the Old Testament. Egyptian hieroglyphs and Babylonian cuneiform needed a long training and frequent practice if a boy was to become a scribe.

When the Phoenician alphabet spread (see *The Alphabet*), writing became simpler, easier, and more common. Still, there were large numbers of people, the great majority, who never learnt to read or write; they had no need to. If they wanted something read or written, they would call on a professional scribe.

So scribes were powerful men. You had to trust them to read or write correctly, for you could not check for yourself — and that applied to many kings as well as commoners.

Their skill gave scribes the opportunity to control affairs of state to a great extent, and their ancient role is reflected in the modern title 'Secretary of State'.

Such a scribe was Ezra, a Jewish employee of the Persian government who won King Artaxerxes' favour and led a major reform in Jerusalem.

According to Jewish tradition, Ezra carried out a major change in Hebrew: he encouraged the Jews to write their language in the letters used for writing Aramaic, instead of the old-fashioned Phoenician letters.

With Aramaic used all over the Persian Empire, his move made it easier for Jews everywhere to read their Scriptures. They no longer had to learn a different style of writing.

Recent discoveries in Israel display the change in process early in the fifth century BC. Over seventy small lumps of clay were found by accident and sold to private collectors.

On one side of each is the impression of a seal. The seals seem to have belonged to governors of Judah and their circle just before the time of Ezra. Old Hebrew writing is engraved on some, Aramaic on others.

In Samaria, to the north, the old letters of Phoenician type were still written. They present the name of Sanballat, governor of Samaria, on his son's seal, and they eventually became the distinctive script of the Samaritans.

In the Bible, Ezra is seen doing another duty of well-qualified scribes in most ancient empires. He translated or interpreted an old written text so that his hearers could understand it.

Aramaic spread as the official language, but the local languages also flourished, so royal decrees had to be translated and explained (see *The King's Orders — In Every Language*). People at Elephantine, far up the Nile in Egypt, read an Aramaic version of the inscription Darius set up at Behistun in three other languages.

Translating went further

than official documents, to include literature and religious books. At Elephantine, scribes read the wise sayings of Ahiqar, a member of the Assyrian court, in Aramaic and in Egyptian. In due course, the Jewish Law was put into Greek.

One of the important tasks of scribes was the accurate copying of old books and papers. It is surprisingly easy to make mistakes if you are copying page after page of a book. Scribes learnt this lesson very early in the history of writing, and soon accepted rules which could help prevent them making mistakes.

In Babylonia a scribe might check his friend's work, or he might count the lines in his copy to make sure it had the same number as the original.

Much later, Jewish scribes followed the same idea, counting the number of words in the originals and in their copies.

Unless extremely old copies of the Hebrew Scriptures are found, it is impossible to measure the accuracy of copyists who worked long before the Christian era. Several hints from the Old Testament itself and from other writings show that they tried to be accurate. Of course, there were bad, careless and lazy scribes. None was perfect. They did make mistakes.

Ancient manuscripts and writing carved on stone enable us to see some of the mistakes, and to see some of the corrections — for instance, words written above the line where they had been left out.

One manuscript which was quite heavily corrected is the famous scroll of Isaiah, found among the Dead Sea Scrolls (see *The Bible of Jesus' Time*).

A rather obscure subject has proved that the Jewish scribes were very accurate in some cases. It is well known that names change when they are taken from one language to another. Often foreigners will alter them to suit the sound patterns of their own speech (compare, for example, Londres for London, Leghorn for Livorno).

Several non-Hebrew names in the Old Testament are known to us from documents written when the names were current. The documents written in the Aramaic alphabet are most helpful for comparison with the Old Testament because that is so close to the Hebrew script.

Scribes of Aramaic had to write foreign names with their alphabet, and it is clear they tried to represent what they heard. When we put the ways they wrote the names of Assyrian kings beside the writings of the same names in the Hebrew text, it is striking to see how similar they are.

In both, the names Tiglath-pileser and Sargon, for example, are written TGLTPLSR and SRGN (the vowels are not certain). In the dialect of Babylon the names were reflected in

𐤀	𐤀	𐤀	'aleph
𐤁	𐤁	𐤁	beth
𐤓	𐤓	𐤓	resh
𐤏	𐤏	𐤏	'ayin
(1)	(2)	(3)	

Letters in forms used in Hebrew handwriting about 600 BC (1) the Lachish Letters (see We Can't See the Signals*), and Aramaic writing on stone (2) and papyrus (3) of the fifth century BC.*

Aramaic documents as TKLTPLSR and SHRKN. Yet, according to common opinion, it was in Babylonia or under Babylonian rule that the Jewish books containing these names were edited later.

The evidence of the Aramaic sources shows that, whatever later scribes did to the texts handed down to them, they kept these names in the old-fashioned forms of the Assyrian dialect and copied them faithfully.

Faithful copying also characterized the Hebrew scribes who preserved the book of Esther.

Among the Persian names in the book are some which seem so strange to commentators (and copies of the ancient Greek translation of the Old Testament write them so differently) that their original forms are thought to have been lost through scribes' carelessness.

In fact, one of the suspect names, Parshandatha, a son of the evil Haman, is a perfect reflection of a good Persian

name. A seal, carved for a Persian citizen in the fifth century BC bears his name in Aramaic letters. It is PRSHNDT, identical with the name in Esther. The Jewish copyists did their work perfectly in this case.

Examples such as these have a very small place in the whole text of the Old Testament. Yet they are the only means of checking the scribes' work in the centuries before our oldest manuscripts were written. They prove that they could copy with great accuracy and, at least as far as foreign names are concerned, they often did.

The importance of God's law, safeguarded by the scribes, is vividly illustrated by the copies worn on forehead and arm by orthodox Jews. A Jewish boy at his Bar Mitzvah wears the small leather boxes (phylacteries) which hold copies of verses from the book of Deuteronomy.

ALEXANDER'S ADVENTURE AND THE GREEK IDEAL

Alexander, king of Macedon, was twenty-one years old when he led his 45,000 Greek soldiers across the Near East to conquer Persia. He marched on and on, and ended up at the Indus river. The brilliant young general was not only a conqueror, he wanted to spread Greek culture and thought. To do that he gave his veteran soldiers land in those distant places, urging them to settle, marry local girls, and build up societies based on Greek ideals.

Alexander's ambition was to a large extent realized. Greek became as widespread a language as Aramaic, city-states organized themselves on the pattern of Greek cities and many used Greek coin values. East of the Euphrates, local languages and customs reasserted themselves in many places within a century or so, but traces of the Greek influences still remained. In Syria and Palestine the impact of the Greeks was stronger. Alexander's generals, who ruled there after his death, sustained it until the Romans came.

Alexander's conquests eventually

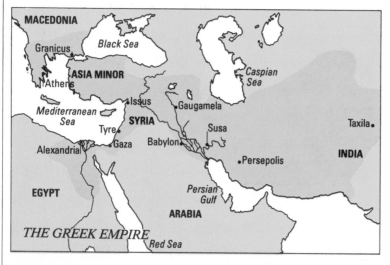

THE GREEK EMPIRE

left a stronger mark on the archaeological record than any other event, apart from the building of mosques after Islam swept across the Near East in AD 634. New approaches to art brought naturalism and individuality in place of formal and conventional styles. Coins carry fine portraits of kings; statues and other forms of art also characterize personalities. Above all, the Greek attitude reveals itself in towns planned on a regular, geometric pattern, the main buildings set up to Greek plans. These features began before the time of Roman rule in the Near East, and continued through it.

Excavations made over a few weeks in 1900 at Tell Sandahanna, between Ashkelon and Hebron, uncovered the whole of a small town destroyed about 40 BC. An inscription in a tomb near the site, and remarks in ancient books, prove that the name of the place was Marisa.

A city wall with square towers enclosed an area roughly 158 × 152 metres/170 × 165 yards. Dominating the eastern end was a large building thought to be a temple, and towards the centre, around two large courtyards, were what seem to have been a market-place and an inn. Other houses varied, from the large ones with central

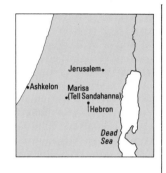

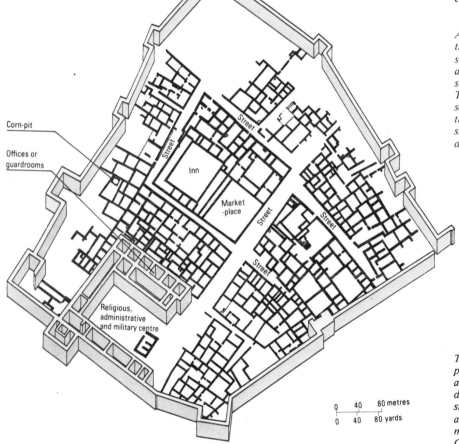

Corn-pit

Offices or guardrooms

Inn

Market-place

Street

Street

Street

Street

Religious, administrative and military centre

0   40   80 metres
0   40   80 yards

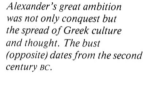

Alexander's great ambition was not only conquest but the spread of Greek culture and thought. The bust (opposite) dates from the second century BC.

Alexander's conquests changed the map. They left an even stronger mark on the archaeological record in Greek styles of art and architecture. The sculpture on the 'Alexander sarcophagus' (opposite) from the royal cemetery at Sidon shows the king on horseback. It dates from the fourth century BC.

The town of Marisa was planned on a grid system. There are strong Greek elements in the design of pottery and carved stonework. Inscriptions, too, are in Greek. Here, as in so many other places, Alexander's Greek ideal was realized.

courtyards to small ones of a few rooms fitting into the space available. The town was clearly planned on a grid system, although in its later stages some of the streets were blocked by private buildings. Pottery and carved stonework have strong Greek elements in their designs, and most of the inscriptions are written in Greek. The most unusual finds were two groups of magic spells, and some richly decorated tombs.

Citizens of Marisa would commission small lead figures of their enemies. These were bent and tied, and left in the temple. On stone tablets they, or a magician, would scratch the words of a curse: 'May the god strike X and Y with dumbness and impotence because they caused A to lose his job.' Several dozen of these spells were found, and a few in Hebrew which are hard to read. Others are prayers to the gods for help.

The names of the people in distress display the variety in the city's population. Egyptian and Semitic names are joined by many Greek and some Roman. Such a mixture was probably normal in all the larger towns outside Judah. The pagan forms of magic were probably typical too.

There were some quite wealthy men in Marisa in the second century BC. Their wealth can be seen in their unique tombs. A long underground hall was hollowed in the rock and cut in its walls were horizontal shafts, each large enough to hold a coffin. Smaller chambers led from the hall to take more burials. On the rock walls were quite elaborate paintings. One depicts a man walking along, playing pipes,

while a woman follows with a harp.

In the largest tomb is a long procession of animals, not only the local ones, but foreign and wild ones. A rhinoceros and a hippopotamus, an alligator and an elephant walk along, a wild ass fights a snake and a lion stalks its prey. Greek letters by some of the creatures spell out their names. So strange was the giraffe that it had a made-up name 'camel-tiger'.

In addition to these real animals there were imaginary ones, a griffin with a lion's body and eagle's wings, a lion with a human face, and Cerberus, the many-headed dog whom Greeks believed guarded the way to the Underworld. All these animals were painted in a fashion coming from Egypt but inspired in the first place by the Greek philosopher, Aristotle. Why they decorated a tomb is unknown. They may represent the rule of death over all creatures.

In the tombs were notices giving the names of the dead and their family history. The wealthy owners came from Sidon and settled, living in Marisa between 300 and 100 BC. They mixed with the local people so that the children born there had local names, some of them Idumean (Edomite) and, as time passed, more and more of them Greek.

Marisa illustrates very well the mixed culture of many Palestinian places just before the birth of Christ. Towns and cities of the Near East have always had a medley of races and beliefs. Alexander's adventure brought new and very influential ingredients to the mix.

JEWISH COINS

Archaeologists are glad to find coins in their excavations because a coin can often give an exact date and so help in working out the age and history of a building.

In the ruins at Qumran, for example, the excavators found two small hoards of copper coins which the Jews issued during their revolt against Rome. The coins have dates on them, many in year 2 and a few in year 3 of the revolt, that is AD 67 and 68 (see *At the Moneychangers' Tables*).

As none were found dated later than year 3, and out of seventy-two coins, four only bore that date, the rest being from year 2, the archaeologists deduced that AD 68 was the year when the Romans captured the place.

In contrast, in the fortress of Masada, where the rebels made their last stand against Rome, some of their coins were found with dates in year 4 and year 5, AD 69 and 70. These coins agree with historical reports that the Romans did not capture the fortress until AD 73, after they had taken Jerusalem, where the

coins were minted.

Coins offer other information as well. From the time when the first pieces were struck, perhaps about 600 BC, in Lydia in western Turkey, they were a good means of communication. In the days before there were newspapers and broadcasting by radio or television, it was not easy for governments and kings to make their policies known. A coin with the name of a king impressed on it, or the symbol of a city, carried the authority of the king or the city.

A new king could announce himself by issuing a large number of new coins with his name on them, or a message about his rule. Greek and Roman coins repeatedly provide examples of coins used to spread propaganda.

After the conquests of Alexander the Great, coins began to be common. For the 300 years before that, they were made of silver or gold only, so most people did not need to use them. When copper or bronze coins were minted, with lower values and in much larger numbers, people of

The silver denarius was a day's wage for the working man at the time of Christ.

A gold coin bears the name and image of Augustus, during whose reign as emperor of Rome, Jesus Christ was born. The census Augustus ordered was intended to bring in more tax.

The coin of Ptolemy V, ruler of Egypt, dates from the second century BC.

The Jews minted their own coins during the Jewish revolt against Rome in the first century AD.

The bronze coins date from Hasmonean times.

Coins discovered on a dig can often give an exact date. The bronze pot and silver coins are from the last centuries BC and the first century AD.

all classes used them freely. The rulers of small and relatively poor states could strike copper coins and so proclaim their existence, even if they could not afford to mint in silver.

This was what the Jewish high priests did when the Greek kings of Syria allowed them to rule Judea, following the Maccabean War. The first to do so was John Hyrcanus (135–104 BC). His small copper coins bear the words 'John the High Priest and the Council of the Jews'. They are written in the Old Hebrew script. Both the words and the writing assert the Jewish nature of the state, and the title marks its religious basis, the

priest sharing the rule with the Council (which later became the Sanhedrin — the Council before which Jesus himself stood trial).

Successive rulers issued similar small coins, using them to publicize themselves. Alexander Jannaeus (103–76 BC) saw their value for this purpose. He made himself king, then had coins struck with his name and title in Hebrew on one side, and in Greek on the other.

Placing Greek on the coins displayed their origin to neighbouring countries. It is also a sign of the deep penetration of Greek in Jewish society.

When Herod gained control, Hebrew inscriptions

were omitted. They only reappeared on the coins of the Jewish rebels in AD 66–70 and in AD 132–35.

The large numbers of small, poorly made copper coins issued by the high priests, and then by Herod, his sons, and the Roman governors implies that they were of little value. They illustrate how very poor was the widow who put the only two she had into the Temple collecting-box. Seeing her gift, Jesus was moved to say, 'I tell you that this poor widow put more in than all the others. For the others offered their gifts from what they had to spare of their riches; but she, poor as she is, gave all she had to live on.'

PETRA, THE HIDDEN CITY

Burning incense was a common act of worship in ancient temples and shrines. The strong, pleasant fragrance was thought to rise up to the deity being worshipped. Smoking incense also masked the sharp smell of animals roasted and burnt as sacrifices. Incense was also burnt to sweeten the air in the presence of Assyrian and Persian kings, and other people may have used it for that purpose too.

Enormous amounts of incense were needed to supply the demands of the Greek and Roman world. The basic ingredient was frankincense, the sap of a tree which grows in southern Arabia. Caravans of merchants with strings of camels and donkeys plodded from south to north through the desert, transporting consignments of incense to Gaza and Damascus for export all around the Mediterranean. They took back, in exchange, fine metalwork, pottery and glassware from the factories of Egypt, Syria and Greece. In southern Arabia the states of Sheba, Ma'in and Qataban grew rich from this trade.

As the caravans travelled, they stopped where there was water and shelter. Some of these resting-places grew into major towns. The most famous of them is Petra. This city was built in a valley between cliffs of red and pink sandstone, where the high desert plateau breaks down to the great rift valley south of the Dead Sea.

In the centuries from 300 BC to AD 150 one of the main incense roads came past or through Petra, turning west to the coastal city of Gaza. The

citizens sold provisions and lodgings to the travellers, and the kings taxed them. So the city grew rich.

The people of Petra were an Arab tribe which had settled and begun to live in the fashionable way, under Greek influence. The tribe was called the Nabataeans. Without the work of archaeologists in Petra and other towns, little would be known about these people.

They were great borrowers. Their towns and temples and tombs have designs and decorations taken from Egypt and Phoenicia, from Greece and Rome. Their language was an Arabic one, but they borrowed the Aramaic alphabet for writing it. From the Nabataeans, that alphabet passed to the Arabs, the shapes of the letters having changed through the centuries.

After the Romans conquered Petra in AD 106, the city lost its power. People lived there for centuries, but earthquakes and neglect led to the ruin of its buildings, until no houses were left standing, and it was forgotten. Modern explorers first reached and identified Petra in 1812. Some excavations have been made by American, British and Jordanian archaeologists, but there is much yet to be learnt about the city.

In its heyday, during the first half of the first century AD, the Nabataean kingdom controlled much of Transjordan, the southernmost part of Palestine (the Negev). Under its most powerful king, Aretas IV (about 9 BC to AD 40) the kingdom even ruled Damascus for a while. (The apostle

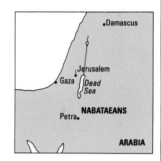

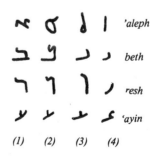

ℵ	⊄	𝌆	ı	'aleph
⊐	𝒴	⌐	⌐	beth
⎤	⎤	⎦	⌐	resh
⌐	⌐	⌐	⌐	'ayin
(1)	(2)	(3)	(4)	

Letters in forms used in Hebrew handwriting of Herod's time (1), Nabataean inscriptions (2), Nabataean handwriting (3), and Arabic (4).

Petra, 'the rose-red city, half as old as time', is built in a valley between cliffs of red and pink sandstone. The magnificent façade of the Treasury (opposite) instantly catches the eye. It is in fact a rock-cut tomb.

On top of a great rock, high above the city, is a Semitic 'high place', designed according to age-old custom for worship involving animal sacrifice. The Old Testament frequently mentions such high places, warning God's people against idolatrous forms of worship.

Once a resting-place for desert caravans, Petra was settled by Nabataean Arabs who adopted a fashionable Greek lifestyle. The city flourished in New Testament times, but lost its power after the Roman conquest in AD 106. Here is a series of tombs, cut in the cliffs.

Paul escaped 'the governor under King Aretas' in Damascus by being let down from the city wall in a basket.)

At this time, recent studies indicate, a grand street was laid through the centre of Petra, and splendid buildings set on terraces beside it. The road led to a square temple, built to the ancient plan of porch, holy room, and shrine that Solomon had followed.

Spreading over the valley from either side of the main street were the houses and workshops of the city. Some were built with finely-cut stones, the plaster on the walls inside decorated with mouldings and paintings.

In one product the Nabataeans

excelled. That was their pottery making. Nabataean potters learnt how to make pottery as thin as porcelain, but made by hand on a potter's wheel, not in a mould. Their dishes are especially fine, painted in brown with floral designs.

Such thin ware breaks easily, so complete examples are very rare. But so many broken pieces are found on Nabataean sites that it is clear this pottery was in quite common use, not made by a single craftsman for wealthy patrons.

The city of Petra was protected by a wall with towers, and by the rocks and cliffs around it. In the soft stone of those rocks, the people of Petra cut the monuments which make their city famous. They wanted to bury their dead so that they would not be forgotten, and they found the sandstone very suitable for carving.

Their masons hacked into the rock, making a doorway to lead to a large room. Some burials might be made in that room, or other chambers might be cut leading from it for the burials. Some of the rooms were apparently

designed so that relatives could visit the tombs to hold celebrations in honour of the dead.

The rock face outside the tomb was prepared for carving, too. In most cases it was cut smooth, carved to look like a stone-built doorway and, high above, like a roof.

The wealthiest citizens, the royal family and their associates, had even more magnificent tombs. For them, the rock was sculptured to take the form of a Roman temple.

Visitors to Petra see the finest one first. As they make their way through the narrow gorge 2 km/1¼ miles long leading to the city they see nothing but the rocky walls. Suddenly, facing them at the end of the crevice is a marvellous pink carving.

Above a pillared entrance are columns carved in the stone with delicate figures in relief between them. On top, on the pediment 30 metres/100 feet above the ground, is a great stone vase. It is solid, but local people shot at it for years, hoping to break it open and find gold inside.

The tomb is still called Pharaoh's Treasury, El-Khazne. Whose tomb this was, no one knows; one leading scholar argues it was made for Aretas IV.

Petra's spectacular rock-cut tombs and the tumbled stones of the once-great city are evidence of the luxury and skill the Nabataeans enjoyed at the time when King Herod was erecting his splendid buildings (see *Herod—the Great Castle Builder*).

In addition to the temple built at the end of the main street, there were other sacred places in Petra, and one is of particular interest. Hundreds of feet above the city, on top of a great rock, is the High Place. This is not a temple in a Greek or Roman style, it is a Semitic 'high place' fashioned after an age-old custom.

A processional road cut through the rock, with carefully hewn steps, led up to the top of the hill. There the worshipper came to the sacred area. Two stone pillars marked it, not built from blocks of stone, but created by cutting the rock away until they stood alone. They are each about 6 metres/20 feet high, and they stand several metres/yards apart — so a lot of rock was removed. These pillars echo the pillars found in Canaanite temples (see *Conquered Cities of Canaan*).

Beyond the pillars the summit of the rock is cut away. A level area about 14 × 6 metres/46 × 20 feet was made, with a bench cut in the rock on three sides. At the fourth side, facing east, is a rock-cut altar, approached by a flight of three steps. To the left of the altar other steps rise to a circular basin cut in the rock. A drain running from it suggests it was the place where animals were slaughtered. Although the altar is big enough for a person to lie on, there is no evidence that the Nabataeans sacrificed human beings.

For long centuries the Nabataeans and their city lay forgotten. Their recovery is another achievement of archaeology, and a contribution to the cultural background of the New Testament.

MASADA — THE LAST STRONGHOLD

The Nabataeans felt safe in their hidden city. King Herod, whose mother came from Petra, wanted to be safe. All his life Herod lived in fear. He knew that no one really liked him. If someone could take his crown and his life, the people would make the assassin a hero. So Herod killed anyone he suspected might be a rival — even two of his own sons and the baby boys of Bethlehem, any one of whom might be the infant king for whom the Wise Men sought (see *Herod—the Great Murderer*). Only the knowledge that Herod had Rome's protection stopped the Jews from revolting against him. His fear made him build fortress-castles: Machaerus and Herodium, the citadel in Jerusalem, and others besides — above all, Masada.

This isolated rock, rising in the wilderness west of the Dead Sea, was a natural fortress. Herod used it to keep his family safe when he went to Rome to win the support of the man who was to become Caesar Augustus, and Masada resisted a siege then. On his return he fortified it strongly, and continued to add to it during his reign so that it should be as secure as possible, and comfortable too.

After Herod died, in March of 4 BC, Masada had a garrison. Then the Jewish rebels captured it in AD 66 and made their last stand there. Roman military camps were set up at the foot of the hill and, eventually, the Romans captured the fort by heaping earth and stones to make a great ramp up one side of the hill. As they breached the walls, the defenders killed their families and themselves, rather than fall into the hands of the Romans. All this Josephus tells us in his *History of the Jewish War*, completed in AD 79.

The rock of Masada was one of the sites Edward Robinson identified in 1834. Various later explorers visited and wrote about it, but only since the outstanding discoveries of the Israeli archaeologists directed by Yigael Yadin in 1963–65 has the place begun to be well understood.

A good water supply is vital for anyone wanting to live on a hill-top in the desert. Masada was well provided with rock-cut reservoirs, and with channels and aqueducts to bring water to them. Even so, men and donkeys would have had to carry water from the lower cisterns to those on the top. Masada's ability to resist attack depended to a considerable degree on its water system.

A side-view of Masada clearly shows the great ramp the Roman forces had to build in order to reach the massive gates and storm the fortress walls. There was no surrender. The invading soldiers were greeted by an eerie silence.

All around the flat top of the hill, right at the edge, ran a double wall with towers at intervals, and four gateways where paths climbed down to the foot of the hill. Inside the walls were barracks, store buildings and living quarters for the staff of the castle. There were also two palaces.

One was on the top of the hill near the western side. This was for official occasions. A hall paved with a fine

mosaic opened on to a small throne-room, and not far away was a small suite of hot and cold baths.

But for relaxation Herod created a second palace, a pleasure palace, at the north end of the hill. On the end of the hill itself were living-rooms with black and white mosaic floors and painted walls. Looking out from the end of the hill was a semi-circular pillared porch where the king and his friends could

A view from the air gives some idea of the impregnability of Herod's fortress at Masada. He built his palace on the terraces in the foreground. Here the Jewish resistance made their last long stand against the might of Rome, and by a final mass-suicide cheated the enemy of the full savour of victory.

look out across the barren hills.

Lower than the surface of the hill at this north end, 20 metres/65 feet below the living quarters, was a terrace on which a round building stood. Only the foundations and pieces of carved stones and pillars remained, not enough for the archaeologists to discover what the building was for. Beside it are ruins of other rooms, including a painted hall.

About 15 metres/50 feet lower still, down the end of the hill, was another terrace. On a square platform were porches with painted walls and gilded pillars, apparently a place for meeting and talking. Yet another small bath-house stood on this terrace, for the comfort and refreshment of Herod and his favoured guests. Broken wine jars in various buildings were labelled in Latin 'for Herod, the Jewish king', with the

The plan shows Herod's palaces and store-rooms, taken over by the Jewish zealots in their last stand.

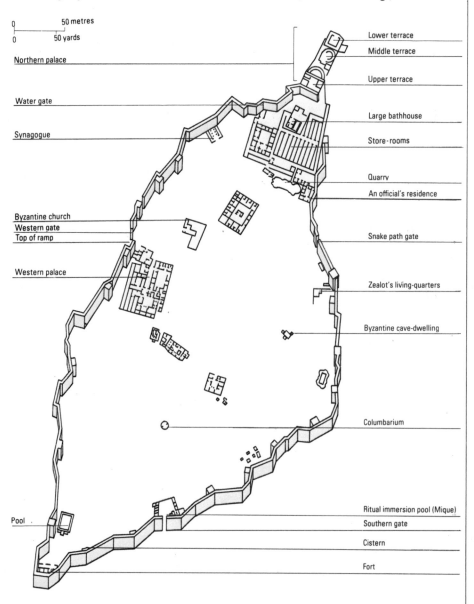

0   50 metres
0   50 yards

Northern palace

Water gate

Synagogue

Byzantine church
Western gate
Top of ramp

Western palace

Pool

Lower terrace
Middle terrace
Upper terrace

Large bathhouse
Store-rooms

Quarry
An official's residence

Snake path gate

Zealot's living-quarters

Byzantine cave-dwelling

Columbarium

Ritual immersion pool (Mique)
Southern gate
Cistern
Fort

date and place of vintage in Italy. Here is further evidence of Herod's love of luxury.

Masada's last phase as a fortress was when the Jewish zealots held out against the Romans. It is from those years (AD 66–73) that the most startling discoveries came. The rebels remodelled some of the buildings. They built a small synagogue for their worship, as they did at Herodium, and they made two ritual baths in other parts of the hill, built according to the rules preserved in later Jewish tradition.

Herod's palace at the north end gave a good supply of timber from its floors and roofs. The other buildings and the rooms in the wall round the hill were turned into living quarters and workshops. Most of them had been burnt. In the rubbish were broken pots and pans and glassware, tools and weapons, piles of dates and remains of other foods. Hidden in some of the rooms were small hoards of the silver shekels issued by the rebels.

The hot, dry atmosphere of the Dead Sea coast allowed unusual things to survive. In the synagogue and nearby, the excavators came upon

fragments of leather scrolls. Some bear biblical texts, parts of Genesis, Psalms, Ezekiel and other books. There are also pieces of Ecclesiasticus and books known among the Dead Sea Scrolls.

In the bath-house on the lowest of the northern terraces were the skeletons of a man and a woman and a child. Beside them were fragments of a woollen prayer shawl, the woman's sandals, and her braided hair. Broken pottery had served as scrap paper; several hundred pieces were found. Dozens bore one or two Hebrew letters. The excavator thought they had been tickets in a sort of food rationing system.

Other potsherds carried names, or were labels for the tithe or for sacred use. Twelve had written on each one a single name, one apparently the name of the commander of the rebels. Yadin believed these to be the actual lots which, according to Josephus, the last defenders drew to decide who should kill the others and then himself. Further study suggests they were tokens, like many others found there, meal-tickets, perhaps, to ensure equal shares during the siege. Nevertheless, archaeology casts one of its most vivid rays of light on history at Masada.

Among the objects which remained from the Jewish Zealot occupation of Masada were these kohl spoons, mirror lid, sandals and a comb.

NO ENTRY — EXCEPT FOR JEWS
The Story of a Stone

The Roman garrison in Jerusalem was used to dealing with riots. For the Jews, religion and nationalism went hand in hand — and that meant trouble. The soldiers had a clear duty to keep order, to control the people, and to try to make sure justice was done.

On one particular day in AD 59, a riot broke out inside the Temple itself. As soon as he heard the news, the Roman commander took some of his men and marched quickly to the scene. Before he arrived, the crowd had pushed its way out of the Temple into the streets and the heavy metal-bound doors had swung shut.

The ringleaders were attacking one man, obviously wanting to kill him. When they saw the soldiers and the tribune coming, they stopped, and simply held on to their victim until the Romans arrived. The mob quietened as the man was chained. They all began shouting again when the officer asked what it was all about. The full account is recorded in the New Testament book of Acts (chapter 21).

The victim was Paul, apostle and preacher. The riot had been started by Jews who had met him earlier in Asia Minor, and wanted him silenced. Now, in Jerusalem, they had seen him going round with a Greek friend. Surely Paul must have taken him into the Temple court? At last they had a good reason to make trouble.

From the beginning of Israel's existence as a nation, the Israelites had known they were God's people. No one could worship God properly except by becoming a Jew and obeying the Law of Moses. No one but a Jew could go into the sacred area of the Temple.

King Herod rebuilt the Temple in Jerusalem between 19 and 9 BC. He made it much larger than it was before (see *Herod's Great Temple*). There was a great open courtyard, with colonnades along the sides, which anyone of any race or religion could enter. It was here that the teachers walked and taught their disciples, and all sorts of business was carried out.

In the middle of the courtyard stood a low wall or fence of stone about 1.5 metres/5 feet high. This enclosed the Temple building, and none but Jews might pass through. To make the position quite clear, notices were placed along the wall. Josephus, the Jewish historian of the first century AD, says they were written in Greek and Latin.

There was a riot when Jews thought that the apostle Paul had taken one of his Greek friends into the Temple court. This was strictly forbidden. Notices, written in Greek for foreigners to understand, forbade entrance to all but Jews, on pain of death. In 1871 one of these notices, engraved on limestone, was found in Jerusalem. Part of another came to light in 1936.

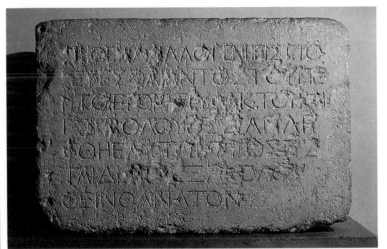

Just over 100 years ago, in 1871, an example of one of these notices, written in Greek, was discovered in Jerusalem. It is engraved on a block of limestone 57 cm/22½ ins high and 85 cm/33½ ins long. Part of another copy came to light in 1936, and shows that originally the letters, each about 3.8 cm/1½ ins high, were painted red so that they would show clearly on the creamy-white stone.

The inscription reads: 'No foreigner may pass the barrier and enclosure surrounding the temple. Anyone who is caught doing so will be himself to blame for his resulting death.' No one could doubt its meaning. And anyone who disobeyed would almost certainly be lynched.

The force of the warning was widely recognized. Josephus reports that the Roman general Titus, later to become emperor, admitted that it even applied to Roman citizens. Rome's authority was supreme and only the Roman governor could order an execution. Yet the Romans respected the Jewish religion and left the control of the Temple area in the hands of the priests. So a blatant offence against religious laws, such as a non-Jew entering the restricted area, could be punished straight away.

But in Paul's case the officer could

The reconstruction shows the western and southern walls of Herod's great Temple, built to win the favour of the Jewish people, who hated him.

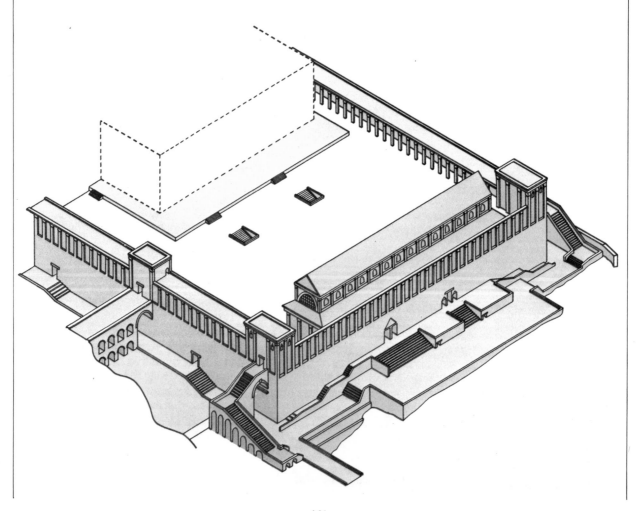

not get a clear case, and so he took him into custody, and, eventually, he was taken for trial in Rome.

This complete copy of the warning is now in a museum in Istanbul, Turkey. (Jerusalem was a part of the Turkish Empire at the time when the stone was found.) For Paul, too, a museum would have been the right place for it. For him, the warning had lost its force.

Paul seems to have had the inscription in mind when he wrote to Christians in Ephesus and other cities of Asia Minor. He told them that the distinction between Jews and others no longer exists. Jesus Christ has taken it away. 'He has broken down the dividing wall.' As a result, anyone can approach God through him. All who

do so are like stones being built into a single temple for God.

The stone in Istanbul, and the fragment in a museum in Jerusalem, appear to have been carved in King Herod's reign. They must have stood in the Temple throughout the time of the gospel story. They are among the most interesting of the few things which we can still see and be sure Jesus and his disciples also saw. And they still have a message for us today: not as a wall of partition, separating Jew from non-Jew, but as witnesses of a new message.

Jesus has broken down the dividing wall. People of different nations and races and backgrounds can be 'made one' through Jesus Christ alone.

PALESTINE AT THE TIME OF JESUS

Mediterranean Sea

Ptolemais

Chorazin
Capernaum • Bethsaida
Gennesaret • Gamla
Lake Galilee
Gaba Cana Tiberias
Sepphoris Nazareth
Nain • ▲ Gadara Abila
Mt Tabor
Scythopolis

Caesarea

Pella

Samaria
Sychar Gerasa
▲ *Mt Gerizim*

River Jordan

Antipatris
Aramathea
Joppa
Lydda

Jericho
Bethany
Emmaus Qumran
Azotus Jerusalem

Ascalon

Bethlehem
Agrippias Herodium Machaerus
Gaza Hebron
Dead Sea
En-gedi

Masada
Beersheba

Caesarea

| 0 | 25 miles |
| 0 | 40 km |

168

Part 2

DISCOVERIES FROM THE TIME OF JESUS

DAILY LIFE

Jesus spoke to people in their houses, in towns and in the countryside. He told stories about the ordinary activities of home and field, about men and women, family and business. Digging up ruined houses from those days, with their pots and pans still in place, helps to give more realism to those stories and to incidents in the life of Jesus. Discoveries in Jerusalem and other towns allow us to say, 'This is what it was like.'

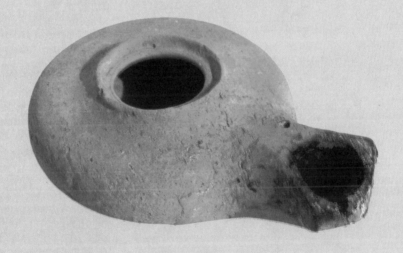

'Show a light!' Even the faintest light helps in a dark place. The common lamps of Jesus' time could be held in the hand. With oil in the bowl and a wick in the spout, a lamp set on a shelf could light a room. Often one was left alight in a tomb, like this example which still has the ancient soot on its lip. The light was a sign of life.

THE BURNT HOUSE

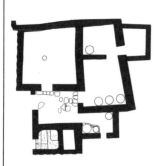

This plan of the Burnt House is based on the original drawings in N. Avigad, Discovering Jerusalem.

The sounds of swords clashing, the screams of the dying, and crackling of flames echo from deep below a new apartment block in old Jerusalem. Foreign soldiers are attacking the city, killing and looting. The sounds are modern, the story they tell is an old one, vividly re-created in the ruins of the Burnt House. Israeli archaeologists shifted a great depth of rubbish piled up over the centuries and uncovered part of the house where a prosperous Jewish family lived until Roman soldiers burnt it down in AD 70.

When the rubbish was cleared away, in January 1970, the walls of rooms began to appear. They covered an area about 10 metres/32 feet square, being apparently the basement of the building. As the archaeologists dug into them they met great quantities of ash and burnt wood, and everything they found was covered with soot. Here was a vivid demonstration of the work of the Roman army. There was no doubt this was a house burnt in AD 70, for scattered on the floor were coins issued by the Roman governors

Among the finds at the Burnt House were stone weights, one of them scratched with the owner's name: Bar Kathros.

of Judea, mixed with others issued by the Jewish rebels in the years 67, 68, 69, and none later. Broken pottery and other objects are also of known first-century styles. Looters had been through the house, throwing what they did not want into heaps on the floors.

Perhaps it was one of the defenders running away who left his short iron spear in one corner of a room. But another did not escape so easily. Against the doorway of one room were the bones of a human arm, the hand spread out to grasp the step. No more of the skeleton remained, but later destruction had carried away everything outside the entrance. The bones belonged to a woman in her early twenties, maybe a servant in the house, who, we may imagine, staggered a few yards to die from her injury.

What did she, and other people, do in those rooms? In the opinion of the excavator, N. Avigad, part of their work may have been to prepare incense for the Temple services. Among the finds pointing to this are many perfume bottles of pottery and glass (see *An Alabaster Jar of Perfume*), some stone mortars and pestles, weights, measuring-cups, and ovens. The heavy soot that clung to everything could have come from oily materials burning. Whether this deduction is right or wrong, two pottery inkpots also found in the ruins indicate that writing was a regular activity in the house.

On one of the stone weights is scratched the owner's name: Bar Kathros. In the Talmud that name is listed among the families of the High

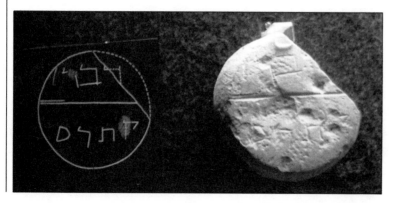

Priests who used their power to line their own pockets. The Bar Kathros family were attacked for misusing their pens, which may mean they spread false rumours or misinformation. Although someone may have carried this weight from another house to the place where it rested for 1900 years (it is only about 8 cm/3 ins in diameter), the Bar Kathros family certainly had a house in Jerusalem, and this one is a good candidate.

The rooms unearthed were workrooms and a kitchen, and a small ritual bath (see *Cleanliness is Next to Godliness?*). Their furnishings were few, apart from ovens, large jars, and stone tables. Before this discovery the furniture of Jerusalem houses in the first century was unknown, for woodwork decays rapidly when buried. Now several stone tables illustrate it. There were tables with rectangular tops about the size of a tea-tray (50 cm/ 20 ins × 75 cm/30 ins), slabs of stone cut smooth and decorated around the edges, supported on a single central leg of stone, about 75 cm/30 ins high, carved like a pillar. Other tables had round tops, about 50 cm/20 ins across, with three carved wooden legs fitted beneath them. Roman sculptures and paintings show the shapes of the legs. They also indicate that people reclined on couches around the circular tables to eat, the food and drink being served from the others.

Stone was also used for making dishes, cups, jars, and bowls, besides the common pottery. Previously scholars had supposed that stone was kept for special, expensive vessels, but the excavations produced so many— some finely finished, others only roughly cut on the outside yet polished within—that another explanation had to be found. Both Jewish writings and

the New Testament gave the clue: stone vessels avoided some of the problems caused by the laws of ritual purity (see *Cleanliness is Next to Godliness?*).

In the Burnt House is preserved an illuminating glimpse of first-century life, and a horrifying reminder of Jerusalem's fall. Staring at the ruined walls, the ovens, cooking-pots and tableware, the visitor can imagine a house of that time more realistically than any words can describe. If the imagination can run a little further, it is permissible to suggest that people who worked in these rooms may have run to wave branches before Jesus as he rode into Jerusalem, or that those who drank from the cups and goblets may have been among those who cried 'crucify him'.

Until 1970 the remains of this wealthy first-century AD Jewish house in Jerusalem lay buried under rubbish. When this was cleared, among the rooms unearthed was the kitchen, with its ovens, jars and stone tables.

RICH MEN'S HOUSES

Mosaic patterns decorated the living-room floors of a very few houses in first-century Jerusalem. This is the finest example of the simple geometric patterns. A coin of AD 67 was found on this floor.

'Sell everything you have and give it to the poor.' That was a key step, Jesus told a rich ruler who came asking him how to get eternal life (Luke 18:18–23). The man went away sad because he was very rich.

Recent discoveries in Jerusalem have revealed how the rich lived at the time. A visitor from another part of the Roman Empire would have found houses furnished as well as those in the major centres of Roman culture. In Jerusalem the best example is so splendid that Professor Avigad, who discovered the ruins, called it the Palatial Mansion. It covers an area almost 30 metres/100 feet long. Later buildings damaged some of the walls, so the position of the entrance has been lost. In the middle was a court-yard. A doorway at one side opened into a passage leading to several rooms. Perhaps because it was a busy place, the passage had a mosaic floor.

Two doorways led into a hall. This was a huge room, over 11 metres/ 36 feet long, its walls covered with panels of white plaster cut to look like fine stone masonry. Pieces of plaster fallen on to the floor seem to have decorated the ceiling. They were moulded with geometric patterns in relief. Our visitor would be familiar with such designs, for they echo the work of interior decorators in houses of the first century BC at Pompeii.

Other rooms were brightly painted. Panels of different colours imitated the marble slabs which only princes could afford. Imaginary windows and columns gave an air of greater space. Able artists painted lifelike fruit and leaves on some walls, and friezes of leaves in regular designs. A lot of this painting was done while the plaster was wet, so that the colours soaked into the wall. (This is fresco painting, the technique Michelangelo used in the Sistine Chapel in Rome.) When a householder grew tired of a design, he could not call a decorator to scrape it off like wallpaper, or cover it with a

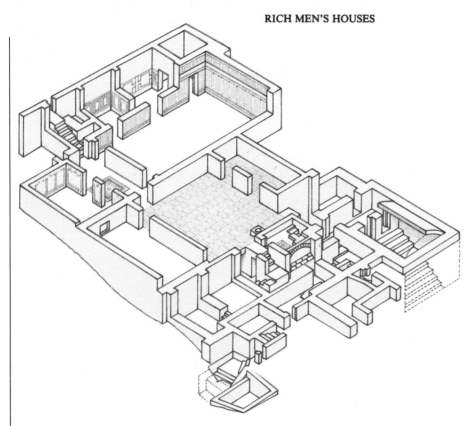

This plan of the Palatial Mansion is based on the original drawing in N. Avigad, Discovering Jerusalem

coat of paint. He had to have a new coat of plaster put on the wall, then painted. Often archaeologists have been able to chip away a damaged layer to uncover an earlier one underneath. Pieces of painted plaster are found in so many places in Jerusalem that it is clear most rich men's houses were decorated in this way.

As in many Roman houses, painters and plasterers worked with a third group of craftsmen, those who laid mosaic floors. They set tiny cubes of stone, black, red and white, into cement to make patterns and pictures. In the Palatial Mansion the passage-way and one reception room had mosaic floors. (Other rooms may have had them but if so they have entirely disappeared.) Where there was little heavy furniture to be moved, floors may have been polished plaster, covered with carpets or mats. Fire and damp would quickly have destroyed floor coverings of this kind, assuming that they were not stolen.

Elegant as these painted walls and mosaic floors were, a non-Jewish visitor from Rome would think them very tame. There are none of the people and animals, gods and goddesses that chase around most Roman walls and floors. Gods and goddesses, of course, had no place in Jewish thinking, but there were ancient Jewish heroes and famous stories like

The colours on the plastered wall of one room in the Palatial Mansion stayed bright, despite the fire that covered the ruins with soot in AD 70.

Well-to-do people had high quality glass vessels on their tables. One famous maker was Ennion. A glass jug from his foundry was unearthed in Jerusalem. This cup came from a tomb in Cyprus. Ennion's name is moulded on the side.

that of David and Goliath which would have made good pictures. Yet there were only geometric patterns, rosettes and waves on the floors, with one or two flowers and leaves, and walls panelled in the styles already described.

The reason for this is religious. First-century Jews were strict in following God's command: 'You shall not make for yourself an idol in the form of anything.' Pictures of animals or human beings might lead to idolatry. Most people applied this rule, but no authority had the power to impose it on everyone. At least one householder dared to disregard it, mildly. Plaster fallen to the floor in a room near the Temple was moulded with pictures of animals running through the countryside.

The visitor to the Palatial Mansion would have found more mosaic floors in the bathrooms. Set on a cement base, mosaic pavements were waterproof, so bathers could move freely in and out of the water. In one elaborate suite in another house the bath-tub itself had a mosaic floor. In other houses, there were rooms with under-floor heating (hypocausts) to create fashionable Roman steam baths.

These were baths for normal washing. What would have surprised the Roman visitor was the number of other baths. They are tanks of various sizes cut in the rock, lined with waterproof plaster, and vaulted with stone. Bathers walked down a flight of steps which often took up the whole width of the tank, and were faced with

a blank wall! They were not stepping into a swimming-pool. If the tank was well filled, the bather could easily go down to the lowest step and duck his head under the water to be totally immersed. That was all that was needed. Then he could turn and climb out. If the water-level was lower, or the bath was small, he would need to crouch to go under the water's surface. These were ritual baths, designed to enable religious Jews to fulfil the laws of purity (see *Cleanliness is Next to Godliness?*).

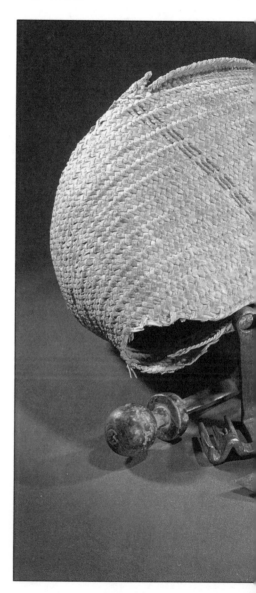

The biggest bath in the Mansion had eight steps running across its 4 metres/13 feet width, and was almost 5 metres/16½ feet long. It had two doorways so that people coming out clean did not brush against those going in unclean. Water for these baths had to be spring or rain-water, so cisterns were essential to collect and store it. Sometimes a cistern fed the bath next to it through a narrow pipe in the wall —so that the pure water which flowed into the bath also purified the water brought into the bath. Baths like these,

and smaller ones, were found in large numbers in buildings near the southern end of the Temple, where its main entrance was (see *Temple Tourists*). Houses in that area may have served as hostels for pilgrims who would want to purify themselves before entering the Temple. The care and expense taken to make these baths inside Jerusalem underlines the central role that ceremonial washing had in the daily life of religious Jews in the first century.

Carefully following religious laws

Archaeologists were astonished at the perfect condition of these objects hidden over 1850 years ago. Jewish rebels fleeing from Roman soldiers had put bronze jugs, iron knives and keys in the basket as they left their homes.

was not a bar to luxury for a rich man. Bits and pieces of stone, metal, pottery and glass hint at the equipment of the houses. Woodwork perished in the destruction, together with leather and fabric. A clue to fine wooden furniture is a cast-bronze foot from the leg of a table, shaped like an animal's paw.

The stone that could be carved into vessels (see *Cleanliness is Next to Godliness?*) also provided slabs for table-tops. Some of these rested on wooden legs, some on a single stone pillar. The latter were side tables for serving dishes. Leaves, flowers, geometrical designs (and in one case a fish) were carved around the edges of the table-tops. A very few tables are inlaid on the top with mosaic patterns. Tables like these could also be seen in Roman houses in Italy.

Jugs, cups, bowls and plates which stood on the tables in Jerusalem also had much in common with those used all round the Mediterranean. Bronze jugs had gracefully curving handles, and beside them were bowls and saucepans and ladles, some in styles known from excavations as far away as Roman London. High-class glass vessels were in use. In the Palatial Mansion were pieces made by the master glass-blower Ennion, who put his name on them. Other products of his workshop have been found in Cyprus and Italy. Local craftsmen were active in casting and blowing glass (rubbish from a glass factory was tipped into old buildings as hard core for a street laid in Herodian times). Fine red pottery with a shiny surface adorned some tables. This was imported from factories on the coast of the Mediterranean, perhaps from Greece.

Local potters made serviceable cooking-pots and storage jars, kitchenware and delicate, painted tableware. They also made the small pottery lamps that could be set on a ledge to light a room after sunset. The rich did better, having bronze stands from which metal lamps could hang like flowers, or on which they could stand.

The remains found in first-century Jerusalem give some idea of the riches which Jesus' inquirer was told to sell. Such a comfortable, even luxurious lifestyle was hard to part with. Nicodemus, Joseph of Arimathea, and some of the priestly families probably lived at the same level of cosmopolitan fashion, while maintaining their distinctive Jewish behaviour.

AN ALABASTER JAR OF PERFUME

Jewish burials from Gospel times do not give great golden treasures to archaeologists, or even dozens of pots and pans, as do the tombs of earlier ages. Often nothing lies in the coffin or the bone-chest except the dead person's bones and a little bottle. These little bottles are commonly made of pottery, sometimes of glass. People often call them 'tear' bottles, although the idea of mourners gathering their tears in them to leave with the dead is fanciful. (The translation of Psalm 56:8, 'gather my tears into your bottle', seems to give some

support, without referring to burials at all.) These simple flasks were made for the cheaper scented oils in daily use. Costly perfumes deserve expensive containers.

The alabaster jar the woman broke over Jesus' feet at Bethany was probably carved from stone, for the 340 gm/ 12 oz of perfume in it was estimated to be worth over 300 denarii (more than a year's wages) according to the account in Mark's Gospel (14:3–5). Pliny the Elder, writing later in the first century, stated that ointments kept best in alabaster boxes. If the jar

in the story had a long neck, like the examples illustrated, it is easy to see how the excited woman would break it off, not stopping to unseal the top, releasing all the perfume at once, so that 'the house was filled with the fragrance of the perfume' (John's Gospel 12:3).

Cheap perfume and oils were kept in small pottery flasks. These examples made in the first centuries BC and AD come from the Jerusalem area and Petra.

These glass perfume flasks were laid in tombs of the first century on the edge of the Valley of Hinnom.

DAILY LIFE

In 132 Jewish patriots began the Second Revolt against Roman rule. After three years they were crushed, and the Emperor Hadrian rebuilt Jerusalem as a Roman city (named Aelia Capitolina) which no Jew was allowed to enter. Caves in remote valleys by the Dead Sea were the last hiding-places for some of the rebels. Israeli explorers found their bones and many of their personal possessions in the caves. The very dry atmosphere had preserved them in excellent condition. People living in Palestine a hundred years earlier used similar things, as discoveries at Masada show.

'After me,' said John the Baptist, 'will come one the thongs of whose sandals I am not worthy to stoop down and untie' (Mark 1:7). 'Wear sandals, but not an extra tunic,' Jesus told his disciples when he sent them out to preach in the country (Mark 6:9). The upper sandal was fastened with a sliding knot, others were tied.

The dry heat at the top of Masada stopped pieces of clothing left in the ruins from rotting away. The blue stripe in this scrap suggested to the excavator, Professor Yigael Yadin, that he had found a prayer shawl (tallith) worn by one of the devout Jewish rebels who held Herod's fortress against the Romans until AD 73.

'No one puts new wine into old wineskins' (Mark 2:22). As skin-bottles grew old, the leather became hard and would not expand with the fermenting new wine. This sheepskin water-bottle was carefully sewn up, the front legs tied together as a carrying handle.

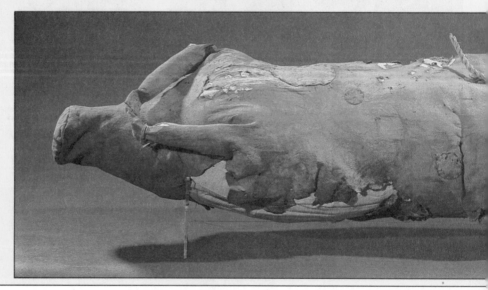

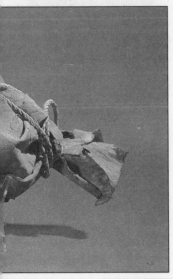

Pottery, bronze and wooden vessels, a wooden spoon and an iron knife with a wooden handle were left in the caves by the rebels. They are good examples of the ordinary kitchenware of a Jewish housewife.

The Jewish refugees took these keys with them to the caves where they hid, hoping to keep their homes and possessions safe against thieves.

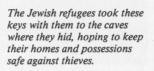

CLEANLINESS IS NEXT TO GODLINESS?

'They don't wash their hands before they eat.'

Many parents may say that about their children today: the Jewish religious leaders said the same thing to Jesus about his disciples. Cleanliness was one of the most important things for religious Jews in New Testament times. It mattered, not simply for health but because anyone who was ritually unclean could not approach God.

The need to avoid uncleanness had led to a great many regulations endeavouring to stop people breaking any of God's commands in the laws of Moses. They had all sorts of results which made life difficult for ordinary men and women who wanted to please God. Eating with un-washed hands made the food unclean, and so the eater became unclean. He would then have to immerse himself in a bath to become clean again. The same thing was required if a man went to the market and touched someone who was not a Jew. On returning home he would have to immerse himself to become clean again.

In recent years archaeology has dis-covered how carefully these rules were obeyed in the first century. Ritual baths have been uncovered in the houses of the rich citizens in Jerusalem as well as in the ruined community

centre at Qumran—and even among the build-ings of the religious nationalists, the Zealots, who occupied King Herod's fortress on the top of Masada in the Judean desert.

Often the baths are quite small, designed so that a person could step down and squat under the water. Some are larger, to display the owner's wealth, or for public use. They may have two doorways with a partition down the steps so that the unclean entered at one side and left, clean, at the other. In every case, care was taken to make sure that rainwater or water from a stream was fed into the pool; water brought entirely in buckets or jars was not satisfactory.

Cleanliness applied to furniture and household utensils, too. They could become unclean in all sorts of ways, developed from the laws in Leviticus, chapter 11. Washing completely in pure water would cleanse them, except in the case of pottery vessels. Most pottery in ancient times was earthenware, so it absorbed a little of any liquid put in it. Therefore it could not be thoroughly cleaned: so, if its contents became unclean, it had to be broken. Metal pots and pans overcame that difficulty, but they were always expensive.

Discoveries in Jerusalem reveal another way of avoiding the need

constantly to replace kitchenware: the production of cups, bowls, jars and trays from the soft limestone of the Judean hills. Stone containers needed washing only if they became unclean. So many examples have been found in Jerusalem that it is clear there was an industry devoted to making them. The best quality pieces were turned on a lathe, beautifully smoothed inside, cut and polished with simple decoration outside. More roughly cut jugs and measuring-cups were kept for kitchen use.

From these discoveries it is easy to see what lies behind various verses in the Gospels. The six large stone jars in the house at Cana where Jesus went for a wedding feast are described as 'the kind used by the Jews for ceremonial washing' (John's Gospel 2:6), and large quantities of water would be needed in order to follow the regulations at a banquet (see *Stone Water Jars*). Mark, relating the

Pharisees' complaint about Jesus' disciples, had to explain for the sake of his non-Jewish readers:

'The Pharisees and all the Jews do not eat unless they give their hands a ceremonial washing, holding to the tradition of the elders. When they come from the market-place they do not eat unless they wash. And they observe many other traditions, such as the washing of cups, pitchers and kettles.'

Jesus answered the complaint quite harshly because, he said, the religious leaders had become so insistent on people obeying all these regulations that they forgot their real purpose. They even invented ways to avoid their effect. What is vital, Jesus said, is the state of the person himself. 'Nothing that enters a man from the outside can make him ''unclean''.' Rather, 'what comes out of a man is what makes him ''unclean''' (Mark's Gospel, chapter 7).

Stone jugs, bowls and dishes were widely used in Jerusalem. They could be washed and used again if they became ritually unclean, but earthenware pots had to be broken.

Wherever religious Jews lived in first-century Palestine they built baths for ritual washing. Many were found in Jerusalem; this carefully plastered example is at Qumran by the Dead Sea.

STONE WATER JARS

At the wedding in Cana there were 'six stone water jars, the kind used by the Jews for ceremonial washing, each holding from twenty to thirty gallons' (John 2:6). The servants filled them with water, and when they drew some of it, and the host tasted it, it was wine!

Excavators have found several stone jars in the ruined houses of first-century Jerusalem. At least six of them stood in the basement kitchen rooms of the 'Burnt House'. They are 65–80 cm/2–2½ feet tall, each cut from a block of stone that could weigh as much as half a ton. They were shaped and finished on a very big lathe, given a pedestal foot and simple decoration. Such stone jars would hold large quantities of water for washing and kitchen needs—up to 80 litres/17 gallons. Flat discs of stone served as lids. The jars at Cana may have been similar to these.

Large stone jars were used for storing liquids. Many were found crushed in the houses of Jerusalem, and have been reconstructed.

CAPERNAUM

Ruins of a fine white stone synagogue were found at Capernaum in 1905. Later the Franciscan owners partly rebuilt them. This synagogue was erected late in the fourth century and was richly decorated with carved stonework. Inside the synagogue the stone step seating can be seen along the walls.

Underneath the white synagogue's walls, archaeologists have found parts of an earlier building of black basalt stone. This was apparently in use in the first century, and so may be the synagogue a centurion gave to the town (Luke 7:4,5). The walls are not well-preserved, so it is not judged worthwhile to remove the later remains in order to uncover them.

Excavations between the synagogue and the shore of Lake Galilee have uncovered several blocks of small stone houses. They were part of the fishing town which flourished from the first century BC to the sixth century AD. Although they were altered over the years, their basic plan did not change. A door led from the street into a paved courtyard and various rooms opened from that, some leading to other rooms. Stone pillars helped to hold up the flat roofs, and there were stone steps to climb up onto the roofs.

Some of the houses had a row of low arches in place of a solid wall. Perhaps these were to let in light or air, or maybe they were entries to animals' byres or to stores.

In the fifth century an octagonal church was built between the synagogue and the Lake. This had been a special place for Christians for a long time. Excavations reveal that the church stood on one of the houses, preserving a central room. The walls of the room had been plastered and visitors coming to it before the church was put up had scratched prayers naming Jesus on the plaster. This was the house, those early Christians plainly believed, where Peter lived —possibly the room where Jesus cured Peter's mother-in-law, or where he had lived.

THE 'JESUS BOAT'

A picture of a small sailing boat was worked into a mosaic pavement at Magdala, early in the Roman period.

There was a drought in Israel in 1985. With little rain, farmers needed more water for their crops. The Israeli water system draws heavily from Lake Galilee, and so more water than usual was drained from it. At the same time, less water than usual flowed into it. As a result the level of the Lake fell. This was bad for the ecology and, if it should happen often, would put the country's irrigation system at risk. But one benefit came from it: the timbers of an old boat appeared, and it was excavated.

The timbers had survived, sunk in the mud beneath the water for centuries. They were black and water-logged, but still kept their shape. After the boat sank, the movement of the water and the anchors of other boats damaged the upper part, so that only the hull remains in good condition. It is 8.2 metres/26.9 feet long and 2.35 metres/ 7.7 feet wide.

Its planks do not overlap in the familiar clinker-built style of many European fishing and small sailing boats: they butt against each other (a style called carvel building). Roman boats, preserved in places spread across the Empire, show that this was the common method at that time. Mortice and tenon joints hold the planks of cedar and oak together. To make the shape of the boat, a series of ribs were laid across the planks, curving from the upper edges to the centre. They do not continue round from one side to the other, as in modern boats. Study of the boat and preservation of the wood will take several years, and full publication will make more details available. Meanwhile, it is kept at Ginosar on the shore of the Lake, north of Tiberias.

What was this ancient boat?

Its style, and objects found with it—a cooking-pot and a lamp—point to an age of about 2,000 years. The 'carbon 14' test applied to the wood gave the same age. Journalists were quick to name it the 'Jesus boat' or 'Peter's boat'. Certainly the boat belongs to the Gospel period, or very close to it.

One suggestion links the boat to the war against Rome. In AD 67 Roman soldiers overran the town of Magdala and sank their boats in the Lake. This could be one of them, for Magdala was the nearest place to the shore where it was found.

Of course, there is no way to prove any connection between it and the Gospel characters. Only a name painted or carved on the side, 'Zebedee and Sons', could do that! Like so many more discoveries, the boat from Galilee's waters allow us to see what something the Gospels mention was like, and to picture the events they record more vividly.

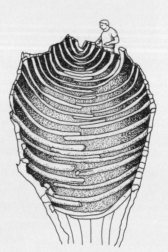

This drawing, made from a photograph, shows the construction and scale of a boat dating from the time of Jesus. The waterlogged vessel was taken with great care from Lake Galilee and each part carefully identified.

A TOWN THE ROMANS CONQUERED

East of Lake Galilee the Golan Heights rise sharply from the shore. In winter and spring, water from rain and melting snow rushes down into the Lake, and over thousands of years the water has cut steep-sided valleys for its course. About 11 km/7 miles to the north-east of the shore is a place where five of these valleys meet at an acute angle. There a promontory stands up, precipitous on one side and sloping heavily on the other. The ridge has a humped outline when seen from the side, joined by a long narrow rock to the Golan plateau at the east. This hill has a good defensive position, and it commands a view directly down the valley to the edge of the Lake, to Bethsaida and Capernaum.

An Israeli explorer went surveying in the hills after they had been seized from Syria during the 1967 war. He found ruins of stone buildings on the sloping side of the promontory. Broken pottery lying among them showed that people had been living there in the first century AD. Round stones the size of a baseball looked like the missiles shot by Roman siege-engines.

What was this place?

Archaeologists often have a problem in identifying the places they discover. In ancient times towns did not usually have convenient signs at the roadside to identify them. Only under the Roman Empire were milestones put along the main roads to help travellers. Anyone arriving at a town would ask where they were. The archaeologist has no one to ask, so he has to search among the records that

survive to see if they give any help.

In this case the explorer's reading suggested the answer. Apart from the New Testament, the only Jewish history-writing to come down to us from the first century AD is the work of Josephus (see *Josephus the Jew*).

Describing the war against Rome of AD 67–70, Josephus tells of a town called Gamla whose citizens defied the Roman army. He knew the place because he himself had built some of the defences at the start of the revolt. The story of its capture is best read in his own words.

'The houses were built against the steep mountain slopes, astonishingly huddled together, one on top of another, and the town seemed to be hung in mid-air.'

When Vespasian arrived he saw that the town could not be surrounded, so he set his legions to begin the siege from the eastern neck. Soon the Roman equipment was in position and the defenders were hard pressed.

'Their leaders encouraged them and led them to the walls. For a while they kept at bay those who were bringing up the siege machines, but the first of the catapults and stone-throwers drove them back. Then the Romans brought battering-rams against these different points and broke through the city wall. With trumpets sounding, the clash of arms, and battle-cries, they poured through and closed with the defenders. At first those in the city held their ground and checked their advance. But the Romans were too many, so the men of Gamla fled to the higher parts of the town where they could push the Romans down the uneven slopes. The Romans were unable to drive back the enemy above them and they could not force their way back through their own ranks pressing on from behind, so they took refuge on the roofs of the enemy's houses. Crowded with soldiers, and not made for such weights, the roofs soon fell in. As one fell it brought down several others below it, and they in turn, carried away those lower down. In this way a lot of Romans were killed because they had nowhere else to turn and went on leaping on to the roofs, although they saw the houses collapsing. The ruins buried many, some were pinned down while trying to escape, and more died choked by the dust.'

Harassed by the citizens, the Romans withdrew. Such a disaster was bad for Roman morale. Vespasian

spoke to his troops to give them fresh courage. Some of them then undermined one of the towers, causing confusion among the people. The Romans pressed in, driving the defenders to the high part of the town. There they threw whatever they could at the Romans, but the wind was against them, deflecting their arrows.

Led by Vespasian in person, 'the Romans mounted the crest and quickly surrounded and killed them. Hemmed in on every side, despairing of their lives, many threw themselves headlong with their wives and children into the ravine which had been dug deep below the citadel.' In fact, more died in that way than at the hands of the Romans. Gamla was left empty; nobody returned to live there again.

The sloping site of the hill northeast of Galilee and its humped shape made it a prime candidate for

identification as ancient Gamla, although there is no definite proof. The name Gamla means 'camel(-town)' and the hill looks like a camel's hump. Excavations began on the hillside in 1976. Running up the slope facing the neck of the peninsula is the hint of a town hall. At one point a gateway leads through it. Within the town are ruins of streets and houses, all built of dark grey basalt stones from the hills, and standing one below another on the slope of the hill, as Josephus described.

The walls against the hillside still stand several feet high; others have tumbled down the slope. Small copper coins found in the ruins show that the town was occupied in the first century BC and the first century AD. The pottery belongs to the same period. Everything points to the place coming to a sudden end. Iron arrowheads lay in the gateway and in other buildings. Some of them have bent points, the result of hitting the hard stone walls. Many of them had evidently been shot into the town by enemies outside the wall.

Arrowheads were not the only missiles that came hurtling in. Scores of stone balls were strewn among the ruins. They were lumps of basalt from baseball size upwards to some half a metre/20 ins diameter, chipped and hammered into shape. These were surely the balls shot by Roman catapults!

Everything agrees with Josephus' description of Gamla and its fate. There can be little doubt, with the evidence of its violent end, that this is the site of that town. It is, naturally, a poignant place for anyone of Jewish descent to visit. It is also of great interest for the study of New Testament times. Here is a town, here are the houses, where people lived who saw and heard Jesus as he moved across the hills of Galilee.

The town of Gamla, devastated by the Romans, was abandoned in the first century AD. This steeply sloping hill north-east of Lake Galilee (which can be seen in the distance) seems the most likely site. Excavation began in 1976.

A SYNAGOGUE OF JESUS' DAY

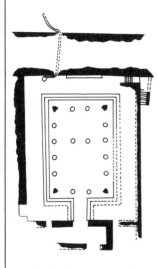

A plan of the synagogue at Gamla, based on the plan from S. Guttman in L.I. Levine, Ancient Synagogues Revealed, *Israel Exploration Society, Jerusalem, 1981.*

One of the first buildings the excavators uncovered in Gamla was an unusual one. It was clearly not a house. A porch led into a pillared hall some 20 metres/65½ feet long. Four rows of stone steps, each about 50 cm/ 19 ins high, ran from the doorway along either side. At the far end they joined a similar row of four steps. A space almost 2.4 metres/8 feet wide separated the walls from the edge of the top step. Stone pillars placed at intervals round the central area held up the roof. The tops of these pillars were carved with geometric designs, and the pillars at the corners were not round but heart-shaped in cross-section. Along the foot of the rows of steps the floor was paved, but in the centre it was simply bare earth. This building was set along the slope of the hill, so one side stood on a terrace high above the street. Here a flight of steps led up into the back corner of the hall.

The ruins showed that this building had been taken over in the siege by the defenders. They had built fires in it for cooking their meals. The reason for that is clear. The east end buts on to the town wall, and just to the north is a gateway through the wall. It was obviously an important position. Further signs of that were the numbers of stone catapult balls and iron arrowheads lying about, especially at the eastern end, where the attack had come. When the town fell, this building caught fire. Iron nails from the roof beams lay in the burnt debris.

In a Jewish town, what could such a building be? There was one obvious answer: a synagogue. If that is the right answer, the ruins of Gamla have yielded the oldest synagogue so far found in Palestine. The New Testament and the books of Josephus tell us that there were synagogues in the towns of the first century, so it was to be expected that remains of one might eventually be uncovered. Yet how can anyone be sure it is a synagogue? Without an inscription no one can be certain, and it is unlikely, in a Jewish town, that there would be a notice on it. (In Corinth a stone was found cut with Greek letters forming parts of the words 'Synagogue of the Jews'.) However, there are two good reasons for identifying the Gamla ruin as a synagogue.

First, the plan of the building is almost the same as the plans of buildings uncovered at other places around Galilee. These date from the third century AD and later, and they were certainly synagogues. In some of them were Hebrew and Aramaic inscriptions recording the gifts prosperous men made for parts of the structures, or their decoration. Words like 'this holy place', and the prayers included, show beyond doubt that these buildings were synagogues. Indeed, it is hard to think of any other use for such halls in Jewish communities. Some of them have heart-shaped columns in the corners like those at Gamla. Examples can easily be seen in the famous ruins at Capernaum.

The second reason for calling the building in Gamla a synagogue is the discovery of what are likely to be two more synagogues of the first century

The ruined hall beside the town wall of Gamla is probably the only synagogue of Jesus' time yet found near Galilee.

AD. Both lie south of Jerusalem, far from Galilee. They were not purpose-built; the Zealots and other Jewish rebels converted parts of other buildings during the revolt against Rome.

In King Herod's fortress and burial-place at Herodium, 6 km/3½ miles south-east of Bethlehem, the Zealots altered the dining-room, a hall 15 metres/49 feet × 5 metres/34 feet. They took stones from other rooms to construct a platform along three sides, with two steps at the inner edge, making benches. A pillar was set at each corner of the floor to hold up the roof. Just outside the doorway a ritual bath was carefully made in a small room. These features together suggest that this room served as a synagogue, although they cannot prove it.

The second building is in King Herod's amazing fortress on top of the isolated rock of Masada beside the Dead Sea (see *Masada—the Last Stronghold*). Herod's architects had designed a double wall to run along the edge of the mountain-top, with guard-chambers and store-rooms built between the walls. One of these rooms in the north-west sector projected inwards from the line of the wall.

When Professor Yigael Yadin's volunteers cleared away the sand and rubble they found a room with four tiers of plastered benches around its sides, and places for pillars in the middle of the room. It was nearly the same size as the hall at Herodium, about 15 metres/50 feet × 12 metres/40 feet. Was this a synagogue? The excavators hardly dared express their hopes. Had they found the place where the last of the Zealots to stand against the Romans had prayed and read the Holy Scriptures?

In one corner a small room had been built, but its purpose is not clear. Careful digging revealed a pit dug through the floor. At the bottom of it was a piece of dry, rolled-up leather. Not far away, patient work traced the edges of another pit. At the bottom of it lay part of another scroll. As soon as the dust was blown off, eager eyes read familiar words from the Book of Ezekiel, chapter 37, the vision of the valley of dry bones! The first piece had to be unrolled in a laboratory. When it was open its words were clear: it contained the last part of the Book of Deuteronomy. Finding two books of the Bible might point to a sacred place, but pieces of others came to light in other parts of the fortress, so they do not by themselves prove that this room was part of a synagogue.

It is all the evidence taken together which points to the conclusion that the bench-lined halls at Masada and Herodium were synagogues. In both cases they were obviously so important to the rebels fighting the Romans that they were prepared to build these clearly non-military structures inside their strongholds. Knowing that the rebels were intensely religious makes the synagogue interpretation all the more plausible.

The likeness of the Gamla building to these halls strengthens the case for identifying this one too as a synagogue. It also makes sense of some of the other features found. Outside the porch was a cistern cut in the rock, carefully plastered, and entered by a few steps, set in a convenient place for the worshippers to wash before going to pray. In the building itself, by the north-west corner, was a recess in the wall. This could be a cupboard for the scrolls of the Scriptures. Across the central floor was a line of paving-stones with a pillar at each end. The excavators think this was the place where a reading-desk stood.

Here then, surely, was a synagogue used by people who were among the crowds listening to Jesus at the lakeside. Gamla's synagogue is the only one of the first century near Galilee. Were others in the area like it? No one can be sure. However, the fact that some of the later synagogues there were similar in many ways suggests that they were. Given that no one can be certain, we may use the Gamla ruins to build a picture of the synagogues Jesus knew.

Luke's Gospel describes him going to the synagogue at Nazareth 'on the Sabbath day, as was his custom'. Citizens of Nazareth had walked along the streets, some pausing to wash at a pool, to the doorway of their prayer hall. Entering, they climbed the steps and walked along to find a place to sit. Men and women may have had separate sections, that is not clear. They sat in rows along the steps, leaving the central area empty. The floor there was probably covered with rugs, giving a splash of colour. Men wore prayer shawls, white, some with long fringes (see Matthew's Gospel 23:5).

When everyone was seated, the leader could begin the service. An important moment was the reading of the Bible lessons. The scrolls of the Law and the Prophets would be brought respectfully from their ark or cupboard, carried through the congregation and laid on the reading-desk in the centre. On that occasion in Nazareth Jesus was reading the second lesson, from Isaiah's prophecy. The Dead Sea Scrolls show us the sort of book he read from (see *The Bible of Jesus' Time*).

The discovery at Gamla helps us to imagine more clearly the setting in which Jesus began his teaching, and the synagogue from which he was expelled.

THE BIBLE OF JESUS' TIME

Jesus 'went to Nazareth . . . and on the Sabbath day he went into the synagogue, as was his custom. And he stood up to read. The scroll of the prophet Isaiah was handed to him. Unrolling it, he found the place . . .' (Luke 4:16,17).

What was it like, that scroll from which Jesus read? Scrolls read in synagogues today are big and bulky. Judging by the Dead Sea Scrolls they were rather smaller in the first century. One of the first of those scrolls to come to light happened to be a copy of Isaiah. It is also the only biblical scroll found complete (see *A Treasure from Buried Books*). If the synagogue in Nazareth owned a similar one, it would have been about 7.5 metres/24½ feet long, and 26 cm/10 ins high. Seventeen leather sheets were sewn side by side to make the roll, and on them were fifty-four columns, each with 29 to 32 lines of writing: 1633 lines in all. The reader held the book and unrolled it with his left hand, taking the outer edge in his right and rolling it again as he read, column by column. To reach Isaiah 61, the chapter he read in the synagogue, Jesus would have unrolled most of the scroll and re-rolled it again.

The dozens of copies of Old Testament books found among the Dead Sea Scrolls suggest that it was not hard to obtain a biblical scroll in first-century Palestine. Of course, the Scrolls belonged to a very devout Bible-reading community, and in a country town like Nazareth probably only a very few people had the leisure to read, or owned any Bible scrolls themselves. Even so, books were not expensive. Calculations put the time needed to copy a long work like Isaiah at almost three days, so its price had to cover three days' wages for a scribe, and the cost of materials.

This is in line with the price of one and a half to two and a half denarii for a cheap copy of a papyrus scroll, unlikely to be as long as Isaiah, which the poet Martial quoted in Rome later in the first century. In second-century Egypt, the cost of copying 1,000 lines of Greek was two denarii. A working man determined to buy a copy of Isaiah would expect to pay three or four days' wages for it. To own a complete Old Testament would cost a lot more, and would mean not a single book but a pile of scrolls.

By the time Jesus read from Isaiah's prophecy in the synagogue at Nazareth, this copy of Isaiah was over 100 years old. It had been read over and over again and repaired where it had torn. Where the copyist missed out some words by mistake, they were inserted afterwards, running down the margin where the space on the line was too short. The join between two sheets of leather is visible to the left. The photograph is of Dead Sea Scroll Isaiah A (the original is in the Shrine of the Book, Jerusalem).

THE LANGUAGES THEY SPOKE

Talitha kumi, ephphatha, abba are all words in Aramaic, the language of Jesus reported in the Gospels. In the days of the Old Testament prophets the Jews spoke Hebrew. When they went as exiles to Babylon, in 586 BC, Aramaic was normal there, and they began to speak it themselves. Aramaic is a sister language to Hebrew and was spoken in Syria. Trade and Assyrian deportations spread it across the Near East and it became important as the administrative language of the Persian Empire. Although Greek invaded the same area (see below), Aramaic remained the speech of most ordinary people.

Those words in the Gospels are important relics of first-century Palestinian Aramaic. Scholars wanting to reconstruct the sayings of Jesus as the disciples might have heard them, had hardly anything else from his time. They had to work back from the phraseology of Jewish and Christian books of the third to seventh centuries, which made their studies

Alexander Jannaeus, the Jewish king who ruled 103–76 BC, struck coins with his name in Greek on one side and Hebrew on the other.

less than satisfactory.

With the discovery of the Dead Sea Scrolls the situation has changed. They include books, or fragments of books written in Aramaic in the first century BC and up to AD 67. Their language lies between the language of the Persian Empire and that known from the third century AD onwards. Among the scrolls are paraphrases of Old Testament books, including some like the later Targums, and several apocryphal and visionary compositions. These all have a formal, literary flavour. Scribblings and notes on pottery vessels, and especially the notices scratched on ossuaries, add examples of the languages in daily use.

If Aramaic was the common language, what was the role of Greek? Alexander the Great's

campaigns left Greek generals ruling and Greek soldiers settled all across the region, so Greek replaced Aramaic as the language of government. Coins minted in Syria, Babylonia, Persia and further east carry rulers' names in Greek. The same was true in Judea. When the Hasmonean priest-kings started to issue their small copper coins, they had their names and titles stamped on them in Greek on one side.

Inscriptions in Greek were set up in Jerusalem to commemorate generous gifts to the Temple. There were also notices in Greek intended for foreign visitors (such as the Theodotos inscription and the 'Forbidding Stone', see *Temple Tourists* and *Herod's Great Temple*).

Again, names or descriptions of contents scratched or painted on

pots and pans, and ossuary texts, show that Greek was not limited to the ruling class. Among the Dead Sea Scrolls are pieces of books in Greek, biblical translations and others, demonstrating that some religious Jews read their sacred literature in that language in first-century Palestine. In the course of their daily duties the Roman governors certainly spoke Greek, and Jesus may have answered Pilate's questions at his trial in Greek.

Josephus recorded the display of warning signs in Latin beside the Greek ones in the Temple. Latin was the formal language of Roman rule, and of military command. (Papyri written in Latin were left at Masada by Roman soldiers.) The priestly authorities would be concerned that Roman officials and their staff should be alerted to the rule forbidding entry to the sacred area. Pilate's inscription in Caesarea is engraved in Latin (see *Pilate's Own Monument*).

Pilate wrote the title for Jesus' cross—'Jesus of Nazareth, the King of the

This inscription in Aramaic, from an ossuary, states that these were the bones of 'Simon the builder of the temple'.

אלהנבנ ו ימ ס

The Greek writing on this ossuary includes the names Joseph and Mary.

Jews'—in three languages: the local language, Aramaic; the official language, Latin; and the common language, Greek.

Aramaic, Greek, Latin . . . was Hebrew spoken, too? For years scholars believed not, or that it was restricted to religious circles, synagogue readings and prayers, and the Temple. Counting in favour of a wider knowledge is the presence of Hebrew inscriptions on the other side of Hasmonean coins. That might mean no more than Latin legends on coins of recent times—a grand style which the educated could understand.

However, recent discoveries have thrown new light on the question. Books in a style of Hebrew imitating the Old Testament yet distinct from it, and some in Hebrew more like that of the Mishnah (see *Jewish Writings*) make up a large section of the Dead Sea Scrolls. They could be dismissed as the products of a religious sect had not other documents been found with them, and in other caves, which come from secular life.

There are letters and legal deeds, admittedly of slightly later date, connected with the revolt of Bar Kochba (AD 132–35). This false Messiah had letters written in Hebrew, Aramaic and Greek. From first-century houses in Jerusalem, from Herod's castles (Herodium and Masada), and from other places have come pots with Hebrew words or names painted on them. There are ossuaries, too, with labels which are clearly Hebrew.

Within each of these languages there were dialects, hard to trace now, plain to those who heard them. Matthew 26 records the serving girl's recognition of Peter's Galilean accent in the High Priest's house. The language used by peasants and by the uneducated workmen was Aramaic. Hebrew was probably taught in synagogue schools everywhere and spoken in some places near Jerusalem, by religious zealots and by nationalists. Except for those in the remotest villages, craftsmen, businessmen and traders would have learnt enough Greek for commercial purposes at least. A Jewish craftsman's son brought up in Nazareth, a town on a main road, could be expected to talk in Aramaic, to use Greek when necessary, and to have more than a reading knowledge of Hebrew.

SMALL IS BEAUTIFUL

A sharp-eyed bedouin picked up this tiny leather packet in the Qumran area. It is a first-century head phylactery. When it was unstitched, it opened to reveal four tiny parcels tied with hair. Both pictures are actual size.

Each of the parcels in the leather packet is a piece of very thin skin containing verses from Exodus and Deuteronomy in minute writing (actual size).

Most people would not have noticed the tiny blackened object. To the sharp-eyed bedouin, hunting for treasure in the caves by the Dead Sea, it was something that they might be able to sell. They were used to finding pieces of old leather scrolls (see *A Treasure from Buried Books*): this was a tiny leather package. Presently they took it to their agent, and it found its way to the shop of an antiquities dealer in Jerusalem. In January 1968 the dealer sold it to Yigael Yadin, then Professor of Archaeology at the Hebrew University. He knew what he had bought, a fascinating antiquity which he set about studying and described in detail in a book published the next year.

The package is a piece of leather, folded in half and sewn together along three sides. It is tiny, 20 mm/0.79 in. long and 13 mm/0.51 in. wide. When it was unsewn, it opened to reveal four minute parcels, tied with hair, each lying in a hollow in the leather. To unwrap these was a delicate task. They proved to be folded pieces of very thin parchment, with lines of very small writing on one side. The largest piece is 2.7 cm/1.06 ins and 44 mm/1.73 ins wide, and carries twenty-six lines of writing. The letters are about 0.5 mm/0.02 in. high.

Although no one was ever expected to read them, a scribe had copied on to these sheets passages from the books of Exodus and Deuteronomy.

Several more tiny sheets were found among the Dead Sea Scrolls. There are also a dozen or so more of the leather packages, but none of them is as well

preserved as the one Yadin bought. All of them are about the same size.

Four times in the 'Law of Moses' a command comes to the Israelites from God: 'Fix these words of mine in your hearts and minds; tie them as symbols on your hands and bind them on your foreheads' (Exodus 13:9,16; Deuteronomy 6:8; 11:18). How should Jews who wanted to obey the Law put this command into effect? Perhaps it was not meant to be taken literally, but many Jews thought it should be.

At least as early as the second century BC devout men had the words of these commands written on slips of parchment to tie on to themselves as reminders of God's Law. By the first century AD this was a custom for religious men. Later, the rabbis laid down rules about them which are still in force today. One package is tied inside the left arm, above the elbow, where it is nearest to the heart. In it is a single piece of parchment with the texts of Exodus 13:1–10, 11–16 and Deuteronomy 6:4–9; 11:13–21. To the forehead is bound a package with four sheets inside, containing the same texts.

Nowadays these are worn for morning prayers, except on the Sabbath and holy days. In the first century it is possible they were worn more often, even all day. Certainly there were some variations in the texts included, although it is not clear if these were definite patterns. The men who wore them would hardly be likely to know exactly which texts were inside, unless they were scribes who made their own. At Qumran we find that a scribe added the Ten Commandments in Deuteronomy 5:1–21 and the following verses 22–33, and several other sections.

The Hebrew name for these packages is *tefillin*, which seems to mean 'prayers'. In the New Testament a Greek word is used for them which has passed into English as 'phylactery'. This word meant a safeguard or an amulet, and it is easy to see how other peoples could think that what the Jews wore were amulets just like theirs. Everywhere in ancient times men and women wore amulets and charms to protect them from accidents and disease, from evil and misfortune, much as they do today. Sacred words engraved on metal or written on parchment supposedly have special value. It is not surprising, therefore, to learn from rabbinic writings that some Jews did treat their phylacteries in the same way. However, their real purpose was clearly to remind their wearers of God's Law.

That is how 'the teachers of the Law and the Pharisees' used them in Jesus' time, undoubtedly. Jesus condemned those religious leaders, not for wearing their phylacteries but for making them wide (Matthew 23:5). Until the example from Qumran came to light, it was hard to envisage what was meant. Now it is clear that some phylacteries were so small that they would hardly be visible on the wearer from a distance. These specimens from Gospel times would surely have won Jesus' approval. Smaller ones can hardly be imagined. By contrast, phylacteries of recent times may be three times as large, with heavy straps to hold them in place. Jesus' teaching is plain: religious duties are to be done without display or fuss. It is not a person's apparent piety which pleases God, but the faithful and humble spirit.

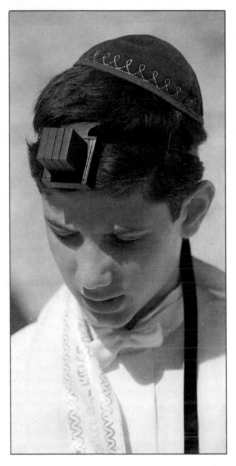

Whereas the first-century phylacteries found near the Dead Sea would have been hardly visible on the wearer's head, modern phylacteries are very obvious.

GEHENNA—'THE EVERLASTING BONFIRE'

Wherever people live they leave rubbish. When they live in towns or cities they have to find a place to dump it. Today you can see piles of refuse outside some towns, whereas at other places it is buried in the ground. Ancient people had the same problem of waste disposal as we do. If a river or the sea ran by the town, it was easy to throw things into the water. If not, heaps of rubbish would build up outside the city wall, or in a convenient ditch. Sensible citizens would make sure they tipped their rubbish where the wind would not carry the smell across their houses.

Archaeologists are often glad to find the rubbish heaps of an ancient town. Ruined houses may have very little left in them, if the owners moved out peacefully. Much more can be discovered about their life-style from the things they threw away. Broken pots, worn-out metalware, pieces of glass, lost coins, waste paper, lie in the soil made by rotting food, decayed clothing, old woodwork and the sweepings of streets and houses. Dead animals might be thrown on a rubbish heap, too, and even, in many places, unwanted children. (The habit of leaving babies exposed to die in this way was accepted in Babylonia, Greece, and Rome. It only ended as the spread of Christianity brought a new appreciation of the value of the individual life. Kind-hearted or childless couples sometimes rescued and adopted exposed babies.) Digging through the layers of a tip can reveal evidence from all types of rubbish, if the earth is carefully analysed for bones, traces of pollen and other organic remains.

The positions of some cities, and their climates, made it unhygienic to leave the refuse rotting in a heap, so it was set on fire. Heat destroyed some of the dangerous by-products of decay (although ancient people did not understand that), and reduced the size of the tip.

The people who lived in houses on the rocky hills of Jerusalem had no river to wash away their rubbish, so they dumped it. At the south of the city, running to the west, is a steep-sided valley which was probably the site of their refuse tip. There they could dump what they did not want, possibly throwing it over the edge of the valley, and set it on fire. Even if flames were not always shooting out, the piles of rubbish would always be smoking and smouldering. Much of what was not burnt, or would not burn, gradually decomposed, as worms and insects gnawed and burrowed, or corrosion and rust ate into it.

That valley was named the Valley of the Sons of Hinnom, or just the

The Valley of Hinnom was Jerusalem's ancient refuse tip.

Valley of Hinnom, in Old Testament times. There Jews who turned to foreign religions performed horrible ceremonies, burning their children in honour of pagan gods (see Jeremiah 7:30,31). In the first century it was the fires of burning refuse that lit the valley. By that time its name had been put into Aramaic as Gehenna, and had become a common Jewish word for hell.

Knowing this, some of Jesus' words strike the modern reader with greater force, as they would have hit their first hearers. He told his followers, 'Anyone who says, "You fool!" will be in danger of the fire of [gehenna]' (Matthew 5:22). And he warned them, 'If your eye causes you to sin, pluck it out. It is better for you to enter the kingdom of God with one eye than to have two eyes and be thrown into

[gehenna], where "their worm does not die, and the fire is not quenched"' (Mark 9:47,48, quoting Isaiah 66:24). Take care, he was saying, that you don't end up on God's rubbish tip!

That was the danger for some of the Pharisees, with their self-righteous stress on the particular details of the laws they had multiplied, contrary to God's intention (see Matthew 23:15,33). It is the danger anyone faces, Jesus taught, who rejects God's way and lives for his own self-satisfaction. The parable of the rich man and Lazarus, recorded in Luke 16, illustrates his point. The rich man has ignored the needs of the poor all his life, and after death it is too late. Tortured by the searing flames he begs in vain for a sip of cooling water.

RULERS OF THE LAND

The country of Palestine, where Jesus and his friends lived, presents a peculiar political picture. There were Jewish kings, then a Roman governor in Jerusalem. The Roman Emperor demanded taxes, and foreign soldiers enforced the law. Learning about the political background makes parts of the Gospel story easier to understand. Archaeological discoveries illuminate the history told by Josephus and other ancient writers.

This head of Augustus in glass is 4.9 cm/1.9 ins high. It is an idealized portrait of the emperor at the beginning of his rule, although it was probably made soon after his death in AD 14.

PEACE AT LAST

Peace, peace at last! For thirty years the people of Palestine had been free from foreign invasion and murderous civil war. A whole generation had grown up without the fear of hundreds of soldiers suddenly seizing their goods and burning and killing, or of flight to the hills and caves while their homes were ruined. Peace meant better food, more time for family life, easier travel, meeting for religious festivals, prosperity and contentment.

That was the picture when Jesus was born in Bethlehem about 6 BC. His grandfather, or his elderly uncle, the priest Zechariah (John the Baptist's father), could have told him of the hardships they had lived through: the brothers raising forces to fight each other for the High Priest's crown; Pompey's invasion; Jerusalem besieged and taken again and again, and squads of soliders enforcing the payment of Roman taxes (see *Caesar's Image*).

In 40 BC armies had come from the east, from Parthia (Iraq and Iran). Bribed by a would-be High Priest-King they marched on Jerusalem and captured it, looting everywhere. Roman power drove the Parthians out of Syria and Roman support in the end helped prince Herod conquer Palestine. He, too, laid siege to Jerusalem, gaining control in 37 BC only after many weeks of battering and fighting.

Since then, peace had reigned, but at a price, for peace is never free! The price was the rule of King Herod, nearly over when Jesus was born.

What had been happening in Palestine? How did the Romans gain control? Who was Herod? And how did he become king of the Jews?

Fighting for the crown

'I want it!' 'You can't have it; it's mine!' The two brothers fought and squabbled. When they were children their mother had intervened. Now she was dead, and they were fighting over their inheritance. The mother in question was Salome Alexandra. When her husband, the Jewish King Alexander Jannaeus, died in 76 BC she took over the rule of Judea. She could be queen, but she could not follow her husband as High Priest, so she had her elder son Hyrcanus put in that position. By right he should have become king, too, when Salome died in 67 BC, but his jealous brother, Aristobulus, was challenging him. With Mother gone, who could stop the quarrel? Outside help was needed.

Aristobulus built up an army and beat Hyrcanus. He gave up his crown and his High Priesthood in return for a quiet life. It did not last long. His father had put a man named Antipater in charge of Idumaea in the south, and Antipater saw his chance of power in siding with Hyrcanus. He took him to Transjordan and won the support of Aretas, king of the Nabataeans.

With a Nabataean army, Antipater and Hyrcanus marched back to Jerusalem and shut Aristobulus in the temple. Before they could overpower him, an order came to break off the siege. The command came from a power neither Antipater nor the Nabataeans could ignore. It came from Rome.

Since Rome had made a treaty with Judea in 161 BC, to help her fight the Syrians, there had been little contact. Now Syria was securely under Roman rule, so the turmoil next door was unwelcome. If Rome could stop it, she would add to her power. The great general, Pompey, who had settled affairs in Turkey and north Syria, sent his assistant, Scaurus, to Jerusalem. There he sent the Nabataean troops home, and made Antipater and Hyrcanus leave Aristobulus in possession of the city.

In 63 BC Pompey came to Damascus. The two brothers went to put their cases to him. Aristobulus sweetened him with the gift of a golden vine, but his actions were too independent to suit the Roman. Pompey followed Aristobulus to Jerusalem, where he gave himself up. Even so, his followers barricaded themselves in the Temple, where they held out for three months.

October 63 BC saw the Roman soldiers enter the Temple. Judea was now under Roman control; Hyrcanus was set up as High Priest again, without the title king. Pompey paraded Aristobulus in triumph in Rome, executed his supporters, and made the land pay tribute to Rome. All the towns on the Mediterranean coast, others in Transjordan, and Samaria, were added to the province of Syria. Aristobulus' ambition left him in chains, his country impoverished, under Roman control and open to Roman interference in its life.

Julius Caesar—the Jews' friend

All was quiet for a while after Pompey left, then Alexander, a son of Aristobulus, raised an army and occupied three forts in the Jordan Valley. The Romans drove him out in 57 BC. The next year Aristobulus and another son escaped from Rome, tried again to pounce on Palestine, and were quickly beaten back. Aristobulus returned to Rome in chains once more. Alexander was still at large, and his soldiers started to kill any Romans they could find. That brought Gabinius, the governor of Syria, to the attack, and Alexander's force was crushed near Mount Tabor.

One of Gabinius' main activities as governor was to line his own pockets. In 54 BC he was called back to Rome and found guilty of extortion. The man who succeeded him was Crassus. He joined with Pompey and Julius Caesar to rule the territories won by Rome. Crassus' aim was military victory over the Parthians pressing in from the east, and he needed money for his war. What Pompey had not done, Crassus did: he took the 2,000 talents of gold from the Temple in Jerusalem, with a great hoard of other treasure kept there. It was all wasted. Crassus' army failed and retreated: the Parthians killed him (53 BC).

The next years saw the growth of civil war in Rome, as different generals jockeyed for power. Each of them used every means he could to gain support and money from the provinces and from client kings. In the turmoil Aristobulus and his son Alexander were killed. After Pompey's murder, Hyrcanus and Antipater joined Julius Caesar, bringing supplies and men to help him out of a tight corner in Egypt, where the Egyptians had shut him up in the palace at Alexandria.

Caesar made his thanks plain. He strengthened Hyrcanus and Antipater as all but independent rulers, making Antipater a Roman citizen and freeing him from paying taxes. The walls of Jerusalem were rebuilt and Jews were allowed to judge Jewish matters. Caesar also gave Joppa and other places by the coast back to Judea, which meant the country had a sea-port again, bringing great benefits in trade and revenue. One other privilege was that Roman legions should not spend the winter in the country or levy recruits there. This was a valuable relief to the people, because the soldiers were usually billeted on them to be fed and housed without making payment.

Caesar had already built up an

enormous fortune through his conquests in France and Germany, so he could afford to be generous. He also understood the benefits to Rome of a peaceful and contented province. Outside Judea he decreed respect for the Jewish faith and liberty for Jewish communities to function in their own way. That meant, among other things, the freedom to send the annual half-shekel tax to the Temple in Jerusalem (see *At the Moneychangers' Tables*). Caesar's decrees stayed long in the memory of the Jews.

After Caesar's murder in 44 BC one of the assassins, Cassius, took command in Syria. He needed money and when some towns in Judea did not pay he sold the inhabitants as slaves. Antipater made sure of Cassius' protection by paying him a large sum himself. Unhappily for Judea, troubles were multiplying rapidly. Antipater was poisoned. His enemy Malichus took command in Jerusalem, ousting Antipater's elder son Phasael. In Galilee, Phasael's energetic younger brother Herod was in charge, and he persuaded Cassius to approve the execution of Malichus (43 BC). The next year Cassius joined Brutus to fight Mark Antony and Octavian, Caesar's heirs, at Philippi in Greece. Defeated, he committed suicide.

After centuries of war, by the time Jesus was born the land knew peace. This picture, looking towards Bethlehem, captures the tranquil scene.

HEROD—KING OF THE JEWS

HEROD'S KINGDOM

Tyre

GALILEE

Tiberias

Sebaste/Samaria

DECAPOLIS

SAMARIA

Jerusalem — PEREA

JUDEA

IDUMEA

NABATAEANS

Herod was born about 73 BC. He was the son of Antipater, ruler of the Idumean people who lived in the south of Palestine. When the Jewish king John Hyrcanus (134–104 BC) was ruling, he had conquered the country and forced the people to become Jews. Later, King Alexander Jannaeus (103–76 BC) set up Antipater's father, an Idumean nobleman, as his governor in Idumea. Antipater seems to have succeeded him. His family was rich from sheep-farming and from its shares in the trade which went across their land from Arabia and Petra to the ports at Gaza and Ascalon. This was the route for the caravans of perfumes and incense going to Rome.

Antipater was shrewd and well-informed. As we have already mentioned, he was quick to use the unambitious Hyrcanus, the legitimate Jewish priest-king, to increase his power. He also foresaw the rule of Rome: his own security lay in becoming Rome's faithful ally. New generals held power in Rome every few years, and Antipater became adept at changing sides to win the favour of the man of the moment, although he did not always succeed.

Antipater strengthened his political position by marrying Cyprus, a noble lady of Petra, capital of the Nabataean Arabs. They named their first son Phasael, their second Herod. They had two other sons, Joseph and Pheroras, and a daughter, Salome.

Many Jews disliked Antipater. Although he was said to be pious and just, he was not thoroughly Jewish. Unlike Alexander Jannaeus before

him, and Herod after, Antipater was certainly not responsible for large-scale executions and massacres. Some Jews preferred to support Hyrcanus' brother Aristobulus and his sons. Others wanted a return to rule by true descendants of their first High Priest, Aaron. All the time groups of men tried to overthrow the rulers, some for religious or patriotic reasons, others simply for their own gain.

When Herod was twenty-five years old (in 47 BC), his father put him in charge of Galilee, with Phasael governing the Jerusalem region. Herod took up his task energetically. Bandits were terrorizing the area, so he rounded them up and put them to death, including the leader, Hezekiah. Naturally, the local people were very pleased to be rid of this burden, and so was the Roman governor of Syria. In Jerusalem there was another view. Herod had acted high-handedly. Only the Sanhedrin, the court in Jerusalem, could pass the death sentence. Jealous for their rights, the priests and nobles called Herod to appear before the court. Antipater advised him to comply.

Herod went to Jerusalem with a strong guard, but the Sanhedrin moved to condemn him. Before they could do so, Herod escaped. The Roman governor of Syria had sent a letter to Hyrcanus, who presided over the Sanhedrin, ordering an acquittal. So Hyrcanus interrupted the trial and secretly warned Herod.

The sequel reveals something of Herod's character. He was furious at this treatment. He got control over

Lebanon and Samaria from the Roman governor, collected an army and advanced to attack Jerusalem and dethrone Hyrcanus. Antipater and Phasael rushed to meet him, eventually persuading him that any such action would be counter-productive—Rome would be bound to interfere again. But Herod had made his mark. For the moment he went back to Galilee, yet within ten years he would be king in Jerusalem.

Still hovering in the background, hoping for power in Palestine, was Antigonus, the younger son of Aristobulus. The vacuum left by Cassius seemed to open the way for him to take his uncle Hyrcanus' place. He had some support, but Herod stopped him. However, the tyrant of Tyre took over some towns in Galilee.

After the battle of Philippi, Asia fell into Mark Antony's hands. Herod immediately went in person to affirm his loyalty, and to make him a generous present. At the same time, a large number of Jewish nobles went to complain against Phasael and Herod, and the way their father had behaved, but Antony ignored them. He gave the two brothers the title 'tetrarch', which meant ruler of part of a province, and he made Tyre give back the towns in Galilee.

This happy situation quickly passed; a fresh storm broke as the Parthians burst out, overrunning Syria. Antigonus saw another chance, bribed the Parthians, and at last climbed on to the throne in Jerusalem. Herod managed to escape. Phasael was caught and died a prisoner of the Parthians. Hyrcanus was taken captive and Antigonus had his ears cropped. This physical maiming disqualified him from being High Priest. Parthian soldiers looted all they could. Although Antony's general soon drove the Parthians out of Syria, Antigonus ruled until 37 BC.

Herod, the Romans' friend

Herod escaped from the Parthians to the safety of Idumea. Then, on hearing that Phasael was dead, he set out for Rome to ask Mark Antony's help. He travelled by way of Alexandria, where he brushed aside an offer of military command from Cleopatra, was almost shipwrecked, and had to stay for some months in Rhodes. At Rome, Antony introduced Herod to his colleague Octavian.

Octavian admired Herod's energies and skills, and Herod reminded him of

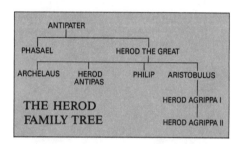

THE HEROD FAMILY TREE

the good relations that had existed between Herod and Antipater and Julius Caesar. Caesar had named Octavian, his grand-nephew, as his heir. When Octavian and Herod met, the Roman was about twenty-three years old, Herod ten years his senior.

Antony and Octavian did more for Herod than he had hoped. Antony saw him as a tool to help defeat the Parthians in Syria and Palestine, and proposed that the Senate make him king of Judea. Whatever his future subjects might think, from now on to challenge Herod would be to challenge the might of Rome.

Early the next year (39 BC) Herod landed in Palestine. He went first to Masada where he had left his wife, his mother, and his mother-in-law safe in the castle guarded by his brother Joseph. Antigonus, the Parthian-appointed king, had tried to capture the fortress, and failed. Herod moved on to Jerusalem but a Roman official's interference obstructed him.

After clearing more bandits out of Galilee, and going to help Mark Antony in Turkey, Herod returned to Jerusalem in the spring of 37 BC. Supported by eleven Roman legions, he laid siege to the city, broke through the walls and fought yard by yard until all was under his control. The Roman soldiers killed the defenders without mercy and only by giving each soldier a handsome present did Herod save the city and the Temple from total destruction.

King Antigonus was captured and sent to Mark Antony, who had him executed in Antioch. It was the first time, people said, that the Romans had executed a king. The king they created, Herod, sat on his throne in Jerusalem.

Although Herod always enjoyed Antony's favour, things became awkward when Antony fell under the spell of Cleopatra. The queen of Egypt wanted to be as great as her ancestors,

and their kingdom had stretched through Palestine into Lebanon. Herod was in the way: he should be removed. That was too much to ask, even of the infatuated Antony. How could he dethrone the king the Senate had so recently created, when he had been a loyal ally? There would be constant rebellion among the Jews, too.

To mollify the queen, Antony gave her a choice piece of Herod's kingdom, the date-palm orchards and gardens of balsam[1] around Jericho. Herod had to agree, even though the Jericho crops were a major source of income for him. He made a neat arrangement by which he continued to farm the region, paying a heavy rent to

[1] Balsam was the sap of a bush. It had antiseptic qualities and a pleasant smell, and was widely used for dressing wounds.

Cleopatra. That meant her officials had no reason to be busy in his kingdom. When Cleopatra made more trouble for Herod, by taking sides with his mother-in-law against him and making charges against him to Antony (see *Herod, the Great Murderer*), Antony still refused to act against a faithful helper.

Cleopatra's hatred prevented Herod joining the army she and Antony gathered to fight Octavian. Instead, they sent him to bring the Nabataeans to heel. When Octavian won the battle of Actium in 31 BC, Herod knew he had to change sides. He went to Octavian and told him he would be as loyal to him as he had been to Mark

Antony, Octavian, who wanted to settle affairs, assured him that his position would not change. Soon afterwards, in 30 BC, with Antony and Cleopatra dead, Octavian gave Herod back the Jericho estates and added other towns to his kingdom, among them Gaza and Samaria.

Herod was quick to make his thanks to Octavian public. In 27 BC the ruler of Rome took the title Augustus. In 25 BC Herod founded a new city where ancient Israel's capital, Samaria, had been. Here 6,000 men from his army of foreign soldiers were given plots of land. Herod named the place Sebaste, the Greek for 'Augustus' town'. High above the roofs of the

The Citadel at Jerusalem stands on the site of a stronghold built by Herod at the north end of his palace. The largest tower remains from Herod's time, the typical large stone blocks having finely smoothed margins.

Herod's castle at Herodium towered over the countryside, a sign of his rule visible to all. Excavations revealed traces of the elaborate arrangements inside Herodium—baths, a dining-room, an enclosed garden, and the great tower.

houses reared a temple. It was dedicated to Rome and Augustus. In 21 BC Herod began another city, a great new port which took twelve years to build. This he called Caesarea.

Augustus gave more lands to Herod —in 23 BC and again when they met in Syria in 20 BC. They met in Italy a couple of years later, and again in 12 BC, when Herod took two of his sons to Rome for the emperor to settle a charge of conspiracy. There is doubt about a third visit by Herod to Augustus in Rome.

Herod sent the emperor many messages on all sorts of matters. When they were not about imperial policy and the intrigues of his neighbours, they were about his family. Herod's problems with his sons were endless, to Augustus they became a nuisance. 'I would rather be Herod's swine than Herod's son,' he said. He was playing on the Greek words for 'pig' and 'son' which are similar (*hys* and *hyios*), and on the Jewish objection to pigs.

Augustus aimed to rule a peaceful empire. By putting down brigands and ne'er-do-wells, Herod extended the peace. In fact, Augustus gave him lands in south Syria, because they were controlled by robber bands under robber barons who threatened the peace. Herod was able to subdue them. Doing that, he went farther than he should have done. His army went into the Nabataean kingdom to catch some of them and the Nabataeans complained to Rome.

Augustus was angry; Herod had broken the peace. The emperor wrote a harsh letter ending their friendship. There was not much hope for Herod without that, so after about a year he sent a favourite courtier to put matters right. The courtier's speech, and events that took place, changed Augustus' mind. He wrote again to Herod, warmly. For the rest of his rule, Herod had the good will of the Roman emperor.

THERE'S NO GOD THERE!

Pushing past protesting priests, the Roman general strode through the heavy curtain and into the Holy of Holies. He stopped, astonished, turned, and marched out. His officers gaped in surprise. 'There's nothing there!'

In Athens the great statue of the goddess Athene stood in her temple, the Parthenon. At Ephesus the famous temple of Diana guarded her ancient stone which had fallen from heaven. Egyptian temples, too, had sacred statues in shrines where only priests could see them. No one knew what was hidden in the heart of the Temple in Jerusalem. There was great treasure there, so surely there would be an impressive holy object. The Roman general Pompey went to see—and found just an empty room!

Pompey won the praise of Cicero in Rome and, later, of Josephus because

he took nothing out of the Temple. He did not touch the golden table and golden lampstand, golden dishes and bowls that stood in the main hall, nor did he seize any of the funds in the stores (2,000 talents of gold—over 52,000 kg/50 tons).

Even so, the fact that he went into the holy place was sacrilege. Not even the most devout Jew could go in there! No religious Jew could overlook this conduct. When the Egyptians with whom Pompey sought refuge killed him in 48 BC, many Jews said it was divine punishment.

The shrine in the temple of Bel at Palmyra, dedicated in AD 32, would have held a fine statue of the god, with valuable ornaments. Like other great statues of ancient gods and goddesses, it was destroyed long ago. Today the shrine stands empty—as Pompey found the holy place in the Temple at Jerusalem.

RULERS

EMPERORS OF ROME

Augustus	31 BC–AD 14
Tiberius	AD 14–37
Caligula	AD 37–41
Claudius	AD 41–54
Nero	AD 54–63
Galba	AD 68–69
Otho	AD 69
Vitellius	AD 69
Vespasian	AD 69–79
Titus	AD 79–81

JEWISH KINGS OR RULERS

Herod	37–4 BC
Archelaus	4 BC–AD 6 (Judea)
Antipas	4 BC–AD 39 (Galilee, Perea)
Philip	4 BC–AD 34 (Gaulan, Bashan)
Agrippa I	AD 37–41 (Gaulan, Bashan, Abilene)
	AD 41–44 (Gaulan, Bashan, Abilene, plus Judea and Samaria)
Herod	AD 41–48 (Chalcis in Lebanon)
Agrippa II	AD 50–53 (Chalcis)
	AD 53 (Gaulan, Bashan, etc.)
	AD 54–93? (Gaulan and Galilean towns)

CAESAR AUGUSTUS

Portrait of Augustus on a silver coin (tetradrachm) from the province of Asia, 19 BC.

The entrance to the temple of Rome and Augustus at Ankara On the walls is engraved the account of Augustus' rule in his own words, in Latin, with a Greek translation. The building survived being converted into a church and later being partly used as a mosque.

Coins were a very good way to spread information. They were easy to make in large numbers, and could reach all the population. The Romans used coins as a means of propaganda, like every other state: Rome ruled and everyone should know it. Soon the emperor's head was recognized everywhere (as Jesus' question about the tribute money proves—see *Caesar's Image*).

Statues of the emperor standing in temples and public places helped to remind people that he was in control. Smaller figures stood in shrines or private houses. In Rome, during his lifetime, Augustus did not allow people to worship him as a god. Rather he was the father or creator and upholder of the state. In the provinces of the east he was treated as a god, which made his portrait or image even more offensive to Jews.

Over 230 statues or busts of Augustus are known to have survived —everything from miniatures to life-sized sculptures. No doubt originally there were more, some placed in the temples Herod built in Caesarea, Samaria, Paneas and other towns of Palestine which were not Jewish centres.

In his lifetime Augustus could make his actions known through his agents. He also took care that they should be remembered after his death. At his tomb in Rome a great notice engraved on bronze sheets set out his own account of his greatness. Copies were made for temples in other towns. The bronze plates are lost, as are most of the copies, but one that is almost complete can still be read on the walls of a temple in Ankara, Turkey. The proud proclamation makes the emperor's position clear: Rome ruled the world.

At home Augustus improved the state of the country and its people. Abroad his armies fought battles to win peace through victory. Kings beyond the frontier of the empire made pacts with him. Ambassadors and princes came from far away with valuable presents: from Persia and India, from Britain and Rumania. The senate and people of Rome honoured him for his 'courage, mercy, justice and piety'. His enemies in Rome did not live to tell a different story.

Augustus was enormously rich. Besides his family estates, he took

over the properties of the enemies
he overcame before his reign began,
including the treasure of Egypt which
belonged to Cleopatra. Important
Romans left money and estates to him
in their wills. With his wealth, he paid
for grain to feed the poor in Rome on
more than one occasion. He improved
the regular grain supply system and
also constructed new aqueducts to give
the city a better public water supply.

Using his wealth for show was
essential to keep his name popular.
He transformed his capital city with
temples, theatres, bridges and
government offices. 'I found it brick
and left it marble,' he boasted. That
meant good employment for craftsmen
and labourers. For the people's
amusement he staged gladiator shows
with as many as 10,000 men, and mock
sea-battles. About 3,500 wild beasts
fell as prey in the mock 'hunts' he
held, 260 lions and thirty-six
crocodiles being killed on one
occasion.

The emperor must live in the
greatest splendour, although Augustus
avoided the excesses of gluttony and
ostentation that began to appear in
Rome. In later years, gold and silver
plate and jewellery from the imperial
palaces were melted down or looted.
Only a few examples survive from the
first century AD to suggest the
magnificence of the imperial
household.

HEROD—THE GREAT MURDERER

Herod then with fear was filled,
'A prince,' he said, 'in Jewry!'
All the little boys he killed
In Bethlehem in his fury.

Bethlehem's babies, the Holy Innocents, were far from being Herod's only victims. He was suspicious of anyone whom he thought could try to take the throne away from him. One-time friends, servants, countless enemies, priests, nobles and all who happened to cross him in some way were killed. In such a crowd, a few baby boys would hardly be noticed. In fact, we would not know about them if the baby Herod wanted to kill had not escaped (Matthew 2:13–18).

The list of Herod's individual victims is horrifying and damns his memory. He had one of his ten wives (the favourite one) executed. And he ordered the deaths of three of his own sons, a High Priest, a former High Priest and ex-king, and two of his sister's husbands. What threat were they to him?

The first to fall victim to Herod's jealousy was an innocent teenager, Aristobulus. He was the son of Alexander and grandson of the Aristobulus who claimed Hyrcanus' crown (see *Peace at Last*). His mother was Alexandra, Hyrcanus' daughter, and his sister Mariamme was Herod's second wife. Aristobulus, as the last eligible male in the Hasmonean family, was the rightful heir to the high priesthood. Herod had appointed someone else in order to limit the power of the Hasmoneans to rival him.

Aristobulus' mother made Cleopatra put pressure on Herod, so he deposed his appointee, making his young brother-in-law High Priest. All the time Herod watched Alexandra, and stopped her when she tried to leave Judea, smuggled out in a coffin with her son in another. When Aristobulus caught the people's attention in the Temple, for he was a good-looking sixteen-year-old, Herod acted. A party was held in the winter palace at Jericho, the guests played in the garden pools—and Aristobulus drowned (36 BC). Herod ordered a fine funeral; Alexandra worked for revenge.

The second victim was Herod's uncle, Joseph, who had married Herod's sister Salome. Salome and Mariamme, Herod's wife, were enemies. While Herod was away with Mark Antony, answering Cleopatra's charge that he had murdered Aristobulus, Joseph had the care of Mariamme. On Herod's return, Salome told him that her husband Joseph was Mariamme's lover. Mariamme convinced Herod that this was a lie, but she also told him that Joseph had disclosed Herod's order that she was to be killed if he failed to return from the meeting with Antony. The order was a secret one, and Joseph could have let it out only if he had been very close to Mariamme. Salome saw her husband Joseph executed and her enemy Mariamme forgiven (34 BC).

The cruellest of Herod's murders was the killing of Hyrcanus. Although he had been king and High Priest, Hyrcanus was now over eighty years old, quite happy to live at peace in his own home, no threat to anybody. Yet Herod feared Hyrcanus might be the focus of a rebellion, while he himself went abroad to make friends with Octavian. Hyrcanus and the Nabataean king had been writing friendly letters to each other. Herod found treason in that, and so had the old man condemned.

In addition to killing his wife's grandfather, Hyrcanus, before he went away Herod shut his mother-in-law and Mariamme in one of his forts, leaving his sons by Mariamme with his mother, and his sister Salome in Masada. They were all safe, but the plotting continued. Mariamme did not welcome the king on his return, and Salome fed him more false tales about her. At length Herod came to believe that his wife had been unfaithful to him. Despite his love for her, he had her put on trial, condemned and executed in 29 BC. So strong was his passion for Mariamme that Herod made himself ill with remorse. It took another plot to cure him.

Herod's illness was the opening Alexandra, Mariamme's mother, wanted. Alexandra thought she could take over the kingdom. Loyal officers of Herod reported her secret moves to him. At his command, his mother-in-law's life was ended, too.

One more execution brought in a calmer period for Herod's family. After the death of Joseph, Salome was married to Costobar, governor of Idumaea. Now she accused him of conspiring against her brother, Herod. Since he had been forgiven previously for co-operating with Cleopatra, when proof of conspiracy was found he was killed (about 27 BC).

Herod and Mariamme had two sons, Alexander and Aristobulus, who were the king's favourites. His eldest son, Antipater, born by the wife Doris whom he divorced when he married Mariamme, was banished from Jerusalem except for special occasions. The brothers were sent to Rome for education in the emperor's entourage.

Herod brought them back in 17 BC, arranging good marriages for them. Their popularity in the country, coupled with their royal descent through their mother, led them to rash behaviour and outspoken statements. They alone had rights to the throne; their mother's murder should be avenged.

Herod's sister Salome hated them as she had hated Mariamme. She started spreading rumours again, with her brother Pheroras to help her: Alexander and Aristobulus were leading a plot to overthrow Herod. He was hard to convince, but to counter them he called Antipater back to court. Antipater saw that he could build up his own cause. Even from Rome, where Herod sent him to meet Augustus, he wrote in concern about his father's safety and his half-brothers' behaviour. In 12 BC, Herod appeared before the emperor with his two sons, charging them with intent to murder him. Augustus saw through the situation, ruled the charge untrue, and reconciled father and sons. However, Herod changed his will: Antipater was to be king, with Alexander and Aristobulus ruling under him.

No one was content, except Herod. The rivalry and intrigue grew worse. Salome, Pheroras, Antipater, Alexander and Aristobulus, Alexander's powerful father-in-law (king of Cappadocia in Turkey), and other characters hatched schemes to hoodwink Herod into thinking this son or that was, or was not, about to assassinate him. Alexander and

Excavations in the area of Herod's palace at Jericho have uncovered the remains of two pools. The archaeologists suggest it was in one of these that Herod had the young High Priest Aristobulus drowned.

Aristobulus were the objects of many accusations. All proved ill-founded. Yet in 7 BC, Herod, suspicious as ever, supported by a letter from Augustus allowing him to act as he saw fit, had the brothers pronounced guilty and strangled. Salome, at least, had some satisfaction.

Antipater could not wait for his father to die. He started to build up support, forging a link with his uncle Pheroras. That disturbed Herod, so Antipater went to Rome to escape attention. Then Pheroras died and some of his servants suspected he had been poisoned. An inquiry found that there was poison, obtained by Antipater for Pheroras to feed to Herod! Antipater was recalled by Herod, who did not reveal to him what had been discovered until he reached the palace. There he was arrested, tried, and found guilty. Herod reported to Augustus and received his permission to execute Antipater. By now mortally ill, Herod rewrote his will. There were other sons still alive. Three were to share the rule: Archelaus was to be king, his brother Antipas tetrarch of Galilee and an area in Transjordan, and Philip, son of a different wife, tetrarch of the former brigand country in the Golan and further east. He gave three cities to his loyal sister Salome.

Herod died in March 4 BC, aged about seventy. The historian Josephus, who preserved so much information about him, commented, 'Fortune made Herod pay a terrible price in his own household for his public successes.'

HEROD—
THE GREAT CASTLE BUILDER

Keeping safe and keeping his crown were Herod's goals. Executing imagined rivals was one way to make sure he remained king. But suppose there were a war or a large-scale rebellion? Against this possibility Herod built castles where he could live securely. Each held stores of weapons, and a strong garrison. His engineers gave them good water supplies. All over his kingdom he built castles. Where there were old ones, he made them stronger, and on strategic sites he erected new ones. Their ruins were identified long ago. With the rise of archaeology in Israel, excavators have uncovered some of the defences and the splendid apartments Herod had designed for himself.

The old fort in Jerusalem was at the north end of the Temple. Herod rebuilt it at the start of his reign and named it Antonia, for Mark Antony. But it has disappeared in the convulsions of the city's history. In the west Herod created his new palace. He could not rest easy in Jerusalem without defences, so he ran a wall with towers around the palace, setting three extra-large towers at the north end.

Josephus said, 'The king made the splendour of these works a means of expressing his own emotions, naming the towers after the three persons he cared for most, his brother (Phasael), friend (Hippicus), and wife (Mariamme).'

Today the lower part of one tower still stands in the 'Citadel', a striking reminder of royal power. The palace itself has vanished, except for traces of the platform on which it stood and

some cuttings in the bedrock. Josephus reports that it was magnificent beyond description, luxuriously decorated and furnished with gold and silver. Its colonnades led past green lawns and trees, round two great pavilions. The palace passed from Herod's son Archelaus to become the residence of the Roman governor, the Praetorium where the Gospels record that Pilate washed his hands at the trial of Jesus.

The richness of Herod's palaces is best revealed in the amazing rock fortress of Masada (see *Masada—the Last Stronghold*). Equally rich and well-protected was Herodium—the castle Herod named after himself. On a hill south-east of Bethlehem his workmen erected an extraordinary round fort. Two concentric walls crowned the hill, with semi-circular towers protruding on the north, south and west sides, and a round one on the east. Towers and walls still stand 10–15 metres/33–50 feet above the inside ground level; their foundations are 5 metres/16 feet or more below. Architects calculate two storeys have fallen, so that the whole rose 25 metres/80 feet above the floor, and the eastern tower certainly soared even higher.

Those who visited Herod here climbed 200 steps to the doorway. They saw the fort not as a massive stone drum but as a great hill crowned by the wall and towers. Hiding the outside, as high as the now existing walls, was a great tip of earth and stones, giving the appearance of a conical hill. Herod's labourers carried away the top of the next hill to heap up this one. From the top of the stairs, the visitor stepped

Ptolemais

Gaba

Strato's Tower, Caesarea

Samaria/Sebaste

ALEXANDRIUM
Antipatris
Phasaelis

JERUSALEM   CYPROS
HYRCANIA
HERODIUM   MACHAERUS

MASADA

★ Herod's fortresses
● Towns built or rebuilt by Herod

through a room in the double walls
into a cloister. The pillared walks
surrounded a space, 33 metres/36 feet
long, which was probably planted as
a garden. On the side were the main
entertaining rooms of the palace.

There was a large dining-room,
which the Zealots apparently turned
into a synagogue during the revolt of
AD 67–70, and a well-built bath-house.
This was the latest Roman amenity,
which Herod introduced. Heated air
circulated under the floor and up the
walls of the hot room, floors were
paved with mosaic, and walls painted.
The domed roof of the warm room
is still complete. Bedrooms were
most likely in an upper storey here.
Courtiers might lead privileged visitors
up to the top of the great tower, where
the king enjoyed the breezes and the
panoramic views over the country he
ruled, right across the Dead Sea to his
castle at Machaerus in the mountains
of Moab.

Anyone building a palace on top of
a hill must solve the problem of water-
supply. At Herodium three very large
cisterns were hewn from the hill below
the palace, near the staircase. They
collected rainwater, or could be fed
from an aqueduct Herod made to
carry water from a spring 6 km/
3½ miles away (at Artas, south of
Bethlehem). A shaft in the palace area
gave access to another cistern from
which water could be drawn by bucket.
That cistern seems to have been filled
by hand from the lower ones.

The castle on the hill was only part
of Herod's grandiose design. On the
ground, at the foot of the hill, spread
other opulent structures. A major
feature was a great pool, 70 metres/
230 feet long, 46 metres/150 feet wide,
and about 3 metres/10 feet deep. A
round, pillared pavilion stood in the
middle. Gardens and a pillared walk
surrounded this big pool, making an
oasis in the dry summer landscape.
There were long halls, and a bath-
house bigger than the one in the castle,
as well as storage and service rooms.
An unexplained narrow terrace runs

for almost 350 metres/380 yards to the
west of this area, overlooked by the
ruins of another palatial building.
Parts of more elaborate structures
await examination.

Herodium was both a fort and a
palace. It was to be more, for this was
Herod's tomb. But precisely where his
body was buried is a mystery explorers
still hope to solve.

Between Herodium and the Dead
Sea was a small fort, Hyrcania. Herod
used it as a prison. Cisterns and a few
walls survive, taken over by monks
who had a monastery there.

Across the Dead Sea, and visible
from Herodium, was Machaerus in
the mountains of Moab. High on a
rocky ridge Herod set up a wall with
defensive towers to enclose another
palace. Again, a series of cisterns
ensured enough water in time of siege.
Limited excavations have uncovered
parts of the building.

Two strongholds watched over the
lower Jordan Valley. Cyprus, named
after Herod's mother, was near
Jericho. On the hill guarding the
south side of the ancient road from
Jericho up to Jerusalem remains of
cisterns, baths and other buildings
show that this fortress was as well-
served as Herodium and Masada,
even though it was smaller.

Some 30 km/18 miles up the
Jordan Valley, atop another commanding hill, lay Alexandrium. As
soon as he entered Palestine, Herod
took this fort and rebuilt it, equipping
it no doubt as well and as strongly as
the others.

Through smaller forts, watch-
towers, and the garrisons of the cities
he ruled, Herod was able to keep a
tight grip on the whole of his
kingdom.

HEROD—THE GREAT CITY BUILDER

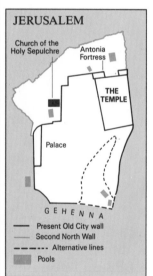

JERUSALEM

Church of the Holy Sepulchre

Antonia Fortress

THE TEMPLE

Palace

G E H E N N A

— Present Old City wall
— Second North Wall
--- Alternative lines
▨ Pools

Castles could impress and control the people; cities provided them with streets and buildings where they could enjoy themselves or carry out their business. Herod, like many other kings, founded a number of cities. His name would live on, he hoped, as a generous benefactor in all the major towns of his kingdom, and a large number of places beyond.

On the way to Rome to meet Mark Antony, Herod had to stop at Rhodes to find a new ship. To that city he gave funds for repairs and he rebuilt the temple of Apollo which had burnt down. When Augustus built his new city of Nikopolis in honour of his victory over Mark Antony at Actium, Herod gave liberally to the work, in part, at least, out of duty. Other cities in Greece benefited from his generosity. Perhaps the least expected gesture was Herod's revival of the Olympic Games. He acted as president for one celebration (12 BC) and gave enough money to make sure they would continue.

In Syria Herod was free with his giving. Citizens of Antioch on the Orontes, once the capital of Syria, walked along a muddy main street. Herod supplied a wide stone-paved road with colonnades on either side, 4 km/2½ miles long. Byblos, Beirut, Tyre and Sidon, Tripoli, Damascus, and other cities too, received walls, halls, theatres and gymnasia.

In Palestine Herod did even more. Towns he rebuilt were named after Herod's family and friends and his patron: Antipatris for his father, Phasaelis for his brother, Agrippias for his friend who was Augustus' right-hand man, Sebaste for the emperor himself. Overshadowing all was Caesarea, also honouring Augustus.

Building began in 22 BC and the city was dedicated twelve years later. Caesarea rivals Jerusalem as Herod's most ambitious project. Although he never saw the Temple fully finished, Caesarea's monumental harbour was ready for the opening. Josephus praised the harbour as one of the biggest in the Mediterranean. Whereas ports usually grow around a creek or bay, here only a small harbour had existed. Herod's engineers had to erect huge artificial breakwaters to provide shelter for the biggest Roman ships.

The new city was to become the major shipping point for trade between Asia and Europe. After Herod's time, Caesarea was the centre of Roman administration and for a long time the major port, despite earthquake damage in AD 130. Neglect and shrinking trade resulted in the gradual collapse of the harbour works, so that today there is nothing to be seen, and some have doubted Josephus' account.

Proof of his accuracy has come from underwater exploration. Archaeologists have been diving into the sea beside the ruined city to examine and map features seen from the air. Two enormous stone banks reach out from the shore, curving round to form a big harbour. The southern one is the longer, about 480 metres/525 yards; the northern is just over half that length. Both were 60 metres/65 yards wide, on average, agreeing with the

60 metres/200 feet Josephus reported. To build the southern breakwater, blocks of stone 15 metres/50 feet long were sunk into the water, he said. Blocks like these, and even longer ones, lie under the sea.

As well as costly stones, the builders fitted timber frames underwater and poured a special concrete into them to make huge masses that would resist the pounding sea. (One is 13.5×3.3×1.8 metres/45×33×6 feet.) Tufa from Mount Vesuvius in Italy was one ingredient of the concrete. Shaped stones tumbled on the seabed are evidence of towers and other buildings once set on the breakwaters. Harbours often face the problem of silting. At Caesarea a

sluice was specially devised to flush sand out of the harbour.

A temple to Augustus, a theatre, an amphitheatre, and immense warehouses made the city as impressive as the harbour. The temple is no more. The theatre, many times renovated and reshaped (see *Pilate's Own Monument*), is once more in use. The amphitheatre lies unexcavated. Near the harbour, vaulted halls grouped in blocks are parts of the warehouse and storage system. The temple of Augustus may have stood on top of them. A great arched sewer beneath the later main street is a witness to the thorough planning of Herod's city. Another is the noteworthy aqueduct. Fresh water had to

From the air it is possible to see the lines of Herod's quay walls as black masses stretching far beyond the modern harbour.

Herod's new city at Caesarea needed a reliable water-supply, so his engineers constructed a great aqueduct. Its last stretch was carried on arches to the city. The part still standing was partly rebuilt by Roman soldiers in AD 132–35.

Later builders took stone pillars from the ruins of Caesarea to build new breakwaters.

flow through 10 km/6 miles of tunnel from springs in the flanks of Mount Carmel, and along an equal length of aqueduct, to supply the city.

Founding new cities, or remodelling old ones, was a good way to increase employment. Thousands of labourers and craftsmen could be put to work, if there was money to pay them. Indeed, when the Temple was finally completed, King Agrippa II set the jobless workmen to re-pave the streets of Jerusalem with fine white slabs. Herod's large income (see *Money and Coins*) covered the expense, drawing on the profits of his estates and businesses, but also on the taxes he extracted from his subjects. Although he cut taxes by a third in 20 BC, then by a quarter seven years later, and went so far as to melt down his own gold and silver plate to buy grain from Egypt to feed his people in the famine of 25–24 BC, the ordinary citizens felt the tax burden so harsh that they burnt the record offices after Herod's death. They were the ones who paid the price for his self-advertisement.

HEROD'S SONS

On Herod's death, only the Emperor Augustus could bring his will into effect. So Herod's sons, the three claimants, hurried to Rome. A party of Jewish nationalists went also, separately, and envoys from the Greek cities in Herod's kingdom. The nationalists wanted no kingdom at all; Herod's reign had been so cruel and oppressive that to be an ordinary Roman province would be better. The Greek cities wanted no king at all. They wanted freedom to rule themselves within the province.

Augustus listened to them all, then divided Herod's kingdom, but not quite as his will set out.

Archelaus was put on probation as ethnarch of Judea, Samaria and Idumea. If he did well, he would become king, Antipas was given charge of Galilee and Perea (in Transjordan) as tetrarch, and Philip the north-eastern territories. Three Greek cities were added to Syria. One was Gadara, which Augustus had given to Herod in 30 BC. Its people had always resented the change of control, for they had suffered under Jewish occupation earlier. By giving Gaza the same standing, Augustus took away from Archelaus an important source of income through trade.

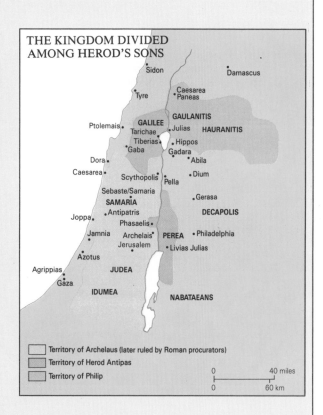

THE KINGDOM DIVIDED AMONG HEROD'S SONS

Damascus
Sidon
Tyre
Caesarea Paneas
GAULANITIS
Ptolemais
GALILEE
Tarichae
Julias
HAURANITIS
Tiberias
Hippos
Gaba
Gadara
Abila
Dora
Caesarea
Scythopolis
Pella
Dium
Sebaste/Samaria
Gerasa
SAMARIA
Antipatris
DECAPOLIS
Joppa
Phasaelis
Jamnia
Archelais
PEREA
Philadelphia
Jerusalem
Livias Julias
Azotus
JUDEA
Agrippias
Gaza
IDUMEA
NABATAEANS

☐ Territory of Archelaus (later ruled by Roman procurators)
☐ Territory of Herod Antipas
☐ Territory of Philip

0 ——— 40 miles
0 ——— 60 km

Herod Archelaus
(4 BC–AD 6)

Archelaus failed his probation. Even before he went to Rome he had killed a crowd of rioters in the Temple. After he left, the governor of Syria had put down more revolts and, when he returned, he found the country cowed. His rule was harsh. Something he had heard about it prompted Joseph, on his return from Egypt, to take his wife and the young Jesus to Galilee rather than into Archelaus' realm, according to

Matthew's Gospel (2:22).

Archelaus changed the high priests as he wanted. He upset many of his subjects by marrying the widow of his executed half-brother, Alexander. She had borne a son to her husband, so there was no question of Archelaus carrying out a levirate marriage to provide an heir for his dead brother. The marriage was illegal in Jewish eyes.

Archelaus' conduct grew so unbearable that a joint delegation of Jews and Samaritans complained to the emperor.

Augustus removed Archelaus from his position, sending him into exile in Gaul, and turned his domain into a Roman province (AD 6).

Archelaus made small coins like his father Herod's. Instead of the Greek words 'of king Herod', these carry the words 'of ethnarch Herod'. The bunch of grapes on the obverse and the helmet on the reverse continue the style of inoffensive designs used by Herod and earlier rulers.

Herod Antipas
(4 BC—AD 39)

Ancient graves, making the site 'unclean', might halt some building work, but it took more than that to stop Herod the Tetrarch! He was going to build his new city where he wanted to. So Tiberias grew up, with its harbour on the edge of Lake Galilee. Today it still has the name Herod Antipas gave it, to honour the Emperor Tiberius. If religious Jews would not live there because of the graves, Antipas could bring in others by force or by promises of land. Building his palace there would attract many who wanted work, and the courtiers and men who needed or wanted his favour. 'That fox', Jesus called him, according to Luke's account (13:32)—a name well earned by Herod's cunning.

Herod Antipas' territory of Galilee was fertile and well populated, the right place for his capital. He also rebuilt the town of Sepphoris, his first capital, to guard the region. Perea, the other half of his realm, was rough and thinly occupied. There he fortified a town and called it Livias, in honour of Augustus' wife. His father's castle at Machaerus was important, as it guarded the frontier with the Nabateans and, like Masada, it was splendidly furnished.

In both regions the people were thoroughly Jewish, forcibly converted a century before. Antipas was happy to follow his father's behaviour, and so adopted the Jewish calendar, taking part in the festivals in Jerusalem. (Luke 23:7 records that he was there at Passover time.) When Pontius Pilate set up the shields in Jerusalem which so offended the Jews, Antipas joined his brothers in writing the petition to Tiberius for their removal (see *Certainly not a Saint!*). A distinct party supported him, the Herodians, made up of those who benefited from the family's rule. They saw it as better than having a Roman governor. At the same time they

Philip (4 BC—AD 34)

Philip received the north-east part of his father's kingdom. This was former bandit country and had fewer Jewish inhabitants. That meant he could put the emperor's head on his coins without causing an uproar. His thirty-seven-year rule was peaceful; his conduct won him the reputation of being the most just and moderate of Herod's ruling sons.

Philip, too, was a builder. His major town was Paneas, by the sources of the Jordan. Herod had built a temple to Augustus there. Now Philip developed the city. He called it Caesarea, to honour Augustus; the addition 'of Philip' (Philippi) distinguished it from the city Herod founded on the coast. The other notable place he rebuilt was Bethsaida, which he named Julias after Augustus' daughter. Set where the Jordan flows into Lake Galilee, Philip's city watched the frontier.

Recent exploration strongly suggests that it is the ruin-mound known simply as 'the Tell', on the east side of the river, a mound not yet excavated. Possibly a settlement on the other bank was the Bethsaida of Galilee mentioned in John 12:21.

Excavations to the south of modern Tiberias have cleared a gateway with a typical Roman paved street. This is the only relic of Herod Antipas' city which has been recovered.

Antipas struck a series of larger bronze coins at his new capital, Tiberias, from AD 19–20 onwards. On the obverse they bear the words in Greek 'of tetrarch Herod' and the date, òn this example 'year 33' (AD 28–29). The reverse has the name 'Tiberias' in a wreath. Although Antipas erected statues in his palace at Tiberias, none of his coins show any human or animal figures.

recognized the need for Rome's protection, and so apparently expected to pay tribute and to uphold her power (see Mark 3:6; 12:13; Matthew 22:16).

As Tiberias had shown, Antipas was not one to let Jewish feelings obstruct his wishes. According to Josephus, when Antipas was visiting his half-brother Herod (who lived as a private citizen), he fell in love with his sister-in-law, Herodias. She left her husband for him. The only other ancient sources of information, the Gospels, say that Herodias was the wife of Philip (Mark 6:17; Matthew 14:3).

Was Herod the same man as Philip?

Herod the Great certainly had two sons named Herod, and one named Philip. Was one Herod known as Herod Philip to distinguish him? The son named Philip was not called Herod, according to the evidence. Archelaus and Antipas did add Herod to their names, but only when they became rulers. Most scholars assume that the

Gospel record is wrong and Josephus right. An argument that Josephus is partly wrong maintains that Herodias was wife of Herod first, then of Philip the Tetrarch, then of Antipas!

When ancient sources disagree like this, it is unfair to all of them to label one as wrong without very strong grounds for doing so. Whoever Herodias had married, he was Antipas' half-brother and she had a child by him. For Antipas to marry her was illegal in Jewish eyes. John the Baptist criticized the tetrarch and was shut up in the fortress of Machaerus for his boldness. Antipas was afraid of John's popularity, yet to kill him immediately might have led to a revolt. Eventually the execution was ordered, at Herodias' request (Mark 6:14–29; Matthew 14:1–12).

Herodias spelt trouble. As proof of his devotion to her, Antipas had divorced his wife, whose father was Aretas, the Nabatean king. Furious at the insult,

Aretas attacked, defeating Antipas' forces in Perea (AD 36). Fighting between Rome's subjects was not allowed, as Herod had learnt (see *Herod—King of the Jews*). The Emperor Tiberius ordered his governor in Syria to attack Aretas but, before he could do so, Tiberius died, so the governor withdrew.

The new emperor, Caligula, was a great friend of Agrippa, Herodias' brother. He made him king of the lands once ruled by Philip the Tetrarch (AD 37). Jealous, Herodias urged Antipas to ask Caligula to give him the title 'king'. In Rome Caligula paid more attention to messages from Agrippa than to Antipas. There was no love lost between them. Antipas was condemned for building up a huge stock of arms, which he could not explain. He was banished to the west and his lands given to Agrippa.

Tiberius' head and title are on the obverse, the front of a temple and the words 'of tetrarch Philip' in Greek on the reverse, with the date between the pillars (here 'year 19', AD 15–16).

Herod Philip built his new city of Caesarea Philippi at one of the sources of the River Jordan, a spring in a cave. In the cliff beside the cave niches were carved for statues of Greek gods. One of them was probably Pan, after whom the place is still called Paneas or Banyas.

THE ROMAN GOVERNORS

The Roman governors made small bronze coins for the people of Judea. This one, struck under Ambibulus, has an ear of corn and the word 'Caesar's' on one side, and a date-palm tree with signs for 'year 40' (AD 10).

Archelaus failed to rule his kingdom properly, so Augustus turned it into a province of the empire. Herod had set up an effective government, all that was needed was a competent manager. The emperor found one among the equestrians, the middle-class businessmen of Italy. His name was Coponius. He answered to the emperor, but the governor of Syria was higher in rank, a senator, so sometimes took charge in Judea. There were other provinces with special local circumstances that had governors of equestrian status, notably Egypt.

'Prefect' was the governor's title until the reign of Claudius (AD 41–54) when it was changed to 'procurator'. Prefect is Pontius Pilate's title on the Caesarea Stone (see *Pilate's Own Monument*) and the Greek of the Gospels reflects that accurately.

The governor had to keep order with the troops under his command, suppressing brigands and rebels (see *Army of Occupation*). He had to administer justice, taking his seat formally in his official residence, either Herod's palace in Jerusalem or the one in Caesarea. In his hands alone rested power to order the execution of a criminal. The governor of Judea had to work with the High Priest if the country was to stay calm. All religious matters went to the priests' court, the Sanhedrin. If that condemned someone to death, the case then had to go before the governor for him to order the sentence. That was why Jesus met Pilate.

Sending the province's tax to the imperial treasury was the other duty of the governor. He was responsible for having the land tax and the poll tax collected; the publicans took the customs duties (see *Caesar's Image*). Governors turned their positions to their own advantage; the greediest bled their provinces white. In AD 17 both Syria and Judea complained to Tiberius that they were too heavily taxed, asking for relief.

Both taxes were based on surveys, the one of land, the other of people. As soon as Judea became a Roman province a census was begun (AD 6). Luke's Gospel places the birth of Jesus in the context of a census: 'In those days Caesar Augustus issued a decree that a census should be taken of the entire Roman world. (This was the first census that took place while Quirinius was governor of Syria.)' (Luke 2:1,2). At present it is almost impossible to reconcile this statement with other reports. Saturninus governed Syria from 10 to 7 or 6 BC and Varus followed him. Quirinius held office from AD 6. Herod was ruler when Jesus was born, according to Matthew 2:1,22 —therefore he must have been born before 4 BC, the year Herod died. The Roman emperor would hardly have ordered a census in Judea during Herod's reign, because he was responsible for collecting the taxes in his own land. No record of Quirinius governing Syria about 6 BC exists. Each of these points, and lesser ones, have convinced scholars that Luke made a mistake. His reference to a universal tax is unexplained. But much is still unknown, and a conclusive answer can only come with new discoveries.

Governors of Judea probably also received money from the High Priests in return for appointing them. The fourth governor, Gratus, put three in office in successive years (AD 15–18), then a fourth who was High Priest from AD 18 until AD 36, Joseph Caiaphas. Ultimate control over the Temple services lay with the governor, for he kept the High Priest's ceremonial robes in the Antonia fortress, releasing them only for the few days of major festivals. In AD 36 the governor of Syria handed them back to the priests, to appease the Jews after he had sent Pontius Pilate back to Rome for misgovernment.

Apart from their names, little is recorded about the governors before Pilate. The first, Coponius, earned Jewish gratitude by repairing part of the Temple damaged in riots at the start of Archelaus' reign. One of the gateways from the Tyropoieon Valley into the Temple was named after him. Pontius Pilate gained a bad reputation (see *Certainly not a Saint!*). Later governors, such as Felix (AD 52–60), were worse, but their story does not belong here.

In the middle of each Roman army camp was a shrine. The legions' standards and the Roman eagle stood there. They were carried into battle to serve as rallying points. For any of them to be captured by the enemy was a disaster. On this Roman coin (a silver denarius) of about 31 BC, the eagle stands between two standards. Under the emperors, the roundels on the standards held imperial portraits. By allowing his soldiers to carry such standards into Jerusalem, Pontius Pilate caused a riot.

ROMAN GOVERNORS OF JUDEA

Coponius	AD 6–9
Ambibulus	AD 9–12
Rufus	AD 12–15
Gratus	AD 15–26
Pilate	AD 26–36
Marcellus	AD 36
Marullus	AD 37–41
(perhaps = Marcellus)	
(King Agrippa I ruled Judea AD 41–44)	
Fadus	AD 44–46
Alexander	AD 46–48
(nephew of Philo)	
Cumanus	AD 48–52
Felix	AD 52–59
Festus	AD 59–62
Albinus	AD 62–65
Florus	AD 65–66

PILATE'S OWN MONUMENT

The town theatre was old. King Herod had built it over 300 years before. Others had changed and rebuilt it, and now there was major remodelling to be done. The architects redesigned the orchestra area so that it could be filled with water for spectacular displays. Extra walls were needed and new arrangements for the entrances.

Cutting new stone blocks for such work was costly, so the builders looked for old or ruined buildings where they could find an easy supply. One they went to was almost as old as the theatre. There was a fine slab of stone there which would fit neatly at the top of some steps they had to build. A small problem was overcome with a few hammer blows. The slab was slightly too thick—people coming up the steps might trip on it—so workmen knocked away part of the surface to make a slope. What they did destroyed some letters cut into the face of the stone, but that did not matter to them. Now anyone coming up the steps would have a smooth passage.

In 1961 a team of Italian archaeologists from Milan were excavating at Caesarea, north of modern Tel Aviv and its suburb Herzliya. For the third year they were concentrating on the theatre which they had decided to clear. Moving away the sand and stones, they found the steps and the stone.

It is a limestone block 82 cm/32 ins high, 68 cm/27 ins wide, and 20 cm/8 ins thick. The right half of four lines of writing was still engraved on one part of it. They had survived the tread of countless theatre-goers' feet and were still clear. To find an inscription was a major event for the archaeologists —not many had come to light in Caesarea. As soon as this one was uncovered it made headline news. This is what can be seen on it:

There was no difficulty in completing the second and third lines as:

Here is a monument of Pontius Pilate, the Roman governor of Judea who gave his consent for the death of Jesus. It is the first one ever to be found.

King Herod built the theatre in Roman style at Caesarea. It was re-modelled several times over the following centuries until a fortress was erected over it in Byzantine times.

To the Italian archaeologists excavating the theatre at Caesarea this battered stone slab was the greatest prize—it is the only known inscription from his life-time naming Pontius Pilate, the Roman governor who ordered the crucifixion of Jesus. Part of his name can be seen in the second line.

Pilate apparently built a temple or shrine in honour of the Emperor Tiberius, called a Tiberieum, and wanted everyone to know it. Exactly what the missing words of the text were is debated. From the point of view of New Testament studies, the surviving parts of the wording are the most important. If they had been the ones hammered away, the other letters would have given less information. The PON of PONTIUS and the PRAEF of PRAEFECTVS might have pointed to the sense, but with less certainty, for the words could be completed in other ways.

A battered stone naming Pontius Pilate may not seem especially important at first, but this is the only one. No other inscription or document written in the first century AD actually mentions him. This is the only contemporary evidence for the existence of Pontius Pilate.

CERTAINLY NOT A SAINT!

The Samaritans worshipped on Mount Gerizim for centuries before Pontius Pilate broke up their pilgrimage. On one part of the mount foundations of a temple built by Hadrian in honour of Zeus have been uncovered. Beneath them are ruins of an earlier building, perhaps the Samaritan temple destroyed by Alexander Jannaeus in 128 BC.

Christians traditionally call outstandingly faithful men and women of the past 'saints'. Among the saints are famous men and women, such as Augustine and Theresa, whom everyone can admire. Other 'saints'—like George who killed the dragon—survive in stories which have little claim to be true, and almost nothing is known of them. There are also people whom some Christians call 'saints', but who do not qualify as saints in most people's minds. King Charles I of England, executed in 1649, is one of them. The most surprising of all is Pontius Pilate, listed as a saint by the Ethiopian Church.

In the fourth and fifth centuries stories were told about the trial of Jesus which put Pilate in a rather

better light than the Gospels do. He was made to seem more reluctant to condemn Jesus. In some quarters there was a report that Pilate committed suicide, supposedly realizing what a terrible thing he had done. Stories like these perhaps grew in the face of pagan attacks, and gave rise to views of Pilate which led the Ethiopians to rank him with the saints.

To the rest of the world, Pontius Pilate was weak, perhaps a villain, certainly not a saint. What sort of man was he really?

The stone from Caesarea is his own declaration of loyalty to the Emperor Tiberius who had appointed him. Nothing less would be expected of any Roman governor. That stone is the only first-hand statement we have from Pilate. Roman, Jewish and Christian writers of the first century tell more about him.

Tacitus is the only Roman author whose surviving books mention Pilate, and the reason is simply to give the date when Jesus was crucified. Jewish authors present a fuller picture.

Philo, the philosopher from Alexandria, spoke about Pilate when he was trying to persuade the mad Emperor Caligula not to set up his statue in the Temple in Jerusalem. He told how Pilate had set up gilded shields in Herod's palace in Jerusalem. They were plain, except for a short notice saying that Pilate had made them in honour of Tiberius. It may have been similar to the inscription from Caesarea.

Something about them offended the Jews. They asked Pilate to take them away. No other Roman official had treated the Jews with so little respect; they were allowed to practise their religion as they wanted to. At length Pilate gave way. The Jews threatened to appeal to the emperor if he did not, and that, Philo asserted, made Pilate change his mind. He was afraid Tiberius would learn of abuses in his rule.

Pilate had begun his period in office by showing the attitudes he would take. He had a fresh garrison march into Jerusalem at night with its military standards covered. Next day people saw them in place, with portraits of the emperor on them. The soldiers paid divine honours to these standards, so they were, in effect, idols. To have those in Jerusalem, near their Temple, was more than devout Jews could bear. They followed Pilate back to Caesarea and demonstrated outside his residence. His reaction was to summon them to the stadium. There he encircled them with soldiers and threatened to kill them all. Their reaction pulled the carpet from under his feet. They would die, they said, rather than see their Law flouted in Jerusalem. Pilate ordered the garrison back to Caesarea.

The books of the Jewish historian Josephus record this episode. They also tell of two other actions by Pilate which resulted in the deaths of many people. The first one started well. Thanks to Herod's prosperous rule, and the protection of Rome, the city of Jerusalem had grown. One thing essential for the growing population was water. The Virgin's Fountain was the only constant supply, so most houses had their own cisterns to collect rainwater, but there was never enough. Some time earlier an aqueduct had been made to bring water from Solomon's Pools, south of Bethlehem, to the Temple in Jerusalem.

Pilate decided to build a new one. Surely Jerusalem would be grateful! There were funds to pay for it, too. Large sums of money were stored in the Temple treasury, offerings from all over the world, so Pilate took some of it to pay for his project. Although Jewish teachings allowed spare funds from the Temple to be used for the good of the city, it was unthinkable for a Roman to take them, however good his purpose. In addition, the Emperor Augustus had decreed that no one should interfere with the Temple tax.

When Pilate went to Jerusalem, big demonstrations were held. The governor dressed his soldiers in civilian clothes and sent them into the crowds, with clubs hidden in their garments. On his order, they drew their clubs and broke up the crowds. Some people died from clubbings, others in the panic.

This occasion may be the same as one Luke's Gospel mentions: 'there were some . . . who told Jesus about the Galileans whose blood Pilate had mixed with their sacrifices' (Luke 13:1). The people of Galilee were very patriotic, although the inhabitants of Jerusalem looked down on them as provincials (see John 7:52). Pilgrims from Galilee could easily have become involved in the protest against Pilate's action. Their fervour would mark them out in the crowd, bringing them to the soldiers' notice. However, Luke may have known of another occasion which no other writer has reported.

Pilate's governorship ended with trouble in a different place. His authority extended over Samaria as well as Judea. There the people worshipped God on Mount Gerizim, maintaining that Jerusalem was the wrong place (see John 4:20). In AD 36 one Samaritan led a crowd to the hill where he said he would show them furniture from the Tabernacle, buried there by Moses.

Pilate heard that the men were going armed, so he sent his forces to stop them. A battle took place, men were killed and the leaders captured. Pilate executed them. He seemed to be doing the right thing, but he soon found it was wrong. The Samaritans protested very strongly to Pilate's superior officer, Vitellius, the legate of Syria. Their people were not rebels, they claimed, rather they suffered so much under Pilate's rule that they planned to emigrate. Their case appeared so strong to Vitellius that he ordered Pilate to leave for trial in Rome before the emperor. Pilate embarked, but it was winter, and when he arrived in Rome three months later Tiberius was dead (March AD 37). That is all Josephus records.

In the fourth century, the church historian Eusebius quoted an earlier writer who said that Pilate killed himself two years later.

Philo, Josephus and the Gospel writers were all naturally opposed to Pilate. Jews did not want Roman rule; Christians knew the part Pilate played in the crucifixion of Jesus. Their stories about him would be likely to show him in a bad light. If his own account were found, what would it reveal?

The Caesarea Stone proclaims his loyalty to Tiberius. One other source of evidence about him does exist, in the coins minted for the land under his control.

CLUES TO PILATE'S CHARACTER

Shiny new copper coins were changing hands in the market-place. They were the small change of Palestine. People were used to them, the Jewish priest-kings had made them as signs of their independence in the first century BC. So had Herod and his sons. The Roman governors had done the same, minting coins with the emperor's name on them, a picture of a tree, a bunch of grapes, or another plant, and the date. They proclaimed Rome's rule, irksome to nationalistic Jews, but accepted.

The new ones issued in AD 29, with three ears of corn stamped on them, looked the same until people turned them over. There on the back, in place of the palm-tree or ear of corn, was a pan or ladle. It was not an ordinary kitchen utensil, but the bowl Roman priests used for pouring wine in honour of the pagan gods.

These were the first coins Pontius Pilate supplied for Palestine. There was not much the Jews could do about it. They had to handle the money with its heathen design. Perhaps they protested to Pilate. If they did, they probably looked carefully at the new coins of AD 30 and 31, and became even more dissatisfied. On the back was a harmless wreath

In a handful of coins issued by the Roman governors of Judea, those made under Pilate stand out from the rest. He issued the coins with a curved staff (at left and right) and a ladle (left). Both were pagan objects, contrasting with the ears of corn and palm branches on the other governors' coins!

with the date in it; on the front was a curling rod, something like a shepherd's crook. One objectionable design was changed for another. This was the mark of office of the Roman augur, the expert who foretold the future. When an animal was sacrificed, the augur would inspect its entrails to tell whether the worshipper should carry out his plans that day or not. By putting such a device on the coins, Pilate could not but offend the Jews.

Out of the five Roman governors who struck coins in Judea, only one other put anything on them which could upset

the Jews. He was Felix, ruling from AD 52 to 60, the man who kept Paul in prison for two years (Acts 24:22–27). Felix was a thoroughly bad governor. He was the brother of the Emperor Claudius' influential freedman Pallas, and, according to Tacitus, when in Judea he 'believed himself free to commit any crime'. Even so, while he was in power the coins made in AD 54 and 58 carried ears of corn or palm branches, and the Emperor Nero's name in a wreath. One type, which was issued in AD 54, was apparently meant to assert Rome's control. On one side it shows military equipment, crossed shields

and spears.

As people spent their money, the coins themselves would remind them how the power of Rome affected their lives. Yet, despite Roman rule, the Jews were free to follow their own religious rules and ceremonies. Pilate's coins, unlike those of all the other governors, could be seen as threatening interference in that exclusive religion. Those coins, Philo, Josephus, and the Gospels, all tell the same story: Pontius Pilate had no concern for Jewish feelings. The coins he issued give their first-hand evidence.

MONEY AND COINS

Enormous numbers of coins made 2,000 years ago still exist. On Mount Carmel in 1960 a hoard of 4,500 silver pieces was found. Most of them are shekels and half-shekels of Tyre, the rest are hundreds of denarii bearing the images of Augustus and Tiberius. Who hid them, and why, no one knows. Perhaps they were part of the yearly tax being taken to the Temple in Jerusalem when disaster struck the caravan (see *At the Moneychangers' Tables*). Even this big hoard is only a very small fraction of the coins current. A carefully calculated estimate puts the amount taken to the Temple each year at half a million shekels.

From Herod's time onwards money was officially counted by Roman standards. Greek and Semitic names were still used, and the great variety of coins circulating gave the money-changers plenty of business. The basic unit was the silver *denarius*, equal to the Greek drachma, a good day's wage. The Good Samaritan in Jesus' story left two denarii towards the cost of the robbed man's board for several days at the inn (Luke 10:35).

For very large transactions or the savings of the wealthy, there was a gold coin, the *aureus*, worth 25 denarii.

The crowds who followed Jesus rarely saw a gold coin. For buying and selling in large amounts they had the denarius and the larger silver coins of the Greek cities, the two and four drachma pieces. The four drachma piece, also called a *stater*, was equal to the Semitic *shekel*.

Copper coins served the needs of daily life. Rome made the sestertius, one quarter of a denarius, and that was the unit for counting money in Latin, even for large sums. Augustus boasted, for example, that he bought land in Italy to give to the soldiers at a cost of 600,000,000 sesterces.

The *dupondius* was half a *sestertius*, but the ordinary copper coin was the *as*, originally named *assarion*. Four asses made one sestertius, sixteen asses one denarius. The soldiers were paid by the *as*, and the average cost of a loaf of bread was an *as*. Two sparrows sold for one *as*, or five for two (Matthew 10:29; Luke 12:6).

The smallest of Roman coins was the *quadrans*, one quarter of an *as*.

In Judea the largest copper coins were issued by Herod Antipas (see *Herod's Sons*). Herod and his sons, and the Roman governors, minted coins which were mostly quadrans size, that is to say, one sixty-fourth of a denarius. This was 'the last penny' which had to be paid in Matthew 5:26.

Mark's Gospel explains that one quadrans equalled two smaller coins, the *lepton*. That was the widow's offering (see *A Widow's Mite*). The Jewish priest-kings, and Herod and Herod Archelaus struck tiny bronze coins a little over a centimetre (half an inch) in diameter, and weighing between 1 and 2 grams (0.05 oz) which were probably worth half a quadrans each, a *lepton* in Greek, or a *prutah* in Hebrew. This was 'the last penny' of Luke 12:59.

Between the poor widow and wealthy King Herod yawned an immeasurable gap. Herod's income was measured in talents, a weight too large to be coined, containing 10,000 drachmae or 40,000 sesterces. His annual income at his death was about 1,050 talents, equivalent to 42,000,000 sesterces. Cicero said an annual income of 600,000 sesterces was needed to lead the life of a gentleman in Rome about 50 BC. That amounts to about 60 talents, or 150,000 denarii, something like one thousand times the income of a Palestinian peasant farmer at the same time! In the parable of the unjust steward recorded in Matthew's Gospel (18:23,24), the ten thousand-talent-debt which the king cancelled was an unimaginably large sum—Herod's income for ten years!

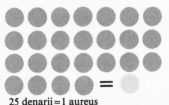

25 denarii = 1 aureus

d.19.05mm/0.75in

This aureus was issued by Augustus in Ephesus about 20 BC to celebrate the addition of Armenia to the empire. On the reverse the figure of victory is cutting a bull's throat.

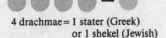

4 drachmae = 1 stater (Greek)
or 1 shekel (Jewish)

d.26.67mm/1.05in

A silver four-drachma (shekel) coin from Sidon, 31–30 BC. It shows the turreted head of Fortune, and an eagle with its foot on the prow of a galley.

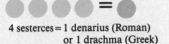

4 sesterces = 1 denarius (Roman)
or 1 drachma (Greek)

d.20.3mm/0.8in

The lost coin of the parable in Luke 15:8,9, was a drachma or denarius. This one was issued by Augustus to celebrate the conquest of Egypt, 28 BC.

4 asses = 1 sestertius

d.35.56mm/1.4in

This sestertius of AD 22–23 carries the letters S.C. 'by permission of the Senate' and Tiberius' titles on the obverse; on the reverse is a text advertising his generous aid to cities in Turkey damaged by a great earthquake in AD 17.

4 quadrans = 1 as (assarion)

d.30.48mm/1.2in

Tiberius had coins struck in honour of Augustus as a god. His bust wears a divine crown and the words mean 'Divine Augustus, Father'. On the reverse is a panelled altar. This is an as.

2 lepta = 1 quadrans

d.16.5mm/0.65in

This is a quadrans of Augustus, 9 BC. On the obverse are the emblems of Augustus as high priest, the ladle and staff which Pontius Pilate put on coins he issued. The inscriptions name the officials in charge of the coinage.

1 lepton (Greek) or
1 prutah (Jewish)

d.12mm/0.5in approx.

On tiny coins minted near the end of Herod's reign appears an eagle which may be the one he had put up in the Temple (see Herod's Great Temple).

CAESAR'S IMAGE

All governments tax their subjects, and Rome was no exception. Wherever Rome ruled, taxes were imposed. There was a tax on the produce of the land, there was a tax on imports and exports, and there was a tax on each person.

Even where King Herod ruled, his kingdom had to pay a tribute to Rome each year in return for her protection and as a sign of subjection. This was the land tax (*tributum soli*), probably amounting to about one eighth (12.5 per cent) of the annual yield of the crops. The well-to-do paid this to the king or,

after Judea became a Roman province in AD 6, to the governor.

All over the Empire there were tax collectors at ports and frontier towns. They had to levy tax on goods passing from one place to another. The rate of this tax is uncertain; it may have been quite low, about one fortieth (2.5 per cent) of the value of the merchandise. Collecting it could be very profitable, for it would be the tax collector's task to estimate the value, and he could easily over-estimate it. The men who did this work were not government

officials but businessmen (*publicani*) who bought the rights to collect in specific areas. They paid the amounts which the government had set as appropriate for each place, then recouped their outlay and made as much extra profit as they could from the merchants who travelled past their posts. (When tax collectors asked John the Baptist what they should do, Luke 3:13 records that he told them bluntly, 'Don't collect any more than you are required to.')

Within any area the actual collecting was done

by employees of the concessionaire. Levi, or Matthew (one of Jesus' twelve apostles), was one of these. At his tax-collecting booth by Lake Galilee he probably assessed the value of goods carried across the Lake to or from other regions (Matthew 9:9–13 records how Jesus called Matthew to follow him).

Not surprisingly, people hated the 'publicans' and their agents. They worked for the occupying power, and they lined their own pockets in the process. No wonder Jesus' conduct provoked hostile comment

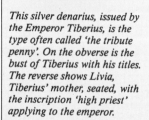

This silver denarius, issued by the Emperor Tiberius, is the type often called 'the tribute penny'. On the obverse is the bust of Tiberius with his titles. The reverse shows Livia, Tiberius' mother, seated, with the inscription 'high priest' applying to the emperor.

Tax-collecting was a part of government everywhere. On this carving from a third-century tomb in Germany, the collector sits with his ledger and piles and bags of coins.

when he met and shared meals with publicans and tax collectors. To the religious people the fact that they worked with non-Jews (Gentiles) made these men 'unclean'.

One customs' post was at Jericho, by a major crossing-place over the River Jordan. The river marked the boundary between the province of Judea and the district on the eastern side, called Perea. In Jericho about AD 30 one of the leading publicans was named Zacchaeus. How much these men might gain from their activities is made clear by the promise the remorseful Zacchaeus gave, after coming face to face with Jesus: 'If I have cheated anybody out of anything, I will pay back four times the amount' (Luke 19:8).

The tax that people resented most was the individual or poll-tax (*tributum capitis*). To discover how much was due, the authorities needed to know how many people lived in each part of the Empire. That was the reason why, as Luke 2:1 tells us, the Emperor Augustus ordered a census to be taken throughout the Roman Empire, at the time of Jesus' birth. To simplify the process, everyone had to register in his own home town. Collecting this tax was a job for the governor and his staff. The annual rate at the time of Jesus was about one day's wage for a workman: one Roman denarius per head.

The teachers in Jerusalem asked Jesus about this tax, to try to trap him into saying something subversive against the Roman rule. They would then have had a case against him to take to the governor. They asked: '''Is it right for us to pay taxes to Caesar or not?'' He saw through their duplicity and said to them, ''Show me a denarius. Whose portrait and inscription are on it?'' ''Caesar's,'' they replied. He said to them, ''Then give to Caesar what is Caesar's, and to God what is God's.'' They were unable to trap him in what he had said there in public. And astonished by his answer, they became silent.'

The Gospel writers do not describe the coin in detail. Many silver denarii issued by the emperors Augustus and Tiberius bore the imperial portrait. One type minted for Tiberius is especially common and has become known as 'the tribute penny' by being identified as the coin shown to Jesus.

The overseers of the Sacred Gate at Aswan in Egypt issued this receipt written in Greek on a piece of broken pottery on 12 July AD 144. Pekysis had paid poll-tax of 16 drachmas.

ARMY OF OCCUPATION

Roman soldiers were highly trained and harshly disciplined. Each man was responsible for maintaining his armour and weapons. A bronze model from the second century AD shows one wearing an iron helmet and leather clothes plated with iron.

Judea was under occupation. Even in peace-time Roman soldiers were to be seen in most places, and officers had homes in small towns like Capernaum (Luke 7:2ff.; Matthew 8:5ff.).

Herod could not command Roman troops. He had his own forces, modelled on the Roman army. Augustus gave him a bodyguard of 400 men from Galatia in central Turkey. Previously they had been Cleopatra's. To garrison his castles Herod hired mercenaries. He also had a squad of archers from Trachonitis, harnessing the skills of the former bandits.

Herod settled a large body of reservists on land around his new city at Sebaste (old Samaria), and others on the Nabataean frontier at Heshbon. He took a troop of Idumeans to the north-east, away from their home area. A troop of cavalry reserves lived at Gabae on the north slopes of Mount Carmel. They were within reach of Galilee should trouble break out there. The Idumean troop could be mustered to put down troublemakers in Trachonitis and nearby areas. The men quartered at Sebaste were convenient for Judea and Jerusalem. Herod's soldiers served his sons and, after Archelaus was deposed, those in Judea and Samaria came under the command of the Roman governor.

Pontius Pilate and the governors before and after him had five infantry cohorts of 500 men each, and one cavalry cohort, making 3,000 men in all. Their main base was the governor's capital, the largely Greek city of Caesarea. None of them was Jewish, because Julius Caesar had decreed that the Jews were exempt from military service, and Augustus had upheld that position. (Military discipline would make it impossible for them to keep the Sabbath or the food laws.) Consequently racial problems arose between the soldiers and the people they had to control. When the troops were on duty at religious festivals in Jerusalem, violence could easily break out as the crowds grew excited.

The auxiliaries were not very well paid, their annual wage being perhaps 100 denarii, whereas a legionary would receive 225 denarii. But the auxiliary had one valuable reward. After twenty-five years' service he could· retire with a gratuity and receive a diploma which gave him Roman citizenship. His children would inherit that status.

Authority and discipline were the basis of the army's function. The centurion who told Jesus how his men obeyed him exemplifies that (Matthew 8:8,9). It is also clear from the camps the soldiers built. From the top of Masada the lines of stones marking tent walls and streets show up plainly. Once the siege was over (AD 73), the camps were left to crumble gradually, an impressive testimony to the basis of Roman power.

On campaign, Roman troops built ramparts around their camps at night. Laying siege to Masada (AD 70–73), they built more permanent camps around the foot of the rock, but out of bow-shot. From the top of Masada the ruins of these square camps are obvious on the bare ground.

RELIGION

Two discoveries have added greatly to our knowledge of
Jewish religion in the first century. One gives visible, physical evidence,
the other brings books which tell of ideas and beliefs. The first is the
excavation of remains from Herod's Temple, the Temple where Jesus
walked and taught. The second is the Dead Sea Scrolls. These books
belonged to a group of religious Jews who were hoping for the Messiah
to come. They are the only Jewish books actually surviving from the
Gospel period.

The seven-branched lampstand, the menorah, *has become a symbol of the Jewish faith.
It was first stamped on coins by Antigonus, the man the Parthians set up as priest-king
in Jerusalem about 40* BC *(see* Herod—King of the Jews*).*

TEMPLE TOURISTS

They stopped and stared, and shouted for joy. There across the valley stood the Temple, white stone walls gleaming, flashing with golden ornaments. That was what they had come to see! From Jericho to Jerusalem the road was steep and hard, hot and dusty for much of the year. For the last few miles a long, tree-covered hill formed the sky-line, with a promise of shade after the bare hills of the desert. As pilgrims reached the top of the Mount of Olives, or rounded its corner, Jerusalem was spread out before them.

From every angle the Temple crowned the city, but the view from the Mount of Olives was the most impressive. The east wall ran for 460 metres/500 yards along the brow of the valley opposite, and the shrine itself stood in the centre. At the corner where the south and east walls met there was a tower. Anyone standing on the top could look straight down into the Kidron Valley, a precipitous drop

estimated by some scholars at as much as 137 metres/450 feet. 'Pinnacle of the Temple' is a name fit for such a dizzy height. That name, used in the account of Jesus' temptations, may apply to this tower or to a high corner of the main Temple (Matthew 4:5; Luke 4:9).

The Temple! That was the pilgrims' goal. To see it, to walk in its court-yards, to bring sacrifices and pray there were the aims that brought them from all over the world. Herod's wide courtyard allowed them into the Temple area in their thousands, but they could not live there. Even the most devout pilgrims had normal physical needs. They had to find somewhere to sleep, to eat, and to make themselves pure for worship.

Jerusalem was always busy with visitors and traders coming and going, so there were inns and lodging houses all over the city. In springtime, when the Passover Festival came round, the whole place became a vast camp, as pilgrims flocked in to keep the feast there. The poor set up tents and shelters outside the city walls, others paid for rooms or sleeping-spaces. According to Josephus there could be as many as three million people in Jerusalem at Passover time! All agree that this figure is too high, but pil-grims could certainly be numbered in hundreds of thousands.

Near the Temple, ruins of first-century houses have remarkably many ritual baths. One excavator has explained their number as evidence that the houses were hostels where pilgrims stayed. The baths on the

The generosity of Theodotus, who built a synagogue and an inn in Jerusalem, is recorded in this inscription.

premises were convenient for them to use before they entered the Temple.

Helping pilgrims was an act of charity. Wealthy men in Judea and abroad gave money to pay for building hostels and synagogues for them. Altogether there were said to be 480 synagogues in Jerusalem in the first century. Attached to them were schools for studying the Old Testament. There the teachers explained how to interpret and apply it to everyday life according to 'the tradition of the elders'. One of these centres is known to us from first-hand evidence.

A French team digging in the City of David, the southern part of the Old City, in 1914, found a plastered cistern. In it were pieces of stonework from a fine building. One has ten lines of Greek letters on it. They announce the building of a synagogue by Theodotus,

a priest and synagogue-ruler. His father Vettenus was also a synagogue-ruler, and his father had been, too. This meant that he was in charge of the affairs of the synagogue, including the choice of those who would read the Scriptures. The Gospels tell us that a man called Jairus held this position in Capernaum (Mark 5:22; Luke 8:41). Theodotus' inscription states that he built the synagogue 'for reading the law and teaching the commandments'. The buildings included an inn for overseas visitors who needed lodgings, with rooms and baths. The style of the letters and the place where the stone was found show that the inscription belonged to the city destroyed in AD 70. Who Theodotus was there is nothing to say. His father's name, Vettenus, was the name of a large Roman family, so he may have been a Jewish prisoner,

The only example of Herod's buildings still standing high above ground is the wall of the Tombs of the Patriarchs in Hebron.

bought as a slave, who took the family name when he was set free. If Theodotus and his father lived in Italy, their concern to help visitors in Jerusalem is easy to understand.

Ruins of synagogues from later centuries often display, engraved on the stones or laid out in mosaic pavings, the names of people who paid for parts of them to be built. Fragments of other Greek inscriptions found near the Temple indicate that the custom was well known in the first century. The names of the donors lived on, and worshippers and pilgrims were grateful.

Even without the gleaming Temple of Herod, the view of Jerusalem from the Mount of Olives enthralls the visitor.

HEROD'S GREAT TEMPLE

'Do you see all these great buildings?. Not one stone here will be left on another; every one will be thrown down.'

That was Jesus' reply to the disciple who was amazed at Herod's magnificent Temple (Mark 13:2), and it has proved to be true. Although part of the platform still stands, there is nothing left of the 'great buildings'.

Happily, Josephus wrote a description of them, and the rabbis remembered a lot of details which were written down in the Mishnah at the end of the second century. Now recent discoveries can join those ancient reports to give a clearer picture of this magnificent place.

Clearing away rubbish and the ruins of later buildings outside the south end of the enclosure and round the corner on the west side, archaeologists reached a paved street that ran along the foot of the walls. About 8 metres/26 feet of rubble and stones had to be moved to reach it, among them great blocks tumbled from the Temple walls. They were beautifully squared, just like those still in position in the lower parts of the platform. Others had fallen from the building on top of the platform at the southern end.

The written records tell that a great columned hall or portico stood there, open on the north side, like a cloister. This was called the Royal Portico because of its size. Four rows of pillars divided it into three long aisles. Josephus reports that each pillar was 8.2 metres/27 feet high and so thick that three men standing with arms stretched out could just encircle it. The tops of the pillars were carved with rows of leaves and the ceiling with leaves and flowers. Pieces of these pillars and decorations were found in the fallen rubble.

It was in this splendid porch that the moneychangers' tables stood, and the traders had stalls to sell animals and birds for sacrifices. To some religious Jews, carrying out such business inside the area of the Temple was objectionable—it seemed irreverent. Jesus dealt with the problem one day: 'Jesus entered the temple area and began driving out those whc were buying and selling there. He overturned the tables of the money changers and the benches of those selling doves . . . he said, "Is it not written: 'My house will be called a house of prayer for all nations'? But you have made it a 'den of robbers'"'. (Mark 11:15–17).

Using the Royal Portico as a market-place was bad enough. But there was worse. Many of the traders charged very high prices, taking cruel advantage of the pilgrims who came from the countryside and from foreign lands. The traders had to pay for permission to have their stalls in this area, and is seems they had to pay the leading priests.

Later Jewish tradition remembered one place as 'the Bazaars of the sons of Annas'. One Annas was High Priest from AD 6 to AD 15, when he was deposed. After him five sons, one of them also named Annas, and a son-in-law, Caiaphas, also served as High Priests (see Luke 3:2; John 18:13–24;

Acts 4:6). The bazaar was called after one of these, and he and his family no doubt took a fat commission from the sales. Both Josephus and the rabbinic writings portray the family of Annas and other priestly families as greedy, extorting money from other priests and beating up ordinary people. Jesus had every reason to be angry at what was done in the Royal Portico! Others grew angry, too, and a mob swept away the whole bazaar a few years before the Roman army took the city in AD 70.

Other colonnades lined each side of the Temple area. The one on the east was Solomon's Porch. When Herod began to make the Temple courtyards bigger, his men found that the old platform wall above the side of the Kidron Valley was sound, so they did not replace it. Solomon's Porch was also left, standing on top of it. Exactly how old that wall was is uncertain, and so is the age of the Porch. In spite of its name, it probably belonged to the time when the Temple was rebuilt under the Persian kings Cyrus and Darius. The Jewish priest-kings of the second and first centuries BC may have altered and repaired it. Piles of earth were removed from the wall in 1965, revealing a junction between Herod's stonework and another style, evidently the older wall.

These covered walks provided shelter from the sun's heat and from chilly winds. People could meet each other and stand and talk in them, as the first Christians did (Acts 3:11; 5:12). Teachers and students would gather there to learn and debate, as Jesus did with the rabbis when he was young, and later with his disciples (Luke 2:46–50; John 10:23ff.).

Glistening in the middle of the courtyard was the gilded Temple itself. A big wall surrounded it, so the Jewish rebels were able to make it their last stronghold against the forces of Rome in AD 70. Like the porticoes, all this has disappeared. Everything we know about it comes from Josephus, who had been inside as a priest, and from memories handed down by the rabbis.

Foreigners were not allowed to enter the Temple courts: notices, written in Greek, forbade entrance on pain of death. In 1871 one of these notices was found intact in Jerusalem. In 1936 a fragment of another was found, showing that the letters were originally painted red.

HEROD'S TEMPLE

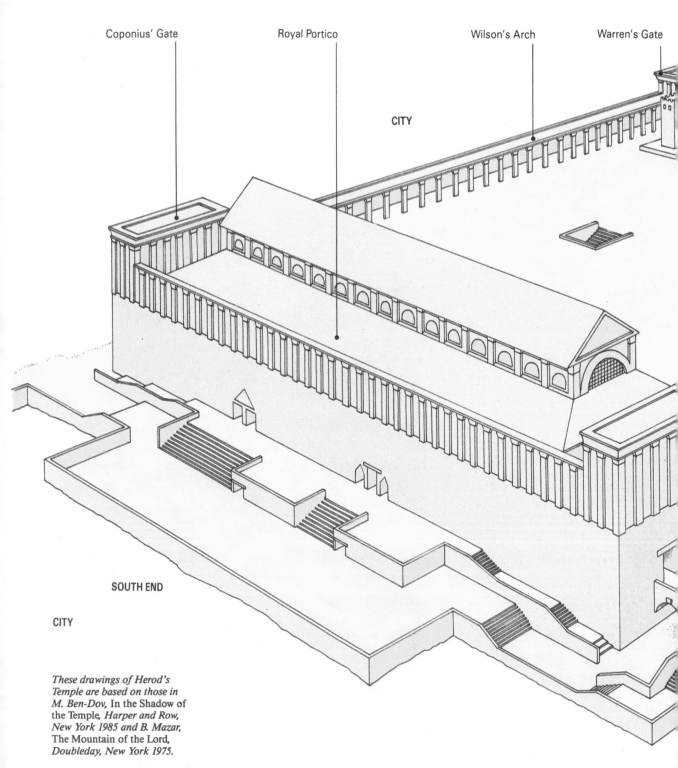

Coponius' Gate

Royal Portico

Wilson's Arch

Warren's Gate

CITY

SOUTH END

CITY

These drawings of Herod's Temple are based on those in M. Ben-Dov, In the Shadow of the Temple, *Harper and Row, New York 1985 and B. Mazar,* The Mountain of the Lord, *Doubleday, New York 1975.*

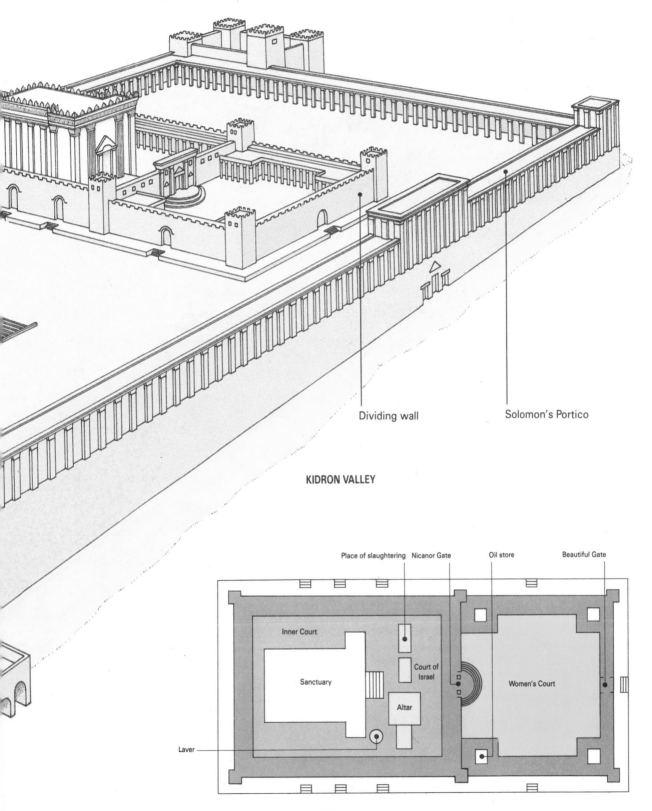

Dividing wall

Solomon's Portico

KIDRON VALLEY

Place of slaughtering   Nicanor Gate   Oil store   Beautiful Gate

Inner Court

Sanctuary

Court of Israel

Altar

Women's Court

Laver

ΟCΤΑΤΩΝΤΟΥΝΕΙΚΑ
ΝΟΡΟCΑΛΕΖΑΝΔΡΕΩC
ΠΟΙΗCΑΝΤΙCΤΑCΘΥΡΑ

This stone ossuary from a large tomb was found at the north end of the Mount of Olives in 1902. The Greek writing on the end says, 'Bones of the sons of Nicanor the Alexandrian who made the doors.' The names of the sons, Nicanor, Alexas, were added in Hebrew letters.

A few details help to suggest the grandeur and glory of it all.

Only Jews could go into the central buildings. A stone barrier about 1.3 metres/4½ feet high divided them from the outer court. Notices written in Greek and Latin warned everyone who was not Jewish to keep out. A foreigner who crossed the line was likely to be lynched (see *No Entry— Except For Jews*).

Steps led up to a platform and on it the high wall around the inner courtyards. More steps led up to gates in the wall. There were four on the north and four on the south. Each one was 13.5 metres/45 feet high, covered with gold and silver plating. Alexander, brother of the philosopher Philo (see *Philo—a Philosopher of Alexandria*) presented them to the Temple.

Another Alexandrine Jew, named Nicanor, gave the pair of gates which stood at the east end, the main entrance. Although its decoration was only bronze, it was a superb example of Corinthian workmanship, which Josephus asserts made it even more valuable than the other gates. They were so heavy, twenty men were needed to push them shut. This 'Corinthian Gate' was probably the 'Beautiful Gate' referred to in Acts, chapter 3, where a beggar sat when Peter and John went into the Temple to pray.

Through the Beautiful Gate worshippers went into the Court of Women, 67 metres/222 feet square. At each corner was a building for storing Temple supplies. Thirteen collection boxes stood there. They were shaped like trumpets turned upside-down. This is where Jesus saw a widow make her humble offering and commended her for giving to God not just what she had to spare, but all she possessed (see *A Widow's Mite*).

Only the men were allowed to climb a flight of steps from the Women's Court and pass through another gold-decorated gate, also a gift of Alexander, to the place where they could see the altar for burnt sacrifices, and beyond into the actual Temple. That had an enormous front 50 metres/164 feet wide and equally high. King Herod put a golden eagle on top of it (see *Money and Coins*).

'You shall not make for yourself an idol,' said the Ten Commandments, and in the eyes of two rabbis, at least, the placing of the eagle broke the law.

When they heard Herod was dying, the rabbis urged their followers to pull it down. They cut it to pieces before the crowds in the Temple. They acted too soon; Herod was not dead. His soldiers arrested the men and took them to the king. Furious, in spite of his illness, the king went out to harangue the crowd, then had the eagle-breakers and their teachers burnt alive.

The golden eagle fell. A different golden ornament was happily accepted. Curling along the top of the entrance to the Temple hung a golden vine. Bunches of grapes dangling from it were as high as a man, Josephus claimed. Worshippers could add a leaf, or a grape, or a bunch of grapes as a gift to God.

Herod redesigned the Temple, as far as he could, to make room for as many people as possible. He dared not change the shape of the holy shrine. He had it rebuilt on the same plan and to the same size as Solomon had built the first one, and just as richly. The walls inside shone with gold, and outside golden spikes kept birds from perching along the edges of the roof. Within the shrine were the golden table for holy bread, the golden lampstand with seven branches (the *menorah*), and the altar for burning incense.

The innermost room, the Holy of Holies, was empty. The Ark of the Covenant, which had stood there in Solomon's day, disappeared when the Babylonian army of Nebuchadnezzar burnt the first Temple. When Pompey, the Roman general, pushed his way into this sacred place he was surprised to find it empty (see *There's no God There!*).

All this magnificence was reduced to ashes and rubble in AD 70. According to Josephus, the Roman commander Titus, whose father was now the Emperor Vespasian, wanted to preserve the Temple. But Jewish resistance groups frustrated any attempt to save it. As the fighting moved from one part to another, fires were started and put out, until a soldier threw a flaming torch through the inner gate and set the shrine ablaze.

So the Temple was destroyed. All the great buildings were thrown down —not one stone was left upon another.

WHAT MASSIVE STONES!

Where two kinds of stonework meet, on the east side of the Temple platform, it seems Herod's builders added their larger stones (left) to an older building.

'Look, Teacher! What massive stones! What magnificent buildings!'

Those were the amazed exclamations one of Jesus' disciples made as they left the Temple in Jerusalem (Mark 13:1). Most of their houses were built of stone. They were used to seeing stone walls and arches. But the stones of their houses were simply fetched from the fields or the hillsides. They were stones a man could carry on his own, one at a time. To build a wall, he would pack the stones together, fitting them according to their shapes, and packing smaller stones and mud into the spaces. The wall could then be covered with mud plaster to give a smooth surface, and whitewashed. For doorsteps and lintels two or three men might have to carry larger, flat stones. A man with a good eye could split some stones to make a flat face, or a square block. Houses of rich people in Jerusalem were built of stones cut more carefully, but not usually very large ones. They, too, were plastered, at least on the inside.

Walls built entirely of cut blocks laid against each other are stronger than walls made of rough stones packed together. They could be taken higher without greater width, and they could carry a heavier load of floor or roof timbers or arches. That sort of building first appeared about the time of David and Solomon. Remains of palaces and other buildings of the tenth century BC at Megiddo show this style of masonry. The stones were so good that later generations took them from the old walls to make new ones. At Samaria the same style of fine stonework can still be seen in the ruins of the palace of Ahab and the kings of Israel who followed him in the ninth and eighth centuries BC. Obviously kings could afford to build in the best way.

That was what King Herod set out to do, with the Temple in Jerusalem. He wanted to make the Temple as magnificent as it had been in King Solomon's time, or more so. When the Jews came back from their exile in Babylon, they rebuilt the Temple which Nebuchadnezzar's army had destroyed (see 2 Kings 25:9ff.; Ezra 1,3). That Temple did not reach the splendour of Solomon's, so Herod declared that he would rebuild it, all at his own cost.

The work began about 19 BC, possibly two or three years earlier. It was made difficult by the need to carry on the services and sacrifices, and by the rule that only priests could go into the inner court and enter the Temple building itself. Herod wanted to do the right thing and not upset the people of Jerusalem. He hired 10,000 skilled workmen and had 1,000 priests trained in stonemasonry, so that they could erect the sacred building. One thousand wagons were needed to cart the stone from the quarries. Jerusalem's hills are all limestone of various qualities, so the material did not have a long way to travel. With everything made ready beforehand, the priestly masons managed to construct the new Temple within eighteen months. Celebrations were held on the anniversary of Herod's accession to the throne, the king himself providing a sacrifice of 300 oxen.

After that central part was finished, the work went on for a very long time. In a discussion with Jesus some Jews told him: 'It has taken forty-six years to build this temple' (John 2:21). That was about AD 28–30. Josephus reports that the whole of the Temple and its courtyards were finally completed in AD 62–64. Herod's plan was to outdo Solomon in the surroundings of the shrine.

Solomon's Temple stood on top of a hill. In order to have a level space around it, Solomon's masons probably put up walls on the east and west slopes of the hill, to hold a stone terrace. Whether or not any of this still existed in Herod's time is disputed. At the eastern side of the Temple, part of a wall can be seen which has stones cut in a different fashion from the stones of Herod's work. Most experts think this is part of the rebuilding after the exile, perhaps as late as the days of the Hasmonean kings in the second century BC, although one or two argue that it is a relic of Solomon's original wall.

The platform these terraces made seemed too small to Herod. His architects designed a much bigger one. At the north end that meant cutting away part of the rock to make the level area larger. At the south end the job was much harder. To raise the platform above the slopes of the hill, Herod's architects designed a series of vaults one on top of another, within a thick wall. At some points the wall was as much as 50 metres/165 feet high because of the unevenness of the rock. The weight of the stonework was so great that the builders had to rest the foundations on the bedrock itself.

In this way the Temple platform was made 32 metres/105 feet longer at the south. How much wider Herod made it has not been discovered. The overall dimensions of the whole enclosure are: east wall 470 metres/1,550 feet long, west wall 485 metres/1,620 feet, north wall 315 metres/1,050 feet, south wall 280 metres/930 feet. That is space enough for thirteen full-size football pitches, or nearly 200 baseball diamonds. It is about two and a half times as long as St Peter's Basilica in Rome, and nine and a half times its area—or five times the area of the Acropolis at Athens.

Parts of these great walls still stand. The most famous is the Wailing Wall, now called the Western Wall or Kotel, where several courses of the

The massive stones of Herod's Temple are visible today in the 'Wailing (Western) Wall'—a place of prayer.

Herodian stones rise above the modern pavement. Along the western side and at the south end excavations made since 1968 have uncovered a lot more of the walls and buildings which stood outside them.

Visitors who saw the blocks of stone in the Wailing Wall realized how well cut they were. Now, with much bigger stretches of wall uncovered, the impact of the massive stones is even more awe-inspiring. The average blocks are a metre or more high/3–4 feet and 1.25–3 metres/4–10 feet long and weigh from 2,000 kg/2 tons upwards. Some stones were much larger. There are many at the south-western corner, where the foundations were particularly deep, almost 12 metres/40 feet long and weighing 50,800 kilos/50 tons or more. The most enormous one was revealed in a tunnel dug illegally under the buildings against the northern part of the west wall. It is reported to be almost 12 metres/40 feet long, 3 metres/10 feet high, and 4 metres/13 feet thick, and the estimate of its weight is about 400,000 kg/400 tons.

Each stone was hewn out of a quarry near Jerusalem. ('Solomon's Quarries', shown to visitors, beneath the north wall of the Old City may have been one source.) Then teams of oxen or men would pull it in a cart to the building site. Some of the bigger stones may have been moved on wooden rollers or even had wooden

wheels built around them so that they would roll. Careful organization and understanding of the principles of balance and leverage, coupled with muscle-power, were the means of bringing the stones to the walls and setting them in place. Roman engineers had developed simple gears and pulleys which would have helped to hoist the stones to the higher parts of the walls.

At the site, each block was chiselled square, so that it would fit tightly against its neighbours without need for mortar between them. The outer side of each stone was dressed with a narrow margin, leaving the centre slightly higher. As a result, the wall did not present a completely smooth, blank face to the viewer. More interest was given to the walls at a slightly higher level by adding flat pillars to the surface of the wall, to give a pattern or relief and shadows. This is not now visible at the Temple area because of later destructions, but it can be seen in the wall of the Tomb of the Patriarchs at Hebron.

Time has proved the skill of Herod's builders. Earthquakes and destructive enemies have toppled all the Temple buildings. The upper level of the vaulted platform was damaged and had to be rebuilt when the Omayyad caliphs of Damascus turned the area into a Muslim holy place in the seventh century. All the rest still stands firm. Visitors can still exclaim, 'Look, what massive stones!'

Stone blocks at Megiddo show that the technique of smoothed margins was in use in the days of the kings of Israel.

AT THE MONEYCHANGERS' TABLES

There was a lot going on in the Temple courtyard. Pilgrims came from all over the world to offer sacrifices and worship God in his only Temple, at Jerusalem. Like travellers today, they had to change their money. Although Rome ruled much of the world, and the emperor's head guaranteed that this money was good (see *Caesar's Image*), there were other states which issued their own coins. Some rulers, like King Herod, had special rights under Rome's control; others, like the Nabataeans of Transjordan or the Parthians in Persia, were beyond the imperial frontiers.

This meant that every city had to have some moneychangers who could rate the different currencies against each other. In days before rapid communication, the rate was very much at the individual moneychanger's will. Basically it was done by weight. Silver and gold coins were standardized forms of bullion, but some places issued coins which were not quite pure silver or gold, so the changers would cut or file them as a test.

Naturally the money-changers looked for a profit when, for example, they bought Parthian coins with Roman ones. It was easy to cheat, so moneychangers were not the best-loved businessmen. Little wonder Jesus chased them from the Temple, telling them they had made it 'a den of robbers' (Matthew 21:13).

Every Jew was expected to pay a tax to the Temple each year. The amount was set at half a shekel of silver, the amount laid down in the Law of Moses for the atonement of every Israelite (Exodus 30:11–16). In the first century half a shekel was reckoned the equivalent of two Greek drachmas or two Roman denarii (see *Money and Coins*). A labourer could earn that amount in two days, according to Jesus' parable of the workers in the vineyard (Matthew 20:1–16).

The priests decreed that payment should be made in coins of the purest silver. Only one sort was acceptable, the silver coins of the city of Tyre. Although Jewish officials had occasionally issued silver coins under the Persian Empire, the independent Jewish kings of the second and first centuries BC did not. These kings, the Maccabees or, better, Hasmoneans, only struck small bronze coins for daily use in the market-place.

Silver coins were minted in large numbers by the Greek kings of Damascus, the Seleucids, but to use them for the Temple tax may have been distasteful. One of those kings, Antiochus IV, had defiled the Temple in 167 BC, causing the revolt led by the Maccabees. After 126 BC Tyre became independent of the Seleucids and started to issue its own shekels and half-shekels, without a king's name on them. The fact that they had the head of Melkart, the god of Tyre, on one side did not matter. Indeed, these coins were so suitable for Jewish use that when the Romans ended Tyre's privilege, about 20 BC, it seems that the Jewish authorities took over the minting of the coins and issued them in Jerusalem. The series only stopped when the First Revolt broke out in AD 66 and nationalistic rebels issued their own silver shekels and half-shekels with inscriptions in Hebrew.

The most common coin from Tyre is the shekel (stater or tetradrachm — four drachms); half-shekels are less often found. This suggests that Jews paid the Temple tax in pairs. That is what happened on one famous occasion. The Temple tax collectors were travelling the country and were in Capernaum when Jesus arrived there with his friends. Asked if Jesus would pay, Peter impetuously answered, 'Yes'. Jesus explained to him that there was no need to pay, but that they should do so to avoid giving offence. Peter was sent to catch a fish and take from its mouth the shekel he would find there to pay for both of them (Matthew 17:24–27).

Everyone who felt it a duty to pay the tax had to obtain the Tyrian coin. The exchange could be made anywhere, but for many it was convenient to be able to do it in the Temple. That is why there were moneychangers there, besides people selling animals suitable for sacrifice, when Jesus visited the Temple (Matthew 21:12).

A silver shekel of Tyre bearing the head of the city's god Melkart on one side and an eagle with the inscription 'Of Tyre, holy place and sactuary'. The date is AD 52, which may imply that the coin was made by the Jewish authorities. Such coins may have been given by the priests to Judas Iscariot (Matthew 26:15; 27:3–10).

When the Jews rebelled against Rome in AD 66 they made their own coins in silver and bronze. This silver half shekel was now the coin for the Temple tax. On the obverse the old Hebrew letters read 'half a shekel (year) 2', and on the reverse 'Jerusalem is holy'.

WHERE THE SAINTS HAVE TROD

'This is where Jesus was kept in prison . . . this is where the soldiers dressed him up . . . this is where they crucified him.'

Guides take tourists to all sorts of places, some likely, some unlikely. Not one of them carries a guarantee that it really is the place. None has a first-century sign, 'Jesus stood here!'

It is almost impossible to identify any place where Jesus, or any other famous person, stood in first-century Jerusalem. The Romans destroyed the Jewish city, and buildings have risen and fallen, century by century, ever since. A strong tradition guided the search for the tomb of Jesus, but no one can be certain the right tomb was found (see *Can We See the Tomb of Jesus?*). Other 'holy places' have far less evidence to support them. Thanks to archaeological excavations, visitors can now go to one site where they can be sure they are walking in the footsteps of Peter, John and Paul, of Jesus himself, and of the great rabbis Hillel and Gamaliel.

These famous people were a few of the thousands who came each year to worship at the Temple. Most would go in by the main entrance at the south end, where Herod built up his great platform on the sloping hill. Its wall rose over 19 metres/60 feet from the street at the south-west corner, and the Royal Portico on top of it made an overall height of over 30 metres/ 100 feet. Two gateways in the 280 metre/ 300 yard-long wall led into the Temple courtyard. A flight of steps led up to each of the gateways, and part of these steps has now been uncovered. The

three arches of one gateway have always been visible. A later building set against the wall hides most of the other, western gateway. The area in front of the gates lies largely outside the city wall, where no buildings have stood for over a century, so it was easy to excavate there.

After digging away a heap of rubbish, Benjamin Mazar's team of archaeologists soon came to the top steps. Following them down the slope, they unearthed the whole length of the flight—thirty shallow steps. The bedrock had been cut to form a series of steps as the bedding for fine stone slabs which made the staircase. Some of the original slabs still lay in their places; masonry falling from the wall had smashed some; and other builders took some for their work. Now new stones have been laid to fill the gaps, so that visitors can climb the stairs just as people did in the first century. Chips and cracks mark out the old slabs from the modern ones—so standing on those stones is truly to step 'where the saints have trod'.

The steps led up, across a paved street that ran along the wall, to the gateways. In ancient times they were known as the Hulda Gates. At present only one edge of the western gateway can be seen, because a tower was built against it when the city walls were redesigned 900 years ago. The only original part of the eastern gateway is the lowest row of stones above the street level. Muslim masons rebuilt both gateways when they took over the Temple area, building the Dome of the Rock and the Al-Aqsa Mosque in the

A wide flight of steps rose up to the gates leading into the south end of the Temple courtyard. The broken ancient stones have been restored so that visitors can climb the steps again.

seventh and eighth centuries. The gateways served as entrances to the sacred enclosure until they were blocked when new defences were put up to keep out the Crusaders. (These new walls proved to be too weak: the Crusaders captured the city in 1099.)

Despite destruction and rebuilding, quite a lot can be learnt about the gateways. The western, double one, was 12.8 metres/43 feet wide, the eastern one was about 15 metres/ 50 feet wide. Inside, the gateways and corridors had domed ceilings. The stone domes were carved with elaborate patterns in low relief, flowers, grapevines, and geometric figures. Behind the rebuilt double gateway these domes remain in place, although they are rarely accessible. Nothing of the three-arched gateway is in position except for one stone of the western-most doorway.

Outside, the excavators recovered scores of broken pieces of carved stone which had belonged to its ceiling. These fragments illustrate the richness of the decoration of the gateways and point to the splendour of the whole Temple. Today the stones are creamy or grey. Freshly carved, they were whiter, and details were probably painted,

making a colourful canopy over the pilgrims' heads.

People could go into the Temple through other entrances. Josephus listed four on the western side. In ancient times the Valley of the Cheesemakers (the Tyropoeian Valley) divided the Temple hill from the hill to the west. Here Herod's architects had to deal with the same problem they faced at the south end, but with less space. Instead of great flights of steps straight up the hill-slope to the gateway, they made different designs.

Excavations since 1968 have made clear what they did where the platform rose high above the valley, at the south-west corner. In 1838 the American pioneer Edward Robinson noticed the stump of an arch sticking out high up in the platform wall. He saw that it was the end of a bridge which led on to the platform near the end of the Royal Portico. Josephus spoke about a bridge across the valley, so scholars thought this was part of it.

When the excavators began to dig opposite the piece of arch in 1968, they thought they would find the first support of the bridge. They did not. Stone blocks from the base of a pier were still in place, but there had not been a row of them making a viaduct. Instead a staircase had climbed up from the street in the bottom of the valley, turning at right angles over arches of ever greater height to a gate level with the Temple courtyard. 'Robinson's Arch' turns out to be part of the last and biggest arch supporting the road. Parts of the lower arches were found to prove the bridge theory wrong.

Josephus' description had been misunderstood. He spoke of the gateway being separated from the opposite part of the city by 'many steps going down into the valley and thence up again to the hill'. At the foot of the steps a paved street ran beside the Temple wall and rooms built into the bottom of the pier were shops. Another road branched off at the corner of the platform, rising by a series of steps to the Hulda Gates in the south wall.

Not far along the western wall from this staircase stood another gate. An architect named Barclay investigated it in 1855–57. It opened from the street into the platform itself, a ramp mounting up to the courtyard in the same way as the ramps of the Hulda Gates. Today only one end of its lintel can be seen, still in place, at the right end of the 'Wailing Wall'. This is an enormous stone block, more than 2.1 metres/7 feet high and 7.5 metres/25 feet long. Its weight is probably over 50,000 kg/50 tons.

Still further along is another arch, found in 1865 by the early explorer, Charles Wilson. 'Wilson's Arch' seems to mark a viaduct which did bridge the valley from the town to the Temple, although the existing arch was rebuilt by early Muslim masons on the remains of the Herodian one. None of the gateway itself survives.

Yet another gate, opening from street level is known. Wilson uncovered the top of it in 1866 and named it in honour of his friend Charles Warren. It has recently been cleared again. Later buildings on top prevent further digging.

Pioneer explorers of a century ago, and their successors from 1968, have found four gates in the western side. Two led at high level on to the platform and were, presumably, entrances for visitors and pilgrims. The two gates at street level were more likely service entrances through which animals, wood for fuel, oil and other supplies could be taken into the Temple. Whether or not there were other gateways on the western side is uncertain at present. A second viaduct and a gate from the castle at the north-west corner may have existed. As to gateways on the north and east, little is known. The 'Golden Gate' is an early Muslim building and the age of the archway once seen beneath it cannot be established. Near the south-eastern corner are traces of an arch which corresponded to Robinson's Arch, and apparently a similar staircase. There were, therefore, many ways for visitors to reach the Temple courtyard and its splendid buildings.

Among stones fallen from the Temple buildings, the excavators found finely carved pieces which had decorated the ceiling of one of the gateways at the top of the steps.

A SECRET TUNNEL

Matthias of Jerusalem was High Priest; King Herod had appointed him. Year by year he carried out his duties as representative of his nation. The high point of the year was the Day of Atonement. Wearing a linen tunic, he would go through the heavy curtain, the veil, into the holiest part of the Temple, to sprinkle the blood of a sacrificed bull and goat on the ground. When he came out, the people knew God had forgiven the sins of the previous year.

In 5 BC it all went wrong. Matthias became unclean; he dreamt he was in bed with his wife, and that was forbidden to him in the days before the ceremony. He could not carry out his duties, he could not perform the ritual. Someone would have to stand in for him—

and a close relative who was also a priest was called to do so.

Religious laws ruled everyone who wanted to worship in the Temple (see *Cleanliness is Next to Godliness?*). Priests had to be even more particular. Every part of their lives fell under special rules, from marriage to mourning to cutting their hair, and many things could make priests unclean. Touching a person with a discharging sore or a wound, or a woman with bleeding, or a corpse, or certain insects, caused uncleanness. If that happened, the priest had to bathe himself and could not take up his duties until sunset. In Jesus' story about the Good Samaritan, the priest and the Levite who would not go near the wounded man

were more concerned to keep themselves ritually pure than to help a fellow human being, and that was Jesus' point (Luke 10:30–32).

Priests living in towns and villages could clean themselves in ritual baths to wash away such impurities, like anyone else. When they were serving in the Temple that was more difficult, for the Temple proper was also pure. Jewish tradition tells of tunnels leading below the Temple to a ritual bath outside the Temple walls. A priest could immerse himself, dry off by a fire, and go back inside without the risk of infecting other priests or the holy place and its furniture.

Deep in the rock outside the south end of the Temple the excavators almost fell into a tunnel

high and wide enough for one man to walk along it upright. Spaced along the walls were little shelves hollowed in the rock. When the archaeologists put candles in them, they saw at once that that was what they were for. Stones blocked the inner end of the tunnel where it ran under the Temple wall, so its route inside the area is unknown. Part of a second tunnel joined the first one, and apparently both led to a ritual bath. Only a precise description or an ancient notice could prove the purpose of these tunnels, so, as with other archaeological discoveries, the most one can say is that the link with the written tradition is likely to be right: these were the tunnels by which the unclean priests could reach the bath.

ZECHARIAH—
PRIEST OF THE ORDER OF ABIJAH

Zechariah's heart beat faster. He had come to the greatest moment of his life: he was the priest chosen to go into the holy place to burn incense. Every day the priests drew lots to pick the man who would carry out this duty. He could only do this once in his career, and some might never have the chance. The chosen priest stood there inside the Temple after the morning or evening sacrifice. He represented the people, and the incense rising from the altar was the symbol of their prayers going up to God.

Wherever they could, the priestly authorities kept to the rules laid down in the Old Testament. According to the First Book of Chronicles, King David arranged all the Temple staff. He divided the priests into twenty-four courses, each named after a leader (1 Chronicles 24:1–19). One course would do the duties in the

Temple for a week, then the next course in order would take over. By this rota every course stood twice a year, taking the priests' share of the sacrifices for those weeks. At the three great festivals, Passover, Pentecost and Harvest (Tabernacles or Booths), members of all the courses shared the ceremonies. In Herod's Temple the rota given in Chronicles was carefully followed.

Jerusalem was home for many priests, and a large group lived in Jericho, but most were scattered through the towns and villages of Judea. Zechariah and Elizabeth lived in one of these hill-towns. Zechariah had made the journey to Jerusalem many times, and had waited for years, hoping his turn would come. He was no longer young, and perhaps was thinking he would never have the honour of burning the incense. He belonged

to the course of Abijah, which was eighth in the list. At last his moment came, and Luke 1 records Zechariah's vision in the Temple and the extraordinary events that followed.

Even after Herod's Temple ceased to exist, the priests kept their list and orders. In some of the synagogues built during the third and fourth centuries, copies of the list were engraved on stone slabs fixed on the walls. Excavations at Ascalon and Caesarea have uncovered fragments of two of them. Beside the name of each course of priests is the name of the place where it had settled after the fall of Jerusalem. Course eighteen, named after Happizzez, made its home in Nazareth. One of the fragments from Caesarea has the name of that village on it, and that is the earliest record outside the Gospels of this then unimportant place.

Among the stones fallen from the southern wall of the Temple, Israeli archaeologists uncovered this stone block nearly 2.5 metres/8 feet long. It had tumbled from the top of a wall, perhaps at the south-west corner. The Hebrew inscription says 'of the trumpeting place' (or 'To the . . .') and may relate to the blowing of a trumpet to signal the beginning and the end of the sabbath, a duty of the priests in their rotas.

The old Temple area and Western Wall, from the air.

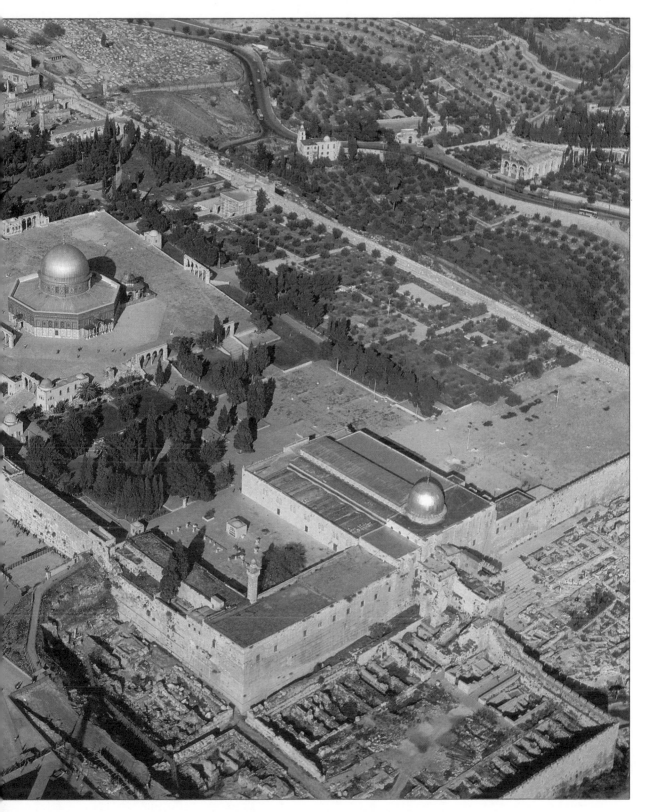

A WIDOW'S MITE

Among many small bronze coins minted by Herod the Great, this type is common. On the obverse is an anchor with the words 'of King Herod', and on the reverse two horns of plenty with a messenger's staff between.

A good day's wage for a workman in Palestine was one denarius, the Roman silver coin. It was the same value as the Greek drachma. One or other of these was the lost coin the woman hunted for in the parable of Luke 15:8–10. It was also half the tax each Jewish man paid yearly to the Temple (see *At the Money-changers' Tables*). Although a denarius was a day's wage, a labourer would not earn 365 denarii a year, because there was no pay for Sabbath days and other holidays. Jesus' parable of the grape-pickers who were each paid the same, one denarius, at the end of the day, assumes that there were workmen waiting for jobs, so some may not have found work every day (Matthew 20:1–16). Not surprisingly, cripples who could not hold a job often became beggars.

If a workman died, his widow could find herself in dire straits. Left alone (her parents also having died), perhaps with no close relatives or adult children and little or no property, she would have no income. All through the Bible, the widow is marked as one of the members of society most at risk. The story of how Jesus raised to life the son of the widow of Nain indicates the desperate state she was left in by his death (Luke 7:11–15).

The worker might receive a silver denarius as his pay, but for daily needs he would change it for smaller coins. They would be bronze pieces minted by the Jewish priest-kings in the first century BC, by Herod and his sons, and by the Roman governors (see *Money and Coins*; *Clues to Pilate's Character*). Sixty-four of them made one

denarius. Their Latin name, *quadrans*, was borrowed in Greek and Hebrew (see *Money and Coins*). Even these were not the smallest coins in people's pockets. The *lepton* was half a *quadrans*—a thin, tiny coin issued by the Jewish kings and Herod. Their value was very small; 128 of them were worth one denarius.

Beside the Temple tax, people made other presents of money to the Temple. Collecting boxes stood in the courtyard to receive them. As worshippers came by and threw in their offerings, Jesus was watching. He noticed a widow and drew attention to the size of her gift (Mark 12:42–44; Luke 21:2–4). She had given something more valuable than others, he said. She had put in all she had: that was two *lepta*, one sixty-fourth of a day's wage!

A TREASURE FROM BURIED BOOKS

'They're coming! Run for your lives! The Romans are coming!'

The message came at last to the edge of the Dead Sea. A commune of religious Jews lived there, isolated from everyone else. Their centre was well built, but it was not a fort where they could hold out against a strong enemy. Packing some food and other essentials, they left.

These people were devoted Bible students, owning hundreds of books. Although they could slip one or two books into a bag or a fold of a tunic, a whole Bible was too awkward to take away—it would be two dozen leather scrolls at least. To leave their holy books, and others, for the Roman soldiers to spoil was unthinkable. They would hide them.

Near the central building was a cave, and in it the people piled their library, 400 or more scrolls, books of the Bible (the Old Testament) and all sorts of others. Some of the people had been living in caves a little further away, and they left scrolls there. In one

cave there was time to wrap the scrolls in linen and put them in jars covered with lids, to protect them better. The people hoped that, when the Romans had gone, the books could be rescued.

If anyone did go back to save some of the scrolls, they left a lot of them behind. Some may have suffered at Roman hands. Among those in the main cave, a few show signs of being torn deliberately, and all were broken or damaged in some way. Winds blew dust and sand into the cave and, even in so dry a place, some damp also crept in. Worms burrowed and bored through the piles of leather. Gradually the crumbling scrolls disappeared under the dirt.

Yet they were not entirely lost to sight. About the year 200, some books of the Bible were found in a jar at Jericho, according to the great early scholar Origen. From 600 years later comes a report of another discovery of scrolls in a cave near Jericho, scrolls which played a part in the rise of a medieval sect of Jewish reformers.

In 1967 Israeli authorities confiscated the largest of all the Dead Sea Scrolls from its owner in Bethlehem. This is the Temple Scroll, 8.15 metres/ almost 9 yards long. It claims to present laws given by God to Moses about building the Temple, its worship, and the conduct of the king. The owners of the Scrolls probably hoped to bring these laws into effect when God gave them victory over their enemies.

The cliffs along the edge of the Dead Sea are riddled with caves. In the foreground of this picture is one close to the ruins of Qumran, Cave Four. About 400 scrolls were hidden here, but the ravages of time had reduced them to tens of thousands of fragments. Ever since their discovery in 1952, scholars have continued to study and fit them together.

After that, the scrolls lay undisturbed for over 1,000 years. In spite of their eagerness to find old manuscripts, neither Tischendorf (see *The Oldest Bibles*) nor any of the hunters like him saw that these stories might lead them to long-lost scrolls. No one thought that very old books would survive underground in Palestine. Only after the discovery of the Dead Sea Scrolls did the meaning of these early reports become clear.

Three shepherds were looking after their goats near the edge of the Dead Sea. Behind them were the crags of the desert cliffs. One of the Arabs saw a small hole in the cliff, and threw a stone into it. He was surprised to hear a sharp clattering noise. It was too late to explore that day, but he told the others about it. After a while, the youngest of them went off on his own and wriggled through a hole next to the first one. He dropped into a small cave, and saw what the stone had hit. An old pot was lying smashed on the floor. More pots stood in the cave. Lifting the lid off one, he found it full of red earth. In another were two small bundles wrapped in cloth, and one not wrapped. Each was a long roll of leather with small black letters all over the inside. The leather was thin and crumbly, not much use for anything. It was the winter of 1946–47 when they found the scrolls. During March 1947 they decided they might be worth some money. They took them to Bethlehem, to a carpenter who also bought and sold antiquities. He kept them for a while, then the shepherds came back.

'How much will you pay for them?'
'Nothing, they're not old!'

They took the scrolls away and arranged with another dealer to try to sell them. They agreed he could take a third of the price as his commission. A few weeks later he was able to give them their money: the three scrolls brought them £16—$65 at that time.

One of the shepherds had gone back to the cave meanwhile, and found some more scrolls buried under stones fallen from the roof. He sold those too. The shepherds had struck a gold mine, without knowing it!

An archbishop belonging to the Syrian Jacobite Church in Jerusalem had bought the first group of scrolls. Fighting in Jerusalem caused him to move to America where he tried to find a buyer for them. After seven years, he advertised them in *The Wall Street Journal*. They were for sale at a price to be agreed.

Someone showed the advertisement to Yigael Yadin, a leading archaeologist from Jerusalem who was visiting New York. He contacted a rich American friend who put up the money to buy them—a quarter of a million dollars. So it was that these scrolls returned to Jerusalem in 1954. There they were reunited with the second group, which Yadin's father,

Professor Sukenik, had bought for £80/$324.

By the end of 1948 newspaper reports had told the world about the discovery and its importance—Hebrew books from the time of Christ had never been found in Palestine before. News that the scrolls were very valuable reached the shepherds and their friends. They went hunting for more caves with scrolls in them until, by 1956, they had located eleven. One cave, Cave 4, had had about 400 scrolls in it. Falling stones, wind-blown dust, insects, and possibly enemies, had torn them into 40,000 fragments. Each one had to be bought from the Arabs who found them, at an average price of £1/$4 per square centimetre.

Museum funds were soon exhausted in Jordanian Jerusalem. The government of Jordan produced a considerable sum of money, and museums, academies and wealthy benefactors abroad gave more. In 1967 the last of the scrolls to come to light was confiscated from the shepherds' Bethlehem agent by Israeli authorities. Afterwards they paid him compensation of $105,000. He and the tribesmen for whom he acted had grown rich because of one idly thrown stone!

Almost all the scrolls are kept in Jerusalem, where an international team of experts was appointed in 1952 to catalogue and publish them. Delays in this demanding task led to public pressure for release of all the fragments. In 1993 the Israeli authorities sanctioned publication of a comprehensive list of all the pieces, with a complete set of photographs, and they are now available on a CD-ROM. These publications scotched rumours about scholars hindering publication because some texts might present threats to basic Christian beliefs; intense searching has failed to find any that do.

A MONASTERY IN THE DESERT

Who were these very religious people? Why did they live in such an uncomfortable, out-of-the-way place?

The shore of the Dead Sea is bare, the cliffs behind are rugged crags. The terrace between, where the buildings stood, is flat and dry. The summer sun makes the rocks so hot it is impossible to stand still on one spot for more than a few seconds. No trees grow there to give shade. Water ran down the cliffs after the winter rains and snow, otherwise fresh water lay 2.4 km/ 1.5 miles way, at the spring of Ain Feshkha. Yet people built quite an elaborate settlement here, in the place now called Qumran.

A small farm had existed there for a short time, about 700 BC. After that the place was abandoned until the middle of the second century BC. The newcomers cleaned out a big cistern and added new ones, leading water to them from the cliffs along stone-walled channels. They set up a pottery kiln and other workshops. Soon major rebuilding began, on a much larger scale.

A strong tower looked over a square of rooms, including a kitchen and a large cistern. Outside were workshops for potters, laundrymen and others, and a long hall where people gathered to eat and talk. Many more people used the new building, so the water system was made much bigger. A dam, a rock-cut channel, and new cisterns were made. Special waterproof plaster stopped the precious water from leaking away. In the tower a staircase led to the first and second floors; another went to an upper storey over some of the ground-floor rooms. The occupants may have slept upstairs.

Josephus reported that an earthquake did a lot of damage in the Jordan Valley in 31 BC. A line of cracks through walls and cisterns at Qumran was the result of the ground at one side sinking by 50 cm/20 ins, most likely because of that tremor. At the same time, fire burnt part of the buildings. Only a few people, if any, went on living there. About 100 years of use came to an end.

After the death of King Herod (4 BC), the whole centre came back to life. Derelict rooms were cleaned, walls strengthened, workshops re-established and the vital water-system renewed. The community was thriving when the Romans attacked it. They shot their arrows at anything that moved and set the buildings alight. Coins from years two and three of the Jewish Revolt, but not later, suggest this happened in AD 68.

In that year General Vespasian reached Jericho. From there he made a visit to the Dead Sea to conduct an experiment. He had heard that no one could drown in the salty water, so he had some non-swimmers thrown in, with their hands tied, to see if the report was true. Of course, they floated on the surface!

The attack at Qumran may be related to that visit. A small Roman garrison made its quarters in the building. From the tower they could watch the road along the shore.

Archaeologists traced the history of the site by excavating in the ruins from

1953 to 1956, under the direction of the French scholar Roland de Vaux. They concluded that the buildings had formed the headquarters of a community. Not everyone who belonged to it lived there. Caves in the cliffs showed signs of occupation. Wooden poles found in them show that tents were used too.

South of Qumran there are several springs, Ain Feshkha being the strongest. There were small oases of palm-trees where the water ran down to the Dead Sea, and ruins of quite a large farm were uncovered beside Ain Feshkha. The produce from this region, and the animals they herded, supplied a large proportion of the people's needs. They could not grow enough grain, however, and had to bring it from other places.

The community's life is clearly seen in the large hall. At one side of it was a small room. This was the china cupboard. Neatly stacked on the floor were over 1,000 pottery vessels; among them were 210 plates, 708 bowls and 75 goblets, the 'dinner service' of the community. In the hall at various points were stands for jars. Clearly the hall was a dining-room, where a large number of people would eat together.

It could also be a place for the community to meet.

Near the ruins was a cemetery with about 1,100 tombs. They lie in tidy rows, with a heap of stones over each burial. The bodies were laid neatly on their backs at a depth of 1.20–2 metres/2–7 feet, the heads pointing to the south. Only a few graves were excavated and each one held a single male skeleton. In an extension of the cemetery the remains of a few women and a child were uncovered. Few of the people buried had lived more than forty years. This was, beyond doubt, the burial place for the community.

Keeping themselves alive took a lot of the members' time and energies, and the workshops show how busy they were. One large upstairs room had a special purpose. When the buildings fell into ruin, things from the upper storey dropped into the room below. Among them were some unusual pieces of smooth plaster. These were taken to the Rockefeller Museum in Jerusalem, and when fitted together they made up a bench 5 metres/16 feet long and about 0.5 metres/18 ins high. Two other objects, one bronze and one pottery, were found with these pieces. They are ink-pots of a shape common

The ruins of Qumran in the desert at the edge of the Dead Sea proved to be the centre of a Jewish sect from the second century BC until AD 68.

This is part of the Commentary on Habakkuk, one of the first of the Dead Sea Scrolls found. The author identified figures in the biblical prophecy with people of his own time. In this section Habakkuk 2:15 is said to refer to the 'Wicked Priest who chased the Teacher of Righteousness to swallow him up'.

throughout the early Roman Empire. One still had dried ink at the bottom! The room was evidently a writing-room or *scriptorium*.

Exactly how the scribes worked is not certain, because ancient pictures and carvings represent scribes sitting cross-legged with the scroll stretched across their knees. At Qumran, probably, scribes squatted in front of the bench, resting the scrolls on it as they wrote on them.

Did the scribes who worked in this room write the scrolls found in the caves? There is no way to prove that they did, yet there is no good reason to doubt it. By comparing the scrolls, scholars have recognized the hand-writing of particular scribes, and so which texts one or another copied. The scrolls show that a large part of their work was to copy important books like those of the Old Testament. But sometimes they produced books which were unique. Since these are unknown outside the Dead Sea Scrolls, and are known only in single copies, they are almost certainly the products of the writing-room. Commentaries on books of the Old Testament are the chief examples.

Prophecy come true

The commentaries the scribes wrote are very revealing. The people who

wrote them read the Bible as if it was written about them. That is a very common attitude. Daniel had already told how a promise made by the prophet Jeremiah would come true in his time.

'In the first year of his reign, I, Daniel, understood from the Scriptures, according to the word of the Lord given to Jeremiah the prophet, that the desolation of Jerusalem would last seventy years' (Daniel 9:2).

So the authors of these commentaries identifed themselves, their leaders, their enemies and foreign powers with figures in the biblical prophecies.

For example, Isaiah promised the Jews, in God's name, 'I will build . . . your foundations with sapphires' (Isaiah 54:11). A commentary on Isaiah interprets the sentence as follows: 'this concerns the priests and the people who laid the foundations of the Council of the Community . . . the congregation of his elect will be like a sapphire among stones.'

These people had no doubt that God had chosen them. Through them he would work out his purposes. In the end, all their enemies would be defeated and they would enjoy the kingdom God would set up. A Messiah like David would be king, and another would be a priest like Aaron. All this they learnt from their study of the Old Testament. As they read their Bibles they found verses here and there which seemed to reflect their history. Through the comments they made about those verses, we too can learn about it.

They called themselves 'the Community' and looked back to a great leader whom they called 'The Teacher of Righteousness'. He did not found the movement but shaped its rules and gave it purpose a few years after it began. His leadership roused others against him. Chief of them was a man the commentaries call 'the Wicked Priest', who could not permit the Teacher to proclaim his very different ideas freely. He chased him to his refuge, perhaps at Qumran, and interrupted him and his disciples in their worship. What happened then is not related, the commentaries make only brief remarks. There is no hint of the Wicked Priest killing the Teacher. In fact, what happened to him is not stated clearly anywhere; he probably died a natural death, perhaps brought on by his enemies' persecution.

The riddle of the Teacher

Who were the Teacher of Righteousness and the Wicked Priest? There was no mystery about them to the readers of the scrolls, so there was no reason to give their names. Two thousand years later that knowledge is lost, so there *is* a riddle for modern scholars. Over the past forty years they have spun various theories. Some of these have collapsed as more documents are published and bring new facts to light.

A badly preserved commentary on Nahum altered the picture. It names a 'Demetrius, king of Greece' who tried to enter Jerusalem. He was invited by 'those who seek smooth things', but failed to reach the city. The writer says no 'king of Greece' came into Jerusalem 'from the time of Antiochus until the time when the rulers of the Kittim came'.

Josephus' history book gives the clue to this riddle. By 88 BC the Pharisees and other patriots were so outraged by the conduct of the Jewish priest-king, Alexander Jannaeus, who had been ruling from 103 and died in 76 BC, that they asked the Greek king of Syria to help them fight him. When Demetrius II (95–88 BC) came and defeated Jannaeus, some of the rebels who had invited him changed their minds, fought on Jannaeus' side again, and drove out the Syrian army. Alexander Jannaeus was not a forgiving man. He had 800 of the rebels crucified in front of his palace, and their wives and children slaughtered before their eyes.

'Those who seek smooth things' were evidently the Pharisees, disguised by a code-name. Whether they got this name because they kept the Old Testament laws less strictly than the Community, or because they were prepared to put up with foreign rule as long as they were left in peace, we cannot say.

Antiochus could be the arch-enemy Antiochus IV Epiphanes (175–163 BC), who set up a pagan image in the Temple in December 167 BC, causing the Maccabean revolt, or he could be Antiochus VII Sidetes (139–129 BC), who pulled down the walls of Jerusalem in 133 BC.

Finally, the Kittim, who occur often in the scrolls, are clearly the Romans. Under Pompey they first marched into Jerusalem in 63 BC.

None of this identifies the Teacher of Righteousness. What the commentary on Nahum reveals is the interest its author had in the events of the second and first centuries BC. Other commentaries seem to point in the same direction. Some time in the second century BC seems a good time to look for the Teacher of Righteousness, after the rise of the nationalist Jewish priesthood. None of the religious leaders whose careers can be traced fits the picture of the Teacher in the scrolls. This man, who inspired others to lives of hardship, devotion, and possibly martyrdom, is still

A few miles down the coast from Qumran is the strong spring of Ain Feshkha. Two thousand years ago a farm and workshops stood nearby. Then, as now, the water also refreshed the herds of the bedouin.

nameless to the twentieth century.

On the other hand, an enemy who could pursue and attack him was clearly in a powerful position, and so may be easier to identify. Two men are particularly suitable candidates, although theirs are not the only names proposed.

The first is Alexander Jannaeus, enemy of the Pharisees and other devout Jews. In his long reign as king and high priest he expanded his kingdom by military conquest, and made his family rich on the loot. Soon after he died, following a long illness, Pompey ended the power he had built

up. The history of Jannaeus accords well with references in the commentaries, and many scholars believe he was the Wicked Priest.

However, the case for the second candidate is even stronger. After Judas the Maccabee had rid the Temple of the pagan idol in 164 BC, he was killed in battle (160). His brother Jonathan took his place as nationalist leader. For some years there was peace and quiet, until a man called Alexander Balas landed at Ptolemais (Akko), aiming to win the throne of Syria. He promised to make Jonathan the high priest in return for his support (152 BC). When

Balas was killed in 145, his conqueror, Demetrius II, confirmed Jonathan's position. Finally, a Syrian general, Trypho, who was fighting Demetrius, took Jonathan prisoner and executed him (143 BC).

This history agrees very well with the hints the commentators give. The Wicked Priest started well, they say, then went wrong. He became High Priest, yet he was not a descendant of Aaron, and he accepted the post from a foreigner. His death, too, occurred at the hands of others, 'they took revenge on his body', in a way which might echo Trypho's deeds.

If Jonathan was the Wicked Priest, another description may apply to Jannaeus. In the commentary on Nahum we read of the raging lion who 'hung up alive' the 'seekers after smooth things', a description that fits his treatment of the Pharisees.

Even though Jonathan seems the better choice at present, as the process of piecing together and translating the fragments goes on, the case for him may improve, or it may disappear entirely, leaving the field to another man.

THE RULE OF THE COMMUNITY

Life in first-century Palestine was rougher than it is for most people in twentieth-century cities. There were none of the modern services. Water had to be carried from a river or pool, a spring or a well. It might not be clean, and proper drainage was rare. Food could not be kept for long unless it was dried or pickled, because there was no refrigeration. Houses could be draughty and damp in winter, dusty in summer. Snakes and scorpions lurked in cracks and under stones, ready to attack the unwary. Insects and parasites of all sorts burrowed into food stores, or made their homes on animal or human hosts.

Most towns and villages stood close to a water supply, with fields, orchards and pastures beside them, providing shade and refreshment. Yet the Qumran people left even that to live in a harsher place, far from ordinary society. What took them to their uncomfortable settlement beside the Dead Sea?

Religious faith can take people to extremes, can spur them to extraordinary acts. The Dead Sea Scrolls speak of those who

trust the Teacher of Righteousness. That was the secret. These people were sure their leader was right, so they would follow his teachings and keep them alive at any cost. One day, they believed, God would demonstrate to the world that they were the faithful ones who had kept his laws correctly. All their enemies would be punished.

The men of Qumran were Jews. They shared their basic faith with all other Jewish patriots. As descendants of Abraham they were God's chosen people, ruled by the laws

God gave by the hand of Moses at Mount Sinai. What made these people distinctive was their conviction that they alone were the 'remnant', they alone knew God's way.

The Teacher of Righteousness was probably the one who started this idea. Before he began to take the lead, the movement was one of several groups that grew up after the revolt of the Maccabees, calling on their Jewish brothers to follow the laws of Moses faithfully. They were 'back to the Bible' missions. Other groups

went along their own paths, one becoming the Pharisees.

They had to resolve the problem all 'back to the Bible' movements face. How does the Bible apply to us today? The Teacher persuaded his group that he had received the answer. God 'made known all the mysteries of his servants the prophets' to him, the commentary on Habakkuk states. His special knowledge divided him and his followers from the rest of Jewry.

If he had drawn vast crowds to his ideas, he might have created a party

The picture shows the opening columns of the Rule of the Community, or Manual of Discipline, which regulated the life of the people of Qumran. This copy was written on a leather scroll soon after 100 BC.

which carried weight in the Jewish commonwealth. He did not succeed in that, so his group naturally became more exclusive. When all the world is wrong except you, it is better to withdraw. For that reason, it seems, the community settled at Qumran. There they could study the Scriptures in peace.

That peace was highly organized, for everyone had his place and his duty. One of the first scrolls to be found is a rule-book, now called the Rule of the Community. It sets out the conditions of entry to the Community, guidelines for conduct in the assembly, and instructions for the leader.

To join the Community a recruit had to pass an examination by the members under their leaders. Before that there was almost certainly a probationary period when an inquirer could learn about the way of life and the rules before committing himself. Josephus says he spent some time in such a state, though not at Qumran. Membership involved total commitment, whole-hearted obedience to the rules, and putting all one's possessions at the Community's disposal. (That does not mean they gave up all their property to live in a form of communism, but they no longer did business with anyone outside.)

Growing food and working to supply communal needs took a lot of the members' time, but their most important task was workship and study. A special time was set for that. The Rule of the Community lays down that 'for a third of the night all through the year the congregation shall stay awake together to read from the Book, to study Law, and to pray together' (VI:7,8).

Some of the normal festivals were held—such as the Feast of Weeks—but not those which involved sacrifices. The men of Qumran had cut themselves off from the Temple and its services by their own exclusivism. They also made any common worship impossible by following a different calendar. Instead of the normal Jewish one, based on a moon cycle of a year of 354 days with an extra month added every three years to keep in line with the seasons, the Community had a sun-based calendar of 364 days, with leap years at intervals. As a result, they did not keep the Day of Atonement, for example, on the same day as other Jews.

The rules for life in the Community were strict.

Three priests and twelve laymen were apparently the leaders, and everyone had to respect them. They controlled the meetings at which every kind of business was discussed. Even then, order was rigidly kept. Everyone could speak, but only in order of rank, and only when called upon. No one could interrupt. The rules of conduct set a penance of ten days for anyone who did interrupt. Other offences drew heavier punishments: thirty days' penance for foolish laughter, or for sleeping during the meeting; six months for deception, bearing malice, or going about indecently dressed. Disobedience to the Community could result in expulsion; so too would the greater offence of speaking the holy name of God, even by accident.

WHOSE VOICE IN THE DESERT?

'God's kingdom is near! Repent, repent!'

Crowds flocked to hear the new prophet preach in the desert. Every few years, it seemed, another man came along with a new message. There was Theudas who was supposed to be the Messiah. He wasn't, the soldiers killed him, and his 400 followers soon disappeared. There was Judas of Gamla, too. He tried to stir people up against the Romans. They made short work of him!

The new man everyone was going to listen to was a strange, wild fellow, wearing camel-hair clothes and eating what he could find—the locusts that landed in the desert with their stomachs full of the farmers' crops, and the honey he took from the wild bees' nests.

'It's time to change,' he told them, 'time to stop cheating, to help the poor, and to be content. It's time to turn to God from evil.' If they did that, he said, they should show they meant it by being baptized in the river. Scores of people were baptized. They liked what John taught. They agreed with his attacks on their religious leaders, for some of them were double-dealers, and the endless rules and regulations they laid down grew tiresome and meaningless. It was time for a new start. People should be ready because God's chosen king, the Messiah, was on his way.

Where had John learnt his message? 'He lived in the desert until he appeared publicly to Israel,' Luke declares, and it was there God spoke to him (Luke 1:80; 3:2). All through the Bible God speaks to people and gives them tasks to do which use their experience and knowledge. Although no one should think John never left the desert to visit his family or talk with others, the desert was his home. How could he learn there, except by his own thoughts?

Before 1947 John's

life in the desert was a mystery. Then, when the Dead Sea Scrolls were discovered, some scholars suggested John had belonged to the group of people that owned them. The settlement at Qumran certainly stood in the desert. Its rule ordered baptisms or bathings to make the members pure for their assembly and meals. At the same time, the rule-book made it clear that such washings were no use unless there was a real determination to follow God's ways. This sounds rather like John's call to repent and be baptized. Also, the men of Qumran were looking forward to the arrival of God's Messiah. Did John live there for part of his life? Did he take over some of the ideas that were in the air?

There is no definite answer to these questions. If John did meet the Qumran people or stay with them for a while, when he began to preach he was not saying things which would have pleased them. He called people to repent and be baptized once, because God's kingdom was coming. At Qumran the bathing was done often, as the carefully-made pools show. There may have been an introductory baptism when people joined the group, as in other parts of Judaism, but there is nothing to show it was a baptism 'for the remission of sins', like John's.

Clearly John disagreed with the lifestyle of Qumran, because he did not tell his converts to leave their homes or obey such strict rules. John attacked the priests in his speeches. But as far as the records tell he did not attack the Temple and its worship in the way some of the Scrolls do. And the ultimate difference is obvious in the Messiah whom John pointed out to the crowds around him, Jesus of Nazareth. So different from the current hopes was he that even John became a little uncertain later, and had to be reassured (Matthew 11:2–19).

Whatever ideas John had heard, wherever he had lived, what he taught was not an imitation or an echo of other men's thoughts. John was independent, knowing that his work was to prepare the way for the Messiah by warning that he was coming. This warning was for everyone, not for a chosen few, as the men of Qumran believed.

People from the villages of Judea and from Jerusalem travelled across these hills and down to the Jordan to hear John the Baptist preach.

THE SCROLLS AND THE TEACHING OF JESUS

No one in modern times had ever seen the actual books people were reading in Palestine when Jesus was there. News of the discovery of the Dead Sea Scrolls led to all sorts of hopes and guesses about what they would be. Perhaps they would bring new knowledge for the history of the Old Testament books. They would certainly pull back the curtain which hid large areas of first-century Judaism, for no other Hebrew writings had survived from those days. Above all, the Scrolls might throw new light on the beginnings of Christianity. No wonder thousands of dollars were paid for these unique documents, even though most are only scraps.

Forty years after the discovery, have those hopes and guesses been realized? As far as the text of the Old Testament is concerned, the Scrolls have brought valuable new knowledge, although it is not as clear as many wished! First-century Judaism has gained a wholly new scene, a life-style not suspected before (see *The Rule of the Community*).

As for the Scrolls and the Gospels, scores of books and studies on the subject have been published. A few writers have made sensational, even outrageous, claims, and other writers have quickly shown that those claims have no foundation in fact. Yet once fanciful, wrong ideas are broadcast, they linger and are hard to destroy, so it is worth repeating some facts.

The Dead Sea Scrolls do not mention Jesus or John the Baptist. They show no links with the New Testament. When the owners of the Scrolls hid their books and ran away from Qumran, they were still waiting for the Messiah to come. They did not recognize Jesus as the Messiah, and would have needed as strong a conversion as anyone to do so. In their view the Messiah would be a warrior, leading them to victory over all their opponents and setting up his kingdom in Jerusalem. Another, priestly, Messiah would then re-establish the correct forms of worship and sacrifice in the Temple. Neither Messiah had any atoning function. Rather, the people who wrote the Scrolls saw their Community and especially its leaders, twelve laymen and three priests, as atoning for sin by just deeds and through suffering. They remained to the end a thoroughly Jewish community which, as far as can be seen, never thought of people from other races joining them.

Essenes at Qumran looked back to their Teacher of Righteousness and followed his teachings. He had died, perhaps naturally, and was not expected to reappear, except in the general resurrection when all the righteous would enjoy God's presence. Christians looked to their Teacher, who had been executed and had reappeared on the third day after he had been buried. They proclaimed him then, not just as a man but as God.

A great gap divides the teachings of the Scrolls from those of the Gospels. No one can justly claim any direct link between them. Even so, they share a lot of common ground, because both have their roots in the Old Testament. The revelation God gave to Abraham, the election of his descendants as the people of Israel to be the special nation of God, with the laws conveyed by Moses, the oracles of the prophets, the history and the psalms—all these were basic to both of them.

Prophecy reached its fulfilment in their own time, both for the Teacher of Righteousness and for Jesus. Each of them viewed the dominant parties in Judaism as mistaken in their teachings and practices. However, where Jesus relaxed religious rules, the Essenes tightened them.

The prime example is in the approach to the Sabbath day. If an animal fell into a pit on the Sabbath, it was not wrong to help it out, according to the Pharisees. In Matthew 12:11 Jesus answers the question, 'Is it lawful to heal on the Sabbath?' with these words: 'If any of you have a sheep and it falls into a pit on the Sabbath, will you not take hold of it and lift it out? How much more valuable is a man than a sheep! Therefore it is lawful to do good on the Sabbath.' At Qumran the animal could not be helped. A man must not even lift his hand to hit a stubborn animal on the Sabbath.

The common ground between the Scrolls and the Gospels was more than the inheritance of the Old Testament. In the Gospels are some expressions not found in the Old Testament which are found in the Scrolls. Here the hope that the Scrolls would shed light on the beginnings of Christianity is met in a small way. Coming from the same time, background, and country, and concerned with the same subjects, they were likely to use similar language. When the angels voiced their hymn of praise at the birth of Jesus, they called for 'peace to men on whom God's favour rests' (Luke 2:14, see *What Did the Angels Sing?*). A scroll of hymns from Qumran, possibly composed by the Teacher of Righteousness, has the phrase 'sons of good will' in two places.

Another hymn, put in the mouths of the victorious 'sons of light' after they have defeated the 'sons of darkness', proclaims 'Among the poor in spirit [there is power] over the hard of heart.' This is not the same as 'Blessed are the poor in spirit, for theirs is the kingdom of heaven', the first of Jesus' 'Beatitudes' (recorded in Matthew 5), but the phrase 'poor in spirit' is. Evidently it was current among pious Jews to denote people who were spiritually humble (compare the Pharisee and the tax collector—Luke 18:13).

When Jesus taught his followers to love their enemies and pray for their persecutors, he commented that others had said 'Love your neighbour and hate your enemy'. He may have meant the teachings of the Essenes. Several times in the Scrolls the faithful are told to hate the 'sons of darkness', an attitude not so clearly stated elsewhere.

Both Jesus and the Scrolls warn those who oppose God's will that they will end up in a place of everlasting fire (see *Gehenna—The Everlasting Bonfire*).

In John's Gospel one of the distinctive themes is light. Jesus is 'the light of the world', who offers light to mankind, although most reject him, preferring darkness (John 8:12; 3:19–21). The Dead Sea Scrolls speak of 'the children of righteousness' who 'are ruled by the Prince of Light and walk in the ways of light.' The 'children of deceit', on the other hand, 'walk in the ways of darkness', and they are contrasted with those who 'do the truth', another term applied to Jesus' followers in John's Gospel (3:21).

The Scrolls correct a common impression that John's Gospel has strong Greek influences in it. Light and darkness, truth and falsehood were equally at home in the thought-world of Palestinian Jews. Thus the possibility of its preserving authentic memories of Jesus' teaching grows a little stronger. The Scrolls underline, at the same time, the novelty of Jesus' teaching which would have struck his hearers; he called for faith in himself first, and flowing from that a life which followed the Law in its principles, whereas it was joining the Community that made someone a 'son of light' according to the Scrolls, and that brought with it a sincere and minute obedience to every part of the Law.

In the ruins of the fortress at Masada, where the last Jewish rebels resisted the Romans until AD 73, pieces of one scroll were found which duplicate a scroll from Qumran. They are part of a hymnbook belonging to the Qumran Community. Their presence at Masada suggests that someone from Qumran fled there, perhaps expecting to take part in the last battle which would see the victory of the righteous.

A GOSPEL AT QUMRAN?

Surprise after surprise has come from the Dead Sea Scrolls, and none more unexpected than a Spanish scholar's announcement in 1972. Tiny scraps of papyrus, he said, come from a copy of Mark's Gospel in Greek, from Paul's letter to Timothy, and from the letter of James.

The pieces of papyrus came from Cave 7 at Qumran. When archaeologists explored this badly eroded cave they found twenty-one minute fragments of papyrus scrolls and the 'negatives' of three others which had been pressed against lumps of mud leaving their ink letters on it, although the papyrus itself had rotted away. The fragments came from thirteen or more scrolls, all in Greek. Enough writing was left on one piece to identify it as part of Exodus, and on a second piece to show it came from a copy of the apocryphal *Letter of Baruch*. Studying the other pieces, José O'Callaghan found he could fit the letters on one of them (numbered 7Q5) into Mark 6:52,53.

If this claim is true, it is an astonishing one. The handwriting of the papyri places them in the middle of the first century AD. Pottery found in the cave belongs to the same time, and is like pottery from other caves where Hebrew manuscripts lay. It would be hard to argue that these scrolls were left behind by people who had no connection with the owners of the scrolls in the other caves. Therefore the presence of New Testament manuscripts would mean that people were reading Christian books at Qumran before the place was abandoned in AD 68.

Numerous people, including the author, would be delighted if a genuine Gospel manuscript of the mid-first century came to light in Palestine, or in Egypt. Many cherished theories would collapse, most histories of Gospel writing would be changed. Arguments for the reliability of the Gospel records would gain strength. Just because the effects of so sensational a discovery would be so far-reaching, the claims of O'Callaghan and of a German scholar Carsten Peter Thiede who has supported them, need to be treated with great caution.

Small scraps of papyrus books can be identified even though the number of words on them is few. The Rylands papyrus of John (see *Oldest of All*) has several whole words (among them 'the Jews' and 'signifying') and distinguishable parts of others arranged on both sides of the page in such a way as to leave no doubt that it comes from a page of John's Gospel. The Qumran piece is smaller and does not contain as many distinctive words.

Two points favour its identity with the Mark passage. In line 4 three letters and remains of a fourth could be the middle of the name Gennesaret (a term for Galilee). The previous line has a space before the word 'And', indicting that it starts a new paragraph (otherwise Greek scribes did not leave spaces between words). These two lines could be part of Mark 6:53, 'When they had crossed over, they landed at Gennesaret', which starts with 'And' in the original. Following this, it is possible to read the letters in the other lines to fit the adjacent sentences in Mark 6:52,53.

An astonishing claim needs an unshakeable foundation if it is to be accepted as fact, especially if other arguments are to be built on it. Statistics count against finding more than one book with exactly the same sequence of letters and spacing over five lines on a page, so the identification seems strong. A computer search through Greek literature found no other passage which showed the pattern of letters O'Callaghan read on the papyrus.

Are his readings satisfactory?

Some of the letters are far from clear, notably in line 2 and after 'And' in line 3. Read differently, the pattern is changed, opening the door to doubt. The letters which fit 'Gennesaret' could equally

The tiny piece of a papyrus scroll which two scholars claim contained Mark's Gospel. Mid-first century AD.

be part of a verbal form. With other letters reconstructed in alternative ways the fragment could come from a completely different book. No one knows how much Jewish literature in Greek from the period 200 BC to AD 70 has been lost to us. Some of these writings are quoted by Josephus, or mentioned by name, others survive in translations into Latin, or Ethiopic. The Hebrew and Aramaic manuscripts from the other caves disclose more books whose existence was previously unsuspected.

With regret, we have to conclude that the fragment is too small, its letters too uncertain, to warrant the label 'A piece of Mark's Gospel from the first century'. And the same verdict applies to the other fragments claimed as New Testament scrolls.

Although it is possible, the identity is not proved. Even if some people at Qumran did read the Gospel, there is no sign of it affecting the teachings of the people living there.

DEATH AND BURIAL

From earliest times people have laid the dead to rest in the
ground with reverence. Jesus' friends did that for him. Christians often
ask what sort of tomb his body rested in, and where it was. The study
of tombs around Jerusalem and burial customs of the time, together
with recent explorations in the city, now bring clearer answers than could
be offered before. As a result the Gospel descriptions grow more vivid.

The bones of the dead were collected into stone boxes or ossuaries,
sometimes ornately carved.

TOMB FASHIONS

Cemeteries and tombs—the town-planner's headache, the property-developer's nightmare—often lie in the path of a motorway, or the site of an apartment block.

What to do with the bodies of the dead has been a problem ever since people began to live in towns. Some buried the remains in their houses, perhaps keeping their families together in that way. Others made graveyards just outside the built-up area and buried the dead there. Cremation, which saves space, was rare in the biblical world until Roman times. For the Jews it was not acceptable because they believed in a resurrection related in some way to the physical body. Over the centuries the number of tombs and cemeteries grew. Sometimes new ones destroyed or re-used the old ones, sometimes builders dug through old burials without care.

Where the soil was deep enough, people could dig simple graves and bury the bodies without fear of wild animals disturbing them. In much of Palestine the spade hits rock just below the surface of the ground, so proper burial was more difficult. One way was to place the person on the ground and pile stones into a cairn, or build stone slabs into a small 'house'—like the dolmens of Celtic lands. That was not very secure. If a robber thought there might be something very valuable in the tomb, he could make his way into it.

What became the usual thing was also the more expensive one, to make a room in the rock big enough to hold at least one corpse. There are plenty of caves in the limestone hills of Israel and Judah, so the smaller ones that could be closed were natural tombs. Already before 2000 BC groups of tombs were cut in the ground near towns like Jericho. A narrow shaft one or two metres/a few feet deep would open into a chamber like a small cave, with enough room to allow the body to be arranged and a few pots and pans put beside it. After the burial, a stone might be used to close the entrance, then the shaft would be filled with earth and stones.

To hollow out a new tomb like that for everyone who died probably cost more time and labour than many families could afford. Often, by making the tombs larger, they could create a family vault. Husbands and wives, aunts and uncles, children and grandchildren could all be laid together, the tomb being reopened whenever one died.

At Jericho Dame Kathleen Kenyon opened several tombs made about 1800 BC. They held up to twenty bodies each, occasionally more. As the later ones were added, the older remains were pushed aside to make space, so that the excavators found only the last burial neatly arranged with its equipment.

This was the time of Abraham, Isaac, and Jacob in the Old Testament. They followed the same custom. The cave Abraham bought in order to bury his wife Sarah later received his body, then those of his son Isaac and his wife Rebecca, and later of Jacob and his wife Leah (Genesis 23;49:31–33). That tomb—so Jewish tradition claimed—

Kings and noblemen of Judah had spacious tombs hollowed in the hills around Jerusalem in the eighth and seventh centuries BC. This chamber in the grounds of St Stephen's Monastery north of the city has benches on either side for the bodies to rest on, and further space beyond. At a lower level is a repository for the bones of earlier burials— only the most recent lay neatly on the benches.

could still be seen at the town of Hebron, south of Jerusalem, in the time of Jesus. King Herod built a great wall around it to mark it as a holy place, a wall which still stands after 2,000 years.

Tombs from the days of the kings

In the centuries of the kings of Israel and Judah forms of burial changed very little. Example of tombs from that time have been found all over the country. Particularly well-made ones can be seen outside the Old City of Jerusalem. One row has been known for a long time. It faces the eastern slope of the original town, now known as the City of David, in the village of Silwan.

Wealthy families paid for chambers to be cut square in the rock face of the valley. Some were even cut as free-standing blocks, to look like houses. Over the doorways, Hebrew letters gouged in a smoothed surface told the names of the dead and, in one case at least, cursed anyone who would open the tomb.

Another row of tombs was made along the southern edge of the Valley of Hinnom, beside the modern St

Andrew's Church. Archaeologists excavated them between 1975 and 1980. They had a long history. Dug in the rock in the seventh century BC, they went on being used as tombs until late in the sixth century BC. Then more bodies were buried in them in the first century BC and the first century AD, above the earlier ones. In the second and third centuries pyres were built on the site for cremations. Cooking-pots found buried there held ashes and burnt bones. Other cremations discovered around Jerusalem belonged to the Tenth Legion, the Roman garrison stationed in the city after AD 70—so these may also be theirs. Further burials were made during this time, too.

In the fifth century, parts of the rock walls of the tombs were quarried away when a church was built nearby. The most recent relics were dozens of rusty rifles, army buttons and oddments left by Turkish soldiers who watched the road to Bethlehem from a guard-post beside the tombs, probably during the First World War. They were lying on the rock bench of one of the seventh-century tombs.

These tombs were single rooms

In the first century BC leading families of Jerusalem had grandiose tombs cut for themselves in the Kidron Valley. The pillared entrance leads to tombs which belonged to priests of the Hezir family (1 Chronicles 24:15) according to a later inscription. The solid square tower with a pyramid on top is part of this monument; its traditional name 'Tomb of Zechariah' has no foundation.

about 3 metres/10 feet square with a step down from the entrance. On either side and at the end were benches over a metre/3 feet high, cut in the rock. On the benches in two of the tombs the stone had been carefully carved to make resting-places for the heads of the corpses. One tomb had three rooms opening off the entrance hall, and on one bench six head-rests were cut in a row.

All this laborious cutting in the rock, done to a high standard, allowed a few bodies to be laid neatly in each of the tombs. Space was too precious to devote one expensive tomb to a very small number of people. Underneath a bench in several of these tombs were smaller hollowed spaces. All of them were empty except one.

In the largest tomb the roof of this space had fallen in, saving what was in it from robbers. As well as scores of pots, pieces of jewellery, and two precious silver amulets, there were lots of bones. Bones of nearly 100 people were collected there. Evidently once the places on the benches were full, the first burials were taken up and bundled into these cellars. Here is a physical illustration of the biblical phrase 'gathered to his fathers'.

A third group of tombs created for rich citizens of Jerusalem in the eighth or seventh centuries BC lies to the north of the Old City. They have the same basic plan as those of the Hinnom Valley, but are much bigger. Rooms with benches for burials and repositories for bones open out of an entrance hall. Seven rooms belong to one tomb, with another larger room that has no benches and may have been a place where the bodies could be prepared for burial. Like the Silwan tombs, these display the work of skilful masons. Near the ceilings, the rock was carved to make a cornice. The doorways were nicely squared with, in one case, sockets for the hinge posts of a pair of double doors. On the walls shallow recesses seem to imitate wooden panelling. Here was truly 'an eternal home' of the highest quality.

Tombs of Jesus' days

Tombs made 600 years before Christ may seem too old to help us understand tombs of the first century, yet they are important. They reveal an attitude to the remains of the dead which was almost the same in the New Testament period. The idea of burying many people in one tomb did not change either. The problem of space grew more acute. Tombs from the first century BC and the first century AD illustrate these points, as well as making clear what sort of tomb the Gospels describe at the burial of Jesus.

To be buried in a rock-cut tomb was no doubt expensive, so only fairly well-to-do people would have afforded them. In the Gospel period the tomb-cutters of Jerusalem made simple tombs, fine tombs with carved entrances, and elaborate tombs with monuments marking them above ground. Simple tombs have a small doorway, 1 metre/3 feet high, closed by a boulder which fitted like a plug, or by a stone slab. It was essential to close tombs tightly, otherwise wild animals, dogs, jackals, hyenas, which were always scavenging outside ancient towns, would enter and tear up the bodies. After stooping or crawling through the entrance, the mourners would go down one or two steps, then be able to stand upright.

Around three sides of a roughly squared room is a bench cut in the rock about waist high. From the bench short tunnels run into the rock walls. They are up to 2 metres/6 feet 6 ins long, half a metre/18 ins wide and 1 metre/3 feet high. Each could hold a human body lying flat on its back. Sometimes stone slabs or rough stone walls closed these tunnels.

Wealthy people might order superior tombs with courtyards in front of the entrances. Plants and shrubs may have been grown in them. The entrances themselves were neatly carved in the rock face to look like the doorways of noble mansions, decorated in some cases with flowers and leaves in low relief. These were full-

The tomb of Queen Helen of Adiabene dates from the Gospel period. Tombs had to be tightly closed lest dogs or wild animals should creep inside and disturb the dead.

Hidden at the back of the Church of the Holy Sepulchre is the 'Tomb of Joseph of Arimathea'. Here are the tunnels and bench typical of a first-century tomb. (Visitors enter on the level of the bench and the grille prevents them slipping down on to the original floor.)

sized doorways, closed with wooden, or occasionally stone, doors. Beyond was a large room opening into other rooms with the short tunnels in the walls for the burials. In one tomb there are eighty of these tunnels. Occasionally these fine tombs were designed for burials in coffins. A shelf was cut in each wall, up to 2 metres/ 7 feet long, with an arch in the rock above it (termed an *arcosolium*). Very rarely the bench under the arch was hollowed out to form a coffin.

Most elaborate of all is the burial place called today 'the Tombs of the Kings'. A royal family from north-eastern Iraq was converted to Judaism and had this large tomb created north of Jerusalem.

An impressive flight of steps leads down to a large courtyard dug out of

the rock. At one side was a pillared entrance, originally crowned with three pyramids, Josephus reports. All this splendour leads to a low doorway shut by a stone which rolled from a slot, like a wheel. Inside is a large room and eight other rooms with burial tunnels.

When the French explorer De Saulcy cleared out the tomb in 1863, he found a big stone coffin. On it was written the name and title of the queen in Aramaic and Hebrew. A few people were buried in stone coffins, but this, too, was something only the rich could afford.

In most tombs the bones were not left lying neatly in the tunnels. Instead, after a year or so, when the flesh had decayed, the bones were collected and put in boxes (see *Their Names Live On*). Six or seven of the boxes could be fitted into the tunnel a single body would occupy when laid out flat, and so a lot more people could be accommodated in a tomb. When the tombs are opened, the boxes are also found on the benches and even on the floor. Although the boxes were made to hold the bones of one person, the remains of several may be in a single box. An inscription on one says, 'Simon and his wife', and on another was scratched, 'The wife and son of Matthia'.

In the light of all this, the accounts in the Gospels of the burial of Jesus and the circumstances of the first Easter Sunday morning can be read more intelligibly. Joseph of Arimathea was a wealthy man, with a new tomb in a garden. He took the body of Jesus to it and laid it there quickly because of the Sabbath. To keep the body safely, everyone was content to close the tomb with a heavy stone. As soon as possible after the Sabbath, some of Jesus' women followers went to anoint the body with spices, to give it the attention the Sabbath had prevented. They expected the stone would be an obstacle, and when they found it had been moved they saw quickly that the body had gone. A figure sitting inside, on the right, told them Jesus had risen.

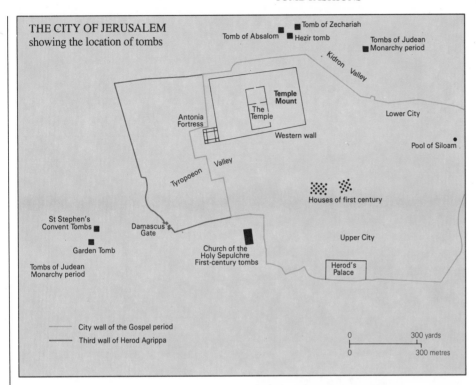

THE CITY OF JERUSALEM
showing the location of tombs

Tomb of Absalom
Tomb of Zechariah
Hezir tomb
Tombs of Judean
Monarchy period

Kidron Valley

Temple
Mount

The
Temple

Antonia
Fortress

Lower City

Western wall

Pool of Siloam

Valley

Tyropoeon

Houses of first century

St Stephen's
Convent Tombs

Damascus
Gate

Upper City

Garden Tomb

Church of the
Holy Sepulchre
First-century tombs

Herod's
Palace

Tombs of Judean
Monarchy period

City wall of the Gospel period
Third wall of Herod Agrippa

0   300 yards
0   300 metres

Jesus' disciples went to the tomb: one peered in, Peter actually went in, and both saw the graveclothes lying there. Then Mary peered into the tomb and saw two angels sitting where the head and feet of the body had been.

The Gospel writers evidently describe a tomb with a small entrance and a rock-cut bench, of the sort now well known as the fashion in the first-century Jerusalem. Jesus' body was not placed in one of the tunnels, as would be expected, because it was brought into the tomb hastily and left without full preparation. It was laid on the bench. After the resurrection, the clothes were left there, easily seen, and the angels could conveniently sit on the bench.

A very elaborate tomb was built to the west of Jerusalem with a monument above ground and four chambers dug in the rock. Some of Herod's family may have been buried there. The entrance was closed with a large round stone slab.

THEIR NAMES LIVE ON

The bones in this ossuary belonged to a man named John, who spoke Greek.

'They have no known grave' are the sad words said of many soldiers killed in battle. They are also true of thousands upon thousands of men, women and children who lived in times past. These people have literally disappeared. Their bones have been scattered, or have completely decayed, or lie in the ground with nothing to mark them. Quite often old burials come to light in the course of farming or construction work, yet they are only a few of those made over the ages. Sometimes things the dead had used in their lives lie with them. They range from a ring on a finger, or a few beads with a child, to the thrones and chariots of Pharaoh Tutankhamun.

In the tombs of important men and women, kings like Tutankhamun, their names may be carved or painted on the wall, or the coffin, or pots and pans. But even very rich tombs may not disclose the names of their dead. A noteworthy example is the group of magnificently furnished burial chambers opened in 1977 at Vergena in Macedonia. The excavator claims that Philip of Macedon, the father of Alexander the Great, was interred there, but not one of the treasures bears a name. It is not surprising, therefore, that the graves of the less important people, the majority of ancient society, are usually anonymous.

Some cultures have had fashions for recording a dead person's identity. Greek citizens set up tombstones, and Romans carved names and other details on stone urns or slabs that covered them. In Palestine during the first century BC and through the first century AD some burials had names on them which give valuable information about Jewish society.

A year after the body had been laid in the tomb the bones were often collected in stone boxes long enough to hold the leg-bones easily. These boxes occupied much less space than a skeleton needed when laid out flat, so more bodies could be put into one tomb. Ossuaries, as the boxes are called, could be plain or decorated. There are patterns of lines and circles on some, scratched with a sharp point, or carved with a chisel. A few have floral decoration and one or two carry carvings imitating stonework.

Hundreds of ossuaries are now in museums, especially in Jerusalem. The majority are plain, but scores of them, plain and decorated, bear names. The letters may be carefully engraved, or roughly scratched, or scribbled in charcoal. They were not public memorials to the dead people, but labels to identify their remains. Usually they give the name of the dead person, often the father's name which served the purpose of a modern surname (many of which, e.g. Johnson, Robinson, Jameson, were formed in just this way), and occasionally a title. There are 'labels' for a rabbi, for priests, for a temple builder, for a scribe, a potter, and for various others. Women's names appear as well as men's, with a description sometimes added, 'daughter of X', or 'wife of Y'.

The Greek, Aramaic and Hebrew languages were all used to give this

The Hebrew inscription states that the remains of Shitrath daughter of Yehohanan lay in this ossuary. (Yehohanan is ultimately the same name as John.)

information. Greek was the least common, and in several cases there is a Hebrew or Aramaic translation of a Greek text. From this it is clear that all three languages could be understood by people living in Jerusalem in the first century (see *The Languages they Spoke*).

The names of the dead reflect this variety. There are Greek names like Andrew and Alexander, Aramaic ones, for example Abba and Yithra, and Hebrew, among them Gamaliel, Isaac and Levi. They show the sort of names parents were giving to their children at that time, and how they were written. What is interesting to see is that the commonest of them all occur in the New Testament. John, Judas, Jesus, Mary, Martha, Matthew are all found, and Lazarus or Eliezer and Simon are among the most frequent.

These were not the same individuals as those in the New Testament, simply others who shared the same name. Finding bones in an ossuary inscribed in Aramaic for Jesus son of Joseph does not affect the Christian belief in the resurrection of Jesus. It shows the same thing—that these names were common at the time. All this is helpful for evaluating the Gospels. As far as the personal names are concerned, there is a striking correspondence; the Gospels reflect well the first-century fashion in names. These simple marks of identification on the stone chests bring us into contact with a few of the people in Jesus' day. Even though scores are named in this way, there were very many more whose tombs bore no names or of whom all trace is gone. They were among the crowds who stood in the Temple or thronged the streets, eager to see Jesus.

CAN WE SEE THE TOMB OF JESUS?

'Jesus was buried here!'
'No, Jesus was buried here!'

Two places are shown to visitors in Jerusalem, each by people who believe this was the tomb where Jesus was buried. The fact that there are two rival sites upsets some pilgrims; others are convinced one is right and take no notice of the second. Is either of the two—the Church of the Holy Sepulchre and the Garden Tomb—the right place? Growing knowledge about the way tombs were made and the fashions in tomb designs around Jerusalem during the centuries (see *Tomb Fashions*) helps to explain why one place may be the right one, and the other not.

The Garden Tomb

In 1883 General Charles Gordon, a famous leader of the British army in the Crimean War, in China and in Egypt, reached Jerusalem. Gordon understood the Old Testament by means of the New Testament. The rites for worship in ancient Israel he saw as pointers to the life and work of Christ. He went to a small hill north of the Turkish wall of Jerusalem. Two caves in the sheer face opposite the city look something like the eye sockets of a skull, so it was called Skull Hill.

Gordon reckoned the priests killed the animals for sacrifice in the Temple there, north of the altar (on the basis of Leviticus 1:11). It would therefore have been the appropriate place for Jesus, the 'Lamb of God', to be killed. In this way he identified the hill as Golgotha or Calvary, and many today still call it 'Gordon's Calvary'. His notes were not printed until 1885. In 1884 Gordon was killed at Khartoum, trying to end the rebellion of the Mahdi.

Quite near the edge of the hill is a tomb in the rock. Forty years before Gordon's visit someone had suggested it might be the tomb of Jesus. Another tomb, not far away, was put forward by a different explorer. With Gordon's idea about Calvary, the first tomb gained favour. A lot of rubbish and Crusader buildings were taken away to reveal the large flat space, cistern and vertical rock wall with a doorway which are visible today.

Inside the doorway is a small room leading to another on the right. This one has two troughs hollowed out of the rock on either side of the doorway, and a smaller one between them at the end. Slots in the rock show where stone slabs made sides and lids for these troughs. Painted on the walls are crosses and Greek letters standing for Jesus Christ, the First and the Last. The paintings belong to the early Byzantine period, the fifth or sixth century AD.

Why should this tomb be identified as the tomb of Jesus, rather than one of the others in this area? The nearness of Gordon's Calvary is one reason. Another is its position—outside the city wall but quite close to it. Emotions also play a part. European Protestants going into the Church of the Holy Sepulchre can feel uncomfortable. The lamps and candles, the gaudy colours, and the black-robed priests are alien to their ways of worship. In its simplicity this tomb, with its well-tended garden, has an immediate appeal; the visitor can imagine the events of the first Easter Sunday morning without difficulty.

Yet there is no real evidence in favour of the Garden Tomb. General Gordon's idea about the hill being the slaughtering-place for the Temple has no historical or geographical facts on its side. He added to his idea the suggestion that the outline of a human figure can be drawn with its skull on the hill, its seat on the Dome of the Rock, and its feet at the Pool of Siloam. When he set out this theory, Gordon himself called it 'fanciful'.

Everyone can see that the Garden Tomb lies outside the city wall, the Holy Sepulchre stands inside it. Where the city wall ran at the time of the crucifixion is something scholars have argued about for years. Of course, the feelings of modern visitors cannot affect the arguments in favour or against the identification.

In recent years archaeological evidence has grown to the point where it can decide the question. Fashions in tomb design are well attested and clearly dated by the objects found in undisturbed burials. Trough tombs were mostly the work of Byzantine masons. However, the Garden Tomb is certainly older than that. Marks left by the stone-cutters' tools are the clues that point to changes inside it. The troughs are not original. Those who first made the tomb left a rock-cut bench around three of its walls, and probably one in the outer room, later chiselled away. Tombs of the first century have rock benches, but running from them in most cases are short tunnels which received the bodies.

The marks left by the stone-cutters' tools are still visible on the walls of the tomb. They are not all the same. Around the upper part, where the walls and ceiling meet at carefully cut angles, they are single long strokes. In contrast, tombs of the first century were normally worked with a toothed chisel which left groups of small parallel lines in the stone. None of these is evident on the walls of the Garden Tomb.

The conclusion is unavoidable: the Garden Tomb is not a first-century tomb. More and more discoveries point to it being much older, as old as the eighth or seventh centuries BC, the days of Isaiah or Jeremiah. Very near to it, on the same hill, are the third group of large tombs from that age, and others lie close by. Here was a burial area at the end of the Monarchy. The Garden Tomb seems to have been part of it. Over a thousand years later, Christians remodelled the inside in order to bury their dead in their own way.

Later still the outside was changed. Perhaps it was the Crusaders who lowered the ground level outside, dug a large cistern with a channel running in the rock to it, and put up some buildings against the rock. All these changes have left their imprints on the Tomb, and now they do seem to make sense: what is missing is any sign of first-century use. The Garden Tomb was not the tomb of Jesus.

This verdict should not upset anyone who has found it a peaceful or inspiring place in which to meditate and worship, for the nature of the place is unchanged, and so is the message of the resurrection. That the angel actually announced the news in a different place is unimportant.

The Church of the Holy Sepulchre
Ropes and crowbars strained at stones, picks and spades thudded into the earth, as gangs of men pulled down an old temple and dug away the soil below it. The year was 326, and the Emperor Constantine had ordered an excavation in Jerusalem. He wanted to build a church in honour of the resurrection. Christians said they knew where the actual tomb of Jesus lay, and obviously that would be the ideal site for the church. They pointed to a rather unexpected place, underneath a temple in the middle of the city.

After the Jews failed to free themselves from Roman rule in their

Second Revolt (132–35), the Emperor Hadrian rebuilt Jerusalem as a completely Roman city. It had a new name, Aelia Capitolina, and no Jews were allowed to enter it. In his new city Hadrian had a temple built for the goddess of love, Venus. That was the one which hid the tomb of Jesus. Hadrian's builders took a lot of trouble to lay a firm foundation. They carried tons of earth to make a level platform over very uneven ground, kept it in place with a huge wall, and set the temple itself on top.

Now, less than two centuries later, this was all being demolished in order to uncover the old tomb supposed to be below it. The Bishop of Caesarea at that time was Eusebius. He wrote a long history of the Christian church, which is his most important book, and some shorter works, among them a Life of Constantine. In that he tells how the tomb was found:

'The Emperor ordered that the stone and wood from the ruins (of the pagan temple) should be carried and dumped as far away as possible, and that a large amount of the foundation earth . . . should be dug away very deeply . . . The task was put in hand at once, and as the subsoil appeared layer by layer, so did the venerable and sacred evidence of the Saviour's resurrection, beyond all our hopes, brought back to life, like our Saviour.'

For over a century Protestant Christians have preferred the simplicity of the Garden Tomb, north of the Old City of Jerusalem, to the ornate tradition of the Holy Sepulchre. Although much research has concluded that the Garden Tomb is not a first-century burial place, the peaceful gardens make it an attractive retreat for thought and prayer.

Constantine's masons chopped the rock away all round the tomb so that it stood free from the hillside. A shrine was put up to protect it, and eventually a ring of pillars and an outer wall supported a dome above it. Next to the shrine was a garden with porches at the sides, and beyond that a large church. At one side another rocky outcrop was trimmed, to be kept in the area as the site of Calvary. Enemy attacks, fires and earthquakes damaged these buildings on many occasions, more or less severely. The rock of the tomb was totally demolished by the mad Caliph Hakim in 1009. As a result, the Church of the Holy Sepulchre is a conglomerate of designs and styles from the fourth century onwards, the greatest part being the Crusaders' work. Pilgrims have prayed at the same place ever since Constantine's workmen discovered the buried tomb.

Is it really the tomb of Jesus?

Did Constantine's men find the right grave? Could the fourth-century Christians who told them where to dig be sure they would uncover the right tomb?

Until the reign of Constantine the Christians were an unpopular and often persecuted minority. Most of those who lived in Jerusalem when the first Jewish revolt broke out in AD 67 left the city. After the Second Revolt, Christians who did not have Jewish connections apparently could live there. In the new city plan the main street ran south from the present Damascus Gate. Hadrian placed the Forum or market-place to the west of the street and attached to it the temple of Venus. The position of the temple was probably just the most convenient one, rather than being chosen to obliterate a Christian holy place. Almost 200 years later, Christians were so certain the tomb was buried there that they persuaded the emperor to order, and pay for, the demolition and excavation needed to clear it. If they had not known a tomb was there, they would hardly have dared suggest the work. What would the Emperor have said if his men had found no tomb? To be safe, the Christians could have pointed to one of the many other tombs outside the city.

Outside the city wall?

The Church of the Holy Sepulchre presents one glaring contradiction. Calvary, the hill where they crucified Jesus, was outside the city walls (see John 19:20), and so was the tomb, for Jewish law did not allow burials inside the city. Yet the Church of the Holy Sepulchre was built, and has always stood, well within the city walls.

The walls that surround Jerusalem today are not the walls of the New Testament period. They were erected between 1537 and 1540 at the command of the Turkish Sultan Suleiman the Magnificent. For a lot of their route they follow the line of older walls. The question that was open until recently concerned the line of the north wall. Supporters of the traditional site of Jesus' tomb, the Church of the Holy Sepulchre, have always argued that there was a change in the shape of the city after the crucifixion, so that the tomb was then included. Others have asserted that the present line of the north wall has not altered in that time, and so the tomb lay north of it.

Archaeological excavations in recent years have ended this debate. The British School of Archaeology in Jerusalem dug at the present-day Damascus Gate from 1964 to 1966. Over 7 metres/24 feet down, beneath old roads and ruined buildings, the excavators reached road surfaces of the first century. Very careful study was made of the different levels and the objects found in them.

Covering the natural rock was soil of farm fields, with a few burials in it. On that the first road was laid. In its plaster make-up was a coin of King Herod Agrippa I, made in AD 42–43. Before the road was put down, foundations had been laid for a magnificent new city wall and gate. As

Ever since Constantine the Great built his church in the fourth century, Christian pilgrims have come to the Church of the Holy Sepulchre. Most of the building which stands today, including the entrance, was put up by the Crusaders in the twelfth century.

so he stopped when he had laid only the foundations. The coin found in the road surface agrees with the witness of Josephus.

If the north wall of Jerusalem was not on that line until Herod Agrippa's time (AD 41–44), where was it before? No one can give a definite answer. No traces of the wall which defended the north side of Jerusalem at the time of the crucifixion have been identified. Josephus indicates part of its route near the Temple. Excavations near the Church of the Holy Sepulchre have added to his information. What they add are clues, not direct evidence. Within the present city walls not many places are free for digging, so only small areas have been explored. One of them is in the market-place to the south of the church (the Muristan).

In 1963, Kathleen Kenyon sank a trench deep into the ground and eventually hit bedrock, 15 metres/ 49 feet below the modern street. She found that the rock had been cut and quarried in the days of the kings. Dumped into the quarry was soil containing pottery from the seventh century BC and the first century AD. A few years after that excavation more digging was done, beneath the Lutheran church nearby, finding the same things. Then repairs to the Church of the Holy Sepulchre made it possible to investigate under its floors. Again there were signs of quarrying, dated by pottery lying on the rock to the seventh century BC or earlier. Vergilius Corbo, the Italian expert in charge of this work, argued that part of the quarry was used as a garden in the first century BC.

Taken together, these discoveries imply that the area was outside the city as long as the quarries remained open (the north wall would have run south of them). Filling up the quarries with earth can be seen as the work of Hadrian's builders, preparing the site for the centre of his new city in 135.

Even so, someone might say that the quarry could have lain within the city walls, and so this could not be the

far as can be deduced from the existing stones, the building of the wall and gate at this point was never finished on its original design. Everything suggests this was part of the new north wall Herod Agrippa began to build. Josephus described this wall. It was planned on so huge a scale that, had it been finished, it would have been pointless for the Romans to lay siege to the city. But Agrippa had second thoughts. When he saw the size it would be, he was afraid the emperor would think he was plotting to revolt, place where Jesus was buried. But stronger evidence rules out any doubt. For years visitors who have known about it have taken candles or torches to go into the Tomb of Joseph of Arimathea. Opening off a chapel in the wall beyond the 'tomb of Jesus' is a dark cave. Although Constantine's builders cut away a lot of the rock, they left enough to show what had been there before.

Part of the rock bench and four of the short tunnels typical of first-century Jewish tombs prove that this was one of those burial places. Two other tombs of the same type are known to have existed quite close to this one, although they cannot now be seen. (One was found a century ago under the Coptic monastery; the other was turned into a water reservoir in the entrance court, but Professor Corbo has found clear traces of its original use.) Since burials had to be made outside the city, these tombs are clear proof that the city wall then stood further south. The rock walls of old quarries were ideal places for the masons to burrow the tombs.

Once again, an objector could argue that these tombs belong to the first century BC, before a city wall was built to enclose the area they occupy. That is possible, indeed it is true, although not in the sense that would

be needed. A wall was built to enclose the area, the wall of Herod Agrippa of AD 41 and after. No records or physical remains exist to indicate any city wall other than Agrippa's that followed a northerly line and was built within a hundred years of that time.

To be sure that any tomb in Jerusalem belonged to Joseph of Arimathea, and so was the tomb in which he laid Jesus' body, we would need a genuine first-century inscription giving his name. No one has found that. The names of the owners of the tombs were very seldom carved in them, so such a discovery is unlikely. With all the evidence available, the Church of the Holy Sepulchre has a very strong claim to stand on the site of Joseph's tomb. There is no way of knowing whether or not the place said to be that tomb is the right place. Perhaps Constantine's men did uncover signs or writing left by Christian visitors before Hadrian covered the cemetery with earth, or perhaps they uncovered several tombs and simply chose one as the most suitable, the easiest one to make into a shrine. Whatever it was they found, they made it into a centre which 1,650 years later still continues to attract pilgrims—pilgrims convinced that the tomb was empty on the first Easter Sunday morning.

HOW WAS HE CRUCIFIED?

An ossuary came to light in a tomb north of Jerusalem in 1968. Scratched on it is the name Yehohanan (John), followed by an unusual phrase. Among the bones in the box was a heel bone with an iron nail through it. After examining that and other bones a group of Jerusalem physicians concluded they belonged to a man who had been crucified. His arms, they said, had been nailed to the cross and his body twisted so that a single nail, driven through both feet, the right above the left, fixed him to the upright. This meant that there had to be a bar part way up the post which bore the victim's weight. A vicious blow had broken both legs.

Several years later an anthropologist and another physician examined the bones and reached different conclusions. The ossuary, they said, held the bones of three people, the crucified man, his son, and another. There was no sign of nailing the arms to the cross, nor of breaking the legs. The nail had been hammered through the heel bone from the side, so that the man's legs straddled the post, rather than one foot being on top of the other. A piece of wood was held against the heel before the nail was driven in, to act as a washer, so preventing the foot from tearing free.

Here is an example of how hard it is to interpret fragmentary remains. However, the more recent study does agree about the unusual nature of the phrase on the ossuary. It appears to describe Yehohanan as 'the one hanged with knees apart'. That suggests this was an unusual position. Written records tell how the criminal was usually stripped and laid on the ground with his arms spread out on the cross-bar. They were either tied or nailed to it, then the bar with the man hanging from it was lifted to be fastened to the vertical stake. After that, the feet were tied or nailed in place. Death came by suffocation, as the victim's chest muscles weakened.

Crucifixion was a death the Jews abhorred. In the Dead Sea Scrolls one author condemns an enemy because he 'hangs up men alive' (the Nahum commentary, see *A Monastery in the Desert*). Another scroll sets it down as the fate reserved for traitors. It horrified Greeks and Romans, too. They kept it as a punishment for slaves and any who challenged the ruling powers. It was as 'king' that Pilate sent Jesus to the cross.

DID HIS FATHER CARRY THE CROSS?

Jerusalem was a magnet for Jews from all over the world 2,000 years ago, as it is today. Pilgrims travelled long distances to attend the festivals, especially the Passover. The book of Acts gives a list of fifteen regions whose languages could be heard in Jerusalem just after the crucifixion (Acts 2:8–11). They ranged from Persia to Rome. Some of these pilgrims fell ill and died in Jerusalem; others, perhaps, came there to die.

A few of the tombs around Jerusalem give evidence that they contain the remains of such visitors. Stone ossuaries which held their bones are labelled not only with their names but also with their places of origin. One ossuary was inscribed in Greek for Judan, a convert or proselyte, from Tyre, another, also in Greek, for 'Maria, wife of Alexander, from Capua'. An unusual memorial cut on the rock wall of one tomb tells how a pious man brought another from Babylon and bought the grave for him at Jerusalem. These finds illustrate the reality behind the list in Acts 2.

In 1941 a tomb was opened in the Kidron Valley which held eleven ossuaries. Nine of them have inscriptions. Although one of the names is Simon, which is among the commonest found on the ossuaries, most of the names were rare ones, e.g. Philiskos, Thaliarchos. Such names were popular among Jews who lived in North Africa, rather than in Palestine. They are found in the inscriptions of Jewish colonies in Egypt and Libya. In fact, the tomb was a burial place for Jewish people from Cyrenaica. Their presence in Jerusalem is mentioned both in Acts 2:10 and in Acts 6:9. One ossuary was marked explicitly in Aramaic 'Alexander of Cyrene'. On the same ossuary is a notice in Greek, giving his father's name—'Alexander, son of Simon'.

Now Mark's Gospel includes a detail in its narrative of the crucifixion which Matthew and Luke do not give. All three tell how Simon of Cyrene was forced to carry the cross for Jesus (Matthew 27:32; Luke 23:26). Mark adds that Simon was 'the father of Alexander and Rufus' (Mark 15:21). Was the Alexander of Cyrene, son of Simon, whose bones lay in that ossuary, the man whose father carried the cross? It may, of course, be a coincidence, yet the identification does seem very likely.

Roughly scratched on an ossuary from the Kidron Valley is the name 'Alexander, son of Simon', in Greek (above). More neatly engraved on the lid is 'Alexander', in Greek, and 'Alexander of Cyrene', in Hebrew (below).

CAIAPHAS' BONES?

In 1990 a tomb was found south of Jerusalem which held several ossuaries. A beautifully carved one, it was announced, has scratched on it twice in Aramaic, 'Joseph son of Caiaphas'. Josephus says one member of the high priestly family was called Joseph Caiaphas, so the excavator has suggested this was the burial of the Caiaphas who was in charge of Jesus' trial (see Matthew 26:57, John 11:49–51; 18:13,14). Further study of the name shows that it is not spelled as would be expected for Caiaphas and that, with the absence of any priestly title, makes the identification very unlikely.

DO NOT DISTURB THE DEAD

'Caesar's order' were the words at the top of the stone. There it was, a marble slab standing in a Paris museum. The words caught the eye of a famous scholar looking over the antiquities. 'Caesar's order' had to be important. What did it say? He read on:

'It is my will that graves and tombs lie undisturbed for ever . . . Respect for those who are buried is most important; no one should disturb them in any way at all. If anyone does, I require that he be executed for tomb-robbery.'

Somewhere people had been opening tombs and moving the bones, and the matter had become serious enough to have the emperor's attention. Where had the stone come from? Which Caesar made the order?

In 1930, when Michael Rostovtzeff, a famous historian, saw the stone and realized it was important, it was on show in the national library in Paris (Bibliothèque Nationale). It had been sent there in 1925 with other objects from a private collection. The

original owner had not let people study his treasures, and he left only a short note about this stone. But it does tell us one important thing. It says, 'Marble slab sent from Nazareth in 1878', indicating that it was found somewhere not very far from Nazareth. Otherwise it might have been thought to have come from Turkey, where large numbers of Greek inscriptions are found.

An imperial decree from northern Palestine forbidding grave robbery may not seem very noteworthy. But when the writing itself is put beside other Greek inscriptions something more appears. The shapes of the letters point to a first-century date for the engraving.

Does the inscription refer to the resurrection of Jesus? Some scholars have argued that it does. They suppose that the

Emperor Claudius (AD 41–54) tried to put a stop to the Christians' preaching by making this harsh decree. If the Jewish claim that 'his disciples came during the night and stole him away' (Matthew 28:13) was right, the followers of Jesus could be punished for tomb-robbery!

Another proposal brings the Nazareth Decree even closer to the time of Jesus' death. Pilate wrote to the Emperor Tiberius, some suggest, to ask how he should deal with the Christian claim about Jesus' empty tomb. Part of the reply was set up at Nazareth, known to be Jesus' home. In either case, the inscription would be the earliest monument relating to the central point of the Christian faith. It would be evidence of the effect which the preaching of the resurrection had on the Roman administration.

Ideas like these are so attractive that they easily lead to the neglect of some awkward facts. No one knows exactly where the stone was found. Nazareth may be the place, but the finder could have carried it there from somewhere else, a few days' donkey journey away, wanting to sell it to Christian pilgrims. Since the nature of the connection with Nazareth is uncertain, no argument linking the stone with the early Christians can rely on it. Unless the stone was set up in Judea and moved northwards later, Pontius Pilate cannot have had it

The Nazareth Decree, a stone slab 60 cm/2 feet high, 37.5 cm/15 ins wide, now in the Bibliothèque Nationale, Paris. It carries a decree of Caesar, translated from Latin into Greek, ordering that tomb-robbers be put to death.

made, because Galilee was in the kingdom of Herod Antipas, where Pilate had no power (see Luke 23:6,7). Indeed, even a decree of Caesar would hardly be displayed in Galilee until after Antipas' reign ended in AD 39. That means it is possible that Claudius made the decree.

Robbing tombs has been a fact of life ever since people began to bury valuable things with the dead. In Babylonia the 'Royal Tombs' of Ur (about 2500 BC), and in Egypt the empty Pyramids and the Valley of the Kings, bear witness to the robbers' activities. All sorts of ways were tried to stop this crime. Often curses were written on the tomb to frighten intruders with the fear of the gods. Greek and Roman law ruled against anyone disturbing burials, and it was impious for the Jews. An emperor's decree could be even more effective if his soldiers were in the area to enforce it.

From the Nazareth Decree we learn about the existence of tomb-robbery on such a scale, or in so sensational a way, that it needed the emperor's attention. The stone illustrates how seriously the Roman government viewed the crime, and how severe its punishment might be. Taking into account only the facts— the erection of this decree somewhere in the Galilee region, which includes the Greek cities to the east, in the first century—we cannot find any reason to link the inscription with the teaching of the resurrection. Even so, it does underline the unlikely nature of the charge that the disciples had removed Jesus' body, disheartened as they were by his death. It also underlines the failure of both the Jewish and the Roman officials to take the action which would be expected if the disciples were accused of a crime that could carry the death penalty.

THE TOMB A PILGRIM SAW

No one can be sure that the Church of the Holy Sepulchre was built over the tomb where Jesus was buried. Today it is impossible to see the tomb the fourth-century Christians identified, because Caliph Hakim's men smashed it with hammers and picks in 1009. Among pilgrims who saw it before then was a man called Arculf, who travelled from France to the Holy Land in about 680. He reported that inside the tomb there was 'a single shelf stretching from head to foot without division, which would take one person lying on his back. It is like a cave with its opening facing the south part of the tomb, and is made with a low roof over it.'

Arculf's description fits very well a first-century tomb of the richer type, with an arched recess for a body or coffin (an *arcosolium*). The tomb of a rich man like Joseph of Arimathea might have had such a recess. Once more, the verdict on the Holy Sepulchre has to be 'possible, but not certain'.

In some grand tombs of the first century around Jerusalem the body was laid in an arched recess, an arcosolium. *Rarely the floor of the recess was hollowed to form a coffin.*

THE MYSTERY OF THE TURIN SHROUD

Thousands of pilgrims have gone to Turin in Italy every year to pray in the cathedral. They have gone there because they believe the shroud in which Jesus was buried is kept there. Now a scientific test has shown, almost beyond doubt, that it cannot be the shroud of Jesus. It is only 700 years old. In spite of this, the shroud deserves a place in this book, to demonstrate some of the difficulties scientists face when they study things made long ago.

In 1898 an Italian photographer was allowed a special privilege: he was to take the first photograph of the Shroud of Turin. This is a piece of yellowish linen 4.34 metres/14 feet 3 ins long and 1.09 metres/3 feet 7 ins wide. On the cloth are shadowy marks which look like the front and back of a man. When the photographer developed his plate, he was amazed to find it had a much more detailed picture than he could see with his own eyes. It was as if the cloth were a negative from which he had made a print. More photographs taken later proved this was not a freak. In fact, every photograph develops in the same way.

What is the Turin Shroud?

The history of the shroud is known from the 1350s. A French knight living near Troyes owned it then, and 100 years later his granddaughter gave it to the Duke of Savoy. A fire in the church at Chambéry, where it was kept, damaged it in 1532. Finally, the Duke of Savoy moved it to Turin in 1578, where it is housed in the Cathedral of St John the Baptist. There is nothing certain about the earlier history. Some think it had none. When the shroud was first exhibited in Troyes, the local bishop denounced it as a fraud. He knew the artist who said he had made it. A few others said the same, but they were ignored.

On the other hand, there are reports of a shroud of Jesus in Constantinople which disappeared when the Crusaders looted the city in 1203. The shroud that came to Troyes might be that one. Six hundred years earlier a cloth marked with a face was taken to be the likeness of Jesus. This relic lay in the city of Edessa, now Urfa, not far from ancient Haran in southern Turkey. A legend said that one of Jesus' disciples took it there soon after the crucifixion. Was the cloth at Edessa the same as the Shroud of Turin, folded up? No one could be sure, because there were too many gaps in the story.

For several years scientists asked for a piece of the shroud to submit to the radio-carbon dating test. (All living things contain the radioactive substances Carbon 12 and Carbon 14. When they die Carbon 14 decays at a regular rate, giving out measurable particles. The particles emitted are counted, and the amount of decay which has taken place can be calculated by comparison with the stable amount of carbon 12. Then the date when the material died can be worked out.) The sample needed would be several centimetres/inches square. The custodians of the shroud feared that cutting so large a piece would cause too much damage, and so

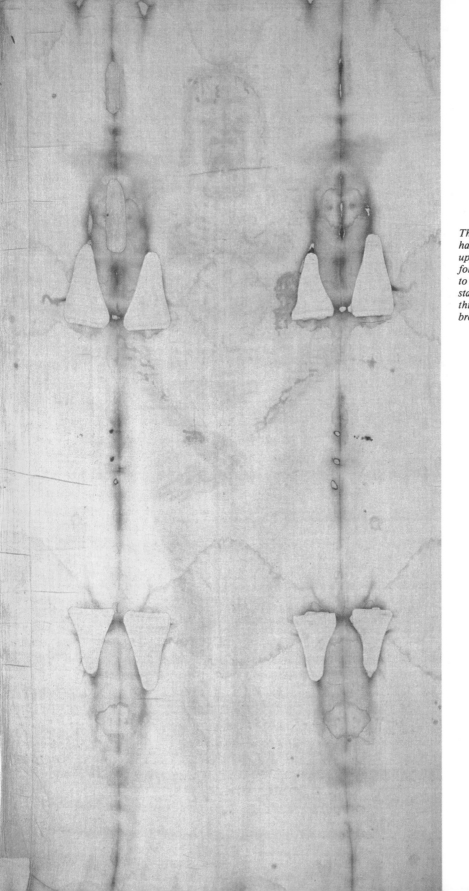

The body was laid on the lower half of the Shroud, then the upper part (shown here) was folded over the face and down to the feet. The apparent bloodstains can be seen clearly in this photograph as faint red-brown stains.

they refused permission.

When technical progress made the tests possible with much smaller samples, the authorities agreed to send tiny pieces of the shroud for examination. Samples went to three centres, in Arizona, Oxford and Zurich. With each fragment were bits of other cloths known to belong to the first century and to the Middle Ages. These were 'controls', to be tested at

When the Turin Shroud is photographed, it produces a startling image like a negative.

the same time and in the same conditions as each of the shroud samples. All of the pieces were sent to the laboratories without labels to tell the scientists which was which. Only when their tests were done could the co-ordinator reveal which pieces came from the shroud.

He made his announcement in October 1988. The results were clear, all three centres agreed. Each fragment of the shroud gave the same answer: the cloth was made from flax cut between AD 1260 and 1390. A first-century date was ruled out. This was a bitter blow for devotees of the shroud.

Although they have tried to prove the conclusion wrong, there seem to be no compelling reasons to discount it. The dating method has been developed and improved in separate laboratories, reducing points of uncertainty. With once-living matter less than 2,000 years old there is very little room for doubt or error. The laboratories agreed on the dates of the control pieces.

Even though the Carbon 14 dates show that the Turin Shroud is not a relic from the first century, it is still a remarkable object, worthy of study.

Believing is always easier if there are things to see and touch. 'Doubting Thomas' explained this clearly, when his friends said they had seen Jesus risen from the dead. 'Unless I see the nail marks in his hands and put my finger where the nails were, and put my hand into his side, I will not believe it' he said (John 20:25). Not surprisingly, as Christianity spread, people began to produce relics of martyrs to help the devotion of worshippers. The first example may be the careful burial of the bones of the elderly martyr Polycarp in Smyrna, in the middle of the second century. The Christians would meet at the place to remember him.

The same need for a visible, physical link with heroes of the past exists in non-religious contexts, too. Businesses flourish by taking tourists to see Shakespeare's birthplace, or Napoleon's tomb, or George Washington's farmhouse. Figures of history become more real when they can be related to a place or an object they used.

Relics were almost 'produced to order' in the Middle Ages, with embarrassing results. So many churches claimed to own fragments of the cross of Jesus that it was said there was enough wood in them to build a galleon! Among the relics were more than forty said to be the shroud in which Jesus was buried.

What makes the Turin Shroud a special case?

Reddish stains scattered over the

image of the body fit the descriptions of the wounds Jesus suffered. Small marks all over the back fit the record of the scourging. For some Christians this was enough. The figure on the shroud, which the photographs show distinctly, is a man who has been crucified as Jesus was, so this must be his shroud.

Not everyone found the case strong enough on this evidence alone, and the marks on the cloth need to be explained, so various tests have been made, especially since 1978. Their aim was to find out as much as possible about the shroud. They produced some more mysteries.

Were the reddish marks blood-stains, or not? One scientist claimed they were paint, others declared they came from an organic substance, which some concluded was blood. When the back of the shroud was studied, these stains were seen to have soaked through the fabric—whereas the image of the body is on the upper surface only.

If these are bloodstains, how did they come to be on the shroud? Blood clots quickly and the flogging and crowning with thorns took place before the crucifixion. Forensic scientists and pathologists, experienced with criminal and accident victims, answered this question with two points. One is the large quantity of perspiration which pours from a person hung by the wrists. This would leave the wounds moist. The other is John's report of Nicodemus bringing a heavy load of myrrh and aloes, which he put on the body of Jesus (see John 19:39,40). Oily or greasy ointments slow down the clotting process.

Even so, the fact that the marks are so clear is almost too good to be true! When the body was taken down from the cross and carried to the nearby tomb, rubbing and movement could be expected to spread the stains much more, especially if the body was carried in the shroud. Another question not finally answered is why the stains have not turned dark brown,

as old bloodstains usually do.

Other tests made on the cloth have brought further claims. Among pollen grains caught in the fabric were some typical of the eastern Mediterranean area, and even the Dead Sea region, a Swiss scientist reported. Yet one of the pollens common there, that of the olive tree, is missing. Mineral particles in the fibres include limestone similar to Jerusalem stone, and the reaction of the hot, crucified body with the alkaline stone might produce the yellowish figure on the Shroud, according to an American crystallo-grapher and an archaeologist. When an Image Analyzer was applied to the photograph of the Shroud, it produced three-dimensional pictures of the body, a result which a painting could not give.

The photograph of the face magnified five times revealed a round mark on each eye. One researcher says he sees part of the imprint made by a coin of Pontius Pilate, placed on the right eye. The coin is the 'crook' type described in *Clues to Pilate's Character*. Yet placing a coin on a corpse's eyes was not customary in first-century Judea, and the repro-ductions of the imprint are not at all convincing to the writer.

With all these points in mind, we have to ask, 'Would the Turin Shroud be anything like the cloth which Joseph of Arimathea took to wrap the body of Jesus?' To the Gospel-writers, the only interesting thing about the grave-clothes was their position in the empty tomb, where they were evidence that Jesus was not there. In the circum-stances of the first Easter we may doubt whether any of Jesus' friends would have gone back to tidy the tomb, or if Joseph would have sent a servant to do it. To keep used grave-clothes would be contrary to normal Jewish habit, because they were 'unclean'.

The Gospels are not precise in describing the burial. Matthew, Mark and Luke all report Joseph bringing a piece of linen. John says he brought pieces of linen, and when Peter looked into the tomb on the Sunday he saw them 'as well as the burial cloth that had been around Jesus' head' (John 20:6,7). What John describes agrees with knowledge of the Jewish burial routine, and Lazarus was treated in the same way (John 11:44).

The body was dressed, the hands and feet tied so that they would stay in place, and the head bound with a bandage under the chin to stop the jaw sagging. But the crucified Jesus had no clothes (the soldiers took them), so Joseph's cloth could be a substitute, a shroud. John's pieces of linen might include it; they were not necessarily 'strips of linen' as the New International Version translates. If this is a correct reconstruction, signs of the bandages around the hands, feet and head ought to appear on the Turin Shroud.

They do not. If the shroud had been tied down there would be clear crease marks, which there are not. It did not fall closely over the sides of the body, and this agrees with the temporary nature of Joseph's and Nicodemus' attentions, for they expected the final burial to be made after the Passover. Then the body would have been more securely wrapped.

Who could have created so convincing a relic in the Middle Ages, and how? Future inquiries may find the answers. Perhaps the best suggestion is that a Crusader brought back this length of linen from his travels. It was a shroud which had been used to wrap the body of a badly wounded man. This suggestion fits the evidence well, even if the cause of the marks is not properly understood. Modern knowledge is far from explaining many curiosities of this world, and the Turin Shroud remains one of them.

The Roman Catholic Church never claimed officially that the Turin Shroud was the burial cloth of Jesus. Like all other relics, it should be an aid to faith, not an object of faith. The announcement that the shroud is not 2,000 years old may disappoint some Christians, but they should not allow it to shake their faith. Rather, it should help them to concentrate on the Person whose shroud it was supposed to be.

WRITERS

When did that happen, and why? What sort of a man was he?
History-writing tries to report and explain the past. It is not a modern
invention. In the first century Flavius Josephus wrote books to set out
the reasons for the Jewish revolt against Rome, and to tell his Roman
friends about his nation's beliefs and past. His books, with the books
of other Jewish, Greek and Roman authors who lived in the first and
second centuries, allow us to weave the historical back-cloth to the
Gospels. They fill out the careers of the kings and rulers they name,
reflecting the opinions of intelligent observers. They clarify some
points which the first readers of the Gospels understood, but modern
readers do not. The following pages offer brief biographies of the two
most important men, describing the value of their works. They also
explain the writings of other authors mentioned in this book. The
section ends with an outline of the sources for early rabbinic traditions.

*Roman ladies liked to be portrayed as writers. This one, from Pompeii,
is thinking carefully before she writes on her wooden tablets.*

PHILO—A PHILOSOPHER OF ALEXANDRIA

Ships approaching the harbour of Alexandria were guided by the lighthouse, the Pharos. A coin of the Emperor Commodus struck in 188–89 records its appearance. One of the Seven Wonders of the Ancient World.

Alexander the Great marched from Macedonia in northern Greece in 334 BC. In 332 he conquered Egypt and the next year made himself master of the Persian Empire. Across this great stretch of land he founded Greek cities. He hoped to spread the Greek way of life and thought over as much of the world as possible, so he settled his soldiers in the new cities. Several of them were named after him— Alexandria. The one that grew into the greatest and most famous is still a major city in Egypt. Alexander himself founded that one in 331 BC, on a neck of land between a lake and the sea. It was an ideal place for a harbour and later developed into the major port for shipping grain to Rome.

Alexander died in 323 BC. His generals took charge of the empire on behalf of his son Alexander, who was born after his father's death. The boy was killed before he grew up, and three of the generals divided the empire among themselves. Seleucus set himself up as king of Syria and Babylonia in 312 BC, then Ptolemy made himself king of Egypt in 305. He took Alexandria as his capital. Ptolemy's dynasty ruled until Octavian, later Augustus, conquered Mark Antony and his mistress Cleopatra with her son, the fifteenth Ptolemy, in 30 BC. Egypt then became a province of the Roman Empire, with the governor's palace in Alexandria.

Alexandria was a Greek city. Many citizens had Greek ancestors. They spoke and wrote Greek, they watched Greek plays in the theatres, they took part in Greek sports, and they wor-shipped Greek gods and goddesses. Alexandria quickly became the greatest centre of Greek culture outside Athens. In its library were half a million books, all written on papyrus rolls. The librarians tried to collect a copy of every book in existence. There was a research centre, too, the Museum, where scholars from all over the world lived and studied at the king's expense.

Beside the Greeks in Alexandria there were native Egyptians. They learnt Greek ways, and began to write their own language (Coptic) with the letters of the Greek alphabet instead of the complicated Egyptian hieroglyphs. The city also held the largest number of Jewish residents outside Palestine. They occupied most of two of the five sectors of the city. Living in a mostly Greek society, these Jews spoke Greek and lived more and more in the Greek way, although they kept the main rules and festivals of their own religion. As time passed, fewer and fewer of them learnt Hebrew so, when the lessons were read in the synagogue from the Hebrew Bible, they could not under-stand them. Jewish scholars began to translate the Law, the Five Books of Moses, into Greek before 250 BC, and gradually did all the other Old Testament books, producing the translation called the Septuagint.

Having their Bible in Greek no doubt helped many to keep to their religion, but the tension between Jewish traditions and Greek culture was too much for some to bear. They took up the Greek way of life, abandoning their religious practices and becoming just like their

302

neighbours. When the Romans took control of Egypt, they allowed the Jews in Alexandria to live as a recognized community, permitting them to keep to their peculiar customs. They were not allowed, it seems, to hold the same rights as Greek or Roman citizens unless they gave up their Jewish status. There were some who did that. One who belonged to a very wealthy family actually became the Roman governor of Palestine from AD 46 to 48, and later prefect of Egypt (AD 66–69). He was Tiberius Julius Alexander, whose father gave doors decorated with gold and silver to beautify Herod's Temple.

His conduct upset the Jews who were trying to keep the faith taught in the Law of Moses. In particular it upset his uncle Philo. Philo, who lived from about 20 BC to AD 45, was a leader in the Jewish section of Alexandria, and a philosopher. His special concern was to explain the Jewish religion and way of life in ways that educated Greeks could understand. By picking ideas from Greek philosophers and knitting them to Jewish traditions he made a bridge between two very different ways of thinking about God and the world. Philo's books were partly intended to help Jews who found Greek thought attractive to reconcile it with their inherited faith, rather than abandoning it. He may have sent some of his books to his nephew, hoping to change his mind.

Philo's sixteen religious and philosophical books are valuable because they are the only Jewish writings of this sort to survive from the Gospel period. They present a way of thought that is different from the style of the rabbis, and show some of the ideas early Christians faced as they preached about Jesus to Greek-speaking Jews.

In Philo's books there are expressions which also occur in the New Testament. One is 'the Word' (*logos*), the power who links God and man. Although Philo's thinking is at

first sight like the beginning of John's Gospel, careful reading makes it plain that they are not the same. Philo's 'Word' was the image of God and the ideal human mind, yet he also identified the Word with the whole intelligible universe. The body, Philo thought, was wicked and an obstacle to knowing God. John, on the contrary, could say 'The Word became flesh and made his dwelling among us,' not as

an idea or an influence, but as the personal Son of God (see John 1:14,17,18). The New Testament Letter to the Hebrews uses language and forms of thought which have more in common with Philo, yet with them the Christian author set out a message about God's revelation which is very different from Philo's.

Philosophers like peace for thinking and writing. Philo's peace was shattered near the end of his life. It was the year 38. Flaccus had been governing Egypt for five years. The Emperor Tiberius, who had appointed

Jews living in Alexandria could not understand Hebrew well, so they had the books of the Hebrew Bible translated into Greek. These fragments are part of the oldest surviving copy of Deuteronomy found in Egypt, a scroll made about 100 BC. In the Greek text the sacred name of God (traditionally written Jehovah in the European languages) stands in Hebrew letters (e.g. line 6). It was too holy to read, so the word 'lord' was spoken instead.

The philosopher Philo was a leader of the Jewish section in Alexandria, the famous Egyptian city named after Alexander the Great. Its position on a neck of land between lake and sea made it the ideal harbour it remains today.

him, died in 37, and Flaccus felt at risk. Gaius Caligula, the new emperor, quickly executed the key figures of Tiberius' court, leaving Flaccus without a powerful friend in Rome. Worse, a Greek, whose political manoeuvres in Alexandria Flaccus had upset, won Caligula's favour. The Greek and his supporters came back to the city and offered to help Flaccus avoid the emperor's displeasure. They had a price for their aid: Flaccus was to let the Greeks of Alexandria have the upper hand over the Jews there.

Apparently the Jews wanted the advantages of Greek citizenship (one being to pay less tax), without accepting some of the responsibilities which ran against their religious beliefs. The Greeks evidently felt the Jews had enough privileges already.

Flaccus was afraid to refuse. Like Pontius Pilate, he needed to be 'Caesar's friend'. So when the Greek mob, annoyed that the Jewish King

Herod Agrippa had paraded through the city, started attacking synagogues, Flaccus did nothing. In fact, he ordered the Jews to live in one section of Alexandria only, the first ghetto. His attitude encouraged the anti-Jewish crowd in their attacks, and many Jews were killed and synagogues burnt.

Suddenly everything changed. In the autumn of 38 a troop of soldiers sailed in from Rome to arrest Flaccus. He was taken aback to find that those accusing him to the emperor were the very people whose help he thought he had bought at the cost of the Jews. He was sent into exile, then executed. Philo and his friends praised God for acting to save them!

Philo's book *Against Flaccus* tells the tale. It reveals the problems Jews faced in pagan society, problems similar in some cases to those the early Christians met. It also illustrates how a pressure group could force a Roman governor to act against his better judgment, in the same way as the priests in Jerusalem did at the trial of Jesus (John 19:12–16).

Philo wrote another 'political' book, *The Mission to Gaius*, explaining how he led a party of five elders from Alexandria to put the Jewish case to the emperor, countering the claims of the Greeks. Gaius met them early in AD 40, and gave no reply. During the summer he made a decree that a statue of himself dressed as the god Zeus should be set up in the Temple in Jerusalem. The governor of Syria, Petronius, sensibly delayed obeying because he realized the trouble that would follow. Then a close friend of Gaius, the Jewish King Herod Agrippa, found out about the order and wrote a letter to him which persuaded him to withdraw it.

Philo declares that the emperor still planned to have the statue put in place in Jerusalem when he visited the east himself—a visit he never made. Later in the year Gaius heard the two parties from Alexandria again, and again failed to resolve the problem. He was stabbed to death on 24 January 41. His uncle Claudius was made emperor and quickly gave the Jews back their previous position in the city. At the same time he told them not to try to get rights which were not theirs. (Claudius' letter to Alexandria, preserved on a papyrus found in Egypt, gives this information.) *The Mission to Gaius* has lost its ending. Comparing it with *Against Flaccus* leads scholars to suggest the last part described Gaius' death, explaining it as an act of God on behalf of the Jewish people.

This book of Philo's contrasts Gaius' behaviour to the Jews with the considerate ways of Augustus and Tiberius. It preserves the letter Herod Agrippa wrote to change Gaius' mind —or Philo's version of it. In that he drew the emperor's attention to Tiberius' reaction when Pontius Pilate brought the gilded shields into Jerusalem contrary to custom (see *Certainly not a Saint!*). Although he lived in Alexandria, Philo heard of events in Judea, and the reports he gives about a few of them are valuable additions to the information preserved by Josephus and the New Testament.

Philo's books were never best-sellers—few philosophers' books are —yet they were not forgotten. As Christianity spread, the question of how to explain Greek ideas in Christian terms became important and Philo's efforts to do the same from a Jewish point of view influenced some of the Christian thinkers, including St Augustine. So it was Christian scribes who continued to copy and preserve Philo's works. Translators made versions of some of them in Latin and Armenian.

JOSEPHUS THE JEW—PATRIOT OR TRAITOR?

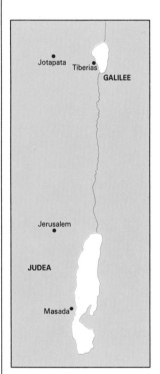

They were just a handful of patriots, facing a well-organized war-machine. What was the point of fighting so strong an army? Why not surrender and save as much as possible? These were the thoughts of the thirty-year-old Jewish commander, Joseph. It was AD 67. He was in charge of the resistance to Rome in Galilee, holding out in the town of Jotapata. He had to keep his thoughts to himself and spur his men on.

After forty-seven days under siege, the town fell. Joseph and forty men hid in a cave. There they made a pact with each other not to be taken alive; they would kill each other. Joseph managed to be one of the last two left. He persuaded the other man that they should not die, then gave himself up to the Romans. Instead of executing the rebel leader who had caused him such trouble, the Roman General Vespasian put him under close guard.

Joseph was a very shrewd and persuasive man. In a private conversation with Vespasian he forecast that he would be made emperor of Rome. When Vespasian's troops did proclaim him emperor, in the summer of 69, he released Joseph from captivity. The new emperor went to Rome to secure control, leaving his son Titus to carry on the war in Judea, with Joseph as one of his consultants. Naturally, the Jews were eager to lay hands on the man they saw as a traitor, and some of the Romans did not trust him, although Titus did. Joseph had to watch, as the Roman soldiers broke into Jerusalem and fought through the Temple courts and sacred buildings.

When they had overrun the whole city, they herded the thousands of prisoners into the Temple courtyard and Joseph was allowed to find his friends among them and set them free. When the revolt was all over, with only the rock-fortress of Masada in Jewish hands, Titus took Joseph to Rome.

In Rome he was lodged in the house the emperor had previously occupied. Vespasian gave him property near the coast of Judea and a pension, and, most valuable of all, the privilege of Roman citizenship. Joseph followed the custom of those who were made Roman citizens in this way and gave his name a Latin form, adding to it the family name of the emperor, so becoming Flavius Josephus. He spent the rest of his life in Rome, dying there about the end of the century.

Unable to return to Palestine, where he had many enemies, Josephus spent his years in Rome writing books. These were copied and published and became particularly useful to Christian writers, because they give the history of the Gospel period in detail. They are still the most important sources of information about Palestine in the first century BC and up to AD 70.

Josephus set out, first, to give an accurate account of the Jewish war against Rome. Others had written about it, he said, at second-hand and unreliably. He would tell the true story. He issued the book in his own language, Aramaic, for Jewish readers in the east. Afterwards he had it translated into Greek, and it is that version which can be read today.

Josephus' *Jewish War* is the most

extensive account of Roman warfare in the first century, so Roman historians prize it. The eye-witness reports of different stages in the war, and of the events leading up to it, make quite lively reading. Josephus relied on his own memory, perhaps his own notes, and claimed he had drawn on the reports Vespasian and Titus placed in the official archives of Rome. He submitted his book to Titus and to the Jewish king, Herod Agrippa II, who both approved it.

Naturally Josephus wrote from his own point of view. He thought the war could have been avoided and so painted the leaders of the Jewish rebels as black as he could. He did not hide his own role, for he apparently believed it was justified by the events. There are some statements and figures which are hard to accept, but most of the book is considered by all scholars as a first-class historical source.

A much bigger book followed the *Jewish War*, for Josephus felt the Roman world was badly informed about his people and their long history. He followed the biblical line from Adam to Moses, through the kings to the Exile, and on to the days of the Jewish kings, Herod, his sons and the war.

The *Jewish Antiquities*, like the *Jewish War*, is especially valuable for the later part of ancient Jewish history. Almost half the book relates events from the times of the Maccabees to the start of the Jewish War. It provides us with a lot of knowledge about the Gospel period. Some of Josephus' descriptions of Herod's buildings and other monuments have proved to be remarkably accurate when archaeologists have excavated their remains. Putting the ancient book and the physical evidence side by side brings a richer picture than either can give alone.

This long work—60,000 lines of writing in Greek, the author stated—was finished in 93 or 94. Josephus dedicated it to a man called Epaphroditus. He may have asked for the book, or stimulated the author to write it, rather as Theophilus (whose name is recorded at the start of Luke's Gospel) may have done for Luke.

Two other books which Josephus wrote survive, both defending him against his enemies. One is his *Life*. In it he concentrates on rebutting an historian from Tiberias, whose own book accused Josephus of stirring up the anti-Roman revolt in Galilee. If people accepted that view, Josephus' favoured position in Rome would be at risk. At the beginning he sets out a summary of his early life. As a young teenager, he boasts, he was so well-

The Roman Emperor Vespasian (AD 69–79) accepted Josephus' surrender and rewarded him for his help in the Jewish War with a house in Rome.

After the fall of Jerusalem, Titus brought back his prisoners and booty to Rome. His triumph was commemorated in the Arch of Titus near the Colosseum. On one wall the carving shows Roman soldiers carrying the table, trumpets and golden lampstand from the Temple.

versed in the Jewish laws that the priests asked his advice. A little later he studied the various parties of Judaism to see which he thought best, and went off to spend three years in the desert with a hermit. When he went back to Jerusalem, he joined the moderate party, the Pharisees.

In 64 Josephus paid a visit to Rome. The governor Felix had sent some priests for trial before Caesar, and Josephus wanted to arrange their release. After escaping from a shipwreck, he reached Rome in the company of a Jewish actor. This man was a favourite at court, so he introduced Josephus to Poppaea, Nero's wife. She agreed to Josephus' request.

The strength and power of the Roman Empire, and its efficiency deeply impressed Josephus, convincing him that to fight against it would be foolish. Even so, events took such a turn back home that, soon after his return to Palestine, he found himself doing just that. Most of the *Life* explains what he actually did, and why.

The fourth book is called *Against Apio*. It is a reply to a piece of anti-Jewish propaganda. Jewish religion and the Jewish race were very old, Josephus declared, and gave proof of this by quoting ancient authors from Egypt, Phoenicia, Babylonia, and even Greece. (Often their writings have disappeared since Josephus' time, so he has preserved the only traces of them.) Further, Josephus argued, the Jewish belief in one moral God who gave just laws for mankind was far better than Greek belief in many gods who behaved disgracefully.

Josephus published his books in Rome, where scribes copied them so that they were widely available. All those copies have disappeared. One third-century papyrus containing a few paragraphs of the *War* has been found in Egypt. In the fourth century Eusebius drew heavily on Josephus' writings for historical details in writing his history of the early church. Ever since, scholars have valued these books for the same reasons.

Scribes continued to copy them throughout the Middle Ages, and some translated them into Latin. A Latin version of five sections of the *Antiquities* is preserved in a papyrus book copied in the seventh century. The oldest Greek manuscripts available, apart from the papyrus, are from the ninth or tenth centuries. They show that the earlier copyists had made a number of mistakes which were passed on uncorrected, and part of *Against Apio* survived only in Latin. The popularity of Josephus' works is clear from the fact that at least six editions of parts of them in Latin were printed between the invention of printing, in 1453, and 1500.

ROMAN WRITERS

As the second century AD began, two Roman authors were at work, composing histories of the previous hundred years. Their books are the chief sources of information about the reigns of the first Roman emperors. Tacitus' *Annals* dealt with the years from Tiberius' accession to the death of Nero (AD 14 to 68). There were eighteen books, but numbers 7–10 and 17 and 18 have disappeared. The oldest manuscript of books 1–6 now available was copied in Germany about 850. Tacitus was a very careful historian, concentrating on the emperors and their policies, which he did not like. As far as the Gospels are concerned, he makes only one direct

In this painting from Pompeii the man holds a papyrus scroll, his wife has hinged writing-tablets and a metal stylus. Painted before AD 79.

The greatest ancient library was at Alexandria, but a hostile king forced many scholars to flee to other cities in 145 BC. They created new libraries and academies, including one at Ephesus. In AD 135 a man from Sardis built a new library there in honour of his father Celsus. Behind the façade, now partly rebuilt, was a reading room 16.76 metres/ 55 feet wide.

reference, commenting that the Christians persecuted by Nero began with Christ 'who had been executed in the reign of Tiberius by the governor of Judea, Pontius Pilatus'.

The Lives of the Caesars by Suetonius is rather different. His book presents biographies of the emperors, from Augustus to Domitian (43 BC–AD 96). Suetonius enjoyed scandal and gossip, yet he was able to include details from the official records of the Caesars because he was secretary to the Emperor Hadrian. Thus his writing has special value. The oldest surviving copy was made in the ninth century.

A century after Suetonius, Cassius Dio put together a long history of Rome from its foundation to AD 229. Two-thirds of his books are lost. A summary, and extracts other writers made, preserve pieces of his work, sometimes recording events other historians omitted.

One historian has left a first-hand account of Tiberius' reign. Velleius Paterculus was a soldier who had fought as an officer in the future emperor's army. Unhappily, he favoured Tiberius wholeheartedly, so that his account is seriously unbalanced. A single copy of his work, made about AD 800, was available in the sixteenth century, but was later destroyed.

Apart from the historians, a lot can be learnt about the Roman world from the *Geography* written in Greek by Strabo during the rule of Augustus. Pliny the Elder, who died observing the eruption of Vesuvius at Pompeii in AD 79, wrote works which filled over sixty books. Only thirty-seven survive, the highly valuable *Natural History*, a sort of encyclopedia of Roman knowledge.

Various other authors, poets, playwrights and philosophers have left writings in Greek or Latin which help to build a rich picture of life in the Roman Empire at the time of the Gospels.

JEWISH WRITINGS

Someone hoping to learn about the period of the Gospels might turn to Jewish writings first. After all, Jesus was a Jew and lived in Palestine. There are large volumes of the rabbis' teachings in Hebrew and Aramaic: the Mishnah, the Talmuds, the Targums, and the Midrash. Sadly, all these books were made long after the fall of Jerusalem in AD 70. They tell stories about events before the calamity, and report teachings of the rabbis in those days, but each of these texts has to be thoroughly assessed.

The rabbis' recollections were coloured by history, and later teachers tended to combine their opinions with the views of their forebears. However, with careful sifting, these writings can supply pieces of information about early first-century life and thought. Even so, the rabbis who taught after AD 70 were almost wholly from the moderate wing of the Pharisees, so their doctrines represent only that section of early Jewish faith.

Any religion that has a sacred book must make its scriptures meaningful to its followers. All the rabbinic writings have that aim. After AD 70 the rabbis had to rethink the way they should apply the Law of Moses to daily life, for there was no Temple in Jerusalem, and after the Second Revolt ended, in AD 135, Jews were not allowed there. New circumstances demanded new interpretations.

About 200, Rabbi Judah the Prince collected the decisions, with supporting discussions, in a series of books which together form the Mishnah. He drew on some older collections in writing, but most of his material came through the traditions of the rabbinic schools. The Mishnah is written in a dialect of Hebrew which may stem from the spoken language of earlier times. It is the written form of the oral law which governed the lives of the pious, the detailed working out of every rule, and the addition of steps to ensure that the laws were not broken by accident. These were carried to such extremes that the Gospels record Jesus' condemnation. (See Mark 7:1–23; Matthew 15:1–20; and *Small is Beautiful, Cleanliness is Next to Godliness?, Did they Wash Beds?*)

As time passed, debates over interpretation continued. The Mishnah itself became a subject for study. Early in the fifth century the opinions of the rabbis in Palestine were put together as a commentary on sections of the Mishnah, to form the Jerusalem Talmud. (Talmud means 'teaching'.) Here the Mishnah text is in Hebrew, the comments in the Aramaic of Galilee. Despite the date of its compilation, this Talmud preserves some much older material.

A similar process took place in the rabbinic schools in Babylonia, ending in the Babylonian Talmud. This was finished in the sixth century. Its language is the Babylonian form of Aramaic, but with some reports in Hebrew.

Aramaic was the common language of Palestine in the first century (see *The Languages they Spoke*), and after AD 70 Hebrew declined further, so the majority of the people did not benefit from reading the Hebrew Bible.

Apart from the Dead Sea Scrolls and fragmentary books from Masada and the Bar Kochba caves, there are no copies of distinctively Jewish writings from the early centuries of the Christian era. This painting from a tomb at Abila in northern Transjordan (modern Quweilbeh) shows a woman writing in a codex. Third century AD.

Aramaic translations or paraphrases had been read in the synagogue for a long time. Officially they were not to be written down. In fact, as the Dead Sea Scrolls prove, some were. Eventually the rabbis accepted some Aramaic renderings and they circulated under the name Targum ('interpretation').

There are three important Targums, Onkelos and the Palestinian Targum on the first five books of the Bible, and Jonathan on the historical and prophetic books. Although they were made about AD 300 and revised even later, they do contain much older traditions. Their closeness to the Hebrew text varies. Some passages are literal Aramaic translations, others are paraphrases or interpretations in the light of current affairs. Agreements between the Targums and the Greek translation (the Septuagint) show that some of these ideas arose in the second or third centuries BC.

Finally, there is the wide range of books called Midrash. These are 'explanation' of Scripture, put in the form of commentaries on the biblical books. They are brief sermons and meditations, illustrating the meanings of the texts as different teachers understood them. Often they fill in the brief biblical stories with colourful details, or bring out the supposed meaning through fanciful word-play. The written books of Midrash belong to Talmudic times and later, although they, also, include much earlier material. Their methods of treating Scripture are seen in the Dead Sea Scrolls, in the Septuagint, and to some extent in the Old Testament Book of Chronicles which calls itself a midrash (2 Chronicles 13:22; 24:27—though the meaning of the word there may not be identical with its meanings in rabbinic circles).

All these writings are helpful in illustrating beliefs and customs in the Gospel period. They are most helpful to someone wanting to trace the influences of Jewish religious attitudes in the Gospels themselves, which is a separate field of study.

GOSPEL RECORDS

Christianity, an illegal religious movement, spread rapidly
across the Roman Empire. Although persecuted by the government,
despised by the intelligentsia and spurned by the Jews, it grew stronger
and stronger. At its base were the books of the New Testament, and
especially the Gospels. When they could lay their hands on them,
officials burnt them. Amazingly, copies survive which were made
during the centuries before Constantine the Great legalized Christianity
in 313. They are important evidence that the Gospel text was handed
down accurately. In some verses they show where misunderstandings
took place later. No other ancient Greek books are known from such a
wide range of copies, written so close to the times when their authors
composed them.

A scene in a Roman school. The master instructs a boy who is reading from a scroll.
From Neumagen, Germany, second or third century AD.

THE OLDEST BIBLES

Britain and France have often been at loggerheads, and sometimes at war. Their rivalry has reached round the globe and affected many people and many aspects of life—even biblical scholarship!

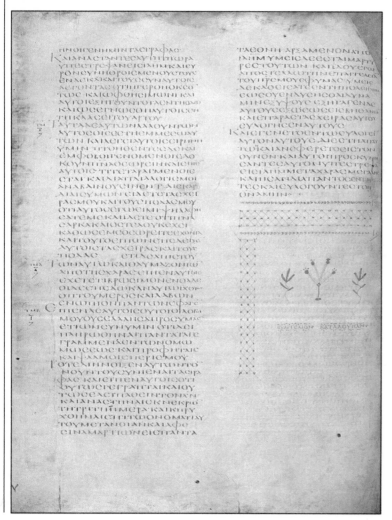

A gift for a king

In the reign of King James I (1603–1625) there was a struggle in Constantinople between the Greek Orthodox Church and the Roman Catholic Church. Who should be more important in the Turkish capital, the Greek Patriarch or the Roman primate? The English ambassador supported the Greek, the French the Roman.

The Patriarch was grateful for the Englishman's support, and helped him to collect old manuscripts and sculptures. To show his gratitude, the Patriarch offered a special present, which he thought the king of England would like. The ambassador wrote to London describing the gift. It was, he reported, a copy of the Bible written by a martyr, Thecla, 'that lived in the time of St Paul'. King James died without receiving the book. His death delayed the affair, but in 1627 the Patriarch delivered the Bible to the ambassador for the new king, Charles I.

The manuscript reached London where it became part of the Royal Library (which King George II gave to the British Museum in 1757). Scholars studied it and wrote about it quickly. Although there was nothing to uphold a date as early as the ambassador had said, it was clearly one of the oldest Greek copies of the Bible to have survived.

Today this copy is named the Codex Alexandrinus, because the Patriarch who sent it to England seems to have taken it from Alexandria, where he had been Patriarch, on his move to Turkey. It is not known where it was originally written. The fact that it includes an introduction to the Psalms by Athanasius, who died in AD 373, shows that it cannot have been written before about the middle of the fourth century. To work out the age of such a manuscript is difficult. From the style of the handwriting a date between 400 and 450 is now usually accepted. That is to say, it was copied less than 350 years after the New Testament was written.

A hidden book

Since the fifteenth century, and perhaps for long before, the library of the Vatican in Rome has owned a very old Greek Bible. The famous scholar Erasmus, who was the first to publish the Greek New Testament in print (1516), was sent information taken from this copy. A few scholars made incomplete studies during the next centuries, but it was not until it left Rome that its value was understood.

The book left Rome as loot; Napoleon carried it off to Paris in 1797. While it was there, a German professor examined it and wrote about its age and importance. When it was returned to Rome in 1815, the Vatican authorities refused to allow scholars to study it freely. The brilliant young Tischendorf was allowed to see it for six hours in 1843, and for a longer time in 1866. A great English scholar had his pockets searched and all his writing materials taken away before he was allowed to look at the book. Eventually the Vatican issued photographs of the whole manuscript in 1890, so that everybody who wanted to could read it.

This copy of the Greek Bible was made about the middle of the fourth century, so it is older than the Codex Alexandrinus. Again, the dating depends to a large extent on the style of handwriting. There is another pointer to the date which applies both to this Codex Vaticanus and to its companion, the Codex Sinaiticus, whose discovery makes a romantic story.

Saved from burning!

In 1844 a German student made a dramatic discovery. Constantine Tischendorf was on a journey round the churches and monasteries of the Near East. Other travellers had brought back valuable manuscripts from some of them, and Tischendorf hoped to find more. In due course he reached the monastery of St Catherine on the north-west slope of Jebel Musa, the traditional Mount Sinai. All sorts of manuscripts were stacked in the library to delight and occupy the young student. On 24 May, however, it was not in the library that Tischendorf experienced his great moment. He described it:

'I perceived in the middle of the great hall a large and wide basket full of old parchments which were to be burnt as fuel for the monastery's ovens. The librarian said that two heaps of papers like these, mouldered by time, had already been committed to the flames. What was my surprise to find amid this heap of papers a considerable number of sheets of a copy of the Old Testament in Greek which seemed to me to be one of the most ancient that I had ever seen.'

Tischendorf told the monks that these old pages were worth keeping, and managed to find 129 leaves altogether. He wanted to take possession of them all but, now that the monks could see they were valuable, they let him take away only the forty-three he rescued from the rubbish basket. Proud that he had made such a discovery and could bring some of the pages home with him, Tischendorf presented them to his patron, the king of the German state of Saxony. The king placed them in the university library at Leipzig, where they are still. Tischendorf printed an edition of this section of the book in 1846, and argued that it was written in the middle of the fourth century AD. He deliberately did not say where he had found it.

Several years passed—how tantalizing they must have been—

The discovery of Codex Sinaiticus was the most important of all the manuscript discoveries of the nineteenth century. The beautiful even script and spacious margins make it a noble book. When the parchment sheets were bought by the British Museum they were carefully treated and re-bound.

then in 1853 he managed to visit the monastery again. His high hopes were dashed! No one would tell him anything about the manuscript. All he found was a scrap with a few verses from Genesis. Had all the other pages he saw in 1844 been burnt? He left frustrated.

Despite that disappointment, the German scholar, now aged forty-three, was back at St Catherine's in January 1859. After a short stay, he was talking with the keeper of the library and gave him a copy of the Old Testament in Greek (the Septuagint) which he had had published. In reply the monk said, 'I, too, have a Septuagint.' He lifted a

package wrapped in red cloth from a shelf over the door of his cell.

To Tischendorf's amazement, there were all the leaves he had seen fifteen years earlier, with very many more. Here was most of the Old Testament and the whole of the New Testament! That night Tischendorf did not sleep. The monk let him take the manuscript to his room to study and, in such a situation, the scholar wrote in his diary, 'that night it seemed sacrilege to sleep'. The monks refused to sell the manuscript, or to let Tischendorf borrow it. Happily, when Tischendorf reached Cairo, he met the abbot of St Catherine's monastery, who was

A NEW DISCOVERY AT MOUNT SINAI

When Tischendorf brought back the Codex Sinaiticus from St Catherine's Monastery, he obtained altogether 390 pages. They contain all of the New Testament and some of the Old Testament in Greek, but much of the latter is missing. Tischendorf's story pointed to the fate of the missing pages: they had served as fuel to warm the monks (see The Oldest Bibles).

In May 1975 another discovery was made in the monastery. A fire had destroyed a chapel and the monks were clearing the ruins. As they worked, they found an old cell. The ceiling had fallen in, burying everything inside. When the monks dug away the rubbish they came upon scores of pages from old books. Some are in Arabic, some in Syriac, and some are Greek. Many of them are 1,000 years old, or more;

others are only three or four centuries old. Why they were in the cell is not known. Perhaps they were rescued from an earlier disaster, stacked in the cell and forgotten.

Long ago, at the foot of Mount Sinai, the monks had a copy of Homer's poem The Iliad, copied about AD 800 and supplied with a translation into Greek prose of that time. They read religious books more often. There were parts of a devotional study by an early abbot of the monastery, parts of a copy of Mark's Gospel from the sixth century, and fragments of Genesis in Greek from the century before. Thirteen pages and fifteen fragments belong to another copy of the Old Testament in Greek. The monks have identified them as part of the Codex Sinaiticus. These, at least, had escaped both the flames and, to the monks'

delight, the eyes and hands of Tischendorf!

Justinian, the great Byzantine emperor ruling from Istanbul (then Constantinople) in the sixth century, founded the monastery, although monks had been living in the area before that time. Whether he gave the Codex Sinaiticus to his new establishment, or whether a monk brought it with him, no one knows. Although the new discovery may give slight hope that other pages lie hidden, no pieces of any older manuscripts have appeared there, as they have in Egypt.

Codex Sinaiticus, one of the most important Greek manuscripts, containing the whole New Testament and some of the Old Testament, was discovered in the nineteenth century at this monastery, St Catherine's, at the foot of Mt Sinai. The story makes exciting reading. On Christmas Day 1933 the British Museum bought it from the Soviet government for £100,000.

visiting the city, and persuaded him to have the book brought there for him to examine. With the help of two friends, he spent two months copying out the whole manuscript—110,000 lines.

What should happen to the manuscript? Could it be kept safely in the Sinai desert? Eventually Tischendorf persuaded the monks to offer it to the Czar of Russia, the protector of the Orthodox Church. On 19 November 1859 the Czar received the 347 parchment sheets. He paid for the text to be printed as part of the celebration of 1,000 years of the Russian Empire (1862).

There was one more journey for this Bible. In 1933 the Soviet government decided to raise money by selling it. After negotiations in America failed, the British Museum bought it for £100,000 (over $500,000 at that time), more than half the money coming from donations made by the general public.

Tischendorf argued that this manuscript, the Codex Sinaiticus, is as old as the Codex Vaticanus. Both were copied, he thought, about AD 350. One reason for thinking this is a report given by the church historian Eusebius who died in 340. He recorded a letter to him from the first Christian emperor, Constantine the Great,

in AD 313, Christians were often persecuted and their books burnt. A complete Bible, handwritten on papyrus or parchment, would be quite a large, thick book, and so be difficult to hide. It seems likely that the books of the Bible were rarely copied into a single volume when there was such a risk of their being destroyed. Once the danger had gone, wealthy Christians or churches could order complete Bibles, handsomely written. They would be expensive. Calculations suggest that one of these copies might have cost more than half a pound in gold coins.

The survival of these manuscripts is a reminder of an important stage in the history of the church, and a major step in the history of the Bible. Although they are not the oldest copies we have of the books of the Old and New Testaments, they are very important for understanding the history of the Greek text.

Codex Vaticanus is the most important Greek manuscript of the whole Bible. Like Codex Sinaiticus, it was copied in the middle of the fourth century, but at a later date someone inked over the letters. The pages are 27 cm/10.3 ins square. The passage shown is John 5:13–37.

asking for fifty copies of the Bible to be made in Caesarea in Palestine, for use in the churches of Constantinople. Perhaps these two were survivors of those fifty.

Nowadays scholars do not believe they are part of that order. There is no evidence that either of them was in Constantinople early in their history. It is thought as probable that they were written in Egypt as in Caesarea.

These two manuscripts deserve to be called 'the first Bibles'. Until Constantine adopted Christianity

BOOKS FROM
NEW TESTAMENT TIMES

A pungent smell filled the air. As the fire crackled and the flames sank, someone threw some more fuel to make it blaze again. Then it was all gone, and the fire died away.

People of every age burn or destroy some of the things they inherit from the past, whether they are buildings or furniture or papers; but this story, told about people in Egypt, is especially sad. What they were burning, 200 years or more ago, were rolls of papyrus, ancient books. The smell of burning papyrus was enjoyed by the inhabitants. The report says forty or fifty rolls were found, a merchant bought one, the rest fed the flames.

Today, when printing produces a book in thousands of copies, the loss of a few by fire or flood is no tragedy. When every copy was made by hand it was common for there to be so few copies of a book that it could easily disappear altogether. Many ancient books are known to us only by name. Every one that does survive, therefore, is precious.

Scholars eventually saw the value of papyrus rolls from Egypt, so the local people began to treat them with more care and sell them to European collectors and museums. Ancient Egyptian books were most attractive, some illuminated with coloured paintings, and there was competition to acquire them. There were other rolls with columns of writing in Greek. The majority of them deal with local government affairs, taxes and conscription. A few are copies of Greek books, in particular Homer's *The Iliad* and *The Odyssey*.

Here was the opening of a new door in the study of the classics. Until these papyri were found, that is up to the middle of the nineteenth century, the works of Greek and Latin authors were known only from medieval copies. Few of those were more than 1,000 years old, the oldest were three copies of Virgil's famous poem *The Aeneid*, made in the fifth century.

Over hundreds of years, as the scribes copied the books again and again, they made mistakes. Sometimes they did not correct their mistakes, and later scribes copied them without noticing what was wrong. If they saw an error, they might be able to correct it, or by trying to do so they might make it worse (see *Finding the True Text*). Certainly, by the time Johann Gutenberg invented printing from moveable metal type (about 1450), there were many mistakes in the texts of classical authors read in schools and colleges, and they were perpetuated in printed editions.

With much older papyrus copies to study, scholars hoped they might see the texts as they were before many of the mistakes were made. That proved to be true, although all sorts of other mistakes appeared, too. Even so, the copies on papyrus have made it possible to reach more reliable texts in many places than the medieval manuscripts could give. On occasion they support wordings in the·medieval copies which modern scholars had condemned as impossible or wrong, and from time to time their evidence disproves modern theories which attacked ancient statements.

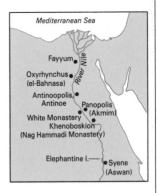

Where did the books come from?

Greek papyri are found at sites throughout Egypt south of Cairo. The biggest discoveries were made in abandoned towns standing round a small lake. Today the area is called the Fayyum. Between 300 and 200 BC, Greek engineers organized an irrigation system for the region. As long as the canals were kept clean and the whole system operated, people could farm the land and prosper. Once the organization broke down, or people lost the will to work together, the flow of water dwindled, people left, and their abandoned houses crumbled and filled with sand.

That began to happen in the fourth century AD and there were only a few towns still occupied by the time of the Arab conquest in 642. Abandoned, the heaps of ruins became quite dry. Papers left in the houses or on the rubbish tips were dehydrated, too, and so survived. Circumstances like these are unusual, but ancient manuscripts have been found in other dry places, for example, near the Dead Sea and in Central Asia.

Greek-speaking immigrants had flowed into Egypt under the kings named Ptolemy, who ruled the country after Alexander the Great (from 304 to the death of Cleopatra in 30 BC). They settled in many places beside the native Egyptians, but the newly developed land in the Fayyum was especially attractive to them. There they spoke and wrote Greek, which was now the dominant language for government and business. Under Roman rule, Greek maintained its status, although Latin was needed for some official purposes.

The papyri are the archives, the collections of books and papers, of these people, usually government officials, landowners and educated men. From the enormous quantity of papyrus documents it is easy to form the impression that most people could read and write. That is false. Those who were literate were a small minority. Another misleading idea is that the papyri make up complete files of papers or libraries of books. Even when they are found in the room of a house, no one can be sure all the papers are there. Occasionally complete rolls of accounts are retrieved and, even more rarely, entire scrolls of literary compositions. For the most part, the papyri are recovered from the rubbish dumps. They were tipped there because they were rubbish, so they are torn, broken, and incomplete. As a result, the books from New Testament times that we can look at today are often very disappointing—only part of a column from this one, a few lines from a page of that.

Finding the age of the books

Greek books did not have title pages, and the scribes who copied them

Papyrus reeds growing at the edge of the Nile were stripped of their outer skin. Then layers of pith were laid horizontally on a flat surface, others laid vertically across them, and the sheet beaten flat and smoothed.

Fresh papyrus was flexible and easily rolled up.

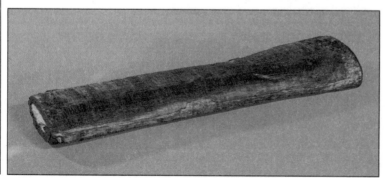

Sheets of papyrus glued together made scrolls to contain books. Here is the end of Homer's Iliad *from a scroll 6 metres/20 feet long, copied in the second century* AD.

almost never signed their work. To give a date to the ancient copies, scholars examine the style of the handwriting and compare it with the writing on legal deeds and official papers which do carry dates. Although these comparisons are a good guide, we have to remember that a scribe might continue to write in the way he had learnt at school for thirty or forty years, at the same time as new fashions were developing.

Further, styles might develop at different rates in separate centres and, although the documents often state where they were written, the books do not. Taking account of all the uncertainties, expert papyrologists can usually tell the century in which a text was copied and, where there are particular characteristics, can reach an even more precise range of years.

What did people read?
Homer's great poems, *The Iliad* and *The Odyssey* were favourites among the Greek books. Between 600 and 700 copies on papyrus are known. Homer's epics are quite long—*The Iliad* is divided into twenty-four books, and one modern English translation is 459 pages long—so each would occupy several scrolls. One scroll, now in the British Museum, is 6 metres/20 feet long. It contained the last two books of *The Iliad* alone.

Writings of famous playwrights, poets, philosophers and historians are well represented. One fragment of Plato's philosophical essay *Phaedo* can be dated to the third century BC, so it was copied within a century of the author's death (348 BC).

A popular dramatist was Menander, who lived just after Plato. His name and work were mentioned by other writers, but only a few quotations survived, until the papyri yielded examples of his work. Now one play is known in full, and six others to a considerable extent.

Greek citizens of Egypt read plays of Aeschylus and Sophocles which later ages forgot, and they had books by Aristotle as well. All these books, and others whose authors are less famous or quite unknown, have been added to modern knowledge of Greek literature by the discoveries in Egypt. They also show us the literature which some of the early Christians would have read.

A reed pen of the Roman period from Egypt. The nib was cut sharp and split.

THE OLDEST CHRISTIAN BOOKS

When the British Museum bought the Codex Sinaiticus in 1933 there was a lot of public interest, because it is one of the two oldest Bibles in Greek (see *The Oldest Bibles*). That copy was made about AD 350 or slightly before. Earlier than that, as far as we know, the books of the Bible were not collected into a single volume. One reason may have been the danger of persecution. A complete Bible would have taken a lot of pages, making a thick book, difficult to hide in times of danger. After Constantine the Great's Edict of Milan (313) it was no longer a risk to possess a large Christian book.

The earlier copies available to us include one which held the four Gospels and Acts (a third-century copy, now in the Chester Beatty Library in Dublin) and another the letters of Paul (except the 'Pastoral' letters) and Hebrews (made early in the third century, in the same library). Today we know of just over thirty papyrus manuscripts of New Testament books which can be dated before the fourth century. That number is small in comparison with the scores of copies of Homer and the dozens of copies of other famous Greek authors. But even though so few, these papyri are very important.

In the first place they show us the form of the New Testament text current in the second and third centuries AD. Each copy has its own oddities and mistakes: no two are completely identical, or the same as the Codex Sinaiticus or other later manuscripts. However, they do fall into groups or families which can be

distinguished among the later copies. A single letter changes the meaning of a sentence, and it is usually just single letters or words that are in question. When all the variations have been sifted, only a few deserve closer examination. In the Gospels there are about seventy places altogether where scholars are doubtful about the original reading—that is to say are unsure whether one group of

Three tiny pieces of papyrus come from one page of a copy of Matthew's Gospel made near the end of the second century. The book had two columns of writing on each page; the words on this side belong to chapter 26, verses 7, 10, 14, 15 (verses 22, 23, 31–33 are on the other side). A visitor bought the fragments at Luxor in Egypt in 1901 and presented them to Magdalen College, Oxford, where he had studied. The fact that they come from the oldest known copy of Matthew was recognized by the papyrologist C.H. Roberts in 1953. Other pieces of the same book, with parts of chapters 3 and 5, are now in Barcelona.

A recent claim that they date from before AD 70 has not been justified.

manuscripts or another has the correct words. Few of these places impinge on any major Christian doctrine, and in no case does any uncertainty affect the Christian faith (see *Finding the True Text*). We can be sure that we read the words of the New Testament books almost exactly as they left their authors' pens.

Books of the New Testament lying forgotten in Egypt are signs that Christians were there. If the books were found only in one place, and all belonging to the same date, they might have belonged to a student of religions or an enemy of Christianity. The range of dates, the variety in handwriting and the different places of discovery weigh against that suggestion. Several of the books are represented by more than one copy on papyrus, which also makes it unlikely.

At least four examples of John's Gospel belong to the third century, and there is another in the book holding all four Gospels. John was perhaps the favourite, but all the Gospels were known. Of the other books of the New Testament, every one is to be found in a third-century papyrus copy, although the only example of Peter and Jude was made at the end of the period, or early in the fourth century. Clearly there were a number of people reading the Christian Scriptures in third-century Egypt.

Those readers had their predecessors in the second century. Parts of copies of Matthew's Gospel, one of John, and possibly fragments of a copy of Paul's letter to Titus, can be placed towards the end of the century on the basis of the writing. One well-known scrap from the Gospel of John is dated before AD 150 (see *Oldest of All*). In addition to these New

Modern Antakya on the Orontes river covers the site of ancient Antioch, where the disciples of Jesus were first called Christians (Acts 11:26) and where, it is suggested, there was a centre of Christian book production by the end of the first century.

Testament manuscripts, pieces from two 'imitation Gospels' are known which belong in the second century, and part of a book about Christian behaviour, *The Shepherd of Hermas*.

The significance of these pieces is seen when they are placed in the context of the history of Christianity. The New Testament refers to churches in Palestine, Syria, Turkey, Greece, Italy, but never in Egypt. From Egypt itself no Christian remains have come to light which are older than about AD 300, apart from the New Testament and related papyri. The papyri, therefore, are the only evidence for the spread of Christianity to Egypt. It follows that Christians may well have lived in other places, where papyrus books cannot survive because the soil is damp, but no trace of them will be identified.

A new sort of book

All these early copies of the New Testament are important for another reason: they are books with pages. This is a striking contrast to the copies of Greek literature on papyrus, and to the earliest Hebrew manuscripts of the Old Testament, which are all written on scrolls. Scrolls were normal for books until the third century AD. Until that time, a book with pages, a *codex*, was used only for note-taking. Only in the fourth century do we find more texts in book-form than in rolls.

Today the advantages of the codex over the roll are obvious. The roll is wasteful because it is written only on the inside, so it can contain only half as much in the same space. It is awkward to carry and use—to find a passage may involve unrolling several feet of it. These facts may have appealed to early Christian scribes and early Christian readers. They evidently did not care about the current customs of the book trade! The gradual change from the scroll for pagan literature may have had its stimulus in this Christian novelty.

In the early New Testament papyri there are some unusual features, little points which set them apart from the other papyri of the first and second centuries. They clearly have a common origin, and recent study has suggested that they began in one place. Somewhere there was a centre where a common pattern was set for copying Christian books, and for copying them as codex books. Wherever it was, and a likely guess is Antioch in Syria, it was surely operating for some time before the oldest copies we can see today were made (and they all survive by accident). That would put its date as early as 100, if not earlier.

The oldest Christian books allow us to read the New Testament as it was within 200 years of its writing—even less for some books. They show that the Greek text of the New Testament was copied faithfully, and they point to the spread of Christian literature on an organized model. They clearly demonstrate the importance the early church attached to its Scriptures.

OLDEST OF ALL

Papyri poured out of Egypt into museums and private collections. They came in such large numbers that it was impossible to study or even catalogue them all straight away. In 1920 one of the scholars who had excavated papyri in abandoned towns bought a collection of pieces for the John Rylands Library in Manchester. While he was cataloguing them fifteen years later, C. H. Roberts — an expert from Oxford — identified all sorts of interesting pieces of Greek books, and even part of a Latin speech by the Roman orator Cicero. Then, looking at smaller scraps, he came to one torn from the top of a page. Parts of seven lines of writing remain on each side. Although it is very small, 9 cm/3½ ins × 6.2 cm/ 2 ins, there are enough words to identify it. Roberts recognized that it belonged to the Gospel of John.

Other copies of John's Gospel written on papyrus had been found in Egypt, some copied as early as the third century AD. To find the age of the papyrus scrap was part of Roberts' job. By examining the style of handwriting, the shapes of the letters, he reached a conclusion. He asked senior and more experienced papyrologists for their opinion, because his conclusion was surprising. The other scholars agreed with him. The shapes of the letters are most like the writing on

documents dated in the first part of the second century, perhaps between AD 125 and 150. Fifty years later this verdict still stands. After half a century of continuing research, this little piece of papyrus is still the oldest known copy of any part of the New Testament.

What survives on this scrap comes from chapter 18 of John, verses 31–33 on the front, verses 37 and 38 on the back. The size of

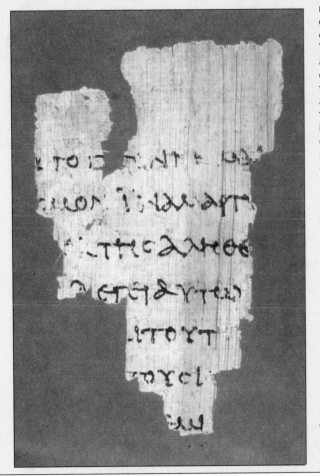

a whole page is calculated to be about 21 cm/8½ ins high and 20 cm/8 ins wide. And the whole book is reckoned to have occupied about 130 pages. Most likely it was complete by itself, not combined with any of the other Gospels.

Why is it important?
None of the Gospels states exactly when it was written. Clearly all come from the time after the resurrection of Jesus, but

there is nothing that shows decisively whether they were written five, twenty or 100 years after. Christian tradition has always believed that the four evangelists composed their accounts before the year 100. John's Gospel was said to be the last, written in the apostle's old age when he was at Ephesus, in the closing years of the first century.

Traditions like these came under attack in the nineteenth century, and one influential school of thought based at Tübingen in Germany argued that John's Gospel came into existence late in the second century, well after AD 150. Echoes of that view can still be heard in some anti-Christian circles today. The Rylands papyrus puts that case out of court.

If this copy of John was made towards the middle of the second century in Egypt, it is a

The few words on either side of this small piece of papyrus fit exactly into the text of John's Gospel (chapter 18). The handwriting is believed to date between AD 125 and 150.

sign that someone was using this Christian book at that time—probably in one of the towns of Middle Egypt 160 km/ 100 miles or more south of Cairo. Unless its owner was a personal friend of the author of the Gospel, the fragment indicates that people knew about the Gospel and that examples had spread from wherever it was composed (traditionally Ephesus), had been re-copied and become familiar. All this points to a date no later than the opening years of the second century for the writing of John's Gospel, and possibly earlier.

Early Christian tradition said John wrote his Gospel at Ephesus on the western coast of Turkey near the end of the first century. The theatre in this view was built in the third and second centuries BC and altered several times in the first century AD. The flat green area beyond the end of the road is the silted-up site of the ancient harbour.

BEFORE THE GOSPELS

For school exercises, notes and reports people often wrote on wooden tablets which could be tied together like the pages of a book. This example was used in Egypt in Roman times.

If the Gospels were already being copied and circulated in a standard form by the year 100, what was their history before that? Exactly when the Gospel-writers did their work is a question scholars are always discussing. By comparing Matthew, Mark and Luke it is easy to see they share a lot of information. Perhaps there was an earlier collection of stories and sayings of Jesus which they all used. (Students of the Gospels call this collection 'Q', from the German word *Quelle*, 'source'.) Each writer added things he learnt from different followers of Jesus and arranged the material to bring out particular points. How they did that is a subject outside the scope of this book.

Another question which is part of the same study is whether the Gospel-writers reported accurately the words that Jesus spoke, or invented speeches and put them into his mouth. If they did make up some of the sayings, they probably included ideas that grew up in the church as Christians thought and talked about their new faith. It would not be easy to disentangle the actual words Jesus spoke from the later additions. This, too, is a subject that cannot be explored here.

What is important to remember in reading any study of it is that all theories about the history of the Gospels are speculations. The only facts available to us are the Gospels themselves and it is impossible to prove that any of their records of the life and teaching of Jesus are wrong or misleading.[1]

Clearly the Gospel-writers had sources of information, whether they were witnesses of the events they described, or were not, like Luke. Did they rely on their own memories and the memories of others who had seen and heard Jesus? One person remembering and telling another is commonly thought to have been the way the Gospel stories spread until they were collected and written down in 'Q' or other forms.

It is easy to imagine the process. Jesus spoke to the crowds, to small groups of people, and to individuals. When they went away, they would pass on to others what they had heard. With his challenging words and sensational claims, Jesus quickly caught the attention of the Jewish religious leaders, and they debated what he was saying. A few were sympathetic, most were angry. There were foreigners who heard Jesus, too. There were a lot of men and women in Palestine, and some abroad, who lived on after the crucifixion with the words they had heard alive in their minds, ready for an inquirer to release.

Learning by memory was the usual way of education in ancient Palestine, and some of Jesus' sayings are obviously short and clear and suitable for remembering. When some of his words are translated back into Aramaic, the language he normally used, they turn out to have a poetic rhythm which also helps to make them memorable. These were some of the ways Jewish rabbis used to teach their disciples, and it is not surprising that Jesus should follow their patterns.

But was word of mouth (oral transmission) the only way the church broadcast its Master's words and works before the Gospels (or 'Q') were written? Were there some who heard Jesus' teaching and said to themselves, 'I must write that down'? This possibility had hardly any place in Gospel studies until recently. Now archaeological evidence for the amount of writing being done in first-century Palestine and new studies of other sources sets it in the balance beside theories about oral tradition.

Tombs in Jerusalem reveal the use of writing for recording the names of the dead so that relatives could distinguish them (see *Their Names Live On*). Other examples were found near Jericho. Excavations in Herod's palaces brought out jars labelled in Greek or Latin with the date and the king's name and title. Other jars found at Qumran and in Jerusalem carry names or labels of contents in Hebrew or Aramaic. There are also a few short messages scribbled on potsherds. These are all very brief, yet they are still signs of people being ready to write, although far removed from books of history or teaching.

Mainline Jewish thought was against writing and collecting the teachings of the rabbis. Although the oral law, the 'traditions of the fathers', had great authority, it was not the same as the written Law of the books of Moses. The basic collection of rabbinic teaching, the Mishnah, was not made until a century after the fall of Jerusalem (AD 70; see *Jewish Writings*). However, other Jewish teachers were prepared to have their own lessons put into writing—Philo and the apostle Paul are examples. Among the Dead Sea Scrolls is a remarkable letter which sets out the opinions of a leader, possibly the Teacher of Righteousness himself, about all sorts of questions

of ritual purity and behaviour. To introduce each opinion, the letter has the words 'About such and such, we say that . . .', which are similar to the repeated 'but I tell you' of Jesus in Matthew 5. In each case the teacher is giving his own, different, instructions.

Even though the rabbis' words were not to be collected, their students were allowed to make notes of them for private study, and we are

told some did so. What is especially interesting is that they wrote in notebooks, rather than on scrolls or potsherds. The Hebrew language had no word for notebook, so it borrowed the Greek word *pinax*. A *pinax* was any sort of board for writing, drawing or painting on. Zechariah wrote on a little one (Luke 1:63; it could also be a tray, such as the one John the Baptist's head was carried on— Matthew 14:8; Mark 6:28.)

Wooden writing tablets of Roman times have come to light in places as far apart as the fortress of Vindolanda, on the line of Hadrian's Wall, and the deserted towns of Egypt. Often they are broken and the writing has disappeared. The writing could be done in ink directly on the wooden surface, or on to a white plaster coating the wood. Alternatively, the tablet was given a shallow recess which was filled with wax.

At many places in the Roman Empire bronze and iron styli have come to light. The points were for scratching letters on wax tablets, the broad ends were for smoothing away the writing for re-use.

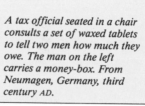

A tax official seated in a chair consults a set of waxed tablets to tell two men how much they owe. The man on the left carries a money-box. From Neumagen, Germany, third century AD.

With a pointed stylus the writer could scratch letters into the wax, and later erase them by smoothing it over with the flat end of the stylus.

Wooden writing tablets of any type could be joined with hinges or thongs to make a pair or, when a lot of space was needed, to make a group of several boards or pages. Such a group of leaves was called in Latin a *codex*, the first-century author Seneca informs us. Ordinarily these tablets were for school exercises, accounts, messages and notes of all sorts. At Rome, shorthand writers took down speeches in the Senate; a secretary slave stood by the scholar Pliny to take down in shorthand anything his master found that would be useful in his studies. Manuals for teaching systems of Greek shorthand have been found among the papyri from Egypt.

Alongside the wooden tablets, notebooks of parchment came into use in Rome by the first century BC. They were lighter to carry than wooden ones, and the poet Martial, in about AD 85, recommended to his friends that they should have the poems of Homer and Virgil written in this type of book. He gave some copies to his friends to try to convince them how much better the book with pages was than the traditional scroll. Regrettably, no books survive from the first and second centuries in Rome, so we cannot tell whether Martial was advertising a growing fashion or was an eccentric a century before his time. Papyrus books from Egypt indicate that the scroll was the more popular form of book for another 200 years (see *The Oldest Christian Books*).

The fact that the Gospels were some of the first books to be copied in the codex form, as distinct from the scroll, leads to the suggestion that they were based on notebooks. Such notebooks could have held reports of Jesus' sayings and actions put down on the day they were heard or seen, even the words of Jesus recorded in shorthand. Taking into account the fact that the places where Jesus worked were often towns, with resident government or army officers, tax collectors and religious teachers, makes this more likely than the common pictures of him on green hills or open lake-sides. (Perhaps the 'parchments' Paul asked for—2 Timothy 4:13—were such notebooks.)

No physical evidence exists to prove, or disprove, this suggestion. It came from C. H. Roberts, a scholar expert in studying Greek papyrus books (see *Oldest of All*), and deserves a place in the discussions of New Testament scholars.

[1] For an excellent introduction to these matters see Craig Blomberg, *The Historical Reliability of the Gospels*, Inter-Varsity Press, 1987

FINDING THE TRUE TEXT

How do we find the true text of something written centuries ago? William Shakespeare, for example, wrote his plays from about 1588–1613. He was both an actor and a playwright, and he wrote some parts to suit other actors in his company. Nothing is known about the way he worked, except that he produced rough drafts in the first place. These do not survive, nor do any fair copies he may have made. Obviously actors with leading roles had to have copies for themselves, at least for their major scenes. The prompter, too, would need a complete text, so that he could help the players who missed their cues or forgot their lines.

Clearly, Shakespeare's plays were not limited to the author's copy for long. As they grew popular, printers wanted to publish them. What they put on sale were sometimes 'pirate editions'. Actors or members of the audience memorized the words, or even made notes of them, and the printers made up a text from that information. This happened, for example, when *Romeo and Juliet* was printed in 1597, *Henry V* in 1600, and *Hamlet* in 1603.

Shakespeare's ideas and words were spoilt in these books, so he or his friends had new editions printed of some of them (*Romeo and Juliet* in 1599, *Hamlet* in 1604–1605, both based on the author's rough drafts).

When Shakespeare died in 1616, twenty-two of his plays were still unpublished. His friends eventually issued a volume containing thirty-six plays in 1623. They wanted to make as

perfect an edition of his work as they could, and so honour his name. They used some of the earlier printings which had been corrected, but, wherever they could, they relied on the author's own copies. Even so, there are lots of printers' mistakes in this 'First Folio' edition.

The 'Second Folio' (1632) corrected some of them while making others. Ever since, scholars have tried to discover what some words and lines mean, or how Shakespeare originally wrote them, because they are unintelligible or sound wrong.

There is wide agreement over the greater part of the text, yet some passages are still hard to understand (the curious might read *King Lear* Act IV, Scene VI, lines 217, 218, or *Hamlet* Act 1, Scene IV, line 37). By ingenious guesses at the ways badly written copies could be misread or printers could make mistakes, sense can be made of some of the hard lines. In *Romeo and Juliet* Act I, Scene IV, line 42, 'we'll draw thee from the mire of this sir-reverence love' can be corrected to 'we'll draw thee from the mire of—save your reverence—love', as many editions do.

For certain plays Shakespeare seems to have added to someone else's work, notably for *Henry VI*, Part 1. There are puzzles left in the text of Shakespeare to occupy future generations of scholars. No one is ever likely to be able to print an edition which they can prove is word for word what Shakespeare wrote.

Shakespeare lived only 400 years ago, yet we cannot be sure that every

The original scribe of the Codex Sinaiticus made several mistakes as he copied. In the third column of the last page of John's Gospel a later scribe made several corrections, especially in John 21:18.

ΙѠΑΝΝΗΝ

line we read of his plays is what he wrote, even though some of them were printed during his lifetime. So no one should be surprised if the same is true in the case of books such as the Gospels and books of the New Testament which were written 2,000 years ago. The authors' manuscripts perished long ago; we can read only copies of copies of them. All the Gospels were written before AD 100, a century or more before scribes made the earliest extensive copies at present available for study.

Did those scribes and their predecessors do their work accurately?

Answering that question is the task of the specialized research called textual criticism. To know a little of the facts which textual critics face, and the ways they explain them, can help anyone who reads the New Testament seriously to understand it better.

Printers may make mistakes, as Shakespeare and his friends found out, and each one is reproduced hundreds or thousands of times. Scribes copying books by hand were just as likely to make mistakes. Yet it is to their labours that we owe the preservation of the New Testament.

The copyist

Try to imagine this key figure in the history of the Gospels. His school record was average, with good marks for handwriting. A career in a government office or a big business was beyond his reach, but he could earn his living as a copyist. People wanted books, so he could provide them.

Of course, he had to borrow the books to copy, or his clients had to bring them to him. In a big city that was not difficult. There were men who had their own collections of books, and it was common to borrow from such a collection for copying. A copyist who lived in a small town might have to ask a number of people before he found the book a customer wanted him to reproduce. He might have to send away for it or travel himself, to use a rare copy in another place.

Copying was a rather tedious job. To be faced with another hundred columns of text was not all that exciting. If the book was one that bored the copyist, or if it was one he had worked with several times before, his attention could easily wander. Then the mistakes would creep in. He might write one sentence twice, or leave out a line that began with the same word as the line before, or he might even write nonsense.

If another man dictated the book to him, mistakes might come from mishearing. If the copyist read from the exemplar himself, he might confuse the words as he transferred them to his own page.

If he was interested in the book, he might work more carefully. Then he might go beyond the limit of his task and try to improve its language. Perhaps the author did not write very fashionable Greek, so the copyist would try to make it more 'stylish'. The book done, the conscientious copyist would check it for mistakes and hope to correct them all, or he could ask another scribe to do it. Quite often the checking was slap-dash and incomplete, as surviving copies show.

The rate of pay for a copyist was apparently about the same as for a farm labourer, although he was paid for what he produced rather than at a daily rate. Naturally, he would be eager to copy as much as possible and, working fast, he would make mistakes more easily.

Late in the first century the poet Martial mentions the price of a cheap book in Rome. It was from one and a half to two and a half denarii. The labourer's daily wage, according to Matthew 20, was one denarius. That was half a century earlier, so perhaps the lower price was about the worth of a day's work. In Egypt during the second century there was a rate of twenty denarii for 10,000 lines, or one denarius for 500.

Very rough calculations suggest

that a copy of John's Gospel would have about 2,000 lines, and so would cost four denarii. Copying would probably have taken three or four days.

Clearly, copying could earn a man his bread and butter if he had regular orders. In a small town it is unlikely that he would. That might mean that someone wanting a book would either have to copy it himself or pay an ordinary scribe to do it. The results of this can be seen in some of the papyrus books recovered in Egypt.

Book copyists were trained to set out their work in a certain style which other scribes did not always follow. When a man who usually wrote accounts and legal deeds copied a book he might easily write numbers as figures and abbreviate common words, just as he did in his daily routine. These things occur in some of the early examples of Christian books, very rarely in others. Evidently some Christians could not obtain or afford the books professional copyists made, or some Christians who could write made their own copies. They read them privately, but the large writing in certain copies may show that they were made for reading aloud to groups of people. Here is more evidence for the need they felt to have the Gospels and other New Testament writings available for study.

Spotting the mistakes

Some of the mistakes the copyists made are easy to see, and often the scribe himself or a colleague corrected his work. The famous Codex Sinaiticus (see *The Oldest Bibles*) has many places where the man who made them put his faults right. After him several other people also made corrections to it at different times.

A scribe copying the Gospel of John shortly after AD 200 slipped fifty-four times by leaving out words when his eye jumped from one word to a similar one (Papyrus Bodmer II). He also repeated words mistakenly twenty-two times. On the other hand, a scribe who put Luke and John into one book

about the same time worked very carefully, making fewer mistakes (Papyrus Bodmer XIV–XV).

When one copy is set beside another these errors are obvious. Two scribes would not always miscopy the same words. Less obvious faults might go unnoticed and so be passed on from copy to copy. These are more serious because they can result in the loss of the original words. One faulty manuscript may spawn dozens of copies perpetuating its error. If that faulty copy was kept in an important library or school, it would be more likely to be the ancestor of many copies than a carefully made copy lying on a shelf in an out-of-the-way town. A single copy made from that one would have much greater value than all the others in preserving the more correct version of the book.

In the same way, there might happen to be copies of the faulty manuscript which are much older than any copy of the careful one. Were that the case, the oldest copies would not necessarily be the best. Neither the number of copies of a text in one form, nor the age need always be weighty arguments in deciding whether that text is better than another one that is slightly different.

Over 5,000 Greek manuscripts of the New Testament survive. They are grouped into families according to their characteristics. A series of family portraits will reveal a large nose or red hair prominent in several generations, yet each person possessed features which made him or her an individual human being. In the same way, each manuscript has both its own features and the marks of its 'family'. The usefulness of any copy depends on an analysis of all the copies. Such an examination, copy by copy, allows scholars to identify these characteristics and to weed out many of the mistakes.

It is reckoned that there may be over a quarter of a million manuscripts of the New Testament books, if translations are taken into account.

That means, inevitably, that the number of differences is enormous. The majority are unimportant. After sifting them, the editors of standard editions of the Greek New Testament give 10,000 or so in their footnotes. Of these, about 1,400 were selected as sufficiently significant to be included in the Bible Societies' Greek New Testament of 1966. Does this mean we cannot be sure that we are reading the words the authors of the Gospels wrote? How does it affect translations of the New Testament?

A THEOLOGICAL DIFFERENCE

Occasionally a change in translation changes the teaching of a verse. Obviously every case deserves careful thought, and such changes are not made without good reason. When a major doctrine is involved, a change in one verse does not alter it, for every important teaching rests on several pasages.

One case is in John 1:18. The Authorized Version translated the traditional Greek text. It has, 'No man hath seen God at any time; the only begotten Son, which is in the bosom of the Father, he hath declared him.' The Revised Standard Version has almost the same, and the New English Bible does, too. The Good News Bible is similar. On the other hand, the New International Version offers, 'No-one has ever seen God, but God the One and Only, who is at the Father's side, has made him known.' A footnote states that 'some manuscripts' have the other version.

Why does this translation differ? The first papyrus copy of John in the Bodmer collection was published in 1956, followed in 1961 by the second. Both of these were copied early in·the third century. Both have the text which the NIV translates, and it is also in Codex Sinaiticus and Codex Vaticanus. Some of the Fathers of the church also knew it.

All depends on one word. Is 'Son' or 'God' the one the author wrote? Nowadays the majority of scholars think it is 'God', because the phrase 'the One and Only God' is harder to understand. 'One and only Son' is found in John 1:14 and 3:16, so a copyist faced with the other phrase might have made this one agree with it, consciously or unconsciously. A change the other way, from the known phrase to a strange one, is less likely. There is no question of an attack on teaching about the deity of Christ here. The opening verse of John and the whole passage make that crystal clear.

334

SIMPLE MISTAKES

A phrase left out

John 13:31 and 32 read, 'Now is the Son of Man glorified and God is glorified in him. If God is glorified in him, then God will glorify the Son in himself . . . '

Some Christians long ago did not read quite the same words. One of the two copies of John now in the Bodmer Library, made soon after AD 200 has, 'Now is the Son of man glorified, and God is glorified in him. God shall also glorify him in himself . . . ' Both Codex Sinaiticus and Codex Vaticanus agree. Yet this is not a real difference. The copyists' eyes simply slipped from the first 'glorified in him' to the second, jumping over 'If God is glorified in him.' This sort of mistake is common in copies of ancient books. (Textual critics give it the technical name *homoioteleuton*.)

A phrase repeated

The opposite mistake is equally easy to make, repeating a word or phrase unnecessarily. In Codex Vaticanus the copyist did that at John 17:18, producing, 'As you sent me into the world, I have sent them into the world, I have sent them into the world.' This common error is called 'dittography'.

'Infection'

There are many chapters in Matthew, Mark and Luke which tell of the same events or speeches in almost the same words. When he was working on one Gospel, a copyist familiar with all of them might unconsciously make it agree with another, because that one was fresh in his mind. Others might deliberately make one Gospel agree with another.

Finding early manuscripts of the Gospels has made it clearer how this happened. Recent translations of the Gospels often draw attention to these places by putting the additions in the margin. When he was warning, 'how it will be at the coming of the Son of Man', Jesus said, 'Two men will be in the field; one will be taken and the other left. Two women will be grinding with a hand mill; one will be taken and the other left', according to Matthew 24:39–41. In Luke's report there are other pictures, then the one about the women grinding. Following that, in the traditional text, is a sentence about two men working in the field, one of whom is taken, ending the speech (Luke 17:30–36).

However, the oldest copy of Luke's Gospel, Bodmer Papyrus XIV, written early in the third century does not have this last sentence. Codex Sinaiticus, Codex Vaticanus, Codex Alexandrinus and other early manuscripts agree. Possibly the scribes who wrote all those copies missed it out accidentally, because it ends with the same words as the sentence before. More likely, a scribe familiar with Matthew added this verse to Luke to make the two reports of Jesus' prophecy more alike.

Examples of harmonization in the same way are plain in Luke's version of the Lord's Prayer. Comparing Luke 11:2–4 with Matthew 6:9–13 in the Authorized Version and in a recent translation shows this clearly.

Copyists made mistakes in various other ways, but these cases are enough to illustrate the value of studying the different manuscripts in order to obtain as accurate a text of the New Testament as possible.

The copyist of Codex Sinaiticus left out the words 'If God be glorified in him' from John 13:32. A later scribe added them in the margin.

335

DELIBERATE CHANGES

When copying, a scribe who was thinking about his work, and had time to do so, might occasionally alter the text or add to it. One working from dictation would hardly be able to do so until after he had written the text. His alterations might stand in the margin. That was a place where any scribe or reader might put notes of all sorts. A careless writer might then copy those notes into his text, as if they were part of it.

An explanatory note, perhaps based on knowledge of local traditions, seems to have entered the text of John 5. The traditional text relates that at the pool of Bethesda 'a great number of disabled people used to lie—the blind, the lame, the paralysed—and they waited for the moving of the waters. From time to time an angel of the Lord would come down and stir up the waters. The first one into the pool after each such disturbance would be cured of whatever disease he had.' The oldest copies of John do not contain this verse, and it has words in it

which are not expressions found anywhere else in the Gospel.

Sometimes a scribe thought he knew better than the text he was copying from. One making a copy of John soon after AD 200 (Papyrus Bodmer XV) was puzzled by 'I am the gate for the sheep' in chapter 10, verse 7, so he wrote, 'I am the shepherd for the sheep' instead. Although this is one of the oldest manuscripts of the Gospel, no one wants to

adopt its reading here. It is an obvious case of simplification by the copyist.

Changes of religious outlook could also lead to changes in the text. Growing devotion to Jesus as God apparently caused scribes deliberately to leave out a word in Matthew 27:16,17. The name of the brigand whom Pilate released in place of Jesus was probably not just Barabbas but Jesus Barabbas. Codex Vaticanus

implies the two names, and Origen knew of them in the third century. Jesus was a common name in the first century (see *Their Names Live On*), so there is nothing exceptional about that man having it. If Barabbas was called Jesus, it is easy to understand why scribes would omit it. Origen expressed it himself: the name of Jesus was not suitable for a criminal like Barabbas. This view prevailed in the church.

Some Greek manuscripts of Matthew 27 name the bandit in whose place Jesus was executed Jesus Barabbas. Codex Vaticanus does not have the name Jesus here, but its wording indicates that it was copied from one that did. This page contains Matthew 26:70—27:24.

WHAT DID THE ANGELS SING?

'Glory to God in the
highest,
And on earth peace,
goodwill toward men'

The angels' song in Luke 2:14 is one of the most familiar of all Christmas texts. Twentieth-century readers of Luke's Gospel have wondered why modern translations are not the same as the Authorized Version in this verse. The Revised Standard Version of 1946 has:

'Glory to God in the
highest,
and on earth peace among
men with whom he is
well pleased.'

In the New English Bible (1961) the verse reads:

'Glory to God in highest
heaven,
And on earth his peace for
men on whom his
favour rests.'

The Good News Bible (1976) and the New International Version (1973) are similar.

The scribe who copied Codex Sinaiticus wrote 'peace to men on whom his favour rests' in the angels' song (Luke 2:14). Later another scribe erased the final 's' of the word for 'favour' to give the sense 'good will toward men'.

One letter in the Greek makes the difference. The word 'goodwill' stands grammatically with 'peace' in the traditional Greek text as something wished for mankind. A Christian named Tatian who was alive about AD 170 knew this interpretation. (He wove a single 'gospel' out of the four, leaving out duplicate sections.) In the fourth century the Christian historian Eusebius also knew it. On the other hand, the fourth-century Greek copies of Luke 2, the oldest available, and the Christian scholar Origen who was active in the third century, have the Greek word for 'goodwill' with a final 's', which gives it the meaning 'of goodwill'.

How can anyone decide which is right? A final answer is impossible. The early manuscripts carry a lot of weight, but the testimony of Tatian and Eusebius partly count against them. Here is a case where scholars maintain that the more difficult form of the text is to be preferred. Scribes would make difficult words and phrases simpler as they copied, not make them more awkward. 'Peace, goodwill toward men' is the easier phrasing in Greek. The expression 'men of goodwill' is now known from the Dead Sea Scrolls as one current among some religious Jews in the first century (see *The Scrolls and the Teaching of Jesus*).

DID THEY WASH BEDS?

'There are many other points on which they have a traditional rule to maintain, for example, washing of cups and jugs and copper bowls' (Mark 7:4, NEB). Mark's Gospel gives this list to explain the way religious Jews carried out the laws of purity. Archaeology has thrown light on the practical effect these laws had in daily life (see *Cleanliness is Next to Godliness?*).

To wash cups, jugs and metal bowls may not seem remarkable, merely an ordinary matter of hygiene. Rather odder is the fourth object which some copies of Mark add, 'and beds'. Among modern translations the Good News Bible has that; the Revised Standard Version and the New International Version have it in the margin. The translation

'tables', in the Authorized Version, is incorrect; the word is the one used for the bed of a sick girl later in the chapter (verse 30), and for the bed of the paralysed man whose story is told in Matthew 9:2,6 and Luke 5:18.

The oldest copy of Mark is a papyrus in the Chester Beatty Library, Dublin, made in the third century. It does not include 'and beds'. Neither does the Codex Sinaiticus nor the Codex Vaticanus. The Codex Alexandrinus, on the other hand, has 'and beds' at the end of the list, as do the Freer Codex in Washington and the Codex Bezae in Cambridge, both from the fifth century. The words continue into the traditional Greek text and so appeared in the older translations.

Did the Gospel writer

put these words in his original text or not? At first sight the evidence of the oldest copies says he did not; the words were added later. Yet there is room for some doubt about that. The very fact that the idea of washing beds seems strange today may mean it seemed strange to ancient scribes, so they left the words out.

Certainly there are laws in the Old Testament that any beds which risked soiling from a bodily discharge should be washed (Leviticus 15:4, 20,26). When the rabbis applied Old Testament laws to every part of life in the first century, they observed the laws of purity or cleanliness strictly. Late in the second century, the Mishnah, a book of their interpretations, was made. In a long section devoted

to rules of cleanliness applying to utensils it discusses the question of which parts of a bed should be washed.

Washing beds might, therefore, be an example which the Gospel writer would give to show the extent of the Jewish concern for such matters. This would be especially appropriate if he composed his book for Roman readers, as tradition claims. On the other hand, a reader of Mark who knew about those customs could have thought in the same way, and so added 'and beds' to the list.

In this case the question can be left open. Whether 'beds' was in the original Mark, or not, the copies that have the word represent the practice of the first century.

Codex Alexandrinus is the oldest copy of Mark 7:4 to say the Jews washed beds. This page covers Mark 6:54–7:23. (The words 'and beds' occur in the half-line two-thirds of the way down the first column.)

ARE THEY ORIGINAL?

Two passages in the Gospels call for comment because they are absent from many early copies, and so modern translations leave them out.

In John's Gospel (7:53–8:11) stands the famous account of Jesus' meeting with the woman taken in adultery and her hypocritical accusers.

'Then each went to his own home. But Jesus went to the Mount of Olives. At dawn he appeared again in the temple courts, where all the people gathered around him, and he sat down to teach them. The teachers of the law and the Pharisees brought in a woman caught in adultery. They made her stand before the group and said to Jesus, "Teacher, this woman was caught in the act of adultery. In the Law Moses commanded us to stone such women. Now what do you say?" They were using this question as a trap, in order to have a basis for accusing him.

'But Jesus bent down and started to write on the ground with his finger. When they kept on questioning him, he straightened up and said to them, "If any one of you is without sin, let him be the first to throw a stone at her." Again he stooped down and wrote on the ground.

'At this those who heard began to go away, one at a time, the older ones first, until only Jesus was left, with the woman still standing there. Jesus straightened up and asked her, "Woman, where are they? Has no one condemned you?"

'"No one, sir," she said.

'"Then neither do I condemn you," Jesus declared. "Go now and leave your life of sin."'

Although most Greek manuscripts of John have these verses, there are some which do not. Among those without the verses are the oldest copies of John, two papyri from Egypt made early in the third century (Papyrus Bodmer II and Papyrus Bodmer XIV). The Codex Sinaiticus and the Codex Vaticanus are also without them. Codex Alexandrinus has lost some pages from John's Gospel, including chapters 7 and 8. Calculation of the number of lines missing shows that there would not have been enough space for the lost pages to have contained the passage about the woman taken in adultery.

As well as several other Greek manuscripts that do not have the passage, translations of the Gospel made in the second and third centuries into Latin, Syriac and the Coptic dialects of Egypt show no signs of it.

The early Church Fathers add their evidence: none of them quotes these verses or comments on them. Moreover, the verses have several Greek expressions John does not have anywhere else.

On the other hand, some Christians of the fourth century knew these verses. Jerome translated them into Latin when he made the Vulgate (AD 384). In one of his books he observed that the verses were found in many manuscripts in Greek and in previous translations into Latin. Augustine, who wrote a little later than Jerome, also knew the verses.

Today the oldest surviving Greek manuscript which contains these verses

Excavations through the rubbish of centuries have uncovered parts of a pool deep below the modern surface just north of the Temple area in Jerusalem. This was apparently the Pool of Bethesda (John 5). There were colonnades around the four sides of the two pools, and between them, making five 'porches'.

men. When they heard this, they left everything on the ground and followed him.' These extra words were taken from the similar passage in Mark 1:17,18.

A few of the Codex Bezae's peculiarities, like the passage concerning the adulterous woman, are more interesting. They may well preserve traditions handed down from the first century, from the friends of Jesus. Why the Gospel writers did not see fit to put them into their four books is not known.

In the present case, the evidence of Jerome, Augustine, some later manuscripts of John, with the Codex Bezae, is strong. Scholars accept the story as likely to be a genuine account from the first century, although not originally part of John's Gospel.

The other passage absent from modern translations, or printed as a footnote, is at the end of Mark's Gospel (16:9–20). These verses pose a quite different problem from the account of the woman taken in adultery.

Codex Alexandrinus and Codex Bezae have them, and so do most later copies. Irenaeus, the bishop of Lyons at the end of the second century, knew them, and Tatian included them in the harmony of the Gospels which he made at that time (the *Diatessaron*). A century later Jerome knew they existed in a few copies. Although he saw many which had the passage about the woman taken in adultery, the majority he had seen did not have the long ending of Mark's Gospel.

Two like the latter survive—Codex Sinaiticus and Codex Vaticanus. By the accidents of survival and discovery, these are the oldest manuscripts of Mark which have the last chapter. There is an older copy on papyrus, at the Chester Beatty Library in Dublin. It is part of a book originally containing the four Gospels and the Acts, made in the third century. Alas, only six of the pages of Mark remain, ending in chapter 12. How the Gospel ended in that papyrus cannot be

is the Codex Bezae, now in Cambridge. This copy of the Gospels was made in the fifth or sixth century, with a Latin translation (older than Jerome's) beside the Greek. The Greek text of Codex Bezae stands apart from the other early copies, because it has a lot of additions found nowhere else. The majority of these additions have little value. They explain or harmonize passages in the Gospels. For example, Luke 5:10,11 has extra words: '. . . James and John the sons of Zebedee. He said to them, Come, do not fish for fish, for I will make you fishers of discovered. The problem about the end of Mark is not simply whether verses 9–20 were part of it or not. Jerome reported a form with extra verses, and one early Greek copy, the Washington Gospels produced about AD 400, preserves them. A few copies of later date, one manuscript of a Latin translation earlier than Jerome's and some other early translations have a very short ending, to which verses 9–20 have been added. Each of these endings uses words which are not used in the rest of Mark.

What do these things mean?

They appear to be signs that the Gospel ended in an unexpected way. Scholars guess that the author's manuscript was damaged; the end of the scroll or the last page of the codex was lost before anyone could copy it. Another guess is that the author never completed his book—perhaps he died suddenly. Of the several attempts to give it a tidy conclusion, the ending in the traditional text was accepted as the most suitable by comparison with the other three Gospels.

NEW KNOWLEDGE—
NEW TRANSLATIONS

One major achievement of the Reformation was the translation of the Bible into the chief languages of Europe. In previous centuries there had occasionally been translations which were made from the Latin Vulgate. John Wyclif's English version was one of these.

With the new learning of the Renaissance more scholars knew Greek, so now translations could be made directly from the Greek New Testament. The one Luther used for his German Bible and Tyndale for his English one was prepared by the famous scholar Erasmus. His Greek New Testament was the first to be printed and published (in 1516).

He put the text together from a few manuscripts which he happened to have to hand. Only one of them had the Book of Revelation in it, and the last page with the six final verses was missing, so Erasmus translated the Latin Vulgate back into Greek!

With some corrections and changes, Erasmus' Greek text was printed over and over again. In the seventeenth century a Dutch publisher referred to it as 'the received text' (*textus receptus*), and that name has stuck. When King James I of England set up a committee to produce an English version without the bias of earlier ones, an edition of Erasmus' Greek New Testament was their basic text.

Although Erasmus' edition became the standard one, scholars soon showed that there were all sorts of differences between it and the Greek manuscripts, notably the older ones. When Patriarch Cyril Lucar presented the Codex Alexandrinus to the king of England he made available a copy older than any other known in the seventeenth century (see *The Oldest Bibles*). Walton's Polyglot, the New Testament part of a Bible in several ancient languages published in London in 1657, noted its variations.

Throughout the eighteenth century the work of examining manuscript copies of the New Testament and listing their variant readings continued. Studying the differences led to better understanding of how scribes made mistakes (see *Simple Mistakes*), and the creation of guidelines to help decide between one reading and another.

With Tischendorf's recovery of the Codex Sinaiticus, his researches on

The great Renaissance scholar Erasmus saw the need for a standard printed text of the Greek New Testament. His work was the basis for most translations until the nineteenth century.

other manuscripts, and the labours of several scholars beside him, the nineteenth century saw a major change of opinion.

The limits of Erasmus' traditional or 'received' text became clear. It did preserve the authors' words, but after they had suffered some changes and harmonization. In order to read or translate accurately what the New Testament writers wrote, that text needed some revision to agree with older manuscripts.

In England the Revised Version of 1881 was the first translation to break away from the traditional text in certain places. Most translations made since then have done the same. For some Christians this is still puzzling. Why should there be these changes in

Preachers aim to 'bring the Bible to life'. To help the illiterate people of the Middle Ages, scribes added pictures to the text of the Bible. The biblical figures were shown as if they lived in the Middle Ages. In the twelfth-century 'Winchester Bible' Christ is shown 'harrowing' hell.

the Bible? How could the church have existed for so long with faulty copies of its foundation document? Are the very old manuscripts really superior to the traditional text?

These questions were asked a hundred years ago, and because they are still asked, they deserve attention. The last one is the key one: with most of the 5,000 or so Greek manuscripts of the New Testament, or parts of it, presenting texts very like Erasmus', why should anyone think a small number which disagree are better?

Age alone cannot put this small minority in first place. Older copies are not necessarily better copies (see *Finding the True Text*). Some people have argued that manuscripts such as the Codex Sinaiticus have survived because they were bad copies. Little used, they were not read to pieces like the good ones which have, therefore, disappeared.

Three lines of argument offer answers to these points. First, if only two or three fourth-century copies existed, like the Sinai or Vatican codices, their survival as faulty copies relegated to store-cupboards might be an acceptable explanation. As it is, their witness is joined by all the other copies of equal or greater age. Where there are differences from the traditional text, they often share them; rarely do any of them support the traditional form in these places. Their number and the circumstances of their discovery make it statistically unlikely that they were all rejects and that every 'good' copy has perished entirely.

Second, there is no democracy in textual studies; the voice of the majority does not dominate. Knowing the habits of scribes and the history of copying makes this plain (see *Finding the True Text*). Almost all New Testament manuscripts were made after the fourth century. Any coming from an earlier time will demand special scrutiny. They will disclose the forms of the New Testament books current in the first centuries of the church's life. If the normal means of

studying ancient texts shows that those have the characteristics of earlier texts by comparison with the traditional text, then obviously they will be preferred.

Third, there is a separate body of very telling evidence. Passages from the New Testament occur often in the books of early Christian teachers and scholars (the Fathers). These men quoted from memory for short passages; longer passages may have been copied from manuscripts— although their memories were probably better than many people today imagine. What is noteworthy is the way these quotations tend to agree with the earlier texts rather than the traditional one, where there are points of difference. If the traditional text had been in use in their day, surely these Christian leaders would have quoted it!

These points are all valid. The traditional text has to be judged by the standards applied to all ancient texts and manuscripts. To claim that the New Testament text falls into a category of its own because it is Scripture is absurd. All of the manuscripts of the New Testament, whatever text they offer, suffer from the failings of their human copyists. Cases of expansion and harmonization are typical of a later text, and easily seen in the traditional text of the Greek New Testament. The Gospels are obvious candidates for harmonization.

One straightforward case is in Luke 23:38, 'And a superscription also was written over him in letters of Greek, and Latin, and Hebrew' (Authorized/King James Version). Modern translations leave out the list of 'letters'. These words occur in various copies in different orders, and are absent from the early third-century Bodmer papyrus and from Codex Vaticanus. This situation is best explained if the words were not part of the original text of Luke but were inserted into it from the account in John. If the words belonged to Luke from the start, there is no way to explain their omission or confusion.

Changes of fashion in piety also had an effect on the copyists. Where the traditional text has, 'Joseph and his mother marvelled at those things which were spoken of him' (Luke 2:23), the older copies have 'His father and mother' (compare RSV, GNB, NIV). As the position of Mary grew in the church, copyists felt a need to remove anything which might cast doubt on the doctrine of the virgin birth of Jesus.

The steps which the nineteenth-century scholars made in unravelling the history of the Greek New Testament text were part of a larger process. Copies of famous Greek and Latin classics found among the papyri from Egypt had similar effects on their study (see *Books from New Testament Times*). As a result, scribal mistakes can be corrected, lines left out can be restored, and phrases wrongly added can be removed, giving texts which are closer to the words the authors wrote.

To separate the New Testament text from this process would be quite wrong. Rather, all who value it should be glad that it can be treated on a level with texts of equal age. In this way its study is made more accurate. On one account it stands above the rest. In many of the classics scholars need to suggest changes to words in order to make sense of lines and sentences. The New Testament text has been preserved so well that not one passage demands such treatment. The New Testament text and all translations made by competent scholars can be trusted.

For 1400 years Christian scribes copied their holy books by hand, as St John is doing in this eleventh-century Greek Gospel book. The invention of printing enabled Erasmus and the Reformers to make the Bible available much more easily and cheaply.

For Further Reading

GENERAL

P. BIENKOWSKI and A. TOOLEY, *Gifts of the Nile, Ancient Egyptian Arts and Crafts in Liverpool Museum*, National Museums and Galleries on Merseyside, HMSO, London, 1995

R.N. FRYE, *The Heritage of Persia*, Weidenfeld and Nicholson, London 1962 and World Publishing Co., Cleveland, 1963

SIR ALAN GARDINER, *Egypt of the Pharaohs*, Clarendon Press, Oxford and Oxford University Press, New York, 1979

O.R. GURNEY, *The Hittites*, Penguin Books, Harmondsworth and New York, 1990

J. OATES, *Babylon*, Thames and Hudson, London and New York, 1986

G. ROUX, *Ancient Iraq*, Penguin Books, Harmondsworth and New York, 3rd edition, 1992

H.W.F. SAGGS, *The Greatness that was Babylon*, Sidgwick and Jackson, London and St Martin Press, New York, 1991

I. SHAW and P. NICHOLSON, *British Museum Dictionary of Ancient Egypt*, British Museum Press, London, 1995

E. YAMAUCHI, *Persia and the Bible*, Baker Book House, Grand Rapids, 1990

The Cambridge Ancient History, 3rd edition, Cambridge University Press, Cambridge, 1973 onwards, analyses in detail the mass of information to hand.

E. SCHÜRER, *The History of the Jewish People in the Age of Jesus Christ* (175BC-AD135), 4 vols, revised and edited by G. Vermes, F. Millar and M. GOODMAN, T. and T. Clark, Edinburgh, Fortress Press, Minneapolis, 1973–87, gives a valuable survey of all written sources and reconstructs the history of the period.

ANCIENT TEXTS AND AUTHORS

Translations of ancient texts are given in J.B. Pritchard (editor), *Ancient Near Eastern Texts*, 3rd edition, Princeton University Press, Princeton, 1968, abridged as *The Ancient Near East*, vol.1, 1958, vol.2, 1975 and in W.W. Hallo and K.L. Younger (editors), *The Context of Scripture*, Brill, Leiden, 1997.

JOSEPHUS, *The Jewish War*, translated by G.A. Williamson, revised and edited by E. M. Smallwood, Penguin Books, 1981

JOSEPHUS, *Jewish Antiquities*, in Greek, with English translation by H.St.J. Thackeray, R. Marcus, L. Feldman, Loeb Classical Library, Harvard and London, 1926–81

PHILO, *Legatio ad Gaium* ('Embassy to Gaius') in Greek, with English translation by E. M. Smallwood, Brill, Leiden, 1961

The Mishnah, translated by H. Danby, Oxford University Press, London, 1933

ARCHAEOLOGY IN GENERAL

N. AVIGAD, *Discovering Jerusalem*, Nelson, Nashville, 1983, Blackwell, Oxford, 1984

M. BEN-DOV, *In the Shadow of the Temple. The Discovery of Ancient Jerusalem*, Harper and Row, 1985

K.A. KITCHEN, *The Bible in its World. The Bible and Archaeology Today*, Paternoster Press, Exeter, and Inter-Varsity Press, Chicago, 1977

A. MAZAR, *Archaeology of the Land of the Bible 10,000–586 B.C.E.*, Doubleday, New York, 1990

B. MAZAR, *The Mountain of the Lord. Excavations in Jerusalem*, Doubleday, New York, 1975

J. MURPHY O'CONNOR, *The Holy Land, An Archaeological Guide from Earliest Times to 1700*, Oxford University Press, Oxford and New York, 3rd edition, 1992

E. STERN (editor), *New Encyclopedia of Archaeological Excavations in the Holy Land*, Simon and Schuster, New York, 1993

E. YAMAUCHI, *The Stones and the Scriptures*, Lippincott, Philadelphia and Inter-Varsity Press, London, 2nd edition, 1978

THE DEAD SEA SCROLLS

F.F. BRUCE, *Second Thoughts on the Dead Sea Scrolls*, Paternoster Press, Exeter, 3rd edition, 1966, 2nd edition, Eerdmans, Grand Rapids, 1964

E. M. COOK, *Solving the Mysteries of the Dead Sea Scrolls. New Light on the Bible*, Zondervan, Grand Rapids and Paternoster Press, Carlisle, 1994

F. GARCIA MARTINEZ, *The Dead Sea Scrolls Translated. The Qumran Texts in English*, Brill, Leiden, 1994

J. C. TREVER, *The Dead Sea Scrolls. A Personal Account*, revised edition, Eerdmans, Grand Rapids, 1977

G. VERMES, *The Dead Sea Scrolls in English*, Penguin Books, 4th edition, 1995

THE GOSPEL RECORDS

K. Aland and B. Aland, The Text of the New Testament, Brill, Leiden and Eerdmans, Grand Rapids, 2nd edition, 1990

J. H. GREENLEE, *Scribes, Scrolls and Scripture. A Layperson's Guide to Textual Criticism*, Eerdmans, Grand Rapids, 1985

B. M. METZGER, *The Text of the New Testament*, Clarendon Press, Oxford and Oxford University Press, New York, 3rd edition, 1992

C.H. ROBERTS, 'Books in the Graeco-Roman World and in the New Testament,' in P.R. Ackroyd and C.F. Evans (editors), Cambridge University Press, Cambridge and New York, 1970, *The Cambridge History of the Bible* I, pp.48–66.

C.H. ROBERTS and T.C. SKEAT, *The Birth of the Codex*, Oxford University Press, Oxford and New York, 1983

Archaeological discoveries are often reported and discussed in *The Biblical Archaeologist*, published quarterly for the American Schools of Oriental Research by Scholars Press, Atlanta, GA, and in *The Biblical Archaeology Review* published bi-monthly by the Biblical Archaeology Society, Washington, DC, also available from Paternoster Press, Carlisle.

Essays in standard reference works, such as D. N. Freedman (editor), *The Anchor Bible Dictionary*, Doubleday, New York (1992), C. Roth (editor), *Encyclopaedia Judaica*, Jerusalem (1962), J. D. Douglas and N. Hillyer (editors) *The Illustrated Bible Dictionary* and *The New Bible Dictionary*, Inter-Varsity Press, Leicester and Tyndale House Publishers, Wheaton, Ill, 2nd edition (1962) give information on specific persons, places and topics.

Index

Acknowledgments

Design
Peter Wrigley

Illustrations
Mark Astle: 69, 95, 120
Dick Barnard: 40, 48, 51, 56, 93, 98, 107, 114, 131, 137, 153, 163, 166, 175, 244 (perspective drawing) and cover illustration
Simon Bull: 164
Pauline O'Boyle: 102, 121, 141
Vic Mitchell: 133, 135, 144
Angela Pluess: 79
David Reddick: 105
Stanley Willcocks: 17
All others Lion Publishing.
Plans on pages 172, 175 based on the original drawings in N. Avigad, *Discovering Jerusalem*, Shikmona Publishing Co. Ltd, Jerusalem, in co-operation with Israel Exploration Society, 1980; Thomas Nelson, Nashville, Tennessee; Blackwell, Oxford.
The drawings of Herod's temple on pages 244-45 are based on those in M. Ben-Dov, *In the Shadow of the Temple*, Harper and Row, New York, 1985 and B. Mazar, *The Mountain of the Lord*, Doubleday, New York, 1975.

Maps
Roy Lawrence and Lesley Passey

Photographs
J.C. Allen: 50, 134
Ashmolean Museum Oxford: 221 (both), 222 and 223 (coins), 251 (shekel), 258, 327
Professor N. Avigad: 174, 175, 184

Biblioteca Apostolica Vaticana: 318, 336
Bibliothèque Nationale Paris: 294
Bodleian Library Oxford: 149, MS Pell Aram bag recto (left), MS Pell Aram IV Int. (right)
British Library: 314, MS Roy I D VIII f.41v, 315 Add MS 43725, 321 (above) Papyrus 114 col 14-16, 331 Add MS 43725 f.260, 335 Add MS 43725 f.256, 337 Add MS 43725 f.229v, 338 MS Roy I D VIII f.10v
British Museum: cover, 27 (top), 52 (left), 104 (right), 116 (both), 130, 155 (below right), 176, 194, 233 (all), 237, 246, 302, 320 (below), 321 (below)
Cairo Museum: 100 (right), 303
Discoveries in the Judean Desert of Jordan III, les Petites Grottes de Qumran, OUP 1962, plate XXX: 175
Dr Gideon Foerster, Department of Antiquities of Israel: 222
Werner Forman Archive: 65, 103, 301
Sonia Halliday Photographs:
Sonia Halliday: 16, 60, 63, 66, 75 (below), 78, 127 (both), 146 (right), 152 (below left), 155 (below left), 156, 185 (above), 206-207, 208 (above), 219, 228, 257, 270-71, 288, 290, 343
Barrie Searle: 151
Jamie Simson: 20, 35, 36, 41
Jane Taylor: 15, 24 (top right), 38-39, 94 (below), 96, 97, 158 (below), 159, 161, 217, 310, 323, 326
Robert Harding Picture Library: 52 (right), 143, 320 (above)
Rainbird: 69 (top and below

left), 71, 72, 73 (both)
John Ross: 37, 105
Georgina Hermann: 29, 144 (both)
Michael Holford: 210 (above), 236
Illustrated London News Picture Library: 19 (above), 24 (below left), 68
Israel Museum Jerusalem: 104 (left), 112 (right), 113 (above), 177, 179 (below), 180 (above and below left), 181 (both), 227, 243 (below), 256, 259, 264, 268
Jericho Exploration Fund: 24 (top left)
Dr John Kane: 213, 295
Kenneth Kitchen: 13, 100 (left)
Kunsthistoriches Museum Vienna: 211
A.H. Layard, *Ninevah and its Remains*, 1849: 21
Lepsius Denmaker III, 40: 58
Lion Publishing:
David Alexander: 22, 89 (right), 107, 129, 171, 198, 243 (above), 307 (below), 340
David Townsend: endpapers, 172 (both), 179 (above), 182, 185 (below), 188, 195, 197, 202, 208 (below), 220 (both), 223 (below), 226, 236 (right), 239, 248, 249, 253, 260, 277, 280, 281, 283, 284, 285, 317
By courtesy of the Trustees of the British Museum: 19 (below left and right), 26, 30 (below), 42, 44, 45 (both), 46 (both), 67, 74, 75 (top), 88 (below left), 89, 90 (above), 91 (right), 108, 109, 110 (both), 111, 113 (below), 118, 119, 120, 121, 122, 124, 125, 126, 133, 140, 141, 142 (both), 145, 146

(left), 152 (below right), 155 (top three)
MacQuitty International Collection: 148
Mansell Collection: 30 (above), 307 (above), 328, 342
Magdalen College Oxford: 322
Alan Millard: 27 (above), 31, 32, 34 (both), 49, 85 (left), 86 (both), 88 (below left), 94 (above), 115 (right), 150, 151, 157, 158 (above), 183, 186, 191, 209, 210 (below), 216, 224, 235, 254, 263, 266-67
Musée du Louvre: 81, 85 (right), 117
Picturepoint London: 55, 57, 61
D. Quatrough, University of Liverpool: 25, 112 (left)
Rheinisches Landesmuseum Trier: H. Thornig; 234-35, 313, 328-29
Römisch-Germanisches Museum Köln: 199
John Ruffle: 77, 106
John Rylands Library: 325, 345
Scala: 309
Barrie Schwortz: 297
Straatliche Museen zu Berlin: 136
Professor J.C. Trever: 193
Trustees of the National Museums and Galleries on Merseyside (Liverpool): 231, 234, 251 (half-shekel), 258
C. Vibert-Guigne: 312
H. Williamson: 115 (left)
Ian Wilson: 298
Estate of Yigael Yadin: 180 (above right), 196 (all)
ZEFA: 12, 117, 240-41, 279, 282, 304